POWER AT SEA

THREE VOLUME SET

INTRODUCTION

Geoffrey Wawro
General Olinto Mark Barsanti Professor of Military History, and Director, Military History Center, University of North Texas

SEA POWER HAS BEEN a critical lever since ancient times, when Greek triremes commanded the Mediterranean, and Athens built a rich, powerful empire by connecting the Piraeus to the Greek islands and Asia Minor with an unassailable navy. The importance of sea power intensified with the "great discoveries" after 1490, when heavily-armed *sailing* ships replaced oar-driven galleys and galleasses. These new caravelles, galleons and frigates—with big sails, scores of guns, and relatively small, sustainable crews (because oarsmen were no longer needed)—pried open every corner of the world to European merchantmen, explorers and warships. Even "fourth-rate" ships could depart the sheltering coasts and beat across the open seas, to the Indies and the Americas, opening up rich new fields of trade and competition.

American Admiral Alfred Thayer Mahan, the most renowned naval theorist, came of age in this new world of "sea powers," which were great powers with big navies determined to defend and enlarge their share of world trade, resources and harbors. Mahan, an indifferent sailor but an excellent thinker, wrote the bestselling *The Influence of Sea Power upon History, 1660–1783* in 1890. The book, which sold heavily all over the world, argued that sea power—

the ability to project power and trade across the oceans and prevent your rival from doing the same—had a profound *determining* influence on history and the fate of nations. Sea power determined which nations rose and which ones fell, which nations got richer, and which ones got poorer.

Mahan's big winner, of course, was Great Britain, which went from a dark horse in 1588—when the Spanish Armada was favored to win the contest with the British navy and seize the British Isles—to the world's clear favorite thanks to a century of wealth creation and maritime empire-building. Gibraltar, Ceylon, Florida, Minorca, Mauritius, Malta, Cape Town, Aden, Hong Kong, Singapore were just a few of the key points pocketed by the Royal Navy. The advantages conferred by these ports, bases and markets only increased with the shift from sail to steam power in the mid-nineteenth century. Britain steamed into the modern age with the densest network of "coaling stations," and was able not only to manage its own empire, but the imperial ambitions of its rivals as well. The French navy was unable to blockade the German ports during the Franco-Prussian War because the British would not sell the French skippers coal from their stocks on Helgoland. Any power that tried to send a fleet around the world, as the Russians did in 1905 or the Americans in 1908, immediately found itself dependent on British sources of coal in every hemisphere.

Lisle A. Rose's three volume *Power at Sea* picks up the story of sea power where Mahan left off. Of course Mahan in 1890 left off in 1783, but all of his readers understood that the book was an extended allegory about his own times. Just as the British, French and Spanish tacked and jibed for naval mastery in the 1780s, the British, French, Germans, Japanese and Americans were striving to snatch a lead from the others in the 1890s. Victory and a chokehold on the world's vital straits, coasts, peninsulas, and harbors would go the nation with the toughest, most venturesome "national character." Mahan frankly admitted that he was a bit of a showman and propagandist: "facts," he once wrote, "must be massed so well as troops and kept subordinate to the central feature." Sea power was to be exalted at all times—heedless of counter-arguments from railroad and later "air power" enthusiasts—to make and sustain the case for ever higher naval spending.

Lisle Rose's facts are deployed more truthfully, as befits a more conventional and learned historian of our day. Volume I *The Age of Navalism 1890–1918* tells the colorful, never dull story of the great navy race of the fin-de-siècle. What makes this volume so absorbing, for casual readers and scholars alike, is its intertwining of military, economic, financial, political, social, cultural and personal strands. "Navalism" was the conviction—spawned by Mahan and acolytes like German Kaiser Wilhelm II and American President Theodore Roosevelt—that great powers had to put to sea and dominate. T.R. was an unabashed "social Darwinist," who believed, like Wilhelm II and the British Foreign Office, that nations had to scrap, fight and expand or else wither away. Sea power, to put it bluntly, was macho. It was also good for business, or so people thought. Colonies were rarely as profitable as people assumed. For every fantastically rich one like South Africa (with its gold and diamonds) there were a dozen pestilential Chads or Samoas that consumed rather than generated cash. But that thought only occurred later; during the race for colonies—90 percent of Africa was carved into European colonies in the twenty years after 1882— none of the maritime powers felt free to pause and reflect on the likely returns of what they were doing. To pause would be to cede a head start to one's rivals.

Sea power also grew on the backs of technology. Steam engines powered hulking steel warships—which no longer needed sails after 1860—and improved metallurgy and casting techniques resulted in big new rifled naval guns, which fired heavier shells out to greater ranges with startling accuracy, even on a rolling sea. Thus, the "Dreadnought Revolution" in 1906 changed everything. With dreadnoughts firing 1,500-pound electronically-targeted armor-piercing shells from well beyond the range of pre-dreadnought battleships, and racing around at 21 knots thanks to 70,000-horsepower turbine engines (the pre-dreadnoughts might manage 18 knots with a tailwind), there was really nothing for a would-be "power at sea" to do but build dreadnoughts, despite their crushing cost.

Of course their crushing cost created great political opportunities in every great power. Just as America's defense contractors today drool over half trillion dollar defense budgets and see nothing but "upside" in them, the Krupps, Thyssens, Mitsuis, Vickers and Schneider-Creusots poured millions into their Edwardian equivalent of "political action committees" to goad parliaments, governments and court camarillas into buying dreadnought navies. Lobbying involved the sorts of bribes and boondoggles that are all too familiar to Americans who have watched the antics of Tom DeLay, Duke Cunningham, and Jack Abramoff, but also "navy leagues" and other apparently (but not really) spontaneous organizations for the propagation of sea power. In Germany, celebrity professors like Max Weber and Hans Delbrück actually signed on as "fleet professors," to tour the Reich and lecture on this historical, strategic and cultural importance of navies and maritime trade. Peasants and landowners who had never even seen the sea supported navies because naval construction bills were traded in the Reichstag for high agricultural tariffs that shut out cheap Russian grain, in much the same way that American rice, corn and sugar producers are sustained today.

For the world's navies, World War I taught lessons altogether different from those expected by the admiralties. The "dreadnought race" had cumbered every power with big fleets of all-big-gun battleships, which they scarcely used! That dispiriting outcome was all the more demoralizing because it was so predictable. Although naval establishments told their governments that the Battle of Tsushima in 1905 (when a fleet of Japanese pre-dreadnoughts had annihilated a fleet of Russians ones by "crossing the T" in Nelsonian style and raking the poor Russians) told all that needed to be told about the future of naval warfare, that was pure casuistry. In fact, those Russian ships had just endured a ten-month, 18,000-mile cruise around the world from the Baltic Sea; the sailors were lousy and demoralized; the decks and gun turrets were literally buried under coal because the British had denied the Russians use of the Suez Canal as well as access to their coaling stations, which forced the Russians to load up with French coal in the rare places like Madagascar and Vietnam where it was stored. Thus, even as the Japanese gunners were zeroing in on the Russian ships at Tsushima, their counterparts were wildly shoveling coal off their decks to reach their guns.

Far more likely than a Tsushima—the *only* battle in history, as it chanced, in which steel, engine-powered battleships fought a decisive fleet action—was at Jutland, the battle in May 1916 between a Royal Navy squadron and a powerful scouting force detached from the German High Seas Fleet. Sparring in the fog and twilight in the North Sea, neither side was willing to put its expensive cruisers and battleships at risk of floating mines or torpedoes. The loss of a single "capital ship" in anything but the most dire invasion scenario would disgrace an admiral and provoke an uproar in the court, press and parliament. Wilhelm II cherished his costly ships, and kept them on a short leash to prevent wastage. The British, who had heard the groans of their taxpayers throughout the naval race, were scarcely less cautious with theirs.

So World War I, Rose explains, became a war of convoys and slow strangulation. American industry and loans kept the Entente well-supplied with food, fuel and armaments, and declined—despite the avowed neutrality of Woodrow Wilson and his po-faced, pro-German Secretary of State William Jennings Bryan—to supply the Central Powers on the wholly disingenuous grounds that

American merchantmen could not reach them because of British patrols. The stalemated war was won by sea power. The Germans and Austro-Hungarians were starved by an Entente blockade of food, fuel and raw materials, and a couple of million American doughboys were hauled over to France in troopships that, a year or two earlier, would certainly have been sent to the bottom with all hands by German U-boats. But convoy art improved so swiftly that the Germans were beaten.

Even the most blinkered, service-proud admiral ought to have descried the future from the facts of the Great War. But they didn't. Navies have always been hide-bound and backward-looking, which is a function of their curious culture. They are the only service in today's egalitarian world where officers and enlisted men wear different uniforms—and quite distinctly different—and navy men and women take command prerogatives to dizzying heights of pride and vanity. Skippers are incontestable, and their judgments are adamantine—a throwback to the days when Fletcher Christians were muttering below decks about the abuses of their Captain Blighs and needed to be slapped down before the rot spread. Somehow that deferential culture persists in our age of information and enlightenment; when admirals say they need something or prefer something it is hard for their peers and underlings to question them, or even redirect them to more fruitful paths.

And so the world's navies continued to build dreadnought battleships after World War I. Lisle Rose writes about people and technologies with a vivacious pen. We get inside leviathans like Japan's *Yamato*-class or Germany's *Bismarck* and *Tirpitz*, and see them from the inside out. The Washington Naval Conference convened in 1922 to save the Western democracies from the heavy, insurgent spending of "revisionist" powers like Fascist Italy, Imperial Japan and Nazi Germany actually leveled the playing field. Conceded only 35 percent of the Royal Navy's surface tonnage, the Germans were permitted open-ended U-boat construction and, in view of naval cuts in Britain and inter-service competition from the army and the Royal Air Force, the Germans at 35 percent would probably overtake the straitened British on the surface as well.

The admirals choked on such projections, but the Royal Navy in the twentieth century suffered the same inter-service pressures as the U.S. Navy in the twenty-first. The air force and the army wanted new money, and generally got it, often at the navy's expense. The U.S. Navy did a bit better, thanks in part to its emphasis on carrier aviation and Marine amphibious doctrine, which proved essential weapons in World War II. Dreadnoughts did not have a good war. Japanese carrier-based planes disabled the bulk of the U.S. Pacific Fleet's battleships at Pearl Harbor on December 7, 1941, and Japanese medium bombers flying out of Saigon sank Britain's H.M.S *Prince of Wales* and H.M.S. *Repulse* on their way to rescue Singapore three days later. Churchill described that disaster as the "greatest direct shock" he felt in the war.

The U.S. Navy's healthy emphasis on carriers, to give cover to otherwise vulnerable surface ships, was almost accidental. There were plenty of "battleship admirals" kicking around in 1941—like Husband Kimmel the defender of Pearl Harbor—and they were plowed under as much by fast-moving events as by any far-sighted plan. Nevertheless, carrier battle groups, their attached Marines, and the titanic "fleet train"—food, drink, fuel and ammo—made possible Admiral Chester Nimitz's "Central Pacific Drive" over and around coral atolls that offered *nothing* to sustain life. No navy could do what the U.S. Navy did. Awed reports home to the British Admiralty confessed as much, and Lisle Rose calls the American feat "industrialism" placed in the water and made to float. Industrialism also made possible the Allied assault on and destruction of the German "wolf packs," those lethal groups of submarines that nearly crippled the Allies in 1942–43 by sinking 200,000 tons of Britain-and-Russia-bound shipping and supplies every month. Convoys, destroyers, aerial surveillance and espionage— the Enigma decrypts—finally wiped out the U-boats, but the sheer quantity of U.S. shipbuilding counted at least as much as the quality of tactics and intelligence in the struggle.

Governments and peoples emerged from the war exhausted. Those not actually maimed wanted at the very least to demobilize, go home and make babies as fast as they could. They wanted government to pay for things like first homes and college, not dreadnoughts or even carriers. Like the Royal Navy after the Napoleonic Wars, the Allied navies after World War II shrank alarmingly, not least because nuclear weapons made them irrelevant, or so air power and army advocates—who saw the chance to punish the navy's foppish pretensions once and for all—convincingly argued. Truman cancelled the U.S. Navy's plans for a nuclear-bomber capable "supercarrier" in 1949—the U.S.S. *United States*—in favor of an inter-continental bomber—which provoked a rather limp "revolt of the admirals." Nothing much came of the revolt, besides a special-pleading piece in *Reader's Digest* titled: "Don't Let Them Scuttle the Navy!"

No one did, of course. The Korean War almost providentially erupted, and new carriers had to be laid down. Navies now pitched themselves as rapid-reaction, expeditionary "platforms." That has been the game of navies ever since the airplane emerged as a major, effective weapon. Mahan wrote before planes, when ships were the only way to control the world's "broad commons." Planes gave a cost-effective option, like the B-36 that killed the first "supercarrier." Rose's third volume shows navies, in particular the U.S. Navy, fighting for funding and a role. He points approvingly to their intervention in the Lebanon Crisis of 1958 and the Cuban Missile Crisis of 1962. In both cases, the navy's carriers conferred flexibility on the American president. He could close sea lanes—the only way to bring Russian materiel quickly into Lebanon or missiles into Cuba—and engage adversaries locally without escalating to a world war. Strategic bombers, intercontinental ballistic missiles, and Europe-based army divisions lacked that flexibility. Rose's masterful three volume history takes us all the way up to Operation Iraqi Freedom, a name that must henceforth be uttered with an ironic sneer. With the wisdom of hindsight, we can say that the Iraq mission should have been left to the U.S. Navy. With its mobility and ubiquity, the navy and its F/A-18s and Tomahawks were able to keep Saddam in his "box." At the same time, naval units deployed to the Persian Gulf—to contain Iraq and Iran—were small enough not to alarm and alienate a world already nervous about American "hyperpower." America could also *afford* such a limited liability campaign, unlike the present one.

Lisle Rose's *Power at Sea* thus steams full circle, from the days of steel Western cruisers with their guns trained on uncooperative "natives," to the days of American carriers parked in vital gulfs and straits ready to enforce their "freedom agenda" from the tip of a laser-guided bomb. The book reminds us at once of the tremendous power, pretensions and responsibilities of the West. On this watery planet, power is wielded and responsibility is still shouldered by navies. It is not all that unlike the days of Mahan.

Power at Sea

Power at Sea

Power at Sea

VOLUME 1

The Age of Navalism
1890–1918

Lisle A. Rose

UNIVERSITY OF MISSOURI PRESS

COLUMBIA AND LONDON

ISBN-13: 978-0-8262-1701-1
ISBN-10: 0-8262-1701-X

Designer: Kristie Lee
Typesetter: Phoenix Type, Inc.
Typefaces: Adobe Garamond, URW Antiqua, Arsis
Book Club Edition

For John Rose

SAILOR, SCHOLAR, SHIPMATE

CONTENTS

MAPS

THE CENTURY JUST past was preeminently an age of warring states and collapsing empires. Industrialism brought not peace but the sword. And the tip of that sword was sea power.

A hundred years ago, great war fleets from half a dozen nations—Britain, the United States, Germany, Russia, France, Japan—roamed the world ocean or rode at anchor, their national ensign displayed in every great port city from New York to Shanghai. They wore no sails, these representatives of proud peoples who beamed upon them. Their graceless hulls and blocky upper works were made of steel now, like the long-range guns that expressed their might. They were propelled through the water not by wind but by great propulsive machinery, engines that seemed the very epitome of the new industrial age. The greatest of the new battleships were adopted by schoolchildren, and their comings and goings often attracted large throngs.

The men who owned them were volatile masters who preached and practiced imperial competition from one end of the earth to the other. Most reveled in an endless game of great-power politics defined by amoral diplomacy in which fighting fleets were the chief expressions of national greatness and purpose. The dispatch of a cruiser to some distant, barely known Mexican or Moroccan bay or the appearance of a small fleet or even a gunboat in a Chinese port or upriver was enough to shift fragile, constantly calibrated and recalibrated balances of power and prestige.

Between 1890 and 1914, Britain, Imperial Germany, Japan, and the United States were or became preeminent naval powers, and their fleets often set the tone and rhythm of international affairs. Other countries, notably Italy, France, and czarist Russia, might have joined them. But whereas Italian warship design and even naval theories were characterized by "great ingenuity," other factors, principally "lack of capital and raw materials," the geographic disadvantage of being confined to the Mediterranean, and lack of technological sophistication, condemned the Regia Marina to a consistently inferior status qualitatively if not quantitatively. Similarly, France and Russia simply could not maintain the hothouse pace of late-nineteenth-century industrial development.[1] Indeed, Russia did not recover for more than a half century from the massive naval defeats of 1904–1905 inflicted by the Japanese.

The great industrial navies that plied the early-twentieth-century world ocean reflected the social and technological strengths and weaknesses of the countries they served. Admiralties and navy departments were both drivers and consumers of the most advanced industrial technologies of the time, from Harvey armor plate and the eleven-inch gun to the dreadnought, "all big gun" battleship. They would remain so throughout the remainder of the century. Navies forced the creation of great public works, including the building and widening of canals, the construction of vast bases, and the dredging and deepening of harbors. By World War I navies required nearly every aspect of industrialization for their survival.

Each of the early-twentieth-century navies served distinct masters and marched to different orders. Britain's Royal Navy remained dedicated to protection of the world's sea-lanes in order to sustain an empire of global dimensions. Kaiser Wilhelm's ill-named High Seas Fleet was primarily designed to promote "Germandom" abroad as the spear point of an aggressive imperial development that would eventually rival if not supplant that of the envied British cousins. The Imperial Japanese Navy was charged with protection of the sacred homeland while leading the way to the acquisition and protection of a vast regional empire in Asia and the western Pacific. Only the United States Navy assumed an ostensibly defensive posture, but its commander in chief from 1901 to 1909 was a rabid navalist who kept a small squadron of warships and river gunboats in China and sent his fleet around the world to demonstrate American maritime power and prowess.

The fighting fleets of Imperial Germany and Japan were faithful replicas of the authoritarian systems they served. The individual was subservient to the immediate needs and whims of the state. Obedience was the prime virtue; innovation, curiosity, creativity were left, if at all, to only a few. Bravery and loyalty were given by men to nations and leaders who sooner (in the case of Imperial Germany) or later (in the case of Japan) failed them. Yet in war and peace they went out on great waters to do their masters' bidding. Whatever problems there were onshore, whatever problems might be encountered at sea, the sailors of emperor and kaiser, like those of the Soviet regime more than a half century on, accounted themselves "real men" once the anchor was slipped and the warship large or small got under way. They were "doing a job that gave them back their sense of self worth and dignity, and instilled in them, in spite of everything, pride in their country."[2] Britain's Royal Navy reflected a society that while certainly free was not truly open. Rigid and cruel class distinctions defined and often smothered British democracy during the crucial early decades of the twentieth century when fate and events forced it to stand at the forefront of opposition to expansive German militarism.

Burdened by various restraints both subtle and overt upon individual initiative, none of these navies, or the societies they represented, could adapt with maximum efficiency to the constantly shifting and growing demands of industrialism with its emphasis upon ceaseless innovation, flexibility, and adaptation. Even the biggest navies became more or less technically deficient because they lacked the broad base of mechanically proficient sailors, shipwrights, and industrialists essential to waging modern war at sea with maximum effect.

The United States eventually proved the one exception. Its open society, incredibly broad and diverse industrial plant, rabid competitive order, obsession with technology and practical education, and exaltation of mass production, distribution, and consumption perfectly positioned the nation to fashion and employ on a massive scale the kinds of weapons that twentieth-century war at sea and power projection ashore demanded. Comparatively well educated and working within arguably the loosest and most decent military command structure ever developed, America's sailors and marines were encouraged to work and think as a team. Initiative was generally encouraged, and from the beginning a sense of professional development was bred into a rapidly industrializing naval establishment. To be sure, snobbery and condescension have never been absent from the U.S. naval officer corps. But they have never been encouraged as a matter of policy, as was the case in every other major sea service with the striking exception of Germany's U-boat arms that were defeated in both wars by superior technology and their own understandable, if in the end inexcusable, blunders.

The years leading to 1914 were devoid neither of conflict nor of drama. The United States battled Spain in 1898, emerging not only with a small empire scattered from the Caribbean to the western Pacific but with a promising industrial fleet as well, while Spain's once mighty maritime power fell below the point of serious calculation. Eight years later, Russia and Japan crossed cutlasses in Far Eastern waters, and the result was the same: victorious Japan demonstrated that it possessed a modern, if modest, and highly efficient navy. The country promptly went mad with navalism, while defeated Russia saw its defeated, depleted navy sink into impuissance that neither the First nor the Second World

War could resurrect. Thirty months after Tsushima, Theodore Roosevelt sent his Great White Fleet of increasingly obsolete pre-dreadnoughts on an unprecedented and chancy world cruise that reconfirmed the rising professionalism and steady growth of American sea power.

Six years later, it was the turn of Europe's fighting fleets, large and relatively small, to be sucked into the maelstrom of war—mankind's first truly industrial conflict at sea that proved midwife to scores of lesser conflicts and one even greater that defined the remainder of the century. The sea war of 1914–1918 was fought all around the Eurasian landmass, on its rivers, and across much of the world ocean. But unlike World War II, the grandest battle fleets remained in home waters, and the newer weapons of war, the submarine and the airplane, proved incapable of projecting their reach much beyond the skies above and the seas surrounding the British Isles and western Europe. So it was that the one great surface battle of the war was fought in waters that lapped both the British and the German coasts, while the U-boat, a sudden new menace of increasingly dire proportions, was confined by the crudity of its technology to sharply limited operational ranges that eventually restricted its effectiveness, then doomed its existence and the navy it served.

This is the tale that unfolds in the following pages. Although it stands by itself, it also forms a prologue to even greater and often more terrible stories of the growth of sea power in the industrial and later nuclear ages to the point where it not only decided wars and the fates of nations and empires but also, finally, with the strategic-ballistic-missile submarine threatened the very fabric of civilization itself. A second volume will carry the story through the end of World War II. The third and concluding volume will examine the new order of sea power that emerged in 1946 with the unprecedented supremacy of the United States Navy on the world ocean and its determination, with unprecedented new weapon systems at its disposal, not only to exercise power *at* sea but also to project power *from* the sea onto and well beyond the coasts of the earth.

The meaning and influence of sea power through the ages have always attracted scholarly interest. In recent years a small army of scholars led by John B. Hattendorf and Norman Friedman in this country and Geoffrey Till in England have attacked the subject. Till's *Seapower: A Guide for the Twenty-first Century* (2004) is especially challenging and comprehensive.[3] But there is no reasonably detailed narrative history of sea power, or, more precisely, power at sea, during the war-drenched industrial-nuclear age that began around 1890. Despite its size, the present effort is neither exhaustive nor an attempt at a final word; the subject is simply too vast. Rather, I have written what might be termed a re-connaissance in force, a needed attempt to bring together in some sort of co-herent narrative and analytical whole the work of many scholars and observers over the past century. I hope it will be considered a starting point, a launching pad for more work, more criticism, and more consideration, and will bring fresh minds and new perspectives to a subject whose fascination is endless.

ACKNOWLEDGMENTS

THE GENESIS OF this study goes back many years to a conversation that an eleven-year-old boy on a train had with a naval aviator about the recent war. At one point the pilot said, "Well, I suppose you know about *Jane's Fighting Ships?*" I did not, of course, but within weeks the deficiency was remedied and I was hooked on a lifelong fascination with ships and the sea.

Three-plus years of sea duty in the Pacific and polar waters between high school and college gave me a firm grounding in the culture of life on the world ocean in general and within the United States Navy in particular. My respect for that efficient, exasperating organization is, I think, apparent on every page of this project, and my affection for shipmates long lost to everything but memory remains strong. Eleven years in the U.S. State Department's Bureau of Oceans, Environment, and Science, especially the year I spent on the U.S. Law of the Sea Delegation, completed an informal but productive maritime education.

The dedicated research that I began in 1995 has been helped immeasurably by the efficient research staffs and open shelves of the Suzzalo and Odegaard Libraries at the University of Washington, Seattle; the National Maritime Museum in Greenwich, England (whose manuscript room is a particular delight to work in); the Nimitz Library at the United States Naval Academy; the Naval Historical Center in Washington, D.C.; and the Naval Undersea Museum at Keyport, Washington. Conversations with the National Park staff of the USS *Arizona* Memorial at Pearl Harbor were also useful in advancing my knowledge of arguably the single most significant event in twentieth-century naval history.

As this work began to take shape, George Thompson and Randall Jones of the Center for American Places in Harrisonburg, Virginia, provided invaluable guidance and support in further developing my ideas and suggesting possible publishers. Their continued interest in my work is deeply appreciated. David Alan Rosenberg, Ted Heckathorn, and John M. Rose shared critically important materials and information that I might otherwise have missed. Robert Ferrell,

Scott Truver, and a number of anonymous readers over the years went through various iterations of the manuscript with great care, providing insightful chapter-by-chapter advice on revision that saved me from numerous sins of omission or commission. Annette Wenda edited the manuscript with great skill.

My gratitude to Beverly Jarrett of the University of Missouri Press for taking on such a "mammoth" (in the words of one reviewer) project is nearly immeasurable, and her editorial staff has transformed manuscript into book with professional aplomb. In its first and final stages, *Power at Sea* became what we used to call in the navy a half century ago an "all hands evolution." My late wife, Maribeth Rose, edited earlier portions of the manuscript with her usual keen eye and brisk efficiency. John Rose, a global information specialist, has provided the maps, while my wife, Harriet Dashiell Schwar, read the final work and provided a number of important suggestions.

With such support from so many, it is clear that I alone am responsible for whatever errors of fact or interpretation that remain.

I would like to gratefully acknowledge the use of ESRI's data and map collection and its third-party vendor ArcWorld for providing the data used in the creation of the maps in this volume.

The World Ocean
and Its Major Choke Points

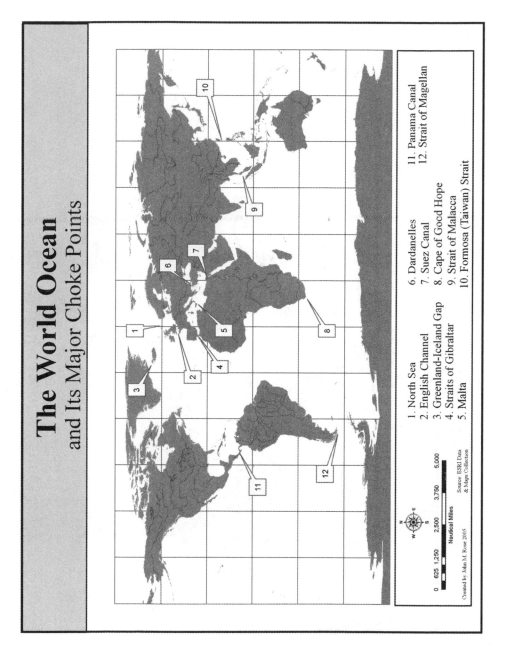

1. North Sea
2. English Channel
3. Greenland-Iceland Gap
4. Straits of Gibraltar
5. Malta

6. Dardanelles
7. Suez Canal
8. Cape of Good Hope
9. Strait of Malacca
10. Formosa (Taiwan) Strait

11. Panama Canal
12. Strait of Magellan

Nautical Miles

0 625 1,250   2,500   3,750   5,000

Source: ESRI Data
& Maps Collection

Created by: John M. Rose 2005

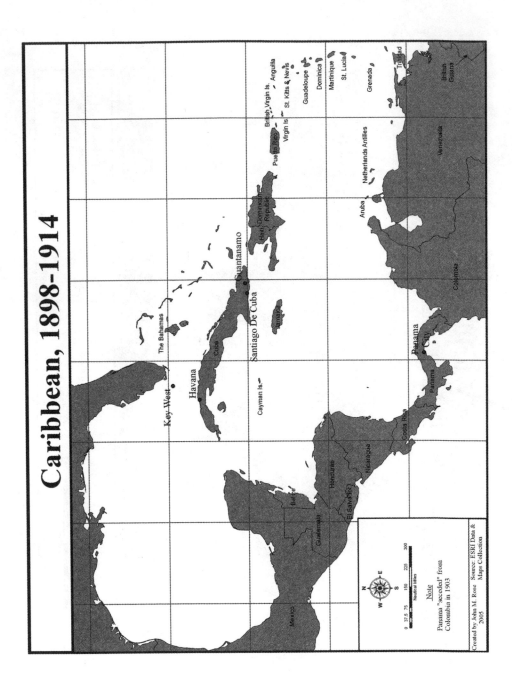

Caribbean, 1898–1914

The Bahamas

Key West

Havana

Cuba

Cayman Is.

Santiago De Cuba

Guantanamo

Jamaica

Haiti Dominican Republic

Puerto Rico

British Virgin Is.

Virgin Is

Anguilla

St. Kitts & Nevis

Guadeloupe

Dominica

Martinique

St. Lucia

Grenada

Trinidad

Venezuela

British Guiana

Netherlands Antilles

Aruba

Colombia

Panama City

Panama

Costa Rica

Nicaragua

Honduras

El Salvador

Belize

Guatemala

Mexico

N
W E
S

0 37.5 75   150   225   300
Nautical Miles

Note
Panama "seceded" from
Colombia in 1903

Created by: John M. Rose   Source: ESRI Data &
2005   Maps Collection

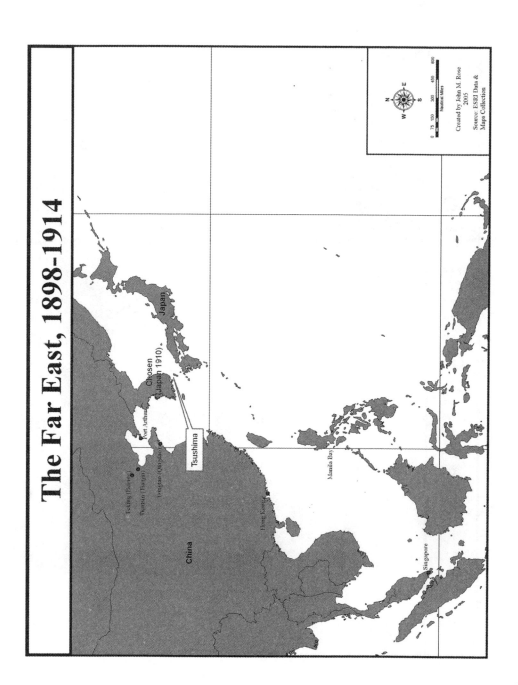

The Far East, 1898–1914

China

Peking (Beijing)
Tientsin (Tianjin)
(Tsingtao (Qingdao))
Port Arthur
Chosen
(Japan 1910)
Japan
Tsushima
Hong Kong
Manila Bay
Singapore

Created by John M. Rose
2005
Source: ESRI Data &
Maps Collection

Nautical Miles
0 75 150   300   450   600

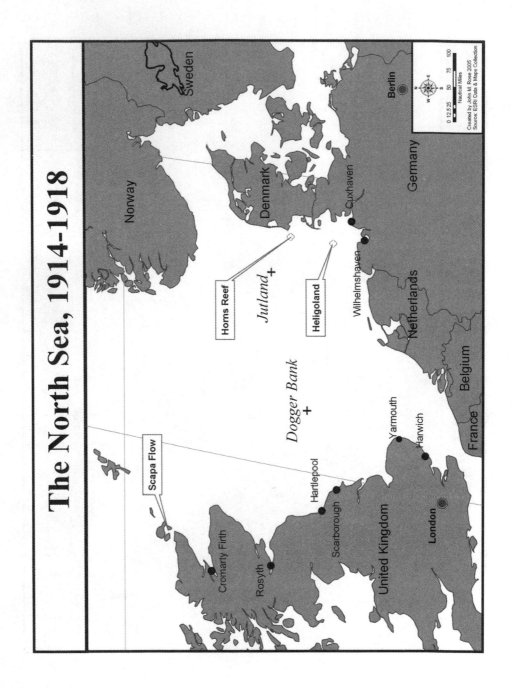

The North Sea, 1914-1918

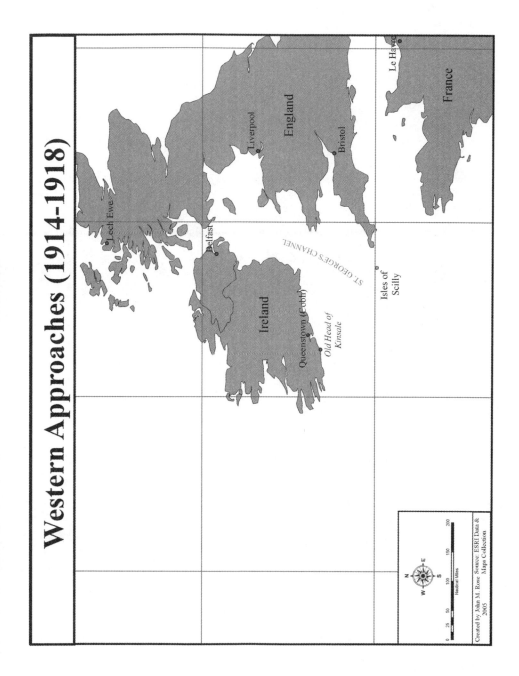

Western Approaches (1914-1918)

Le Havre

France

Liverpool

England

Bristol

Loch Ewe

Belfast

ST. GEORGE'S CHANNEL

Ireland

Queenstown (Cobh)

Old Head of Kinsale

Isles of Scilly

N
W   E
S

0   25   50   100   150   200
Nautical Miles

Created by John M. Rose   Source: ESRI Data &
2005   Maps Collection

Power at Sea

The Master

Alfred Thayer Mahan

ON A LATE AUTUMN DAY in the year 1888, an obscure, middle-aged officer then teaching at the U.S. Naval War College in Newport, Rhode Island, wrote a friend about a project that he was developing. Industrialism was reaching flood tide, and America's sailors, nearly a quarter century removed from any sort of combat, had become far too attached to "the tendency of the age" toward "material" matters. The new steam and steel navy with its powerful guns, engineering plants, and electrical systems had become so bewitching, Alfred Thayer Mahan told Charles R. Miles, that navy men had lost any desire for serious study of their "proper business . . . the art of fighting." The "New Navy," as the small U.S. industrial war fleet eventually came to be called, had taken its first step forward in 1873, when fifteen officers met at the Naval Academy in Annapolis to form the U.S. Naval Institute. The Navy Department, however, understood that this first impulse toward professionalism in the dawning industrial age was not enough. In 1882, it established the Office of Naval Intelligence "to collect, compile, record and correct information on fourteen categories of naval intelligence from descriptions of foreign warships to data on coastal defenses." Two years later, the Naval War College was established "to create and disseminate a system of naval war." The U.S. Navy was clearly moving toward modernity, but the college curriculum initially lacked a coherent intellectual framework—a vision of what sea power and sea warfare would become in the industrial age. Mahan sought to develop such a vision through a series of lectures, then converted them into a book that appeared in 1890 as *The Influence of Sea Power upon History, 1660–1783*. Navy secretary Benjamin Tracy was the first recipient of Mahan's opus. Henry Cabot Lodge, then a rising Republican congressman from Massachusetts, soon had his own copy, and young Theodore Roosevelt, author of *The Naval War of 1812* and a comer in Republican Party reform circles, reviewed it for the *Atlantic Monthly*. He pronounced Mahan's effort "distinctively the best and most important and also by far the most interesting book on naval history which has been produced on either side of the water for many a long year."[1]

Like all important theses, Mahan's argument was stunning in its simplicity.[2] Although *The Influence of Sea Power* was ostensibly a dispassionate look at the lessons of naval history and policy derived from the Age of Fighting Sail, the book at once reflected and ratified the ruthlessly competitive spirit that had grown up with the industrial era, turning that spirit into an apparently immutable set of historical laws revolving around a single theme: national expansion or national death. Mahan began his work with the observation that "the history of Sea Power is largely, though by no means solely, a narrative of contests between nations, of mutual rivalries, of violence frequently culminating in war." Sea power was both the expression and the chief reflection of national greatness, and "the single-minded use of a navy in the service of rational state policy would overcome structural deficiencies in a nation's relative status among others."[3] Throughout history, the strongest nations had been acquisitive trading entities that had created wealth at home while continually seeking riches and fame abroad. The ideal culmination of such activities was the hermetically sealed, tightly regulated, smoothly functioning regional or global commercial system known as empire. In the modern world of powerful industrial states managing extensive overseas empires, a nation could not remain strong if it did not join the global scramble for colonies. And if a nation did not remain strong, it would inevitably become prey to those that were. Waging a *guerre de course* (war against enemy seaborne commerce) with a handful of cruisers against an enemy's imperial supply lines and trading routes did not constitute sea power. Only a large, concentrated battle fleet of the mightiest warships, prepared to slug it out for command of the world ocean against enemy battle lines of equal size and weight, would provide the influence and respect that an ambitious country desired. Indeed, the most successful world sea power would not only ensure the integrity of its own mercantile empire but also possess the naval force and economic attractiveness to trade outside its own colonial sphere.

Naval power could be neither squandered nor ignored. The French and Dutch

had lost most of their global empires because they either paid only sporadic attention to their fleets or had used them to fulfill objectives in Europe or in unsuc-
cessful wars against Britain. Countless British governments of varied political
persuasions had never made the mistake of using their fleet for anything other
than the protection of the realm and the maintenance of imperial commerce
and integrity. Although England had turned to free trade in the nineteenth
century, Mahan conveniently overlooked this fact by focusing his argument on
its earlier imperial era. But even this paradox fitted comfortably within his thesis,
for any nation could pursue whatever trade program it wished and still remain
a world power as long as it possessed the naval strength to enforce its policies.

But for all his genius and insight, Mahan offered little guide to the future.
"Steam navies," he admitted, "have as yet made no history which can be quoted
as decisive in its teachings. . . . Hence theories about naval warfare of the future
are almost wholly presumptive." Later, however, he wrote that no naval battles
of the Age of Fighting Sail were "wholly devoid of tactical instruction," and,
moreover, they provided "mental training" for "student[s]" of the present day
"in the forming of correct tactical habits of thought."[4] The overriding "tactical
habit of thought" that Mahan derived from the Age of Fighting Sail was the line
of battle in which columns of ships blazed away for glory and empire. Mahan's
vision became locked in the minds of an entire generation of industrial-age
sailors. As late as the Battle of Jutland in 1916, every weapon system in the
growing arsenals of the world's great navies was deemed subordinate to and in
support of a nation's line of battleships.

Mahan's tome landed like a bomb in international political, diplomatic, military, and naval circles, not least because in a time of general peace and tranquillity
it dealt frankly and dispassionately with war, whose horrors had not received
much recent attention. Seventy-five years of international stability had created
a planet in which "Nations and Empires crowned with princes and potentates
rose majestically on every side, lapped in the accumulated treasures of the long
peace" that was guaranteed by a diplomacy of civility, restraint, and discretion.
Winston Churchill later wrote of an almost impossibly tranquil era in which "a
sentence in a despatch, an observation by an ambassador, a cryptic phrase in a
Parliament seemed sufficient to adjust from day to day" the global balance of
power.[5] But that balance was rapidly eroding, and Mahan provided the intellectual and conceptual tools for its demise.

He had sown the seeds of revolution in his own country and around the
world, and he could gauge the extent of that revolution and his own influence

by the presence of his book on wardroom tables and shoreside libraries from Portsmouth to Norfolk, from San Diego to Kiel and around to Sasebo. Soon, three powerful figures would step forth to shape his thoughts into an age of rampant, unstable navalism that would unhinge and stain the new century just coming into view.

CHAPTER 1

The Architects

Theodore Roosevelt, Alfred von Tirpitz, and John "Jacky" Fisher

BY THE LAST DECADE of the nineteenth century the world had reached a dangerous imbalance as the new force of industrialism delivered into the hands of foolish monarchs and ignorant warriors hitherto unimagined engines of destruction. For thousands of years human life had centered around meadows, farmlands, barnyards, and quiet villages, which had been ruled from temples, palaces, castles, churches, small and widely scattered commercial towns, and a handful of cities. Humanity's innumerable wars had been limited both spatially and technologically. Men had fought and killed each other on foot and on horseback using chariots, swords, bows and arrows, battle-axes, and later muskets and small cannons. At sea they had destroyed each other in slow, cumbersome fleets of oars and sail. But while generals and chieftains possessed the means to eliminate whole groups of peoples, be they Carthaginians, the various victims of the Mongols, or the hapless seventeenth-century Hurons who perished at the hands of the Iroquois, the human community with only a few exceptions (the Thirty Years' War in Germany being the most egregious example) failed to develop the means to destroy the fabric of civilization itself.

After 1500 Europe had become the cockpit of world power, defined by a nation-state system held in precarious balance through frequent conflict and constant diplomacy while its explorers, soldiers, and colonists expanded the dimensions of Western influence and settlement to global proportions. As

William H. McNeill has observed, European inhabitants of the sixteenth-century Atlantic seaboard "possessed three talismans of power... a deep-rooted pugnacity and recklessness operating by means of... a complex military technology, most notably in naval matters; and... a population inured to a variety of diseases which had long been endemic throughout the Old World ecumene."[1]

The volatility and fragility of Europe's political system required a guarantor to prevent it from collapse. As early as 1527, an Englishman named Robert Thorne residing in Seville intuitively perceived both the requirement and its solution. He wrote a "Declaration of the Indies" to Henry VIII that spelled out in unmistakable terms who the guarantor must be and in implicit terms what the guarantor must do. "God and nature," he told the king, "both provided to your Grace... this Realme of England, and set it in so fruitful a place" in the seas 20 to 400 miles off the coast of northwestern Europe as to be "free from foreign conquest." England was not able then, or for more than a century and a half thereafter, to exploit the opportunity that geography granted it, though in 1588 its fledgling navy, together with favorable winds and tides, was able to turn aside Spanish imperialism in the form of the Armada. Once England became Britain, however, under the Act of Union with Scotland (1707), its fleets began to exert decisive maritime power, dominating the sea-lanes to and from the Continent, thus controlling the world ocean as well. The superiority of the Royal Navy throughout the Age of Fighting Sail, fragile and vigorously challenged as that superiority often was, had two momentous consequences. The first was pointed out by Sir Walter Raleigh in 1608. "Whoso commands the sea commands the trade of the world," he wrote, and "whoso commands the trade of the world commands the riches of the world."[2]

Hatred and envy of Britain's commanding global position were compounded by its command of European affairs as well. German admiral Wolfgang Wegener wrote shortly after World War I that Britain's strategic position in 1914 was nothing short of "brilliant." Its commercial lanes lay in the Atlantic, well beyond the reach of a German fleet based on the Elbe estuary. Germany's trade routes, on the other hand, came up the Channel or in from the North Sea and "could be easily severed by a navy based on the British Isles." Britain's strategic position "was so perfect" that it "never once" had to adjust its wartime naval dispositions. "The English fleet might have been three times stronger or half as strong as it actually was; the proportion of forces between us might have been exactly reversed: the English Operations Plan would have remained exactly the same, always defensive, because the primary mission of the English fleet consisted of defense of England's strategic position." Admiral Sir John Fisher summed it up in a phrase shortly before the war, telling his monarch, George V, that with possession of the vast harbor of Scapa Flow in the Orkney Islands at the top of the North Sea, and the narrow Straits of Dover compressing the English Channel to the south, Britons were "God's chosen people."[3]

British sea power thus naturally compressed ambitious European tyrants from Philip II to Hitler within continental limits. Even there, unifying aspirations could be frustrated by balance-of-power politics as London consistently threw the weight of its financial, political, and, when necessary, military might onto the scales in defense of Europe's weakest nations. On the eve of his disastrous Russian campaign Napoléon remarked ruefully that "as long as there is no peace with England, all other [that is, continental] peace treaties are no more than armistice agreements."[4]

British coalition diplomacy and warfare reached their apex at Waterloo. With Napoléon's disappearance, Britain remained the ultimate arbiter of European affairs while fashioning the greatest global empire the world had ever seen. The second French empire that emerged in the nineteenth century was a pale shadow of the first that had been destroyed by British sea power a hundred years before, while Spanish, Portuguese, and Dutch overseas dominions existed at the sufferance of Whitehall.

After 1850, the relatively stable system of international trade and commercial production was abruptly revolutionized by endlessly inventive scientists, technicians, and engineers in Europe and North America. In a rush they created dynamic new machine societies of enormous wealth and power, progressively binding them together by telegraph lines and transoceanic cables. The world's economically and socially advanced nations were suddenly defined by huge factories, long-range railroad and steamship lines, internal-combustion engines, and enormous, teeming, impersonal cities. Coal and increasingly oil became the driving forces of the new technology, while information, formerly carried by sail and horseback to distant points in weeks or months, now sped around the world in hours through the medium of electrical wire. After 1870 the Industrial Revolution was carried halfway around the globe to Japan through the medium of the Meiji Restoration.

Armies were now transported by railroad and supplied with carbines, rapid-fire "machine" guns, explosive shells, barbed wire, telephones, and huge rifled artillery pieces. Navies were transformed from wood to steel, from sail to steam, their offensive power increased twentyfold from small smooth-bore cannons to large long-range guns. The old wooden ship of the line became the industrial battleship bristling with armament, charging dramatically through foaming waters and trailing long plumes of foul, dark smoke. After 1900 the possibility of war in three dimensions became a reality with the appearance of the first crude submarines, propeller-driven "aeroplanes," and great zeppelin airships.

But if the generals who commanded the new industrial armies adopted the more superficial forms of modernism, their hearts and habits remained in a feudal past. Although absolutely dependent on advanced industrial technologies, they continued to proclaim the glories of hierarchy, courage, and sacrifice embodied in hand-to-hand combat, the bayonet, the cavalry charge, the sword and stirrup—"the mystique of unflinching attack." A British general proclaimed that "war represents motion and life, whereas a too-prolonged peace heralds in stagnation, decay and death."[5]

It was the increasingly huge steel-clad steamship that symbolized, as no gun, flashing saber, or even railroad engine ever could, the spirit of steadily advancing technology, the reality of massive engineering, and the sheer force of the Industrial Revolution as perceived in the courts of Europe and Japan and in the White House at Washington, D.C.

Between 1840 and 1870 "all the ancient lore of naval architecture, the selection and treatment of woods, the hewing and scarfing of the timbers, the mode of construction for maximum strength, and a whole catalog of subsidiary arts, were swept into the scrap heap." Iron and later steel frames proved immeasurably superior to wood in terms of lightness, tensility, and compressive strength. Metal plating made possible the construction of longer, narrower vessels without sacrificing strength, thus increasing ships' speed dramatically. Finally, steel hulls, with their unprecedented toughness and integrity, permitted the fastening of protective armor and the carriage of large naval rifles without undue loss of either stability or mobility.[6]

The steamship rekindled the passion that the peoples of Europe and the United States had long felt for adventure, empire, and the sea. With the last of their territorial frontiers finally settled, there was little room at home to vent personal energies or to dispose of the cornucopia of goods that the industrial economies were producing. But the exotic lands at the end of the world ocean continued to beckon the acquisitive and the naive. Steam and steel passenger vessels took them where their wanderlust dictated; steel-clad battleships protected them en route.

Steam power at sea transformed international commerce and opened formerly remote areas to flourishing trade. Unlike their predecessors in the Age of Sail, steamships were unencumbered by problems with winds or tide. Their owners could confidently promise regular schedules to any port, harbor, or bay in the world. Shippers and merchant captains no longer had to worry about their vessels lying nearly dead in the water for days at a time with sails drooping forlornly in the equatorial calm west of South America or in the Indian Ocean. They did not have to draw up vague schedules to account for constant tacking through the weak, variable breezes of the Mediterranean and the northeast and southeast trade winds of the Atlantic. They did not have to deal with the often howling westerly gales around Cape Horn that for weeks could prevent a sailing vessel from traveling from the Atlantic to the Pacific.

In 1800, seven years before Robert Fulton first placed a steam engine in a ship's hull, the total value of the international import and export trade was estimated at roughly $1.5 billion. Fifty years later, as stout ironclad steamships were just beginning to appear on the world's sea-lanes, the figure had risen to $4 billion. A half century after that, in 1900, with nearly 50 percent of global trade carried in steel bottoms, the value of internationally exchanged goods reached $24 billion. Thus, while the world's population trebled in the nineteenth century, its international exchange of commodities rose sixteenfold.[7]

The size of both passenger vessels and warships increased exponentially almost every decade. HMS *Warrior,* the first officially designated armor-clad seagoing warship, completed in 1859, displaced about 30 percent more than the greatest sail-powered "line-of-battle ship" and was nearly half again as long. Warships grew inexorably thereafter as ordnance designers built ever heavier guns to pierce ever thicker armor plating, and engineers built ever more sophisticated propulsion machinery to push the steel monsters through the waves.[8]

By the time Alfred Thayer Mahan published, the influence of industrialism upon sea power had become decisive. Warships were complex fighting machines demanding men at least minimally versed in one or more facets of the new technology. Chemical propellants (which turned out to be tragically unstable) together with scientific gunnery made the early-twentieth-century battleship "lethal at four times the fighting range of its armorclad predecessor." The growing efficiency of steam engines after 1880 permitted the creation of new warship types like the comparatively fast, lightly armored "protected cruiser" (ideally suited to serve as scout for the battle fleet) and the surface torpedo boat. Finally, the coming of the "wireless telegraph" seemed to reduce if not dispose of the need for visual communications since a commander could swiftly concentrate widely dispersed fleet units and scouts could report their findings via radio from far beyond the horizon.

But perhaps the most important revolutionary element in industrial warfare at sea was the lightening and hardening of armor. As Karl Lautenschläger has emphasized, all naval conflicts prior to 1900 save one—the Battle of Ushant in 1794 five hundred miles west of Brest, France—were fought within sight of land and usually within sheltered waters. This was because wooden and early ironclad warships could fight only in moderate seas due to the open gun port construction of their hulls. Even then, waves and spray interfered with the loading and aiming of guns. The introduction of alloy steel armor and subsequent "cementing" (carburizing) allowed the placing of a ship's guns above an enclosed, adequately protected armored hull without imposing a dangerous excess of top weight. Battleships and cruisers could now be provided with high sides and high-mounted guns whose loading and aim were free of spray and waves except in the most foul weather. Harvey process armor began coming into the new industrial fleets after 1890, and Krupp cemented alloy steel followed five years later. By the time of Victoria's jubilee and the Spithead Naval Review of 1897, the vessels of Britain's most modern battleship squadron were protected by cemented steel armor, and "no nation could challenge British naval supremacy without adopting the new technology."[9]

Not everyone, however, was enamored of the new beasts of war; some viewed them as a "synonym for disaster." At a time when a new generation of American journalists was about to unveil the evils of industrialism—foul, disease-ridden slums; unsavory capitalists; corrupt government officials; and, above all, faulty machines and unprotected workers—newfangled steam and steel warships seemed uncertain, unwieldy, and dangerous. Just before the outbreak of the Spanish-American War, journalist Ira Nelson Hollis wrote that "the friends of our sailors are awaiting anxiously the experiments which must determine" the modern battleship's "place in the system of national defense." Fantasists and illustrators forecast terrible conflicts between battleships, depicting huge vessels "crashing into one another, and plunging into the depths, carrying men and guns down with them."[10]

Conflict between fleets of modern battleships in the waters off the Continent might be years, even decades, in the future, but in the Far East, Japan and China went to war in 1894, each possessing a small squadron of up-to-date steel-clads. The battle between the two small fleets off the mouth of the Yalu River was poorly reported in the West and thus was ripe for exaggeration. Japan's victory seemed to confirm every danger and horror predicted for battleship warfare. European and American editors eagerly copied the fanciful depiction first set forth in a Tokyo periodical in which bombs burst in air, ships sank, "and men in submarine armor were hacking at one another with battle-axes" on the bottom of the ocean.[11]

Two dramatic events would place the new industrial navies in a more positive light. The first took place in 1897, the second a year later. In the summer of Queen Victoria's jubilee year, the British Empire honored her with a magnificent series of celebrations, including a review in which the major portion of her fleet gathered at Spithead off Portsmouth. The Royal Navy at that time comprised 330 ships (53 of them modern ironclads) manned by 92,000 smartly attired seamen. International observers were supposed to conclude that the British fleet exemplified overwhelming sea power and advanced technology gracefully mixed with imperial majesty and the civic virtues of the English common man.[12] And so they did. The British navy was judged to remain "beyond all compare." An American visitor gushed that "all agree that no such spectacle of strength and splendour was ever before seen." Whitehall's ability to muster a huge accumulation of warships at home, "while maintaining her naval service all over the world at its usual height of efficiency," was especially impressive. That week the Italian monarch, visiting his own fleet, which was only half the size of the Royal Navy, ordered a twenty-one-gun salute in honor of Victoria and told the flagship commander to hoist the royal ensign in tribute to British sea power. The Royal Navy was universally acknowledged as the planet's mightiest military service. Certainly, the French, with the world's second-largest navy, thought so. A prominent Paris newspaper thanked Britain for "the naval *fête*," observing gratefully that whatever tensions might exist between the two nations (and they would climax the next year at Fashoda), British sea power would never again be turned against its former enemy across the Channel. Everyone in 1897 admitted that Albion's naval superiority was the essential cornerstone of international peace.[13]

Sea power had suddenly acquired a cachet it had not enjoyed since the end of the Napoleonic Wars. "Ten years ago," a young writer named Fred T. Jane remarked in October of that year, "even in England, where the navy has a peculiarly vital importance, comparatively few people had more than the barest acquaintance with the units of their fleet; in France, the next naval Power, the warships were then scarcely known to the civilian; in the United States, memories of naval actions in the [Civil] War lingered feebly." Now the industrial world had fallen prey to an "all-pervading naval mania." Such mania, of course, would naturally lead to war at some point, but Jane admitted that "we are still blindly groping when we dream of the naval warfare of to-day or to-morrow." The past was of little help. "In history, as I read it, 'strategy' so often seems to have been, at the best, only on very broad and general lines." The young observer who would go on to found the most authoritative annual guide to the world's fighting fleets ever published added that "a vague desire to get at the enemy, and beat him, without much thought to subsequent issues seems rather to have been the dominant idea. The strategical advantages would seem to have been first noted and made use of *after* the victory." Groping in an admitted fog of ignorance about the new navies, Jane concluded that the "naval battle of to-morrow may be a terrible thing; but there is reason to believe that it will be far less dreadful than people are so fond of imagining." The new warfare between "ironclads" might "not be very sanguinary" since it precluded the kind of bloody, close-in fighting that characterized the Age of Sail, while science and technology had yet to solve the problem of "how to hit at long range—except at target practice." Quick-firing four- to six-inch naval guns were effective since they did not have to be relaid after every discharge, and thus sighted themselves, as it were. But shells from such comparatively small guns "cannot reach a ship's vitals."[14]

Within a year the U.S. victory over Spain began to clarify if not resolve the issues that Jane raised, while reconfirming the primacy of ironclad warfare in the Western mind. Americans had been slow to grasp the geopolitical implications of the post-1870 revolution in world naval power. For many years, evidence from the War of 1812 notwithstanding, a majority chose to believe that the vast oceans lapping the shores of North America constituted an unbridgeable moat that no foreign invader would try to cross. Not until 1883 did Congress, "tired of being embarrassed by a nonfunctional, decrepit, wooden navy," authorize funds for "our first four steel warships," three modest-size "unarmored cruisers"— *Boston, Chicago,* and *Atlanta,* together with the "dispatch boat" *Dolphin.*[15] However, these strange, handsome vessels with their two tall brown funnels, brilliant white hulls and upper works, and high masts still rigged for sails did not reach the fleet for years. When they did, they were commonly referred to as "the White Fleet." In the meantime, young Edward L. Beach, who graduated from Annapolis in 1888 with only thirty-four other young men, discovered that his beloved service anticipated having room for no more than half that number because of a personnel system so backward and chaotic that its books carried the names of officers who had not been on active duty for years, many of whom had died or acquired criminal records. Beach's first ship was the "wooden Civil War sloop-of-war" *Richmond,* an "old and thoroughly rotten" vessel whose crew was frankly ashamed of the "decrepit engineering plant" and "feeble smooth bore guns." The vessel "was a laughingstock for all who observed her." The men writhed in agony every time they encountered foreign sailors who served in brand-new "modern warships built of steel, with good engines and high powered guns." The navy, "superannuated" in every way, was filled with comparatively elderly time servers who clogged the promotion ladder.[16]

Even in the new steel and steam vessels that appeared in increasing numbers after 1890, eight to ten junior officers were crammed into tiny dark holes near the coal bunkers or in the fo'c'sle at the bow of the vessel. The crew's quarters could be only imagined. Everyone slept in curved, uncomfortable, and closely slung hammocks (which remained standard issue for enlisted men to the very eve of World War II) or on thin mattresses on the steel decks beneath easily stowed tables. The officers—who enjoyed the status of wearing pajamas—were "forced to sleep, if at all," with their garments "tied tightly about our ankles and sleeve ends about our wrists, and with the further protection of gloves, socks and head guards. The bedbug is a mighty beast." Air-conditioning was, of course, unknown, and all suffered day and night during frequent cruises to the Caribbean. "Every meal was a torment," and uniforms were ludicrously elaborate, dreadfully tight, and always hot and uncomfortable.

Captains and commanders "went by the book." Even then the strain of command or the fear occasioned by capricious orders from Washington could overwhelm the most confident skipper, leading him to bizarre behavior, nervous breakdowns, and relief from command. "The enlisted man of those days was magnificent as a fighter and a seaman," Beach recalled, "but tough and hard to control." Because naval life was so unappetizing, citizenship could never be a requirement for enlistment, and many a brawling drunk from the depths of the immigrant population found his way on board Uncle Sam's warships. The abolition of flogging in 1851, though clearly mandatory on humanitarian grounds, nonetheless made disciplining the recalcitrant exceedingly difficult. When Lieutenant George Dewey, who would later gain immortality at Manila Bay, went aboard the ancient steam-driven side-wheeler *Mississippi* as executive officer in 1861, "he found over a hundred men in chains between the guns and rioters in possession of part of the lower decks."[17]

But change was on the way. When Benjamin Harrison came to the presidency in March 1889 he brought with him the dedicated imperialist Benjamin F. Tracy who proved to be a superb administrator of the Navy Department and a formidable politician who could sustain and build upon the modest momentum already generated in and beyond Congress for a modern sea service. In the late eighties legislators had loosened the purse strings further, and between the spring and late autumn of 1889 the last of the three original unprotected cruisers was joined by four larger armored sisters, three gunboats, and a bizarre "dynamite ship." One of Tracy's first acts was to create a policy board that Mahan (then completing his magnum opus) advised but could not dominate. The board submitted a report at the end of 1889 calling for the creation of two fleets—one a coastal-defense force, the other "for long range offensive action." Under Tracy's lash, the first two seagoing but coastal-defense battleships, *Texas* and *Maine*, were afloat by 1891, with a half-dozen more battleships and armored cruisers being built in national and private shipyards from New York City to San Francisco. The later battleships, starting with *Iowa*, were conceived and designed to fulfill the long-range offensive role. When Beach returned to sea duty in 1890, he thus found the brand-new cruiser *Philadelphia* to be a "splendid ship," possessing "a magnificent assemblage of modern machinery" that included triple expansion and ten thousand–horsepower engines "with wonderful air pumps, circulating pumps, condensers, [and] Marshall valve gear." Ten years later, the authoritative *Jane's Fighting Ships* placed the new U.S. steel navy behind only Great Britain's mammoth imperial fleet.[18]

Great forces, some scarcely understandable to the American people themselves, were shaping these developments. The United States of America was not only the first new nation of modern times but also the only one that rested on no large indigenous population. More than nine out of ten Americans of whatever racial or cultural stock were either immigrants or at best second- or third-generation native born. A sense of nationhood thus had to be forged out of common experience, and only one such experience was available either as something personally lived or as romantically conceived—westward expansion and the frontier. The year Mahan burst on the scene, with the nation rapidly transforming into an urban-industrial giant, a young historian named Frederick Jackson Turner wrote that "our early history is the study of European germs developing in an American environment. . . . The frontier is the line of most rapid and effective Americanization." But Turner proceeded to emphasize the recent conclusions of the superintendent of the federal census. By 1890, a clear "frontier of settlement" was no more. For the first time ever, and forever more, "Americans would be forced to live within a closed space."[19] There was only one way out of this admittedly vast continental confine, and Mahan had shown the way.

The captain's genius lay not only in showing his people the way to a seemingly endless frontier out on the world ocean and on the far distant coasts of the earth but also in stimulating their fears of continued vulnerability from predatory European nation-states. A powerful, often overlooked, element in Mahan's work was his insistence that the balance of global military and naval power in 1890 had swung decisively against the United States. There was abundant evidence to support the supposition. France coveted Central America and during the American Civil War had established a brief puppet government in Mexico under Maximilian. In 1881, Count Ferdinand-Marie de Lesseps began what would prove to be a failed effort to dig an Isthmian canal in Panama. Germany's rising interest in establishing colonies in the Western Hemisphere and the Pacific was well known. Britain's enmity toward its former North American colonies had flared anew when Whitehall supported the Confederate cause for as long as it appeared promising; in their hearts Britons had never yet accepted the United States of America, and there was no reason to suggest that they ever would. Even Spain, weary and dispirited, its ancient New World empire crumbling under native insurrection, seemed able to defy the Americans with impunity. In 1873 a Spanish warship seized *Virginius,* almost starting a war, even though it quickly became apparent that the gunrunner was flying the American flag illegally. If Europe could so consistently and humiliatingly dismiss or ignore American hemispheric interests, where did that leave the venerable Monroe Doctrine? Finally, the United States could not even impose its will upon fractious hemispheric neighbors. As late as 1879 the U.S. fleet was so inferior to that of Chile that Washington could not intervene on behalf of friendly Peru when the two Latin countries went to war.

Only a modern industrial navy could preserve and promote expanding American overseas interests, and only an Isthmian canal could guarantee the shuffling of fleet units from one ocean to the other that would ensure a rapid response to hemispheric and Pacific crises. Mahan became almost morbidly preoccupied with the strategic importance of the Isthmus and its Caribbean and Pacific approaches. At the time he wrote it seemed that the Colombian government would grant France the right to complete de Lesseps's project. From an Isthmian base France or any nation that might ally with it would threaten America's Gulf Coast and the Mississippi River, the nation's great internal highway. Mahan also articulated a more vague fear that an unforeseen war with a European power would expose America's large, completely defenseless coastal cities to a possibly devastating naval attack either by bombardment or by outright invasion. The British burning of the Capitol and White House was only seventy-six years in the past when Mahan published *The Influence of Sea Power,* and young Theodore Roosevelt's recent naval history of the War of 1812 had reminded American readers of its horror. In 1898 panic would sweep the cities of the eastern seaboard when it was learned that the Spanish fleet had sailed westward from home waters, its destination unknown. Might not Cervera mount a naval bombardment of Boston, New York, or Charleston on his way to Cuban waters?

Mahan clearly set forth the rationale for a powerful defensive fleet. The main thrust of his argument, however, involved expansion. In the modern world of powerful industrial states managing extensive overseas empires a nation could

not remain strong if it did not join the global scramble for colonies. And if a
nation did not remain strong, it would inevitably become prey to those that
were. Did this mean that the United States had to build a big navy to use as its
own aggressive expression of national interest? Navy secretary Benjamin Tracy
seemed to suggest so when he enthusiastically accepted the findings of the 1889
policy board that the nation should, in effect, put aside its military isolation for
a forward strategy. Rather than waiting for an enemy to approach U.S. shores
where he or they would be presumably repulsed by a combination of a coastal-
defense force and onshore forts, the navy should take the fight to the enemy
with extended battle-fleet operations in foreign waters.[20] But a closer look at
the "new," still numerically small steel-clad, steam-driven navy that began to
emerge from American shipyards after 1883 raises some serious doubts.

In contrast to the global sailing fleet of the immediate pre–Civil War era, the
new navy seemed "a defensive answer to European developments." Overwhelmingly concentrated on the East Coast, the fleet "reflected a shrunken
rather than an enlarged strategic perimeter"; its orientation was toward protecting
the great cities of the Atlantic seaboard and secondarily the Caribbean and
eastern Pacific (that is, Hawaiian) sea approaches to the Isthmus. The "'search
for bases'" that preoccupied much public debate was in fact a search for a few
rented "coal piles" in two or three Asian and Pacific ports (Yokohama, Pago
Pago, and Honolulu) in contrast to the earlier days, when Washington had
maintained naval agents and storekeepers in London, Marseilles, La Spezia,
Buenos Aires, Saint Thomas, Rio de Janeiro, Lima, Valparaiso, Honolulu,
Macao, and Shanghai.[21]

America's first three new battleships that came into service after 1890 were
deliberately designed and built as smaller, less powerful, and shorter-range ver-
sions of their most up-to-date European counterparts and were used in effect as
coastal-defense ships. Only a few protected cruisers such as those found with
George Dewey at Manila Bay were given the enormous fuel capacity to conduct
the historic mission of a weaker navy—the *guerre de course*. In the beginning,
not even Mahan could reverse the trend. As the first new short-range battleships
came into service in the midnineties, the Naval War College continued to restrict
its studies to Atlantic trade routes, "the strategic geography" of the Gulf of
Mexico and Caribbean, the defense of Hawaii, "and the maintenance of the neutrality of an isthmian canal." Soon after his book appeared, Mahan was ordered
by the Navy Department to Washington, D.C., "to draw up contingency plans
for hostilities with Great Britain or Spain." But the world's chief philosopher of
expansive navalism was given the task of drawing plans for a defensive war in

the Western Hemisphere rather than the eastern Atlantic, North Sea, or Mediterranean. Among his responsibilities, Mahan was directed to ponder the possibility of a sudden German naval assault against Dutch possessions in the Caribbean. Thus the surge to imperialism that overtook the United States in 1898 came not as a powerfully gathering force before that year but as a sudden eruption in that year, largely the result of Dewey's spectacular and wholly unanticipated victory in the Philippines.[22]

No one understood the implications of Mahan and Turner better than Theodore Roosevelt, who in a brief but vigorous lifetime had direct experience both in the frontier West and in the Navy Department. To Roosevelt the prospect of America isolated and confined in a world of predator nations was anathema. Together with Lodge, Secretary of State John Hay, and a handful of others in government, Howard Beale has observed, he "plunge[d] the nation into an imperialist career" in 1898 "that it never explicitly decided to follow." The pugnacious young "TR" believed that a man just wasn't a man without a six-gun and a nation just wasn't a nation without a fleet of battleships. Should the nation be forced to go to war with either European meddlers or hemispheric predators, a large steel-clad, big-gun navy, he argued, would allow it to emerge "immeasurably the gainer in honor and renown. . . . If we announce in the beginning that we don't class ourselves among the really great peoples who are willing to fight for their greatness, that we intend to remain defenseless, . . . we doubtless can remain at peace," but "it will not be the kind of peace which tends to exalt the national name, or make the individual citizen self-respecting." In an amoral world of nations maneuvering incessantly for power, prestige, and position, peace could be preserved only by periodic threats of sword and gun. "If we build and maintain an adequate navy and let it be understood that . . . we are perfectly ready and willing to fight for our rights, then . . . the chances of war will become infinitesimal."[23]

But the navy could not be simply defensive and reactive; it had to be the spearhead of a vigorous, healthy national empire that stretched to the ends of the earth. "Every expansion of a great civilized power," Roosevelt wrote at the end of 1899 in a typically Mahanian tone,

> means a victory for law, order, and righteousness. This has been the case in every instance of expansion during the present century, whether the expanding power were France or England, Russia or America. In every instance the expansion has been of benefit, not so much to the power nominally

benefited, as to the whole world. In every instance the result proved that the expanding power was doing a duty to civilization far greater and more important than could have been done by any stationary power.[24]

Although Europeans that year generally viewed the upstart Yankees as bullies who exploited Spanish imperial weakness to grab a modest Asian and Caribbean empire, the citizens of the United States were convinced that they had rescued the hapless peoples of Cuba, Puerto Rico, the Philippines, and even Guam from the yoke of oppression and that the navy had been the chief instrument of righteousness. All the nightmarish scenarios of helpless men in thrall to whimsically exploding machines that had emerged from the Sino-Japanese conflict evaporated during the euphoria of victory in a "splendid little war" over a chivalrous if incompetent and often disheartened opponent.

Unlike the earlier clash off the China coast, the Spanish-American War was fully reported throughout the Western world and thus became the first naval conflict of the industrial age that both the public and the experts understood. The dominant perception was of industrial man's mastery of his creations. Well-handled warships run by well-trained crews were no menace to anyone but their enemies. Such an impression helped stifle initial public concern in the United States and abroad that the loss of *Maine* might have been due to faulty industrial technology. The ensuing naval triumphs over Spain convinced the Americans and Europeans that the ship's destruction had been an act of Spanish sabotage.

Although in 1898 shipborne radio was still some years in the future, "for the first time in naval history, a government directed the action of distant ships at sea, communicating by telegram" to Commodore George Dewey at Hong Kong and later Manila and to Admiral William T. Sampson and Commodore Winfield S. Schley at Key West and Cuba. When Sampson finally found Admiral Pascual Cervera's fleet huddling inside Santiago harbor, he ordered that his major warships take turns illuminating the channel at night with searchlights. "It was the first such use of light by naval forces."[25]

But contemporary observers were less impressed with the use of the new technology of electricity for communication and illumination than with the overall power of the modern warship and, above all, the technical competence displayed by the American seamen in running it efficiently. At Manila Bay, Dewey coolly brought his small squadron through the minefield off Corregidor in the dead of night and early the next morning quickly maneuvered his handful of steel and steam cruisers and lesser war craft into a coherent battle line against the few enemy warships lurking behind the guns of the narrow Cavite Peninsula. Already under steady but wildly inaccurate bombardment, Dewey calmly informed *Olympia's* captain, "You may fire when ready, Gridley," and after seeing his gunners methodically pulverize the enemy, he withdrew and sent the men to breakfast. The supposedly hellish elements of the battle—stokers locked and crammed into dark, feverishly hot propulsion compartments with hissing steam pipes, clattering engines, and roaring furnaces—in fact did not bother the men involved at all. According to one participant, the engine-room crew aboard the cruiser *Baltimore* spent the time when not engaged in answering orders and moving dials smoking cigars, chewing tobacco, and "swapping yarns." Only one man died (an engineer suffered a heart attack), a few wounded, and the casualties were understandably obscured by total victory.[26] Thousands of miles from home and help, Dewey nonetheless proceeded to fend off by bluff and bluster the handful of European warships that soon arrived to scrounge for any potential imperial scraps they could lap up, thus preserving Manila Bay and the entire Philippine archipelago for Yankee occupation.

Off Santiago some weeks later, Schley ably handled his small squadron of battleships and cruisers. As Vice Admiral Pascual Cervera y Topete's cruisers emerged from the harbor, Schley chased them down and mortally wounded them one by one after a spirited run that in this instance did demand the final ounces of energy from the poor devils who toiled away passing coal and tending boilers in the engine rooms of *Iowa, Indiana, Oregon, Texas, New York,* and *Brooklyn.* When the last Spanish cruiser captain despairingly crashed his vessel against the rocks of eastern Cuba, America had won itself a modest Caribbean empire to go with its new holdings in East Asia. Almost as an afterthought, Washington finally annexed the Hawaiian Islands, which had been under the control of a planter "republic" for the previous five years.

The same American writer who only weeks before had questioned the safety of battleships was now ecstatic. "Military prowess passed away from Spain many years ago, and her organization to manage the modern ship, composed principally of machinery, is wretchedly deficient," Hollis told his readers. The U.S. Navy, on the other hand, understood the value of "education and technical training to a specific end" and had triumphed. Sailors, officers, and marines had performed superbly in their highly technical tasks of machine tending. If the war with Spain had demonstrated anything it was that the United States needed more battleships of *every* type. The cost would be high, but "these ships are well-nigh impregnable, and they must continue to hold their own as our main reliance for offense and defense."[27]

Hollis spoke the new conventional wisdom. After 1898 maritime rivalry became the great game of international politics, and every king, prince, and president believed he had to possess a fleet of modern battleships and supporting vessels to impress himself, his people, and his fellow rulers. The relative position of nations on the international naval list changed with dizzying speed. Even countries that could not truly afford and had no real need for great industrial navies built them nonetheless, ignoring the iron laws of geography. This was true of Russia whose Eurasian coastlines were so intermittent that no coherent naval force could be built and whose continental stretch was so great that no blue-water fleets had to be built. In 1900 the czar possessed either the third- or fourth-largest navy in the world. It was true of France whose global empire was great but whose Mediterranean coastlines fronted on a restricted sea and whose Atlantic ports could be (and historically had been) closely blockaded by enemy squadrons. France constantly vied with Russia for the number two, three, or four position in the world. It was true of Italy, who might dominate the Mediterranean with a big fleet but who was hemmed in from reaching the world ocean by Gibraltar and Suez and was forever restricted from playing a major role in European affairs by the mountain barriers that defined its northern boundaries and those of the adjacent Balkan Peninsula. Even the Austrian Empire ordered battleships from British yards; so did the Greeks and the Turks.

But such fleets were fearfully expensive to construct and maintain. Only Britain, France, the United States, Japan, Germany, and Russia could sustain the pace and thus win the title of great power.[28]

No one read Mahan with greater care or attentiveness than Germany's Kaiser Wilhelm II. A typical feudal warrior—strange, nervous, hypersensitive, and easily swayed by impulse and passion—Wilhelm carried awkwardly an arm withered at birth and believed this slight deformity rendered him incurably afflicted. It was a potentially explosive self-image, one that his young, uncertain nation shared, for Germany itself was a politically deformed patchwork of kingdoms, grand duchies, duchies, and three ancient free cities: Hamburg, Bremen, and Lübeck. A "baroque Catholic south" had been joined to an "austere Protestant north." But despite these potentially crippling divisions, the country was united in a "common pursuit of money, power and status." Wilhelm's realm numbered forty-eight million people in 1889; a quarter century later, without territorial expansion, it contained sixty-seven million. During this same period German iron and steel production expanded eightfold (passing that of Britain in 1900), coal output grew threefold, and exports and food production more than trebled. By the turn of the century Germany had become the industrial and military giant of the Continent.[29]

Most monarchs and peoples would have been more than satisfied with such stunning power; Wilhelm and his citizens were not. From its inception, Germany reached out for military and industrial mastery of Europe. At the same time crown and people suffered from an incessant, thinly veiled inferiority complex toward the "Anglo-Saxons." Germans soon became convinced that Britain—and the United States—hated them and would do everything possible to deny Germany its rightful place atop the new world industrial-imperial order. Wilhelm's cousins in the British royal family seemed to dominate affairs beyond the North Sea with effortless arrogance, and after 1890 the slowly emerging American industrial giant was apparently ready to join them in a tacit "gentlemen's agreement" that would forever confine Germany to continental limits, thus denying it access to the world's major trade markets. Somehow Berlin had to find a way to challenge the British Empire on the world ocean and in the rich, exotic lands that bordered it.[30] Here was the stage on which the future of the planet would be decided, where the rivalries for global dominance would be played out.

Wilhelm soon concluded that Germany had a "bitter need" for a navy.[31] His predecessors were not averse to a modest expansion of the tiny German coastal fleet, but before 1889 the young nation was still a fragile giant whose defining tradition was the Prussian army. Neither the first Wilhelm nor Frederick III was inclined to challenge Great Britain on the international sea-lanes. Wilhelm II, however, clearly had other ideas. As a boy he spent many summers at his grandmother Victoria's summer place, Osborne House on the Isle of Wight, close to Portsmouth harbor and Spithead. There each day the impressionable youth walked beneath a "garish allegorical fresco" above the main staircase depicting "'Britannia receiving the crown of the sea from Neptune' attended by 'Industry, Commerce, and Navigation.'"[32] He watched the frequent naval reviews unfold under his window and walked the shores watching Her Majesty's earliest ironclads majestically clatter and clank in and out of Britain's greatest naval base. Sometimes he even found his way on board his grandmother's warships. He thus obtained vivid, enduring impressions of the might and majesty of sea power exemplified by the emerging industrial navies of steam, steel, and cannon.

As the new kaiser he was enthralled when in 1888, during his first visit to the annual Cowes Regatta of the Royal Yacht Club, Victoria conferred on him the rank of admiral of the British fleet, an honor never before and never again bestowed on a foreign ruler. He had brought with him a small German naval squadron, nearly all the warships his nation possessed at the time. After returning home he wrote Victoria: "I am now able to feel and take interest in your fleet as if it were my own; and with keenest sympathy shall I watch every phase of its further development, knowing that the British ironclads, coupled with mine and my army, are the strongest guarantees of peace."[33] But, of course, Germany possessed relatively few ironclads, and in the early years of his reign Wilhelm struggled with himself, his advisers, and the army over whether to strain Germany's resources and challenge the Royal Navy with a high-seas fleet that would take years to build. In 1890, however, as Mahan's tome was reaching the comparatively few wardrooms of the Imperial German Navy, Wilhelm discovered his own apostle of modern sea power in the rather bristling personage of Alfred von Tirpitz, whom Winston Churchill would later characterize—quite correctly—as a "sincere, wrongheaded, purblind old Prussian."[34]

It was Tirpitz, holding the impressive title of state secretary of the German Imperial Navy Office from 1897 to 1916, who articulated a series of powerful if not always coherent justifications for the kind of fleet that both he and his kaiser yearned to use as a club against the noxious Anglo-Saxons. Whatever he may have lacked in vision or insight regarding Germany's position and relations with the outside world, Tirpitz possessed sufficient intellectual flair and conviction, political courage, and administrative tenacity to fight the army and the Reichstag for the necessary funds and personnel to build and man the battleships and armored cruisers deemed necessary to one day humble arrogant Albion.

Tirpitz's beliefs were first shaped by a revered father who harbored a profound dislike of "selfish Great Britain." The young Prussian soon became deeply affected by the prevailing ethos that equated the German political community and national character with the ideals of pure blood and a superior "race." But he entered the tiny Prussian navy in the late 1860s, when its "real supply base" was Plymouth, where German cadets were treated kindly and implicitly trained as British midshipmen. Tirpitz was never able to reconcile the dilemma that these two perspectives created in his own mind. Should Germany build a high-seas fleet for war or for peace? If for war, it would have to be concentrated in European waters, presumably to hold off the Russians in the Baltic while preparing for a climactic battle with the Royal Navy. If for peace, it should be deployed on the world ocean in the service of the mystical ideal of "Germandom" and the imperial ambitions of the German "race."[35]

Germans were superior beings, he later wrote, who paradoxically suffered from a lack of patriotism because of repeated fragmentation and rivalry orchestrated by selfish interests from without. Moreover, the impersonality of the industrial age was destroying the German soul.

> One could notice the harmful influence of the materialism which was penetrating into the upper classes of Germany, in the shape of a weakening of character, a diminution of that positive idealism which the German nation will always have to exert in the interests of its own self-preservation. For it is only by proud, unselfish devotion to the State that [Germany] can counterbalance the deficiencies of its geographical position, its bad frontiers, its limited area, its jealous neighbours, its religious differences, and its too young and too uncertain national sentiment.[36]

The national birthrate was rising each year, but newly united Germany was forever hemmed into the northwest quadrant of Europe. In the midst of increased crowding, scores of thousands of Germans were forced to go overseas to pursue their destinies not only in the United States but also in Asia, Latin America, and even Africa. In the process they lost their sense of national and "racial" identity. These émigrés possessed the means of creating a world empire to rival that of Britain or France. Unfortunately, they apparently lacked the will to do so. There was thus the terrible prospect—indeed, the sin, the moral crime—that they would be forever lost to the fatherland as it struggled "through to real world-political freedom." Germany's global position remained "artificial," and national greatness and destiny depended on "whether people could remain proud of the fact that they were Germans." Only one potential agency, one possible instrument, was available for "linking up German sentiment" overseas "and instilling into it pride of the homeland." That instrument was the navy, the "pioneer of Germandom." Sailing the world ocean, linking disparate German colonies into a global empire, a high-seas fleet would keep Germany from ultimately falling "to the mercy of the Anglo-Saxons."[37]

Tirpitz never found in his own utterances or writings quite the right phrases to define what he was thinking and planning, but he got his message across to subordinates, who returned it to him with precision and eloquence. In his memoirs he admiringly quoted from several letters he had received from one of his cruiser captains early in the First World War:

> There is so much German blood abroad which must be kept German and reinvigorated. Why should not the time come when this blood should pulsate again? . . . [N]ot to form states that might be annexed, but to take effect in the development of the race and to establish natural markets for

our mother country, without which we must ultimately stifle at home. . . . Embassies and consulates . . . don't win back Germandom or quicken German blood, and [German] schools [in Asia or Latin America] even can only preserve it in cases where the family still feels German. . . .

Only the navy can bring to a conclusion the great work of restoring the essential character and nature of the German[s] to their rightful place in the world. The navy is made to carry out into the world the national strength which reposes at home upon our monarchy and our strong army; it was born for the people out of this idea.[38]

Here was Tirpitz's grand unifying theme—the navy as the primary expression of national destiny—elements of the *Kriegsmarine* riding at anchor in foreign harbors from Capetown and Cairo to Shanghai and Lima, stirring the hearts of all German émigrés who saw the gray warships of their distant homeland floating proudly before them, even as the bulk of that fleet lay in home waters, a perpetual menace to and brake upon perfidious Albion. It was a superb argument to use at court and in the Reichstag in the always fierce competition with the army for funds and men, for if Tirpitz was right, the historical position of the Prussian army as the prime agent and exemplar of Germandom would be overthrown. Frederick the Great would have to give way to a more imposing figure; perhaps Tirpitz saw himself in that role.

Tirpitz's first move to position himself as the father of a "high-seas fleet" had been to ask for the creation of a "strategic-tactical Admiralty Staff" as "a main task in the navy"; such a move was essentially a declaration of independence from the Prussian army's firm control of German sea forces. He also implicitly argued for construction of a large German "war-fleet stationed in European waters" as an adjunct to the "annihilation strategy" being developed by Alfred von Schlieffen and the German General Staff for the defeat of France through the Low Countries. Wilhelm listened to this exciting new philosopher of navalism. In early 1892 Tirpitz, now an admiral, was appointed chief of staff at Supreme Headquarters with instructions to develop new "strategic directives" for a fleet that barely existed. Tirpitz promptly produced a memorandum arguing the need for "concentration on an annihilation strategy and on a fleet consisting chiefly of battleships and torpedo-boats." Time, however, was critical if Germany was not to be hopelessly outdistanced in constructing a battleship fleet, for England, Russia, and Japan were either engaged or about to be engaged in "huge programmes" of their own.[39]

In December 1897 Tirpitz began work on Germany's First Navy Law. He told the Reichstag that a high-seas fleet had become a question of survival *(Existenz-*

frage) for Germany. "Failure to build a mammoth battle fleet would result first in an economic, then in a political decline of the Reich." Chancellor Bernhard von Bülow added that Germany was entitled to "'its place in the sun'" and that only a high-seas fleet could guarantee that place.[40] On April 10, 1898, the Reichstag passed the First Naval Law, calling for the construction of nineteen battleships, eight armored cruisers, twelve large cruisers, and thirty smaller cruisers by April 1, 1904. Moreover, capital ships would be automatically replaced every twenty-five years to guard against obsolescence in an age of rapid industrial and technical advances.

At first foreign observers were not unduly alarmed by the German initiative. The nature of the fleet set forth in the law seemed to imply that Wilhelm and Tirpitz intended only to strengthen Germany's existing coastal-defense forces. But within months the international picture changed. As Britain's war against the South African Boers intensified, the Royal Navy was ordered to interdict foreign vessels off the African coast. When British cruisers stopped the mail steamer *Bundesrat* and several other merchantmen, popular German opinion against Britain became a "white heat."[41]

In June 1900, after more strenuous prompting from Tirpitz, the Reichstag approved his Second Navy Law, which was designed to double the size of the fleet by 1906. Moreover, there would be no parliamentary limit on the funds expended to build this prodigious naval force. In setting forth his rationale for the Second Naval Law, Tirpitz told Wilhelm:

> As soon as the aim is reached Your Majesty has an effective strength of forty-five ships of the line along with complete accessories—so powerful . . . that only England [will be] superior. But also against England we undoubtedly have good chances through geographical position, military system, torpedo-boats, tactical training, planned organizational development, and leadership united by the monarch.
>
> Apart from our by no means hopeless conditions of fighting, England will have lost [any] political or economic . . . inclination to attack us and will as a result concede to your Majesty sufficient naval presence . . . for the conduct of a grand policy overseas.[42]

Convinced now that he would ultimately possess a high-seas fleet second only to that of Britain, Wilhelm successfully forced his country into the final imperial scramble for world power. The kaiser and his diplomats and admirals began to dream of a German empire stretching from Europe to the Near East, Africa, Asia, and around to South America. In 1895 Wilhelm joined Russia and France in denying Japan southern Manchuria, which "that pushing Eastern nation" had just won by the sword. Having achieved a foothold in Far Eastern affairs through trade and diplomacy, Wilhelm next turned to expansion into the Middle East. By participating in settlement of the most recent of the seemingly interminable wars between Turkey and Greece, Germany gained for its bankers control over Turkish finances, which led to the creation of a Turkish-German consortium to construct a railroad from Berlin to Baghdad.[43]

In 1897 the kaiser used the murder of two German missionaries by Chinese bandits as an excuse to seize the strategic port and hinterland of Tsingtao (Qingdao). The next year German diplomats secured a ninety-nine-year lease on the port along with exclusive development privileges throughout the adjacent Shantung (Shandong) Peninsula. Tsingtao was chosen as Germany's Far Eastern bastion, and Wilhelm immediately sent part of his small fleet to Asian waters, boasting at its departure banquet that "the German Michael" had "firmly planted his shield upon Chinese soil." Admiral Prince Heinrich replied that "the gospel of His Majesty's hallowed person ... was to be preached to every one who will hear it and also those who do not wish to hear." Years later former chancellor von Bülow wrote that Germany's "establishment on the coast of China ... was in direct and immediate connection with the progress of the fleet, and a first step into the field of world politics ... giving us *a place in the sun* in Eastern Asia."[44] By 1900 Berlin had acquired the mid-Pacific Caroline Islands with their magnificent harbor at Truk (Chuuk). In Africa Wilhelm's acquisitions were confined to the most arid regions or, in the cases of Togoland and the Cameroons, areas with the most murderous climate. But he nonetheless acquired strategically important harbors and coaling stations, which could help secure and maintain an imperial lifeline between Europe and Asia.[45]

Berlin suffered some humiliating rebuffs along the way. Wilhelm had wanted more and better territories in Africa than he had been able to gain. In 1889 and again ten years later London and Washington denied Berlin control over Samoa, whose possession seemed essential to protect any imperial lifeline between China and substantial German populations in Latin America. Washington's interest in and ultimate seizure of Cuba as a result of the war with Spain infuriated Wilhelm. Cuba had belonged to Spain for centuries and was therefore in the kaiser's eyes a "European state." The United States seemed determined to rob Europe of at least some of its property "by fair means or by foul—seemingly the latter," he observed angrily. Wilhelm quickly became convinced that "Yankee money" and "Yankee audacity secretly supported by John Bull," that is, Great Britain, threatened not only Spain but the entire European imperial edifice as well. His ire was further raised by events in the Philippines in 1898 when, after defeating the Spanish squadron in Manila Bay, newly promoted admiral George Dewey successfully resisted pressure from British, French, and German naval squadrons to claim at least part of the archipelago. Admiral Otto von Diederichs, who commanded the small German squadron at Manila Bay, was especially bitter about his repeated failures to intimidate Dewey and the even smaller American squadron, and he expressed his anger in terms of scorn at American naval and military pretensions. The United States with its slovenly ways of war would never constitute a real military threat, Diederichs claimed in several cables home.[46]

Across the North Sea, there was no need of a Mahan to preach the cause of naval supremacy. Naval mastery remained for Great Britain what it had been for nearly two centuries, the essential guarantor of both unmatched imperial glory and basic national security. Ever mindful of the nation's position at the portals of Europe, Britain's seventeenth-century Articles of War proudly proclaimed that "it is upon the Navy, under the good Providence of God, that the Health, Wealth, and Safety of this Kingdom do chiefly depend." In the 1920s Winston Churchill, looking back at the years immediately before the Great War, defined the central place of the Royal Navy in world affairs:

> Consider these ships, so vast in themselves, yet so small, so easily lost to sight on the surface of the waters. Sufficient at the moment, we trusted, for their task, but yet only a score or so. They were all we had. . . . All our long history built up century after century, all our great affairs in every part of the globe, all the means of livelihood and safety of our faithful, industrious, active population depended upon them. Open the sea-cocks and let them sink beneath the surface, . . . and in a few minutes—half an hour at the most—the whole outlook of the world would be changed. The British Empire would dissolve like a dream; each isolated community struggling forward by itself; the central power of union broken; mighty provinces, whole Empires in themselves, drifting hopelessly out of control, and falling a prey to strangers; and Europe after one sudden convulsion passing into the iron grip and rule of the Teuton and of all that the Teutonic system meant. There would only be left far off across the Atlantic unarmed, unready, and as yet uninstructed America, to maintain, single-handed, law and freedom among men.[47]

What the Royal Navy did need in 1900 was a reformer. After decades of general peace, England's seamen fancied themselves more world policemen than members of a warlike institution. "We considered that our job was to guarantee

law and order throughout the world," one officer wrote, to "safeguard civilization, put out fires onshore, and act as a guide, philosopher and friend to the
merchant ships of all nations." The vast majority of Victoria's and Edward's
aristocratic officers were convinced that tradition, arrogance, and indolence
constituted the best education. Such education often ended where it began—at
the academy at Dartmouth, so expensive that no boy could expect to attend
unless his parents' income was at least seven hundred pounds a year, a princely
sum in those days of sharply uneven prosperity. "It takes three generations to
make a gentleman," one of them wrote. "The present naval officer is in every
way quite suitable for the needs of the Service, and it is a good maxim to 'let
well alone.'" Such an attitude led to the kind of blind discipline that Filson
Young, a great friend of the Royal Navy, characterized in 1914 as "the bleak,
noble attitude of the naval officer towards whatever his superiors decreed to be
his duty."[48]

Most officers exhibited unbridled contempt for the foreigners they encountered and the enlisted men they commanded. "Robert Arbuthnot was so absolute
a martinet that when, soon after he had handed over a ship to his successor a
seagull defecated with a plop upon the quarterdeck, the Chief Bosun's Mate remarked without a smile, 'That could never 'ave 'appened in Sir Robert's day.'"
When William Packenham was sent ashore in Asia Minor to quell an uprising
and found himself "surrounded on all sides by angry brigands," the incensed
officer turned on his Turkish interpreter and burst out, "'Tell these ugly bastards
that I am not going to tolerate any more of their bestial habits.'" When later, at
a "civic luncheon," an elderly lady inquired if he was married, Packenham
"replied courteously: 'No madam, no. I keep a loose woman in Edinburgh.'"
Most Englishmen were satisfied to embrace Gilbert and Sullivan's pleasing con-
ceit that such eccentrics as this ruled over a group of jolly tars. In fact, as late as
1905 a British sailor's fate was completely controlled by such characters, many
of whom proved cruelly capricious, successfully fighting to prevent any reforms
of the lower deck, or, indeed, any reforms at all.[49]

Late Victorian officers and men had been trained in sailing ships for service
in steamships. Every ironclad carried relics of the Age of Fighting Sail such as
marline- and handspikes, and nearly every captain and officer adhered to the
"paint and polish" school, which caused widespread neglect of gunnery because
practice dirtied up ships' decks. One admiral in the eighties and nineties customarily judged the efficiency of Her Majesty's ships by the cleanliness of his
white kid gloves after an inspection. By 1890 the mania for cleanliness had

reached such a ridiculous—and dangerous—degree that whenever a vessel left the dockyard,

> one of the first tasks of her crew was to take all the watertight doors off their hinges and carry them to the engine room where artificers would grind down the surfaces to a state where they would take a high burnished polish. It counted for nothing that their watertightness might well be destroyed in the process.... Successive naval administrations had shrunk from the changes which science in its application to warfare, and improved conditions of life ashore, especially among the working classes, rendered inevitable, and time and again energy and subterfuge were employed to bolster up the old conditions, and to put off the day when the Service would have to admit that a new era had dawned.[50]

To knowledgeable contemporary observers like Archibald S. Hurd, the litany of woes seemed endless. Training schools, ships, and academies "forced useless knowledge on" bewildered students. Gunnery was abysmal; so was engineering. Firing drills had been given over junior officers, and their initiative and energy in training the guns' crews "were restricted so as to cause a minimum of inconvenience to those who considered that the general cleanliness and smart appearance of a man-of-war were the first desiderata." Competition between ships "was in particular tabooed." As in Germany, engineers responsible "for the whole mechanical equipment and mobility of the vessel" were placed in an "entirely subordinate department" and social class. "The enthusiasm of the Fleet and the emulation between ship and ship were kept within old, narrow conservative channels." For those in command, further promotion resulted from smart handling of a single clean, shiny vessel on the few occasions when it set sail. In 1902 "Lord Charles Beresford, the probable Commander-in-Chief in a naval war of the near future, was reported to have stated...that 'he was now 56 years old, with one foot in the grave, and he had only tactically handled three ships for five hours in his life, and that was a great deal more than some of his brother admirals.'"[51]

The apparently magnificent navy that had gathered for Victoria's jubilee and excited the world's awe was thus a rather hollow shell despite what many considered a lavish amount of money spent on it. Indeed, during the latter two decades of the nineteenth century, the Royal Navy had declined precipitately relative to the navies of the other great powers. As late as 1883 Britain possessed new ironclad battleships that had comfortably exceeded the combined total of the next three European navies—41 to 33. By the 1897 jubilee the balance had "radically altered." The Royal Navy could muster but 62 battleships as against 66 total for France (itself an expansionary imperial power in both Africa and Southeast Asia), Russia, Germany, and Italy.[52]

Moreover, most of the vessels were not of good quality. The navy remained stocked with "a heterogeneous collection of largely inefficient ships of different sizes, different speeds, different guns, and different capabilities, impossible of organization into an efficient fleet capable of mutual support in battle." They had been ordered by "successive Boards of Admiralty, nostalgically wedded to the Nelson tradition and the heroic days of sailing navies" who "were hopelessly lost amid the technical clamor for advance." The board had belatedly realized the necessity of building ships in classes, but the first cluster to appear, the five-ship *Admiral* class of 1889, was not good. The first successful design, the nine battleships of the *Majestic* class, were just reaching the fleet when it gathered at Spithead for the jubilee.[53]

Most of the ships so smartly turned out at Spithead had been hastily gathered to provide a full complement for the jubilee; they were actually reserve vessels with skeleton crews or ships that had been completely abandoned until they might be needed, another relic of Nelson's time but one that played havoc with both material upkeep and crew efficiency in an age of steel hulls and increasingly complicated machinery. Moreover, the fewer than 140 ships of all classes in full commission at the time of Victoria's jubilee seldom left port. According to one contemporary critic, only a little more than half the officers and men of the Royal Navy were on sea duty, and "the time which, on the average, the *personnel* at sea spent actually cruising varied between sixty and ninety days each year." The Royal Navy's total expenditure in 1895 for coal was only a half-million pounds.[54]

British sea power was saved from precipitate decline by a small group of vibrant if divisive reformers energized in part by Tirpitz's First Naval Law and in part by French advances in design and strategy. They were driven by Sir John "Jacky" Fisher, commander of the Mediterranean Fleet and after Trafalgar Day 1904 first sea lord. "Whether Fisher himself was a great genius or a great menace is a point upon which opinions still differ," a British admiral wrote years later. "That he was a great man is indisputable."[55]

Fisher and his colleagues intended to bring in the new era with a rush. Their war cry was economy, efficiency, and preparation. To their great good fortune, Whitehall and Parliament had already bestirred themselves and after 1894 provided the funds to send the world's most advanced pre-dreadnought battleships to sea in ever larger numbers. Fisher and his allies could thus work from a solid base. Still, there was much to do. They began by abolishing sail drills and other remnants of the wooden navy. Fisher's ally Percy Scott "introduced a new routine in the Second Cruiser Squadron, economising the time men spent on house-maiding duties, in order to obtain further opportunities of training them in their war duties." Fisher encouraged his subordinates not only to study battle formations and naval strategy but also to write essays about them. He ordered long-distance, high-speed steaming trials and, in the words of Lord Beresford, transformed the Mediterranean squadron "from a 12-knot Fleet with numerous breakdowns" into a "15-knot Fleet without breakdowns." In 1901 Fisher was finally able to convince his superiors to authorize joint operations between the Mediterranean and Channel Fleets. As first sea lord he reformed the naval edu-cation system and in the process encouraged—with only limited success—an infusion of the middle class into the officer corps. Later, he was instrumental in transforming the entire navy from coal to oil, which brought Whitehall into the turbulent politics of the Middle East, and he directed major changes in gunnery practice carried out by Scott, first in the Mediterranean and later on the China Station. Scott's three new inventions—the dotter, the deflection teacher, and the loading tray—doubled fleet efficiency in gunnery in just two years. Many traditionalists in the fleet resented Scott's imperious ways, and large numbers of his fellow reformers disliked him. But Fisher was not deterred: "I don't care if he drinks, gambles, and womanizes; *he hits the target!*" Though Scott was rude and demanding, no one could deny that he was, in a phrase of the day, frightfully keen. In most postings he inspired subordinates with his en-thusiasm and persuaded them of the "essential rightness of his ideas."[56]

Under constant drill and practice the Royal Navy slowly but surely became ever more proficient in accuracy of aim and rapidity of fire. The steady improve-ment in gunnery efficiency seized the public imagination, and in 1902 the Admiralty itself took up the cause. By that year it was clear to Fisher, from his experiences observing French fleet exercises off Toulon, that rapid advances in torpedo technology promised high-speed accuracy up to four thousand yards and more. In the 1870s and '80s the French and British had developed "torpedo boats" (small, fast, lightly armed surface ships carrying one or two torpedo tubes) that clearly posed a threat to cumbersome lines of battleships, especially the Royal Navy's Channel Fleet. Fisher soon concluded that the submarine might in the end prove the undoing of all surface forces. French submarines, however crude, were superior to those being produced in the United States, the only other substantial builder.

By 1904 special exercises by the Channel Fleet suggested to the lords of the Admiralty that with extensive training, the "torpedo-boat destroyer," which the Royal Navy had developed in the nineties to catch and kill torpedo boats, could serve a multipurpose role. Larger than the boats it was meant to annihilate, the torpedo-boat destroyer itself carried torpedoes, thus posing a threat to enemy battle fleets as well as torpedo boats. For this reason alone, the torpedo-boat destroyer soon came to be called simply a "destroyer." Might not such a ship also serve as an effective antisubmarine platform in protecting the nation's priceless capital ships as they stood in line of battle against the foe? Fisher was not wholly convinced, and he pushed strongly to incorporate submarines into the Royal Navy. He wished to build a flotilla and more of small submarines as effective coastal-defense and anti-invasion weapons and larger undersea boats both to attack enemy battle lines and for close, inshore blockades of enemy coasts.

As late as 1913, however, the British submarine force remained small (only two British yards could build the boats), and Admiralty opinion remained deeply divided on their use both tactically and strategically.[57] Nonetheless, the torpedo and submarine had made a suitable impression upon and within the Royal Navy. Henceforth, His Majesty's ponderous battleships could not count on "closing more closely" to blast and finish off an enemy battle line without fear of running into an effective submarine or destroyer defense or both. Long-range fleet gunnery simply had to be improved dramatically if the Royal Navy was to remain supreme at sea.

When Fisher became first sea lord the reform movement became a tidal wave. Fisher was "arrogant, stern, unrelenting, and, when serious mistakes were made, even cruel." He harbored unbridled contempt for the traditionalists upon whom he was rumored to have set spies and snitches. He could and did destroy or deflect many of their careers. Worse, he deliberately cultivated a sense of whimsy and secrecy that some clearly found bracing and others just as understandably interpreted as a threat. "I never in all my life have ever yet explained, and don't mean to," he declared on the eve of the Great War. Widely hated and feared, Fisher nonetheless, in Winston Churchill's words, "hoisted the storm-signal and beat all hands to quarters. He forced every department of the Naval Service to review its position and question its own existence. He shook them and beat them and cajoled them out of slumber into intense activity." As one of Fisher's colleagues recalled forty years later, "He succeeded in making us *think*." Not surprisingly, the navy was frequently an unpleasant place to be while these essential changes were being effected. Under Fisher's steadily lashing tongue and pen the Nelsonian image of a "Band of Brothers" crumbled away to be replaced by a "Fishpond" of loyal subordinates and bitter enemies. The result was "open hostility" and "venomous intrigues." Yet for all that, Fisher, like Tirpitz, was widely lauded as bigger than life, a man who "got things done." In a time when sensationalist "yellow journalism" extolled naval power as the key to national greatness, Fisher's and Tirpitz's "decisive and colorful personalities" made them media stars and gave them great power.[58]

Fisher also sought to revolutionize British naval education, abolishing distinctions in both social class and professional specialty. The fees at Dartmouth and Osborne naval academies (the latter closed shortly after World War I) were greatly reduced in an effort to democratize the cadet corps, and the demoralizing disparities among engineering, torpedo, gunnery, and navigation officers were eliminated. In the new system of education "all . . . distinctions are now being swept away, and the officer of the future, whether it is intended that he shall specialise as a sea soldier [that is, marine] or in gunnery, torpedo, navigation, or engineering, will undergo the same course of study." Henceforth, young cadets would enter Dartmouth or Osborne in their twelfth or thirteenth year to begin a rigorous decadelong training.[59]

Once cadets completed their initial four-year course, they were sent to sea at age sixteen or seventeen for six or seven months on cruisers, where they were instructed by specialist officers. At that point the cadets, now midshipmen, were reassembled into groups of no more than a dozen and assigned to various ships in the fleet for three years, during which "a specially selected instructional lieutenant [was] placed in charge of them." While one group of midshipmen was being educated by gunnery, torpedo, or navigation lieutenants, another was receiving instruction in command and administrative functions from the executive officer, and a third group was with the engineer down in the engine room. After a year each group switched so that at the end of the thirty-six-month training session everyone had been equally exposed to all aspects of shipboard life. The midshipmen were then sent ashore for further study in piloting, gunnery, and torpedoes, and after being confirmed as sublieutenants the young men went to sea for training as watch keepers on the bridge. Only after they had passed this stage in their careers at age twenty-two or twenty-three were the young men commissioned as lieutenants and allowed to study one specialty intensively. As a result of this intense and prolonged training, "the Fleet will obtain officers with an acquaintance with all departments of activity on board ship."[60]

Fisher and his colleagues also reformed advanced education. At the ancient Royal Naval College in Greenwich they bypassed the narrow technical curriculum for midlevel officers and established an eight-month "war course" whose basic syllabus included naval history, strategy, and tactics and international law. Unfortunately, most of the senior lieutenants and commanders of Fisher's day were relics of the rapidly passing marlinespike age, and before the Great War few matriculates at Greenwich were able to benefit from the updated instruction. Nonetheless, in October 1912 a number of "Admiralty officers of middle rank" formed the Naval Society, and Herbert Richmond began publication of a quarterly journal, the *Naval Review,* "to encourage junior naval officers to write and discuss matters of naval interest." By 1913 the society numbered 60; two years later it had 1,260 members.[61]

In an atmosphere of liberal reform and growing class antagonism, Britain's comfortable circles were horrified at the changes Fisher had forced on the navy's officer corps. And they viewed with undisguised loathing his efforts to humanize lower-deck life. But Fisher cared only for the efficiency of the fleet, and he (and later Churchill) espoused and carried forward the demands of civilian reformers such as journalist Lionel Yexley and other vigorous champions of Jack Tar. Fisher and his reformers really had no choice, for industrial navies demanded seamen of increasing intelligence and competence. Although the coming of the modern warship had forced some navies to acknowledge the need to expand the training of enlisted men, the Royal Navy had characteristically rejected the idea for many years.

In 1900 (and for decades thereafter) England's common seamen continued to be recruited from two sources. One was the naval enlisted families in the home ports of Plymouth, Portsmouth, or Rosyth. The other much larger pool came from the working classes of the country's large towns and cities. Just who these chaps were is becoming a matter of contention. To characterize them as "the otherwise unwanted lads of Britain—the waifs, the strays, the abandoned bastards, the untamable, the Artful Dodgers of Queen Victoria's realm"—is a bit much, even coming from one of their own, Tristan Jones, though historians have traditionally assumed such bias. Peter Kemp, himself a Royal Navy veteran of the early twentieth century, wrote that although service on the lower decks of the Royal Navy "was never popular and generally avoided except as a last step, poverty and unemployment made sure that any vacancies in the ships were always filled. The food was poor, the pay meagre, the work on board mainly dull and repetitive. Discipline was strict" and corrupt; Tars could pay off the ship's police to stay out of trouble. Most captains invoked "the statutory minimum of 48 hours every three months" when it came to allowing the men ashore. The argument of American professor Christopher McKee that the Royal Navy's "recruiting methods—its testing for literacy and basic computational skills, its re-

quirement of a character reference from a clergyman or constable before joining—
make it clear that it preferred to recruit from the upper, respectable end of the
working class" may have some merit insofar as ideal conditions were concerned,
but ideal conditions seldom obtained in late Victorian England. The three
hundred–plus-page 1904 *Manual of Seamanship for Boys and Seamen of the Royal
Navy* was clearly written for youngsters of reasonably good intelligence who had
to master a fair amount of material on basic seamanship and were expected to
develop a rudimentary acquaintance with the mechanical functioning of modern
industrial battleships, cruisers, and smaller war craft. But anyone familiar with
recruiting practices in the industrial age—even in the United States as late as
the early twenty-first century[62]—knows that when the enlistment pool starts
to shrink and ships become undermanned, standards are often substantially relaxed for the sake of making quotas. Certainly, "polite" society in late Victorian
and Edwardian Britain viewed its seamen as "so called scum of British earth," and
from that perspective they certainly were, however "respectable" their working-
class origins may have been. Many came from backgrounds that they themselves
described as "really hard times. Almost Dickens' days wasn't it?" Alcoholism
was an essential part of their lives (some had begun imbibing as children), as were
families broken and reconstituted by early deaths and remarriages and a routine
reliance on heavy corporal punishment that our age finds understandably shocking. Finally, a handful of superior minds were crushed by economic necessity
and class prejudice. "Several of the sailors" whose records McKee investigated

> were superior students and were eager to continue their educations beyond
> the mandatory school attendance age of fourteen. Some won scholarships
> that would have permitted them to go on to secondary school and prepare
> for higher-status lives than their parents had known. In every case but one,
> the boy's parents, driven by the family's economic needs—and perhaps by
> other unspoken motivations, such as jealousy that a child should rise out of
> the class in which they were trapped—demanded that their sons leave school
> at the permitted age, go to work, and contribute to the family income.

Work for these future sailors invariably proved to be "a series of low-paying,
dead-end jobs ... followed by a decision to join the navy." In short, most of
Victoria's and Edward's Tars were the same "shilling-a-day men of no birth and
scanty education" as the "old contemptibles" who perished in their several thousands on the western front in 1914 stopping the Germans cold.

  Whatever their moral fiber or intellectual capabilities, all were treated like
the scum that polite society assumed they were. More often than not used to

receiving or at least witnessing rough treatment, recruits were sent first to HMS
Ganges, a former eighty-four-gun man-o'-war become rat-infested hulk that in
1865 was designated a training ship at Falmouth. There the wretched boys were,
in Jones's words, "bullied, beaten, bashed, scourged, half-starved, tormented,
pummeled, lashed, keel-hauled, cudgeled, thrashed, swinged, trounced, lam-
basted, hurt, manhandled, battered, thumped, scared and terrorized into a total
submission to the almighty will of My Lords Commissioners of the Admiralty."
After a year's ordeal they emerged to become, in the fond assumption of themselves and their nation, "the finest naval seamen the world has ever known." It was
a questionable boast at best. As late as 1940 Jones witnessed the routine weekly
removal of "three or four trainees, HO's [hostilities only] or boys, off their
heads, to the mental hospital in Chatham." These occasions, Jones later wrote,

> were spoken of quite casually, in passing, as if the boy or man in question had
> contracted measles or flu and had gone off for a week's rest by the seaside.
> There was never a thought of commiseration for the loony or his family. It
> was looked upon as inevitable that some people would go crazy and show
> it. Others went crazy—and managed to hide it from authority—and, they,
> in the long run, were even crazier than those who were carted away.[63]

Jones is certainly firing for effect with his last observation. As captured by
McKee, former ratings' recollections of life in the Royal Navy ran the gamut
from "harsh, savage, 'ours not to reason why'" and "extremely severe" to occasionally "cruel and sadistic and out of all proportion to the crime," from "too
rigid and in many instances unfair" to "strict but generally fair" and "If one did
one's job and behaved, no trouble at all." Did this mean that the vast majority
of Her and His Majesties' sailors quickly resigned themselves to a life of mind-
numbing docility to escape the lash? Not quite. One thirty-year veteran of both
world wars quoted by McKee seems to have summed up matters perfectly. "The
navy had its own brand of discipline," he recalled. It was "based on the fact that
men were for days and weeks on end in what you could describe [as] a steel
box: calm, storms, tropical heat. No ice water. No cool air system. This called
for a special brand of discipline, a different type of man."[64] Indeed it did. But
throughout the first half of the twentieth century, the United States Navy also
sent men to sea in un-air-conditioned steel boxes through calm, storm, tropical
heat, and mind-numbing cold, and they became far different and eventually
better sailors than their British cousins who endured a harsh world of deliberate
stringency. Though undeniably tough mentally and physically, Jack Tar with his
professional life begun under the cane and the whip was instinctively discouraged

from becoming an innovative problem solver. He was far more liable to anticipate orders, not events. The kind of initiatives that bubbled up from the comparatively well-treated enlisted ranks of both the U.S. Army and the U.S. Navy
before, during, and after World War II was beyond Jack Tar's comprehension.

Following their ordeal on *Ganges,* Royal Navy recruits learned their gunnery,
clerical, or other specialty skills in the fleet. But boys from such unpromising
backgrounds were seldom capable of absorbing training in the advanced technologies of the early twentieth century. Thus, technical ratings such as engine-
room artificers were drawn directly from private industry, where the workers
had already been trained. Whereas common seamen usually joined the Royal
Navy between the ages of sixteen and seventeen and a half and were expected to
serve for twenty-two years (an initial twelve-year enlistment followed by a ten-
year extension), the artificers were generally recruited for five-year service (often
extended through reenlistment) in their early twenties.[65]

Len Wincott, who joined the Royal Navy in the late twenties, clearly enjoyed
the ordeal of basic training. Despite canings on occasion, "the discipline appealed
to me." What rankled and riled was the absolute sense of class, of "them and
we," that pervaded the service. Once in Hong Kong, when a heroic British seaman rescued several children and adults from a hotel fire before falling to his
death, the sailor and his mates were accused by the better sort in the city of
looting. Wincott, a ringleader in the 1931 Invergordon mutiny, found it expe-
dient to emphasize that he and his mates generally loved the service and had
been goaded past endurance because of the follies of a few. But the navy he de-
scribes was clearly too grim a place for intelligent, ambitious, and even minimally
sensitive souls to develop a sense of progressive professionalism.[66] Fisher and
the reformers dimly grasped this fact and were determined to transform life on
the mess decks as thoroughly as in the wardroom.

As late as 1904 Jack Tar's basic training remained largely frozen in the Age of
Sail. He was expected to know the basic structure and layout of a pre-dreadnought
industrial battleship, including its framing and plating and the stresses placed
upon a steel hull by heavy seas and gunfire. He was expected to understand
compartmentalization and how to operate simple watertight-door machinery
and the marginally more difficult sea cocks. But such information was always
basic and perfunctory, while the bulk of the manual was devoted to such relics
of the Age of Fighting Sail as signal flags, small boats and hitches, rigging, knots
and splices, sail making, and the like. Only nine pages were devoted to a discussion of "mechanical work," including the use of such basic tools of the industrial
age as the screwdriver and the nut and the bolt.[67]

Fisher and his colleagues promptly expanded enlisted men's education to take into account the realities of working on a modern steam and steel big-gunned ship. Training schools for ratings were established to advance the professionalism of those on the lower decks, and by 1914 gunners and torpedo men routinely moved back and forth between fleet maneuvers and shore schools. Indeed, the need to keep to this schedule or risk disruption of naval routine complicated the maintenance of fleet mobilization during the tense weeks of crisis leading to the outbreak of world war in 1914.

After a series of wrenching battles between 1904 and 1914, the pay of enlisted men in the Royal Navy and Marines was raised to an almost livable standard, and the most brutal and capricious punishments were outlawed. Gross corruption in the canteen service was cleaned up, and the worst excesses of the wretched naval penal system were abolished. Perhaps the most striking advance came in the dramatic improvement in food. As late as 1904 the lower deck of the Royal Navy subsisted on roughly the same rations that had been issued in 1797: bread or biscuit, salted pork, sugar, butter, cheese, peas, and oatmeal. Rum (for grog) had largely been substituted for beer, together with the addition of jams, mustard, pepper, coffee, and, perhaps most important, milk. The latter must have been just introduced, for one of Fisher's first orders was to install bakeries and refrigerator rooms in the new warships so that British sailors no longer had to choke down worm-laden hardtack and salted meat. (It was said that sailors in Nelson's fleet always had raspy throats from the cold worms that stuck in them after a meal.) By 1914 "Daily Standard Naval Rations" included a pound of "fresh vegetables" for each man, together with a half pound of "fresh meat" and three-quarters of an ounce of condensed milk. But dietary stringency was still maintained. Each week saw one "Salt Pork Day" and one "Preserved Meat Day."

Finally, there was the matter of promotion. Toward the end of the period it became possible for the most talented enlisted men to move into the warrant and lower commissioned ranks, although, as historian Stephen Roskill points out, this "Mate Scheme" was a failure "partly because it stigmatized" enlisted men promoted to officers "as being different from those who had entered as cadets" and partly because the "Mates" proved too old to hope for attainment of higher rank.[68]

Despite these reforms, Britain's modern seamen were treated little differently from their great-grandfathers in the Age of Fighting Sail who had been impressed from the bars and brothels of London and the port towns of the southeast

coast to fight Yankee rebels and Bonaparte's sailors. As late as 1914, the lifestyles
of officers and enlisted men aboard David Beatty's battle-cruiser fleet remained
dramatically different. Whereas ensigns, lieutenants, and commanders often
"motored" from Rosyth into nearby Edinburgh for an afternoon of shopping,
tea, "cinema," or golf or walked the nearby hills for exercise, the Tars in their
thousands were confined to ships large and small, doubtless gazing longingly at
the bleak shoreline. Occasionally, their petty officers would take them off for a
brief football, that is, soccer, match with their fellow "matelots" at some make-
shift field, but thereafter they were promptly marched back aboard. In peacetime,
the men were usually granted a month's leave each year following fleet maneuvers. During wartime they could be given very little if any such indulgence.

The upper classes ashore and in the wardroom insisted on viewing the almost
inhuman life of the lower deck in the jolliest of terms. "It is amazing," British
journalist Filson Young recalled of his days with the battle cruisers in 1914–
1915, "to consider how happy and how healthy" the enlisted men "had kept in
the trying conditions of ship life." So they had, but it was due to their indomitable character rather than their oppressive circumstances. Such men
would fight with incredible perseverance at Jutland, and their sons would fight
with equal bravery off Norway and Crete a generation later. But efficiency beyond basic seamanship was often quite another matter.[69]

In the end Fisher and his fellow reformers largely failed to overcome the
rigid tradition and narrow outlook of a volunteer long-service profession. Fleet
intelligence, for example, was at once derided and largely ignored as one more
onerous "innovation," though largely through the efforts of Admiral Beatty's
secretary and flag commander "an attempt was made in the [battle cruiser]
Lion to organize the information with which we were being supplied into as
full and useful a form as possible." One senior officer, writing to another in
1930, summed up the Royal Navy's prewar malaise perfectly. "I look back on
my own experiences at Osborne and Dartmouth with somewhat mixed feelings,"
T. G. N. Haldane recalled.

> Although the training was in certain respects excellent it is easy to see
> now that certain vital elements were missing. Of these far the most im-
> portant was the absence of differentiation of interests and outlook. Such
> differentiation is impossible if you herd together from the age of (in my
> case) 12½ onwards four or five hundred boys all being trained in the same
> way for the same profession. Inevitably you get a mould turning out a type.
> I don't think the type produced is wholly bad—in fact it is very good in

certain respects—but it is a *type* and the resulting limitations become more obvious in later life.[70]

Jutland would prove Haldane right. Britain's seamen were insufficiently trained and prepared for modern war. Neither were their adversaries across the North Sea. Nor, as events would demonstrate, did the industrialists provide either side with decent weapons with which to fight.

CHAPTER 2

Scorpions in a Bottle

OVER ALL THE EVENTS and crises that crowded the European calendar
between 1905 and 1914 lay the growing specter of the Imperial German Navy.
It was never the biggest fleet in the world; Britain would not permit it. But it
quickly became a large, well-balanced organization that rapidly acquired the
sharply limited professionalism of its day. Above all, despite the dispatch of several armored and battle cruisers to distant stations in East Asia and the Mediterranean, Germany's ever growing inventory of capital ships, cruisers, destroyers,
and, eventually, submarines was overwhelmingly concentrated in several North
Sea ports less than a day's hard steaming across often stormy, murky, and relatively shallow waters from the east coast of England.

The establishment and rising power of a "High Seas Fleet" thrilled Kaiser
Wilhelm and his people, even as it induced mounting dread within ever widening circles in Britain, on the Continent, and to a lesser extent in the United
States as well. The German navy, while young, was modern looking and brim-
ming with confidence and aggressiveness. Once Germany began construction
of a blue-water fleet, the other powers felt compelled to respond. Despite his
many protestations to the contrary, Alfred von Tirpitz had set out to destabilize
the European political and military balance, and he succeeded. The coming of
the dreadnought era in 1906 ignited a blatant arms race, turning the British
and German fleets into scorpions, and the North Sea into the narrow bottle
that contained and increasingly defined them. Finally, the rise of the German
navy not only accelerated Fisher's reform impulses within the British fleet but also
stimulated revolutions in naval architecture, design, ordnance, and propulsion
that dramatically accelerated the development of new warship types like the

submarine while increasing the size, power, and influence, though not always
the effectiveness, of the capital ship.

The universal unpopularity of the Boer War abroad forced the British government to rethink its withdrawal from continental affairs that had followed the
defeat of Napoléon more than eighty years before. The industrial-military rise of
Germany no longer permitted a careful exercise of balance-of-power diplomacy.
Practical isolation from the increasingly turbulent affairs of Europe was no longer
feasible. Indeed, empire itself, as generally understood in Europe for the past
thirty years ("the great game of [global] expansion which had been played without major mishap"), might no longer be feasible. Whitehall's initial search for
allies focused on Berlin. His Majesty's government proposed to the kaiser nothing less than an Anglo-Teutonic agreement to rule the world ocean. But Wilhelm and his diplomats concluded that the scheme actually reflected a tacit
British agreement to join the United States in keeping Germany out of Latin
America, despite the insistence of the German ambassador in Washington,
D.C., that the Yankees would reject any such British initiative and defend the
Americas on their own. It was clear that influential circles in the United States
did not like or trust Germany any more than they did the British. "'Leading
Americans,'" the ambassador sniffed, especially President William McKinley,
found Germans to be "as distasteful as ever."[1]

Once London's offer of an Anglo-Teutonic alliance with Berlin was rebuffed,
the Balfour government went to the French, who were much more receptive,
and an entente cordiale was forged in 1904. Almost immediately, the British
and French general staffs initiated "conversations" to explore the possibility of
joint operations in any future war on the Continent, while the foreign offices
informally agreed that Britain would have a free hand at Suez and in neighboring
Egypt in exchange for practical French control of Morocco.

From a naval point of view, His Majesty's government should have approached
the French from the beginning because an Anglo-French (soon to be Anglo-
French-Russian) alliance fulfilled British interests far better than any rapprochement with Berlin could have done. Germany's growing industrial might
and commercial prosperity masked a chronic financial weakness within the
government that, along with the always heavy spending on the army, left comparatively few resources for naval expansion. Moreover, its lack of long-range
cruisers and overseas bases drastically reduced Germany's threat to both British
merchant shipping and the Royal Navy. The Russian navy, on the other hand,
was large and the French navy technologically innovative in a way that severely
challenged the initially somnolent British. In 1896, the French had laid down

the first of several fast armored cruisers whose plates could withstand the six-inch shells of those numerous but unarmored British vessels designed to protect imperial trade on the far sea-lanes of the earth. François Fournier, perhaps the most influential admiral in the French navy, argued at century's end that a squadron of French armored cruisers, swift enough to evade British battleships and able to prey on British imperial shipping, could in a short time bring England to its knees.[2] Eventually, the British Admiralty bestirred itself to respond with equally impressive armored cruisers of its own. But the French threat (when linked to the Fashoda crisis of 1898) and the rising numerical strength of the Russian navy provided the first, if ultimately not the most important, warning to Britain that despite its impressive display of sea power at the diamond jubilee, the Royal Navy's long and unquestioned supremacy at sea could and would be seriously challenged.

The dramatic new technologies afforded by industrialism promised not only new warship *types* but also the possibility of new warship *functions,* and therefore a revolution in naval force *structures* (though the armored cruiser was designed to pursue the kind of war against commerce, or *guerre de course,* that had been a traditional component of naval warfare for centuries). The excitement and ordeal of sudden, unanticipated change thus confronted admiralties all across the newly industrialized world at the beginning of the twentieth century, even as naval construction and maintenance costs suddenly spiraled with the advent of the heavily armored and heavily gunned warship. The Anglo-French entente of 1904 thus fulfilled Britain's needs and ambitions militarily as well as diplomatically. Whatever dangers might exist in suddenly assuming continental security, responsibilities were more than offset by obtaining the alliance of an advanced naval power that could have seriously challenged Britain's control of the global ocean.

Wilhelm felt outmaneuvered and ignored by the Anglo-French agreement and was incensed that London and Paris had bilaterally disposed of Germany's substantial commercial interests in Morocco. The kaiser petulantly told the king of Italy that during "all the long years of my reign my colleagues, the Monarchs of Europe, have paid no attention to what I have to say. Soon, with my great Navy to endorse my words, they will be more respectful."[3] Wilhelm proved to be a bull who carried his own china shop around with him. In the spring of 1905 he strutted off his yacht at Tangier to declare that Germany was ready to unilaterally guarantee Moroccan independence. Flagrantly bullying France with the prospect of war, Wilhelm forced the French government to oust its foreign minister and persuaded both London and Paris to agree to an international conference to determine Morocco's status.

By February 1906 the deadlocked Algeciras Conference left Europe poised on the brink of an Anglo-French war against imperial Germany and Austria—or so doleful British and French diplomats believed. Asked to provide good offices, Theodore Roosevelt determined that Austro-German demands had exceeded what France could decently accept, and he pushed the kaiser and his diplomats hard to retreat. Speck von Sternburg, the German ambassador in Washington, D.C., cabled home that "Germany has entirely lost its originally strong position at Algeciras and is in danger of losing the confidence of the world"—rather heady stuff for a president and a country only recently emerged on the world stage. Confronted by an American fleet that had already placed decided limits on German aspirations in the Caribbean, Wilhelm backed down and Europe backed away from war. Emerging American sea power was beginning to have an influence on the balance of international politics.[4]

Although it has generally been assumed that the Boer War and the Moroccan crisis marked a sinister turning point in Anglo-German relations, perceptive observers then and later glimpsed deeper forces at work. Queen Victoria's death in 1901 shattered the fragile confidence of an island empire that "had now lost its imperial mother figure." The Britain of 1902 and 1913 was increasingly unsure of its place in the world; Englishmen became prone to fits of anxiety, to outbursts of sudden anger and "ripples of uncertainty and self-doubt." It was a time, according to H. G. Wells looking back shortly after the outbreak of war in 1914, "of badly strained optimism. Our Empire was nearly beaten by a handful of farmers [the Boers] amidst the jeering contempt of the whole world—and we felt it acutely for several years." As the country struggled to emerge from its slough of despondency it was battered by the trip-hammer blows of the Scott party's tragic destruction in Antarctica and the sinking of *Titanic,* both of which occurred in 1912 (though Scott's fate was not determined and communicated to the world until the following year).

> There's a whisper down the field, where the year has shot her yield,
> And the ricks stand grey to the sun,
> Singing: — "Over then, come over, for the bee has quit the clover,
> And your English summer's done."[5]

Within this context—at once melancholic and excitable—the German challenge was inevitably overdrawn.

Across the North Sea, Tirpitz struggled with impossible problems of his own even as he and his eager young subordinates suffered from a severe case of hubris. The admiral understood from the beginning that his dream of a High Seas Fleet contained seeds of disaster. A service whose primary mission was to express na-tional will and power on the world seas could never be risked in war where a battle of annihilation was always possible. Yet Germany's putative enemies— Russia, France, and especially Britain—would never respect a fleet that was *not* built and ready for war. Tirpitz unwittingly emasculated his beloved navy at its birth by presenting to his kaiser the image of pretty ships, not expendable fight-ing vessels. He confused his British adversaries by talking of and planning for a naval war he never really wanted to fight.

Tirpitz, "himself . . . relentlessly offensive minded from the very start," was agonizingly aware of the paradox he had created. Germany must build a *big* fleet of appropriate warship types to implement any global policy. An offensive spirit must suffuse the training of German naval officers from their academy day onward. Yet the fleet must avoid a battle of annihilation in any war that might develop from Germany's aggressive actions either in Europe or beyond. Thus, when he first came to power in the early nineties, Tirpitz drove his young subordinates to study the dynamics of modern naval warfare such as could be gleaned from the few actions between fleets or individual units of steel-clad steamships and to develop sophisticated maneuvers that would keep his beloved navy from destruction in combat. "Such rigorous and disciplined work laid the groundwork for two further decades" of development under Admiral Hans Koester and others that would culminate in Reinhard Scheer's brilliant seaman-ship under fire at Jutland. But although Germany might be able to build a fleet of sufficient size and efficiency to defeat Russia or France, the Royal Navy was always another matter. Tirpitz concluded, however, that there might be a way out of his dilemma. A High Seas Fleet designed to express in material form the spirit of "Germandom" around the world might also attract valuable allies to Germany's side in times of international tension. "In those days, the middle of the 'nineties," Tirpitz later wrote, "we had to increase in general power all round; i.e. to qualify ourselves for an alliance with the Great Powers. But alliance-value could only be achieved by a battle fleet." Tirpitz hoped desperately that as his beloved fleet grew and matured, "one single ally at sea" would emerge to allow a decisive showdown with the Royal Navy somewhere in the Channel or the North Sea should an Anglo-German war materialize.[6]

Nonetheless, Tirpitz and his planners had to develop a general doctrine as well as specific tactics for a High Seas Fleet that could operate alone in the event of war. Their thoughts inevitably revolved around Mahan's assumption that a future war at sea between modern ironclad steam battleships would roughly replicate the battles of the Age of Fighting Sail, that is, two lines of warships would blaze away at one another until one side or the other gave way *(Grosskrieg)*. Tirpitz envisioned heavily armored ships of not great speed whose "heavy artillery was to be used at a close range against the vital parts of enemy ships and at all ranges against particular enemy ship types, rapid-firing middle artillery was to play the major role in most battle situations, and light artillery was to be used against enemy torpedo-boats. In addition ships of the line were to be armed with torpedoes and a ram."[7]

From the beginning Tirpitz understood that he might occupy a more favorable strategic position than many imagined. Because Britain did have worldwide responsibilities, its great fleet had to be dispersed. Because Germany did not yet possess a global imperium, its fleet could be concentrated on the British doorstep. At the outbreak of war a German fleet could gather in the Heligoland Bight and move out smartly against the enemy, be it Britain or France. Tirpitz placed "strong emphasis . . . on offensive action against the enemy at the very beginning of a war, for then the morale of the attacker was the highest." He clearly hoped that German diplomacy would be able to keep Britain and its home fleet out of any future European war. In that case the German navy would sweep down the Channel to destroy its French counterpart while Berlin applied diplomatic pressure on London to keep the Royal Navy not only neutral but in port as well. "A victory in the Channel creates for us after a successful war the right to become a fleet of the first rank, as required by Germany's world mission and world position."[8] Navy planning dovetailed neatly with the army's emerging Schlieffen Plan, which stipulated that the neutrality of Holland and Belgium would be deliberately violated to give the German army the precious maneuvering room needed to outflank and eventually defeat the French army in Flanders or metropolitan France. This same violation of the Low Countries would provide the German navy with the ports it needed to secure permanent control of the English Channel.[9]

Tirpitz and his colleagues suspected that such reasoning, however appealing, was unrealistic because Britain could never allow a great power to occupy the Channel coast. The Royal Navy would surely sortie upon a German invasion of Holland or Belgium, and the British and French fleets, if concentrated and combined in home waters, were sufficient to brush aside German naval forces for decades to come. Moreover, if war ever materialized when the German fleet remained inferior to those of Britain and France, the two enemies would not move in for a decisive naval action but would simply blockade Germany, deny its imports, and starve it to death. Tirpitz admitted as much in a memorandum to Wilhelm in the early summer of 1897, reporting on a major change in German naval doctrine. "The operations plan of the High Command bases itself on the strategic defensive in the Baltic and North Seas. One wants to await the enemy and to defeat him here. The purpose is to keep open our imports."[10]

Indeed, except for the Americans, who built a fleet without a significant merchant marine to protect, maintaining open-sea communications to the homeland had been the basis of naval power for millennia. Mahan had recognized this principle and given it eloquent expression. Tirpitz could not deny it in arguing the necessity for a great fleet. "But I believe now that the enemy will not come at once," he told his kaiser, "and that we will then wait with our large fleet while France, without much loss, cuts off two-thirds to three-quarters of our imports in the Channel and North of England. But this is not my business."[11]

Despite his last throwaway sentence, protection of Germany's vital overseas trade *was* Tirpitz's business, and as historian Ivo Lambi has stated, the admiral "placed his finger on the most vulnerable point in the operational planning against Britain before World War I and on the futility of his own program."[12] A German High Seas Fleet, unless materially larger than its British or French counterparts, simply could not steam out and effectively break a certain Anglo-French blockade in wartime. Yet the breaking of such a blockade was the most important service that a German fleet could render. To build a comparative handful of battleships to advance the cause of Germandom around the world or to use as bargaining chips for an alliance with France, Italy, Austria-Hungary, Russia, or perhaps even the United States was a gross waste of precious German national resources, as Tirpitz apparently realized. He and his colleagues in the navy ministry failed to resolve the problem of how to employ a High Seas Fleet that, no matter how large and powerful, could not match that of its chief adversary and thus had to remain essentially a neutered coastal-defense force. The problem existed in 1900, it existed in 1914, and, indeed, it existed in 1916 both before and after the Battle of Jutland. It would continue to plague Hitler's admirals.

Not only did Tirpitz and his colleagues fail to resolve this key strategic problem. They compounded it by planning a possible naval war with the United States, then stirred up the German public to accept such a possibility. As events in Manila Bay played themselves out to Germany's detriment in 1899–1900, strategists in Berlin began drafting naval studies targeting the hated Monroe Doctrine, the future of Cuba, the Philippines, Central America, and the American mainland. The studies were soon broadened to include detailed planning for a possible invasion of the United States (concentrating on either Chesapeake Bay or Long Island) or a naval bombardment of New York City or both. The

author of these plans was Otto von Diederichs, George Dewey's antagonist at
Manila. By 1904 German naval planning had expanded further to include possible operations in the Caribbean against either Panama or the West Indies. "In
the coming century," a prominent German economist wrote, "we must desire
at all costs a German colony of some 20 to 30 million people in South America."
But such an enterprise, Gustav von Schmoller concluded, would be impossible
"without warships, which provide secured maritime communications and a
presence backed by force." The U.S. naval attaché at Berlin quickly perceived
what was going on. As early as the summer of 1898 Commander Francis Barber
reported that Germany regarded the sacrosanct Monroe Doctrine as "gall and
wormwood" and recommended that Dewey's small squadron at Manila Bay be
immediately strengthened from Washington's limited naval reserves since the
Germans respected only raw power bluntly employed. The American press soon
picked up on the story, and one paper not surprisingly characterized Germany
as "our bitter, relentless, uncompromising enemy."[13]

Many on both sides of the North Sea in 1900 and even 1910 could agree on
one point: the kaiser's rapidly emerging *Hochseeflotte* was a young, thrusting,
aggressive service; the Royal Navy, in contrast, was old, tired, and hidebound.
In fact, the services were almost mirror images of each other, burdened with
dangerously archaic social structures and hobbled by outmoded prejudices while
striving to master and exploit the revolutionary new technologies that their engineers and industrialists had bestowed upon them.

Aping Germany's senior military service, the emerging *Hochseeflotte* was
steeped in the worst aristocratic assumptions and pretenses of its time, despite
the fact that until 1908 or so "naval officers were drawn from young men of
middle-class backgrounds who would or could not enter... the army." This
preference actually proved a blessing, for it allowed Tirpitz to tap the nation's
large "reservoir of urban middle-class talent." Nonetheless, service in any part
of a military establishment conferred high status in garrison states like Germany.
Moreover, the entire thrust of German domestic policy from 1871 to 1918 was
dominated by the determined effort of the kaisers, their court, and its supporters
in the middle class, bureaucracy, and armed forces to maintain the status quo
against socialism. What tensions there were between the monarch and his sailors
revolved around Tirpitz's constant drive for more and more independence. But
Wilhelm's unflagging, boyish enthusiasm for warships and their men won him
the love of the naval officer corps whose chief objective during the years leading
to World War I was to elevate their service to equal rank and status with the

army. Under the circumstances, few if any German naval officers were willing to question the determined thrust of state policy, which emphasized unquestioning obedience to ancient feudal-monarchical norms and traditions.[14]

The curriculum at the German naval academy, which was first established at Kiel and later moved to Mürwik near Flensburg, reflected such thinking. Courses were designed not to instill or promote liberal principles but to reconfirm the ideal of the modestly educated gentleman warrior. Ten years after its founding in 1871 the German naval academy admitted young Franz von Hipper, the son of a deceased middle-class shopkeeper. Fifteen years after Hipper matriculated, young Erich Raeder, son of a schoolteacher, followed him to Kiel.[15] As biographer Tobias Philbin has observed, the generation of Hipper and Raeder "was the first to experience massive popular education and the new urban way of life which followed the Industrial Revolution," and the training and career paths of both boys were somewhat typical. Young Franz and Erich were recruited into the navy at age eighteen—five years later than their British counterparts—by means of a rigorous entrance examination. Wilhelm had earlier told academy founder General Stosch "not to pay too much attention to the number of cadets accepted; the main issue remains the quality and internal homogeneity which the young men bring to their profession from their family background, for this is the foundation upon which the firm coherence of officer recruits can later be achieved."[16]

After attending a five-week springtime introductory course ashore, which included general military knowledge as well as hours of rifle practice, the new cadets were sent to sea for the remainder of the year. There they learned general seamanship and navigation on deck and engineering in the boiler rooms.[17] Their training vessels, usually the oldest cruisers in the fleet, sailed home waters for several weeks, then set off for the West Indies or the Mediterranean to give the boys a taste of international life. At the conclusion of the voyage the cadets took an examination, and those who passed became midshipmen. Their second year was spent entirely at the academy, where they received mainly theoretical training in naval science, engineering, and "electrical technology." By 1912 laboratories had been constructed to enhance the educational experience. But sport, games, and socializing were also emphasized as means of character building; work and play with comrades and officers was considered an essential part of the education process.

After another examination the survivors spent six months at gunnery school, on a torpedo vessel, and at marine infantry school, after which they took another test, which not only completed their careers as midshipmen but provided "definite determination of seniority." A further year on a ship in the High Seas Fleet or one of the kaiser's big armored cruisers sailing abroad gave cadets the opportunity to win a coveted certificate of achievement, which gained them promotion to sublieutenant *(Leutnant zur See)* and set them on their career paths. The young men were then sent on to purely technical schools.

Captain von Kühlwetter, who provided the most comprehensive discussion of German naval training in the years before 1914, stated proudly that sublieutenants thus spent two of their three and one-half years of formal education on board ship. Although he did not emphasize it, formal training could be longer, for it was essentially the captains at sea who determined whether and when a cadet qualified for his final certificate. After acquiring a commission, German naval officers spent varying proportions of their time serving at sea, ranging from 45 percent for commanders and captains to 93 percent for lieutenants.[18]

But the German naval officer corps was never exposed to the prolonged if much too narrow training that Jacky Fisher and his reformers after 1904 imposed on their young men across the North Sea. German sailors suffered, too, from the persistent inability of the kaiser and Tirpitz to articulate a satisfactory role for the fleet, despite the introduction of courses for midshipmen in history and political science and for midcareer courses in naval strategy, tactics, industrial economics, and war gaming. At the same time the admiral admonished his subordinates that technical training had to remain preponderant, and he made it clear that he was "against being allowed to rear scholars who were not capable of turning out spick and span."[19]

Tirpitz clearly wanted well-rounded officers who were superb technicians. But because of his own uncertainties and disinclination to challenge the prevailing culture, he got something else instead: a service that instinctively reflected the rather indolent, feudal-aristocratic mores of the regime it served. Lieutenants and captains were neither required nor expected to dirty their hands or fill their minds with specialized aspects of the day-to-day running of a warship. Hipper, Raeder, and their colleagues were instead given a broad but not deep education regarding overall ship operations, and their sole task, the aim of all their training at Kiel or Mürwik, was general oversight of shipboard activities. Hipper, for example, received forty-six and a half months of formal training ashore and afloat before finally qualifying for a commission. During the rest of his career of more than thirty years (which did not include the midlevel training courses) he received only fourteen and a half months of additional training.[20]

The gentleman German naval officer was expected to rely exclusively on the talents of specialist assistants, warrant officers who formed "a class between petty officers and officers, composed of individuals whose practical knowledge of one single subject"—navigation, gunnery, engineering, electricity, or torpedoes—"is being constantly improved by frequent alternations of practical experience and teaching in the schools." As the Imperial German Navy expanded in size, its warrant officers were deliberately rotated among ship, classrooms, and factories so that they retained a hands-on understanding of the most advanced weapons and technology employed in the fleet. But all their professional lives were spent pursuing rigid specialization. They were "highly trained by constant and exclusive employment of the one machine," and their professional development was "perfected in the schools by theoretical instruction limited, in extent, but of great efficiency."[21]

The dramatic expansion of the German navy after 1900, with its inevitable growth in status and prestige, brought a decided change in the internal social structure. The class of 1912 at Mürwik, which enrolled at least twenty-five noblemen as well as bourgeois officers in the upper and middle ranks of the service, "threw overboard" any lingering liberalism and approval of social mobility they might have possessed "and anxiously closed ranks with the aristocracy to protect themselves against infiltration by 'the lower classes.'" Formerly approachable officers now "ape[d] the airs of the feudal Junker class, by looking down upon their social inferiors, and by cultivating an excessively gruff and somewhat ludicrous military tone." More care was devoted to recruitment of the officer corps, and before a cadet was admitted "every aspect" of his family's political, social, and financial record was investigated with the help of government officials and the police.[22]

Contempt for specialization in the officer corps became more pronounced. The "general" officers sought to "suppress and thwart the drive toward advancement of inferior social groups," such as engineering officers and the essential warrant-officer corps. In 1911 the inspector of the navy's education department suggested that future engineers be deliberately drawn from Germany's lower classes so they would surrender social pretensions and accept the inferior social positions "'they deserve.'" The director of the engineering school agreed enthusiastically. As late as 1914 engineers were denied access to officers' clubs, and while at sea or dockside not even the highest-ranking engineer on board one of His Imperial German Majesty's ships—a captain—was permitted to give orders to a lieutenant of the "general" service.[23]

Treatment of the warrant officers was even worse. These devoted, long-term, highly skilled servants of the kaiser, who truly kept the fleet running smoothly and efficiently, were not even given the courtesy of being addressed with the polite

Sie. They were forbidden any social contact with regular officers and were denied the right to have their own meeting rooms or clubs. During the 1914–1918 war, with manpower shortages acute, not one of them was promoted to the officer corps to fill a critical billet. As historian Daniel Horn notes, even the Prussian army "was more liberal than this."[24]

The training of enlisted men in Germany was no better. Before 1898 the small German navy had been able to rely on long-term enlistees from fishing villages and coastal towns, boys well acquainted and often experienced with the sea. As the fleet multiplied this source began to dry up, "and it became necessary to tap the vast manpower reservoir of the industrial cities." Young men were now drafted into the navy for three years. The conscription was conducted each October after the fleet returned from summer maneuvers, so that each autumn one-third of the nonrated seamen in the Imperial German Navy were mustered out and another one-third brought in. The draftees were sent not to training ships or stations for indoctrination but directly to the cruiser, torpedo boat, torpedo-boat destroyer, or battleship on which they would serve. Thus, each year from October to May, while the German fleet was in winter port, warrant officers and petty officers were busy "licking into shape these embryo sailors," and "the fighting ships of the Empire [became] practically training vessels." Reinhard Scheer wrote in 1920, "The result . . . was that a continuously high standard of preparedness in battle-practice was not to be attained under our system." The man who would rise to command the High Seas Fleet at Jutland in 1916 added that the outbreak of war in the late *summer* of 1914 was particularly disadvantageous because the fleet was about to obtain a new influx of raw recruits who would require intensive training.[25]

Because of the complexity of even the smallest modern warship, the navy could not draft rabble. After 1900 half the enlisted men in Wilhelm's navy could be classified as technicians. Once they were conscripted, special efforts were made to retain them, including the provision of higher pay, better rations, larger clothing allowances, and much more rapid advancement than was available for enlisted men in the army. But, according to Horn, such coddling did not assuage the resentments of intelligent, well-trained enlisted men toward an officer corps that was steadily broadening its aristocratic pretensions. Even before the hunger, starvation, and other privations of World War I, the navy was threatened with crippling divisions, as two classes "extremely conscious of their positions and power confronted each other. The officers, determined to preserve their privileges and to enhance their power, demanded absolute obedience, respect, and discipline, while the men were equally resolved to improve their lot, to raise their status, and to win greater freedom."[26]

As Tirpitz mounted his naval campaign, the small circle of talented young officers whom he gathered as a planning group became absorbed with preparing annual budgets and lobbying key industrialists, politicians, court favorites, and others instead of developing a coherent strategy that would have given real purpose and effectiveness to the new service.[27] Tirpitz understood modern advertising and mounted a prodigious propaganda campaign. The few existing naval magazines were changed from technical journals to popular weeklies and monthlies propounding the heady message of Germany as a world naval power. As the Royal Navy preened at Spithead, Tirpitz created the "Division for News Services and General Parliamentary Affairs" within the Naval Office to popularize the navy among the German press and intelligentsia. He sent agents into all the universities "to successfully woo many political economists" who promptly set to work demonstrating that expenditures on a blue-water navy "would be a productive outlay" in view of the "insecure politico-economic foundation of our whole civilization and power, and the danger that our superfluous population might become an intolerable burden instead of a source of wealth." Finally, under Tirpitz's prodding, Friedrich Krupp, the great munitions maker, joined other industrialists and publicists to establish the German Naval League *(Deutscher Flottenverein)* in 1898. "The members of the League came predominantly from a bourgeois background. Many were employed in the upper civil service, the clergy, the teaching professions, commerce, and industry."[28]

Strident propaganda helped obscure the weaknesses within a rapidly building High Seas Fleet. So did the very act of building that great fleet, which substantially advanced Germany's material and political position in the world, a fact that sensitive and uneasy Englishmen were quick to grasp. Even in the Age of Fighting Sail, the largest warships had been "moving towns, supporting community life for months on end, and capable of surviving the worst the sea could throw at them. They carried more and heavier cannon than accompanied whole armies." Navies thus required vast support facilities ashore—ship- and dockyards, arsenals and casting shops, barracks, canteens, administrative offices, store- and warehouses, and the like. Industrialization dramatically accelerated the shore establishments of the great powers. In 1909 British maritime writer John Leyland observed that the recent dramatic expansion of the German fleet— carried forward despite the nation's precarious finances—had generated "a corresponding development of the shipbuilding, armour-plate and gun-making,

and harbour and docking facilities of the country." The kaiser's own Imperial
Yard at Kiel had been expanded to include two building slips more than 425
feet long plus a patent slip for torpedo boats, four floating docks, and six dry
docks nearly 600 feet long. Germany's two other large yards at Danzig and
Wilhelmshaven had been similarly enlarged. "All the Government yards" were
"fully supplied with steam, hydraulic, pneumatic, and electric power and their
shops and works . . . fitted with the latest and most efficient machinery. The private establishments have more than kept pace with those of Government."
Moreover, the Kiel Canal, linking the Baltic and the North Seas, would soon be
widened and deepened to accommodate the new class of dreadnought battleships and battle cruisers. Leyland articulated a theme that would become familiar
in twentieth-century military and naval thought, one that might be called the
myth of the invincible foe. German shipbuilding technology seemed to have no
flaws or weaknesses, and the kaiser's increasingly mighty navy appeared an irresistible force. Britons felt in their very marrow that Germany, with its exuberant,
crowded population, mounting prosperity, and incessant demands for markets,
coveted some of the most precious imperial real estate in England's possession.
The kaiser's repeated acts of recklessness, along with the steady expansion of the
German fleet, seemed to confirm this impression. In 1904 and again in 1908
"violent agitations against German naval expansion . . . swept England."[29]

A sympathetic American writing in the latter year noted that the recent cruise
of the High Seas Fleet into the Atlantic (the only time it ever did so) was a
"mere peg" on which the British public hung a much greater "pique" over Germany's incredible industrial and commercial development since 1870. Respected
political observer Maurice Low observed as early as the autumn of 1906 that
"on both sides of the North Sea the feeling is one of intense dislike and distrust."
Four years later Low's colleague Sydney Brooks wrote that "a fusillade of almost
identical charges" was being hurled back and forth between Britain and Germany. "Every suspicion that is entertained in London about the Kaiser is entertained in Berlin about King Edward. Great Britain sends a squadron to visit the
Baltic, and multitudes of Germans look upon its advent as scarcely less than a
declaration of war. Germany increases her navy, and the British Teutophobes at
once warn their countrymen to prepare for a German invasion."[30]

Over the previous several years, Britons had learned to cultivate generally
sound relations with the rest of Europe. But the English stubbornly retained a
distaste for the foreigner, and that repugnance was now concentrated on Germany. "Allied with this dislike, which rises to the dignity of hatred, is fear," Low

observed. "Germany, with her magnificent army and her fast-growing navy, is the bogey to frighten the mind. Nine Englishmen out of ten honestly believe that the sole purpose of Germany in creating a navy is to menace England. The Germans cordially reciprocate this feeling. English statesmen, they believe, lie awake nights thinking how they can best spoil the German game." A British political observer noted in 1908 that the old Concert of Europe, "which a few years ago might be compared to a group of snarling hypochondriacs bound together by mutual suspicions," had become, insofar as British policy was concerned, "a great convivial dinner-party with only one skeleton at the feast—Germany."[31]

During the first years of the new century, technology continued to favor the Royal Navy decisively.[32] German yards simply could not match, much less outbuild, their British counterparts. In 1914, Britain's foremost naval analyst, Archibald Hurd, and his colleague Henry Castle stated that between 1897 and 1904 England laid down 27 battleships and 35 large armored cruisers, a total of 62 heavy ships, or an average of 7.75 ships a year. In the same period Germany built 16 battleships and 5 armored cruisers, a total of 21 heavy ships, or an average of 2.62 ships per year, only about one-third of the British total.

Not only were the Germans unable to match their British adversaries in numbers, but their battleships were always hopelessly outclassed as well. Geography proved a decisively limiting factor for German pretensions and production. The North Sea is shallow, and the German coast is surrounded by sandy stretches. The rivers are tortuous, and the big naval harbors at Cuxhaven and Wilhelmshaven lack depth. Until it was widened, the Kiel Canal also restricted mobility, making it difficult to avoid dividing the fleet between the Baltic and the North Seas and fighting a two-front war. For all these reasons Germany's battleships had to be somewhat smaller than those of Great Britain. And year after year, "with mathematical precision" under the provisions of the 1898 and 1900 naval laws, German yards built consistently inferior war vessels. Before 1900 the largest German battleships displaced 11,130 tons, 4,000 tons less than their British counterparts; they mounted 9.4-inch guns, whereas British ships had 12-inch naval batteries. By 1904 the Germans were building the *Braunschweig*-class battleships, which displaced 13,200 tons and carried four 11-inch guns. But Parliament had already authorized the British Admiralty to construct more vessels of the *King Edward* class, which displaced 16,350 tons and had more powerful 12-inch guns that could penetrate more inches of steel armor than the German battleships possessed and could do so far out of range of any 11-inch shells the Germans could rain on them.[33]

Tirpitz and his gunnery officers had become enamored of the "quick firers," which Japan had used to wreak havoc on the Chinese fleet in the Battle of the Yalu. The Germans loaded their battleships with this light armament, usually 6.6 inches or 5.9 inches in gun-barrel diameter. But experience in the 1904–1905 Russo-Japanese War indicated that such traditional quick firers could no longer penetrate the reasonably well-armored upper works of a modern battleship or armored cruiser. Effective secondary batteries against enemy battleships and armored cruisers would have to be at least 7.5 inches in diameter. The most modern British warships in 1905, *Lord Nelson* and *Agamemnon,* carried in addition to four 12-inch main batteries no fewer than ten 9.2-inch guns.[34]

Germany had also initially failed to match British construction of a new class of warship (originally developed in France), the armored cruiser. Instead, the Germans had built countless smaller, weakly gunned protected cruisers. "If the German fleet is thus analysed," Hurd, writing as "Excubitor," insisted in 1906, "it must be admitted that it is not yet a very formidable instrument of warfare in comparison with the ships which have been built in the last six or seven years for the British fleet."[35] In fact, the British Admiralty simply waited each year to find out what kind of heavy ships Germany was building and then proceeded to plan battleships of its own that were comfortably larger, stronger, and faster. Before 1906 the one true High Seas Fleet belonged to the Royal Navy.

In the end, no amount of human ingenuity could overcome Britain's dominance of the sea approaches to northwestern Europe, though Wilhelm and Tirpitz had done their best. In 1890, the two induced Whitehall to give up Heligoland in exchange for Zanzibar, thus transforming the critical island that dominated the estuaries of the Elbe River (with the port of Cuxhaven) and Jade Bay (with the port of Wilhelmshaven) from an enemy threat to a defensive bastion. A German fleet might enjoy some maneuvering room in the Bight. But to ensure the breakout of at least a portion of a high-seas fleet into the Atlantic and beyond, Germany would have to seize a substantial part of the European coastline from Scandinavia to Iberia in order to spread sufficiently thin an inevitable British blockade. This the kaiser was unable to do either before or during the Great War of 1914–1918.

Out on the world ocean the British Empire and British naval bases lay astride all but one of the key choke points that gave ready access to and from the Atlantic, Indian, and Pacific Oceans. Whereas Germany possessed not one important coaling station on the long sea routes to the Far East, British stations were located at various strategic points from Gibraltar to the Cape and Suez and on out to Singapore and Australia.[36] From the Falklands the British dominated the

Cape Horn Atlantic-Pacific passageway, from Gibraltar and Suez they controlled access to the Mediterranean (including the crucial Dardanelles passage from the Black Sea), and from Malta they could command the narrow waters between Italy and Africa. The naval base at Simonstown, South Africa, governed the shipping lanes from the South Atlantic to the Indian Ocean, and Indian Ocean trade routes were easily observed from naval bases in India and Ceylon (Sri Lanka). Singapore and Perth dominated all the approaches from the Indian Ocean to Southeast Asia and the South Pacific, while Hong Kong lay astride the key sea routes from Southeast Asia to Japan and China. In 1914 the only potential choke point on the world ocean not owned by the Royal Navy in fact or theory was the Isthmus of Panama, which had at last been annexed by the United States in 1903 and became strategically vital when the canal was completed at exactly the moment in which war broke out in Europe eleven years later. Despite initial tensions with all the European powers over the adjacent Caribbean basin, American presidents from Theodore Roosevelt to Woodrow Wilson were firm friends of Great Britain (although not yet totally antagonistic to imperial Germany).

Looking back from 1930, Hurd concluded that even the ostensibly disastrous Boer War in South Africa between 1899 and 1901 had been "a vindication of British sea-power which the world's other great powers . . . could not help notice." The three-year conflict in South Africa "was carried on six thousand miles from the base of supplies. Transports and store-ships continued throughout that long-drawn-out struggle to pass without interruption between the Mother Country and the base of operation. This triumph of sea-power was not without its influence on the naval policy of the other countries."[37]

Indeed it was not. Unable to contest British control of the world ocean, Germany also had the problem of the Baltic. When the Reichstag passed the first two naval bills in 1898 and 1900, the Russian fleet comprised a mix of fifteen elderly and modern battleships and perhaps two dozen effective cruisers. Some of the units were at Vladivostok in the Far East; most, however, were based at Kronshtadt on the Gulf of Finland. The completion of the sixty-one-mile-long Kiel Canal in 1895 and its subsequent expansion to accommodate the larger battleships had assured Tirpitz that he could easily shuffle his heavy as well as light fleet units between the Baltic and the Heligoland Bight. But in any general European war the German navy would have to fight a two-front conflict, just as would the army. With all these factors added to the German government's strained finances, the kaiser's practical threat to British sea power seemed overdrawn in the extreme.

Moreover, British sea power certainly offered a threat to Germany. In a future war, the Royal Navy might well seek to force its way into the Skagerrak and Kattegat and invade the Pomeranian coast. It could also seek to conquer "the Belts," that string of small, low, sandy islands off the Netherlands and Dutch coasts south of Heligoland whose occupation would flank the Bight and dominate the Elbe estuary, Jade Bay, and the great German North Sea naval bases at Wilhelmshaven and Cuxhaven. Britain might even seek to use the Belts as a launchpad to invade the Elbe estuary itself. Berlin's nightmare scenario was that London might try to do both, that is, occupy the Belts with light forces while the main fleet units escorted transports into the Baltic for an invasion of Pomerania, or use the Belts as a staging area to invade the Elbe estuary. The navy took these threats quite seriously—indeed, far more so than did the army. In 1899, even as Tirpitz was rushing full speed to construct both a High Seas Fleet and the aggressive philosophy to go with it, the newly formed German Admiralty Staff presented a counterargument: use of the future fleet largely for the "Defensive Against England." Under this scenario, the chief job of the fleet was either to remain in the Baltic to protect the fatherland, concentrate at Wilhelmshaven to frustrate any enemy occupation of the Belts, or split the fleet between Wilhelmshaven and Kiel-Danzig to repel both thrusts. The Admiralty Staff planners (and Tirpitz) were frustrated by never knowing British intentions: would a close-in blockade in case of war (implying occupation or at least control of the Bight and the Belts and a possible thrust into the Baltic) or a distant blockade in which case none of the three scenarios (invasion of the Belts, the Baltic, or both) be possible? Tirpitz and his people asserted that even under the defensive scenario, the fleet was incapable in itself of stopping the Royal Navy single-handedly and urged the army to keep troops in reserve to occupy Denmark if necessary to outflank any possible British thrust through the Skagerrak.

Helmuth von Moltke and his people took quite another—and relaxed—view of the matter. Germany must concentrate its forces for a decisive swing through Belgium into France to end a future European war quickly and decisively. No other considerations should be allowed to deflect this aim and purpose. Reserving two or more divisions for an investment of Denmark was out of the question (though in the event, the kaiser so ordered). As for a Baltic invasion, Pomeranian beaches were well fortified by 1905, and "reserve" units, along with the fleet, could hold off any British Baltic thrust. London knew this also, and a British staff paper that autumn noted: "The coast defense system of Germany is very thorough and complete. It is to a great extent now under control of the Navy. . . . Special troops will be allotted for the purpose" of defending the German Baltic coast. "If necessary Germany has 850,000 trained men of the Landstrum, available for home defence only."[38]

Tirpitz understood the issues posed by geography on the one hand and possession of a strong, powerful fleet on the other. No naval action in the distant Atlantic would be required to break Britain's anticipated wartime blockade. Whatever battles would be fought would be close to home. Tirpitz therefore decreed that the cruising radius of German ships could be limited to the borders of the North Sea, though in fact the ships of the High Seas Fleet were provided with significant steaming capabilities.[39] Except for a brief expedition into the Atlantic in 1908, the Imperial German Navy never moved out into the world ocean as a unit. Rather, the kaiser's squadrons spent their summers cruising either the Baltic or the waters off Norway (Wilhelm loved spending the hottest months of the year in cool, beautiful Sogne Fjord). Flotillas and divisions often made visits to the New World, while the big ships made the usual round of naval reviews in Russia, Italy, and France. Cadet cruises around the world in one or two cruisers continued to occur each year, and the Naval Office maintained a surprisingly powerful squadron of two new armored cruisers and a handful of support ships on the Asia-Pacific Station.[40] But as a coherent unit the German navy spent too much of its time swinging around its anchor chains at Kiel and Wilhelmshaven to be considered a seasoned professional force. It might yet prove to be efficient and competent in battle, but no one could be sure.

This was the message that England's foremost naval analyst, Archibald Hurd, tried to drum into the minds of increasingly apprehensive Britons as he pleaded for calm and understanding. "No one can study the comparative strength of the British Fleet and other European Fleets as they exist to-day," he wrote at the end of 1906, "without realising that Great Britain's position is so strong, in spite of German effort in the past eight years, that there is no possibility of Germany risking her huge commerce and great industrial prosperity by crossing swords on a direct issue with the world's greatest sea Power. . . . At this moment the British people are in absolutely no danger from the German Fleet."[41]

His words went unheeded. Even as Hurd pleaded, Sir John Fisher, amid dramatic and, as events proved, disastrous secrecy, unveiled his greatest reform, the dreadnought battleship and very shortly thereafter its faster but weakly armored sister, the battle cruiser.

Although the international naval community had been moving inexorably toward an all-big-gun vessel (the Italian Vittorio Cuniberti had written an article for *Jane's Fighting Ships* in 1904 calling for a seventeen thousand–ton vessel with twelve twelve-inch guns, and reform-minded U.S. naval officers had already

urged a class of such ships, soon to materialize as *South Carolina* and *Michigan*),
HMS *Dreadnought* encapsulated nearly all the technological advances in large
warship design up to that time.[42] The vessel's particulars were never officially
made public before the outbreak of war in 1914, but the February 9, 1906,
issue of the British magazine *Engineering* contained a long article about the ship
that was undoubtedly devoured eagerly by admiralties from Paris to Tokyo.[43]
Dreadnought's propulsion plant and hull design were unprecedented. It was rated
at twenty-one to twenty-two knots, an astounding speed for a fully armored
battleship of the day, at least two to three knots faster than the latest pre-
dreadnoughts, *Lord Nelson* and *Agamemnon,* which were generally acknowledged to be two to three knots faster than the best of the kaiser's big ships. The
secret of *Dreadnought's* speed lay in its water-tube boilers and two high-pressure
and two low-pressure gas turbines, which represented a giant leap forward in engineering efficiency. Turbines provided a substantially advanced power output
over the old reciprocating engines without greatly increasing the volume of
machinery. They were also much easier to maintain because of reduced strain
during high performance. Before *Dreadnought* a day's steaming at high speed by
any warship required at least several days' overhaul of machinery in the harbor.
Turbines reduced the amount of overhaul time dramatically.[44]

Turbines also improved the maneuverability of the ship. Designers adopted a
four-shaft power plant with dual rudders placed within a double stern, which
provided remarkable balance and stability through the sea. Moreover, although
the boilers ran on coal, *Dreadnought* possessed "an auxiliary oil-spraying appa-
ratus" that would permit limited flexibility in propulsion. The U.S. battleships
Delaware and *North Dakota,* which were also in the building stage, had the
same feature. The world's navies had already grasped the enormous advantages
of fuel oil as a propulsive agent, and all who could afford it were moving as
quickly as possible to convert at least their major fleet units to oil burners.

Dreadnought was fully armored, and at five hundred feet it was eighty feet
longer than *Lord Nelson,* which allowed for magazines directly under the twelve-
inch turrets without interfering with the vessel's five submerged torpedo tubes.[45]
Thus, for various reasons *Dreadnought* rendered every battleship in the world
(except the soon-to-be commissioned *South Carolina, Michigan,* and their later
sisters) more or less obsolete. As soon as the ship began its sea trials in October
1906 the world knew that forevermore there would be dreadnoughts and pre-
dreadnoughts. Britain seemed to have trumped every possible and potential
opponent.

Dreadnought was not simply an "all-big-gun ship"; it also incorporated *and integrated* just about every advance in naval technology that had come into being in the previous half decade. Nowhere was system integration more apparent or important than in gunnery. With its optical range finders, observers aloft to spot the fall of shot, central control for aiming and firing, uniform-caliber main armament, and a telescopic bearing indicator, *Dreadnought* and its successors transformed the combat capability of the large industrial warship. Centralized fire control permitted several heavy guns to hit a target consistently "at distances where individual control for the guns was inaccurate," thus extending effective engagement distances from between five to seven thousand yards to between ten to fourteen thousand yards.[46] Until the coming of radar-controlled firepower, this was the maximum range at which the human eye, enhanced by telescopic sighting, could effectively penetrate.

But Fisher and the Admiralty proved too clever by half. HMS *Dreadnought* compelled every other nation with pretensions to sea power to match it in every particular, including size and width (forcing the Germans, for example, to widen the Kiel Canal, which Tirpitz could not have otherwise found either the rationale or the funds to accomplish). Thus, while *Dreadnought*'s immediate effect seemed to overwhelm the entire German naval building program, the revolutionary new ship simply elevated the Anglo-German naval race to a technologically higher and above all *level* playing field.[47]

Despite Fisher's undoubted genius, one prominent naval historian has recently noted that it was "never" possible "with absolute clarity" to trace his thought processes since his ideas were often a distillation of the thinking and recommendations of others. Moreover, the admiral's grasp of technological matters was shaky. "Fisher was quick to see the advantages of new developments in technology but slow to appreciate the disadvantages and limitations that usually accompanied them. He has often been described as a visionary because of his early and enthusiastic promotion of such innovations as the steam turbine, diesel engines, water tube and oil-fired boilers and submarines. But he tended to do this with *all* new developments and more often than not, his predictions were somewhat less than accurate."[48]

Not only did *Dreadnought* trigger a major international naval race, but Wilhelm and his people also felt betrayed by the revolutionary new ship and its half sister, HMS *Invincible,* the first of several classes of British battle cruisers. German naval designers quickly began to "transition" (in Tirpitz's phrase) to dreadnought battleship and battle-cruiser construction. The kaiser angrily wrote

Lord Tweedmouth, then head of the Admiralty, that *Dreadnought* had been built in secret and that when it appeared, the Admiralty and British press had announced that it could sink the entire High Seas Fleet. Germany had no choice but to reply to the challenge with all the speed and vigor that its new shipyards and gun factories could muster.[49] Even before Tirpitz's 1908 naval bill, Germany had begun work on the first of four *Nassau*-class dreadnoughts. The 1908 legislation duly provided for the construction of four dreadnoughts per year through 1911 and two per year thereafter, along with half a dozen or so battle cruisers, a host of lesser ship types (including armored cruisers), along with funds for major dredging and port- and canal-improvement programs to accommodate the dramatically larger warships.

Berlin went further than that. In 1908, Vice Admiral Baudissin assumed command of the German Admiralty Staff and immediately began agitating for revival of an offensive naval strategy. "Whether the Royal Navy instituted a close blockade or a more distant one, it would have succeeded in cutting off Germany's maritime commerce with the outside world." A "waiting strategy" by the fleet would provide no remedy. The rising German navy possessed effective, efficient seagoing warships, though admittedly not in the same numbers as Great Britain. The purpose of such warships was offensive, and the sooner they were employed aggressively in that role against a close or distant enemy, the better. Baudissin managed to gain an audience with the kaiser on March 12, arguing that the most recent British maneuvers indicated that the Royal Navy had no intention of imposing a close blockade of the German coast with its battleships. Enemy "light blockading forces" should be vigorously attacked, possibly with the entire High Seas Fleet, in order to reduce Britain's numerical superiority at sea. Even "a full fleet action should be risked if circumstances permitted it." The chief of the Admiralty Staff then proceeded to win over the navy itself, firing the imagination of the new fleet commander, Prince Henry of Prussia, with talk of a raid against the Scottish coast. Baudissin told Admiral von Fischel, commander of the North Sea Station, that "to use a High Seas Fleet for the local defence of river mouths would be the same as if we allotted our Field Army to defend our fortresses." A new doctrine appeared: the task of the German fleet would be "to do the greatest possible damage to the enemy, risking all the forces" available. "If you do not encounter the foe during the first sortie," Baudissin told Prince Henry, "then some of his coastal areas...are to be strewn with mines and hostile shipping is also to be destroyed by other means as far as is possible."[50]

A variety of factors soon weakened Baudissin's offensive, not the least his transfer to another equally exalted post and the realization that Germany's newest dreadnoughts were too big to pass through the Kiel Canal until it was widened farther. Since Germany's warships always worked up to full battle capability in the comparatively protected waters of the Baltic, concentrating the High Seas Fleet at Wilhelmshaven and Cuxhaven would risk the newer dreadnoughts to attack by the Royal Navy as they steamed the forty hours through the Skagerrak and down the Danish and northwestern German coasts in time of war. Hitler and his admirals would confront a similar dilemma thirty-odd years later during World War II when operational imperatives practically split the handful of battle cruisers and battleships between the Baltic and the port of Brest on the Atlantic coast. After prolonged wrangling within naval circles between the proponents of an offensive and a defensive doctrine, Tirpitz cracked heads and in November 1909 got his fractious colleagues to split the difference with the thoroughly unsatisfactory compromise of a "waiting offensive."[51] But Baudissin's influence and arguments never entirely disappeared, and when war came in 1914 the more venturesome commanders in the navy, led by battle cruiser commander Hipper, and later fleet commander Scheer, were able to employ Baudissin's arguments and ideas to advance their own plans.

Responsible British officials soon concluded that under the kaiser's building plan, Germany would possess no fewer than nine dreadnoughts by March 1911 and at least thirteen and perhaps seventeen a year later when Britain would possess but twenty. The German naval threat thus seemed both pronounced and immediate. For the next four years, British naval officials and analysts, Parliament, and the general public engaged in an obsessive game of hull counting and parity rating with the High Seas Fleet. Britons charged the kaiser and his sailors with building battleships secretly in excess of published fleet laws, and they worked themselves up into a frenzy that prefigured the hysteria precisely a half century later in the United States over the nonexistent "missile gap" with the Soviet Union. Convinced that Berlin was plotting a war against France that would inevitably draw in the British Empire, London opinion makers toyed with the idea of a preemptive strike. In 1908 one unidentified publicist, "a man of large experience in both political and commercial circles," suggested to a group of friends that only such a blow by the Royal Navy against the German fleet at Wilhelmshaven could avert future disaster. "If England were ever going to check the rapidly-growing German navy, the sooner she did it the better, before it got any larger; the smashing would be easier now than later." Fisher concluded that 1914 was the real danger year, when the new German naval program of seventeen dreadnoughts and battle cruisers would be completed along with the widening of the Kiel Canal. He confided to the king that war would surely come in the autumn of that year after the harvests were gathered. Perhaps it would be best if the German fleet were "Copenhagened," that is, struck an un-provoked, sudden, and shattering blow, before then.

Reviewing the construction schedules and figures, John Keegan has concluded that in fact Churchill, Parliament, and the British people, however panicked they may have been, were right to demand eight capital ships in the 1909 build-ing program ("We want eight and we won't wait"), else Germany might well have enjoyed a narrow margin in dreadnoughts and battle cruisers by the be-ginning of the Great War. In fact, Britain consistently outbuilt Germany and at the outbreak of war enjoyed a thirty-one-to-twenty edge in modern capital ships. By the time of Jutland two years later, Britain had added another ten battle-ships and one battle cruiser to its stock, whereas the Germans managed to add but three battleships and two battle cruisers.[52]

Thrilling as they were to behold, HMS *Dreadnought* and its successors under the White Ensign dramatically increased the complexity and instability of the modern capital ship and harbored unsuspected and potentially catastrophic flaws. The chances for enormous system failures grew exponentially with the intro-duction of each advance in dreadnought technology. As the world braced for Armageddon, naval designers, engineers, and technicians on both sides of the North Sea and across the world struggled to understand and perfect the mon-strous aquatic machines they had fashioned.[53]

The German dreadnought battleships of 1907–1912, though fewer in num-ber, would prove to be strong, effective vessels that significantly exceeded their British counterparts in armor protection, beam, and internal subdivision. In contrast, British dreadnoughts, especially the battle cruisers, were comparatively weak-hitting floating bombs in some ways more dangerous to their crews than to the enemy. In the magazines of German heavy ships, for example, the main cordite charges were kept in a heavy brass case, and the black-powder igniter at the bottom of the charge did not come into contact with the other charges from the time it left the magazine until it was fired from the gun. The risk of accidental explosion was thus greatly minimized. "In British ships the igniter was sewn in a small pocket of silk at both ends of all charges, and the very fine high-quality gunpowder tended to seep through the silk, eventually coating the outer covering of the cartridges. If charges were placed end-to-end during the loading sequence a flame at one end could pass very quickly down the line of charges." Moreover, the British and French navies used cordite made of gelatinized nitrocellulose. If this compound was incorrectly made, it became highly volatile and "had a nasty habit of exploding without warning." In 1907 and 1911 French warships abruptly blew up at their piers. "Not for many years would it be discovered that a small quantity of iron pyrites in the atmosphere could result in serious instability." Other solvents used in British propellants proved dangerously volatile, whereas the German navy developed a far more stable propellant using nitroglycerin and a compound called centralite. The problem of ammunition volatility was accentuated in both British and German heavy ships by the lack of protection for the shell hoists from the kind of flash explosions caused by unstable propellants and by the British practice of having ships in action leave the doors to magazines open in order to speed the rate of fire.[54]

The flaws in British dreadnought design—and operation—were compounded by the comparative weakness of British naval ordnance. "German guns were much lighter than British for an equivalent performance," Correlli Barnett has noted. German 12-inch guns weighed only forty-eight tons, yet yielded a battle performance comparable to British 13.5-inch guns weighing seventy-six tons. The decisive difference seems to have been in the process of making steel guns and shells that displayed a "general obsolescence and want of modern research facilities" in the British steel and ordnance industries. "The steel for German guns and shells was made in special electric furnaces, giving a very high quality steel," whereas in Britain naval ordnance was still fired and molded by the old Siemens-Martin open-hearth process. Remarkably, even with the intense interest devoted to gunnery improvement, British batch testing of shells was extremely careless. Thus, the tendency of the Royal Navy's heavy naval shells to both volatility and weak penetrating power because of either poor steel, overhardened nose caps, or faulty fuses (or all three) was never fully understood before the great sea battles of 1914–1916. At the Battle of the Falklands, at Dogger Bank, and, most crucially, at Jutland, British shells striking the heavily armored German ships too often burst on impact or blew holes in the armor plate and superstructures rather than plunging into the enemy's vitals before detonating with fearsome impact. Smaller German shells, on the other hand, wreaked havoc.[55]

The flaws in British heavy naval ordnance might have been irritating rather than disastrous if there had not been another generally overlooked problem in capital-ship construction: the advent of the big, long-range naval gun meant an increase in "plunging fire," that is, shells landing aboard a vessel not in a straight line that would take them into heavy side armor but in a looping trajectory that caused them to detonate on upper works and decks. The advent of plunging fire meant that battleships now had to be heavily armored on the upper decks and also around the magazines and engineering spaces or risk being suddenly blown up by heavy shells crashing through from above to detonate among shells and powder. The Germans, Japanese, and Americans more or less solved this problem by armoring their upper works and the decks immediately adjacent to the propulsion and ordnance spaces accordingly. The British did not. This oversight would be pitilessly revealed in the crucible of battle.

The final flaw in British capital-ship design reflected the financial strains that His Majesty's treasury felt all too keenly after 1907 and the cost cutting that consequently resulted from the naval race with Germany. The millions of pounds devoted to new construction meant that money was not available for enlarging the Royal Navy's dry docks. Increasing their length to accommodate the steadily growing size of His Majesty's capital ships was no problem; widening them was. As a consequence, new capital vessels right down to the *King George V* battleships of World War II had limited beams that in turn restricted both internal compartmentalization and the depth of their underwater protection. The size of British carriers built in the 1930s and early '40s was similarly restricted.[56]

Recent scholarship has suggested that the *Dreadnought* battleship design was merely a step Fisher very reluctantly had to take to attain his real interest, which lay in the *Invincible* class of "battle cruisers" that followed immediately thereafter. Indeed, both contemporaries and some historians employ the term *dreadnought* to mean both "all-big-gun" battleships and their equally heavily armed but faster and only lightly armored battle-cruiser cousins. Combining the hitting power of the battleship with the speed and light armor of the cruiser, the three *Invincibles* and their later sisters—in some ways merely upgraded armored cruisers, in other ways a new design—were meant to be the "supreme combination of speed and power" at sea and as such "the strategic cavalry of the . . . Royal Navy." They were the heart of Fisher's solution to the mounting challenges confronting Britain in the first decade of the twentieth century. Under the lash of an economy-minded Parliament and an ongoing naval race with Germany, Fisher wished nothing less than to overturn Mahan, replacing a traditional concept of sea combat based on squadrons of cumbersome, slow, costly battleships blazing away at each other in battle lines by a system that combined speed, nimbleness, and innovation. Fisher was inordinately proud of his battle cruisers. To him they were the "big cats" of the Royal Navy, the "New Testament" vessels that would replace the "Old Testament" battleships. Even a small squadron of such vessels could easily outmaneuver slower enemy battle lines and shoot enemy battleships to pieces from vast distances while nimbly pirouetting across the seas, avoiding enemy salvos that could destroy them because of their weak armor. The future Royal Navy would be based on a surface force of battle cruisers and destroyers together with stealthy submarines lurking below to ambush invasion forces or enemy fleets. The submarines and destroyers, along with squadrons of cruisers, would keep Britain's narrow seas and vulnerable coasts safe from enemy incursions, while a squadron or two of fast long-range battle cruisers would fulfill the dual purpose of protecting Britain's far-flung trade routes and successfully dueling slow, blundering enemy lines of battleships whether encountered in the North Sea or out on the world ocean. Such a navy would be far less costly to build and maintain in terms of both men and money than a huge fleet of dreadnoughts.[57]

In fact, Fisher's battle-cruiser design proved a poorly conceived—indeed, disastrous—idea. First of all, its ostensible distinguishing characteristic, speed, proved a hoax. Fisher equated speed with armor—or, more precisely, substituted speed for armor. But for this to work, British battle cruisers would have had to be faster than enemy battleship lines by at least five and perhaps as much as seven or eight knots to gain in maneuverability and nimbleness what they had lost in protection. Prior to 1914, however, all of Fisher's battle cruisers, though attaining twenty-eight to twenty-nine knots on sea trials, could make twenty-six to twenty-seven knots at best under battle conditions, whereas *Dreadnought* and its successors were rated, and could generally sustain, twenty-one knots. Britain's last prewar battle cruisers, HMS *Tiger* and *Queen Mary*, were rated at thirty knots, but at least one of the *Queen Elizabeth* class dreadnoughts of the same period was rated at twenty-five, though they seldom if ever achieved such a speed and sacrificed what advances there were at some cost in armor.[58] In the end, Fisher refused to face the brute realities of physics. Ships could be protected by armor, but not by speed. The power needed to push twenty-five and thirty thousand–ton steel vessels through the seas was so immense that at the upper ranges an enormous amount of additional propulsive force was required to obtain one or two more knots. Thus, in shedding nearly their entire armor protection, all but the last prewar British battle cruisers obtained at most a minimal advantage over the most advanced battleships of the time, which was insufficient to guarantee any security from well-directed gunfire. When hit by even a single heavy shell in a vulnerable spot, Fisher's battle cruisers would literally disintegrate, sending a thousand men winging into eternity.

Moreover, as Jon Sumida has emphasized, Fisher's battle-cruiser revolution depended absolutely on superior fire control and accuracy in gunnery. Despite

the formidable reforms of Percy Scott, John Jellicoe, and others, these critical
elements of naval power remained weak not only in the Royal Navy but in all
the world's fleets. It was a problem that would bedevil every navy until the
coming of the proximity fuse in the middle of World War II. To ensure destruction of distant enemy battle lines maneuvering at best speed, British capital
ships, especially the battle cruisers and new *Queen Elizabeth* class of fast battleships, themselves twisting and turning at high speeds, would have to "acquire"
the enemy, then keep their gun sights and gun barrels firmly locked on. Scott
began to successfully address the problem with his mechanical fire-control director, operated by a single sailor or officer, who would track distant targets,
bringing his ship's guns in train with the director. According to Scott, a hide-
bound Admiralty moved "heaven and earth to prevent director firing being
adopted." When Fisher's stubborn ally nonetheless managed to get a successful
test of the director carried out in January 1911 aboard HMS *Neptune,* Home
Fleet commander in chief Admiral Sir Francis Bridgeman still refused to support
its adoption. Despite Churchill's support, Scott was unable to arrange another
test until November 1912 when the battleships *Thunderer* (equipped with a director) and *Orion* (without) steamed into the Atlantic some twenty miles off
Bantry Bay, Ireland, and had at it.

> The range was nine thousand yards, the ships were steaming at twelve
> knots' speed, and the targets were towed at the same speed. Immediately
> the signal was made to open fire both ships commenced, the *Thunderer*
> making beautiful shooting and the *Orion* sending her shot all over the
> place. At the end of three minutes "cease fire" was signalled, and an exami-
> nation of the targets showed that the *Thunderer* had scored six times as
> many hits as the *Orion.*

Churchill and Jellicoe were completely won over; incredibly, Fisher and his
first lord were unable to budge conservative elements in the fleet, and it was not
until the first weeks of war in 1914 that directors began to be hastily installed on
bridge tops all over the Royal Navy. Most capital ships had director-controlled
firing by the time of the Dogger Bank action early in 1916, and the Royal
Navy was fully equipped by Jutland.[59]
    Regrettably, the reformers could go no further, though one, civilian design
engineer Arthur Hungerford Pollen, tried heroically to advance still further the
fledgling science of fire control. Between 1905 (when *Invincible* was laid down)
and 1912 (when Scott at last made some headway in getting his fire-control di-

rector accepted), Pollen slowly and painfully "developed a wholly original system of fire control," employing a variety of data acquired from gyroscopically stabilized range finders, plotting units, mechanical calculators, "and an electric data transmission system." According to Sumida, Pollen's system was premised on three major principles: "first that the requisite rapidity of operation and reliability could only be obtained by the automation of as many functions as was possible; second that the mathematics of relative motion had to be solved exactly, not approximately; and third, that success in practice could not be achieved without instruments built to high standards of mechanical workmanship." Alas, an effective mechanical "fire control computer development" (for such it was) lay beyond the technical and administrative capabilities of the prewar British Admiralty. Pollen's system proved expensive to develop and imperfect in operation. "Consistent results with optical range-finders were difficult to achieve," Sumida notes. "High speed and changing courses resulted in ship motion that interfered with gun-laying even when director firing was employed, and neither rate nor probably true-course plotting by themselves were capable of producing satisfactory results under difficult conditions."[60]

Fisher soon became an increasingly erratic patron who could not overcome the entrenched and unimaginative interests within the British naval establishment. Earlier gunnery reforms had been accepted grudgingly, but the quantum leap to Pollen's system proved too much. What finally doomed Pollen's effort were high system costs, Fisher's dim grasp of how difficult yet rewarding the invention would be, and Pollen's own growing bitterness over what he conceived to be Admiralty blindness and stupidity. In fact, their lordships were seeking to control if not reduce spending in the years immediately leading to the Great War; reduced costs were the whole notion behind the ideal of the battle cruiser with its big, deadly accurate long-range guns. Yet the development costs of Pollen's fire-control system were immense. For one of the first but far from last times in the twentieth century, those seeking ways and means to cut expenditures failed to understand that money had to be at first spent before it could be saved. Pollen's system, for all its failed promise as a wonder weapon, was far and away the best fire-control system available at the time.[61] Had the Royal Navy pushed development of the Pollen system, its battleships and battle cruisers would have had an enormous advantage over any possible future adversary, enabling "British ships to hit more often—perhaps even much more often—when range and bearing rates were high and changing," as they often proved to be at Jutland in 1916 and even at Dogger Bank the previous year. *Invincible* and its successors, hobbled by fatal design flaws and gunnery control inadequate to their needs, proved far less satisfactory, and effective, than the other dreadnoughts of their time.[62]

These included, as it turned out, German battle cruisers. The kaiser's naval architects proved that the design, per se, was not infeasible if certain concessions were made to reality. Although the German ships were smaller and one to two knots slower on average, they were more stoutly and imaginatively constructed. Britain's *Queen Mary* class of battle cruisers, for example, displaced 27,000 tons compared with 24,610 tons for the Germans' *Seydlitz*. Yet the *Queen Marys* carried only 3,900 tons of armor, whereas the *Seydlitz* had 5,200 tons. Moreover, German ships were better subdivided because their engines took up less space and weight due to smaller but equally powerful and efficient tube boilers.[63]

Not only were Britain's early dreadnoughts prone to internal flaws of one sort or another, but they would also prove frightfully vulnerable to other new weapon systems, most notably the torpedo and its new carrier, the submarine. For nearly a century clever inventors had tinkered with systems of valves, ballast tanks, and pumps to create a true submersible, and by 1910 "the broad outlines of the modern submarine were settled. However much the boats of the various navies might differ in detail the main problems had all been solved. . . . [T]he electric accumulator battery, the diesel engine and the self-propelled torpedo were to be steadily improved as the years went by, but no other fundamental change was necessary for another 50 years."[64] Progress and developments had varied within each great navy: the Germans, for example, were early submarine enthusiasts, though they did not equip their *Unterseeboot* with diesel engines until 1912, the year that marked the first modern submarine attack. On December 9 during the Balkan war, a 295-ton Greek submersible named *Delphin* fired an eighteen-inch torpedo at a Turkish cruiser off the Dardanelles. Not surprisingly, the missile failed to find its target, and *Delphin* hurried away. The inevitable failures and frustrations attendant upon the introduction of any new weapon system gave heart to those reactionaries within the Royal and Imperial German Navies who had little patience with advances beyond their ken and knowledge. But a cadre of submarine enthusiasts emerged within both services, and long before the guns of August 1914 spoke, Jacky Fisher and his sailors would be forced to an agonizing reappraisal of this most sinister new weapon system.

The rush amid cost cutting, the haste in the context of penny-pinching that produced massive, powerful, but fatally flawed dreadnoughts, need not have happened. Although Britain's battleships and battle cruisers were indeed more expensive than their smaller, slower, less powerful predecessors, the government and people had reached a moment of high irresponsibility in which they expected a global empire that had reached its apex to be run without either bother or expense. If Niall Ferguson's figures are correct, Britain's "total defense budget" for 1898 amounted to forty million pounds, "a mere 2.5 per cent of net national product...far less than the equivalent percentage spent on the military during the Cold War." Between 1906 and 1913, His Majesty's government sent down the way and out to sea no less than twenty-seven dreadnoughts and battle cruisers at a total cost of only forty-nine million pounds, "less than the annual interest charge on the national debt. This was world domination on the cheap."[65]

Though Britons did not realize it, matters were much worse across the North Sea, where the carefully crafted German warships of 1907–1912 were terribly expensive. The five battleships of the *Kaiser* class, for example, cost 2.4 million pounds, whereas its rough counterpart in the Royal Navy, battle cruiser *Lion*, was built for roughly 75–80 percent of that amount. The Socialist faction in the Reichstag, to say nothing of the army, became progressively uneasy over navy expenses, and this restiveness had a decisive impact on the shaping of Germany's last prewar naval bill.[66]

Nonetheless, by 1908 the naval race had assumed an irresistible momentum of its own. Sir Henry Campbell-Bannerman's Liberal economy-minded administration cut back that year's naval estimates slightly, only to discover that Germany was dramatically increasing its capital-ship construction. Parliament's decision to fund the building of ten dreadnoughts or battle cruisers in 1910 to be followed by five more each in 1911 and 1912 was undercut by stories that Germany planned to build no fewer than sixteen such vessels between 1908 and 1911 alone. The result was an abrupt naval scare in 1909 that drove the British Admiralty, Parliament, and ultimately the people into what one recent historian has characterized as "a frenzy of competition."[67]

Both sides in the immediate prewar years maintained their frantic dreadnought construction pace in large measure by holding to basic designs while improving each successive class as much as possible. Fisher and his architects and engineers realized that HMS *Dreadnought* had been conceived and built so quickly—and secretly—that some defects were inevitable. Among the very few quickly recognized were the layout of the main armament and the placement of the tripod mast, with its gun-control platform, between the funnels.[68] The

12-inch-gun turrets had been set with the intention of providing maximum gunfire fore, aft, and broadside. Thus, *Dreadnought* possessed not only centerline turrets but also forward-wing turrets next to the bridge superstructure. The blast from the wing guns, however, disrupted human concentration, electrical communication, and delicate machinery. The Germans built likewise and discovered that as they advanced from 11- to 12-inch guns, the bigger wing turrets also severely encroached on the antitorpedo protection. The gun-control platform between the funnels was constantly shrouded in smoke from the forward funnel at high speed, choking and blinding the gun layers. In January 1908 Henry Reuterdahl, American editor of *Jane's All the World's Ships,* published an article in *McClure's Magazine* describing further generic problems in the overall dreadnought battleship and battle-cruiser design. In both American and British ships (and presumably those of Germany as well; Japan was still buying its capital ships from British yards), secondary batteries were placed within hulls whose freeboards were too low, ammunition hoist shafts were open, and armor belts were badly situated. These design flaws led to severely wet and uncomfortable ships in heavy seas. At the beginning of the Great War, John Jellicoe, newly appointed commander in chief of the British Home Fleet, found that his dreadnoughts were so wet that partial bulkheads had to be fitted in the rear of the lower gun compartments to confine the water. Some of the less well-positioned secondary batteries were removed from the hull altogether and placed in the superstructure, a design feature that after 1912 or so would become mandatory. Jellicoe's battle-cruiser commander, David Beatty, complained to his wife at the same time that during the Grand Fleet's initial sweep of a gale-lashed North Sea, "I haven't a dry spot in my cabin. The deck leaks like a sieve and it's like lying under a perpetual shower bath. It reminded me often of *Typhoon* by Conrad."[69]

British designers were more successful in dramatically improving the size and caliber of dreadnought main batteries. By 1908, the 12-inch gun, long the mainstay of the fleet, had reached its optimal level of development. Efforts to extend range by keeping shell weight low and increasing muzzle velocity by lengthening the gun barrels had created substantial rifle wear and produced barrel whip, which caused the light shells to begin to wander near the end of their flight. Fisher and his colleagues addressed these problems with their usual energy, and the result was an advanced dreadnought design, the four-ship *Orion* class, whose lead vessel appeared in 1909. Adopting American practice, the Admiralty placed the *Orion*'s entire main battery on the centerline; two superimposed turrets were located forward, a single turret was placed amidships, and two turrets were superimposed aft. This arrangement not only ensured a maximum broadside but also allowed the most efficient placement of magazines.

The main battery itself was increased from 12 to 13.5 inches, and the new gun was proclaimed "an outstanding success." Not only did it shoot a much heavier shell farther, but lower muzzle velocity also meant much less barrel wear and no whip effect. Soon designers had increased the weight of the 13.5-inch shell from 1,250 to 1,400 pounds. Although the *Orions* and their successors suffered from poor antitorpedo protection and a continued placement of the gun-control platforms squarely in the face of funnel smoke and exhausts, they were very formidable warships.[70]

The Royal Navy retained the 13.5-inch guns in the *Lion* class battle cruisers and *Princess Royal* class dreadnoughts of 1910–1911, but gun-director platforms were finally moved forward of the funnels to the top of the bridge structure, which improved British gunnery "immensely." As the *Lions* and *Princess Royals* were being built, the Admiralty asked the Elswick Ordnance Company to begin feasibility studies of a 15-inch gun that would make His Majesty's ships supreme on the seas for years to come. Word came back quickly that both the gun and the ships to carry it could be built almost immediately. The result was development of a new fast battleship, the *Queen Elizabeth* class, the first of which appeared in 1914 and in many ways represented the zenith of early-twentieth-century dreadnought design. The four 26,000-ton ships mounted eight 15-inch guns and could theoretically move at twenty-five knots. They were not flawless, however. Although certainly not tin clads, their armor and internal protection were markedly less than that of the slower (twenty-one-knot) *Nevadas* of the U.S. Navy and the new German *Derfflinger* and *Lützow* classes of battleship and battle cruiser.[71]

Despite undoubted achievements in exploiting the technology they possessed, the inability of German naval designers, engineers, and builders to match British capabilities in the sheer size and range of guns proved a deficiency that could not be ignored in the midst of a frantic naval race, and they reflected a weakness in German industrial capability that nearly matched that of Britain. Tirpitz's obsession with capital ships and a High Seas Fleet did not extend to the details of battleship design and construction. The admiral accepted and employed what German private enterprise gave him. "If a particular innovation in maritime technology easily complemented his capital ship strategy, he became its champion." However, Tirpitz believed that the development of and training in advanced technologies should take place entirely in the private sector. The German Naval

Office's sole responsibility was to stay informed of current research. The fate of the German navy thus reposed exclusively in the hands of the kaiser's industrialists, and "the real problem lay in the fact that [Friedrich] Krupp's factory at Essen could not turn out guns very quickly—a penalty paid for excellence."[72]

Germany's other twentieth-century gun, munitions, and electronics makers shared Krupp's weakness and tended to let the navy down in the kind of products they provided. Between 1900 and 1942–1943 Germany introduced naval guns and optical and radar systems that were at first almost invariably superior to but always more complex than those of its enemies. Once a particular system had been developed, however, German manufacturers seemed incapable of either producing it quickly and in quantity or constantly improving and simplifying it. Not until 1912 was Krupp Works finally persuaded to abandon the 11- and 12-inch guns with which the German navy had begun the century and build the larger (15-inch) and longer-range models that first appeared in 1916 (too late for Jutland) in *Bayern*.[73]

As the great Anglo-German naval race gathered momentum, it continued to generate irrational fears and hysteria. The British public in particular never understood the terrible constraints on German naval power. Instead, it indulged in wild fantasies of national disaster and internal subversion. Opinion soon focused on the notion of a sudden armed invasion, and a popular literature flowered on both sides of the North Sea. Its antecedents could be traced back to the dawn of the German Empire, declared at Versailles in 1871 at the close of the Franco-Prussian war. Later that year, Sir George Tomkyns Chesney wrote a fictional account of a Teutonic assault on England titled *The Battle of Dorking*. First serialized in the popular *Blackwood's* magazine, it was quickly issued as a novel and became a best-seller. A sleeplessly malevolent Germany invades England at the moment when British armed forces are distracted by uprisings in India and Ireland while confronted in Canada and on the North Atlantic by a still belligerent United States. The Royal Navy is spread across the globe supporting suppression of these crises, and the home country is wide open to assault. "From 1871 onwards Chesney's story showed Europe how to manipulate the new literature of anxiety and nationalism. Between 1871 and 1914 it was unusual to find a single year without some tale of future warfare appearing in some European country." Prospects for construction of a Channel tunnel convinced London pamphleteers as early as 1882 to concentrate on France as Britain's impending enemy. But after the entente of 1904, France was immediately replaced by the German peril. Erskine Childers's *Riddle of the Sands*, which appeared in 1903, prefigured that revival. It was swiftly followed by a translation of the sensational German novel *Der Weltkrieg*, which appeared in 1904 as the *Coming Conquest of England*. "During the ten years before the First World War the growing antagonism between Britain and Germany was responsible for the largest and most sustained development of the most alarmist and aggressive stories of future warfare ever seen at any time in European literature." By 1908, William Le Quex's *Invasion of 1910* had become the latest popular fright novel in England. Whereas the book placed the invasion two years hence, a contemporary wrote that "the more conservative folk, including military experts, incline to 1912." American writer Edwin Mead discovered that a number of high-ranking officers in the British army were convinced on the basis of "authentic knowledge . . . that German experts have mapped England in such detail for military purposes that the number of cavalry horses which can be stalled in the stables of every manor-house from Penzance to Berwick-on-Tweed is registered." Many German youths "who were innocently supposed by most of us to have come to London to earn a living as waiters in restaurants were really, according to the truly wise, in on this business." One of the highest-ranking officials in His Majesty's government solemnly assured Mead that if Britain had voted during the recent Hague Conference for the inviolability of ocean commerce in war, Germany would have been at Britain's throat within two years.

"No rational motive has been assigned for the apprehended German invasion," Mead wrote in the spring of 1908. Indeed, despite the kaiser's bluster and the fanciful dreams and plans of his military and naval staffs, Germany had prudently kept out of war for the entire thirty-seven years of its existence. Nonetheless, alarmists insisted that war would come, although "there is to be no provocation for it on England's part; it is to be undertaken" by Germany "in the fullness of time, on general principles, in sheer wantonness, for the purpose of crippling England's prosperity, spoiling her commerce, and seizing, it may be, some of her colonies—precisely that is the nightmare." The essential first step in Germany's humiliation of Britain and its empire "would be a German naval victory" over a British fleet that was three times the size and power of all the war vessels that Wilhelm could put to sea. Next Germany would have to defeat a three million–man French army, and if all that happened and the entire Continent and British Isles lay at Berlin's feet, then surely the U.S. Navy would cross the North Atlantic and enter the battle.[74]

Fearmongers in the British press and public refused to heed such realities. Instead, their hysterical warnings about the imminent storming of the Hun onto

English beaches stimulated a broad movement to augment the county militias to an "immense degree," fill the countryside with emergency gun clubs, militarize the schools, "and even turn parish houses and church basements into centres for target practice." Mischief-making brigadiers, "honestly stupid . . . fighting parsons," and panic-stricken titled ladies crusaded for a "'Nation in Arms.'"[75]

Statesmen and admirals heard the cries and felt the pressure. After 1904, Fisher gradually imposed one final, and characteristically controversial, reform on his beloved navy—he brought it home. In 1906 the Atlantic Fleet, hitherto based on Gibraltar with the largest and most powerful vessels in the fleet, was moved to home waters. Two years later Alfred Thayer Mahan estimated that 86 percent of Britain's biggest naval guns were facing the German High Seas Fleet. In 1912, seeking to counter the effects of the newest German naval law, Churchill ordered the last six British battleships out of Malta to Gibraltar, where they could operate either in the Atlantic or in the Mediterranean but with the tacit understanding that in case of war they would sail to England. At the same time Britain's entente ally, France, transferred its last battleships from Brest on the Channel to the Mediterranean to keep an eye on the small but growing Austrian navy and unstable Italy's larger fleet. Few British ships remained beyond home waters: one old battleship on the East Indies Station, a demobilized battleship at Hong Kong, and a battle cruiser or two patrolling the narrow seas between Gibraltar and Suez. Never again would British dreadnoughts routinely cruise Far Eastern seas, and not until the 1930s and the rise of Mussolini's Italy would the Mediterranean Fleet again rival the Home Fleet in size and strength.[76]

Critics charged that the concentration of the fleet not only was a disaster for British strategic, economic, and diplomatic interests in Europe, the Mediterranean, and the East but also devastated the professional morale, character, and competence of the navy itself. The old imperial motto was often recalled: "What do they know of England, who only England know?" Officers and men who year after year sailed and mastered only the approaches to the British Isles would soon lose that keen edge in seamanship that came from navigating the world ocean and confronting its many treacheries, including tropical hurricanes, coral-choked harbors, and the wintry blasts of the North Atlantic. "If the Fleet loses tone," naval writer Varne Light scolded in 1913, "if it ceases to exhibit those qualities which have rendered it the envy of other nations—every interest, home and Imperial, will suffer. The security of our trade, our food, and our shores will be jeopardised; the Dominions will cease to have faith in our power of protecting them, and our prestige and theirs will fall."[77] The nearly hysterical relief with which the citizens of Auckland, Sydney, and Melbourne had greeted the U.S. battle fleet in 1908 suggested that imperial ties with far-distant Australia and New Zealand could be reaching the breaking point. And if these two increasingly prized possessions fell into the American orbit, would Canada be far behind? Certainly, Japan and the United States might carve up the Asian-Oceanic region before Britain could spare the heavy fleet units from home waters to redress the balance.

In 1911, with the Royal Navy's Mediterranean squadron badly weakened by the need to reenforce the Home Fleet in the face of the German peril, the Italian army suddenly lunged across the Middle Sea in a huge amphibious assault against Turkish holdings in Tripoli and Cyrenaica (Libya). This "bolt from the blue," launched across sea-lanes no longer than those that linked Britain with Germany, dramatized the capability of modern industrial states to make sudden sneak attacks, landing on unsuspecting shores "before the inhabitants were awake in the morning, or any adequate measures could be taken for defence."[78] The power of the kaiser's growing fleet over the British mind grew exponentially.

Germans harbored their own fears. Why was Britain reacting so bitterly to Germany's legitimate desire to become a world power? Why did it seem so bellicose? As early as 1903 Britain's own distinguished military and naval analyst T. A. Brassey chided his countrymen for what he considered excessively liberal spending for the Royal Navy. Parliament was voting huge sums each year, and "we have pointed out again and again that Great Britain is practically maintaining her fleet on a war footing in time of peace."[79]

In 1908 King Edward VII visited Berlin, and one of his entourage, Lord Hardinge, had a lengthy conversation with the kaiser about British concerns. Wilhelm dismissed them. He alone controlled German foreign, military, and naval policy, and he loved England. Despite his anger over British foreign policy, had he not forestalled a proposed French-Russian-German alliance at the time of the Boer War? "The German Navy represented no danger to England, and [its battleship construction] program must be carried through." A year later a senior German diplomat remarked to a Russian counterpart that "of course, Germany could not admit that a foreign Power should dictate the extent of her naval armaments; but the present situation could become dangerous, if protracted, for which reason an amicable solution must be found."[80] It never was.

In the summer of 1911, Wilhelm's rashness pushed Europe to the brink of war. That spring, a French expedition had expanded the boundaries of Morocco by seizing Fez and the surrounding territory on Morocco's Atlantic coast.[81] Mannesmann Brothers, a large German firm active in European and North African affairs, claimed that it had a large interest in the previously untouched

sandy bay of Agadir within the newly seized territory. The kaiser's foreign minister, Alfred von Kiderlen-Wächter, immediately took up the Mannesmann
cause. Paris denied the German claim but was prepared to listen to Berlin's argument if negotiations could also include discussion of the Congo frontiers. The
German press railed against the French for meddling in Germany's imperial interests, and then on the morning of July 1 Berlin announced that the kaiser had
sent the gunboat *Panther* to Agadir "to maintain and protect German interests."
Tirpitz later revealed that the move had been instigated by Kiderlen-Wächter.

Terror engulfed Europe. For three weeks the Liberal government in London
dithered; then David Lloyd George, the fiery, controversial chancellor of the
exchequer, erupted into the foreign policy realm, delivering what Berlin interpreted as a firm warning that if Germany challenged French rule in Morocco in
any way, Britain would be on the side of France. The appalled world waited for
the German response. Tirpitz later claimed that he had realized from the beginning that Kiderlen-Wächter had made a major blunder, "and I was strengthened
in my belief when I learned that England had not been consulted." Germany
had never intended to seize territory in Morocco, but Kiderlen-Wächter had
not made that clear, and Lloyd George's warning forced the Wilhelmstrasse to
emphasize its peaceful intent and thus give the appearance of a humiliating
backdown to a show of British power. Germans were embittered once more,
while anxious Britons braced for the worst when Berlin's initial reply to the
Lloyd George speech was that "if France should repel the hand offered her by
the Emperor's Government, the dignity of Germany would compel her to secure
by all means full respect by France for German treaty rights."[82]

Churchill, who had just assumed administration of the Admiralty, promptly
beat the fleet to quarters. The German message that seemed "so very cautious
and correct" masked "deadly words." Soft voices had purred quietly, courteously,
gravely in large, peaceful rooms. But similar "exactly-measured phrases" in the
past had set cannons flaming without warning, "and nations had been struck
down by this same Germany." Were the Germans now preparing the long-
dreaded secret attack against Britain?

> The Admiralty wireless whispers through the ether to the tall masts of
> ships, and captains pace their decks absorbed in thought. It is nothing. It
> is less than nothing. It is too foolish, too fantastic to be thought of in the
> twentieth century. Or is it fire and murder leaping out of the darkness at
> our throats, torpedoes ripping the bellies of half-awakened ships, a sunrise
> on a vanished naval supremacy, and an island well-guarded hitherto, at
> last defenceless?[83]

Agadir proved to be the nothing that Britons and Europeans hoped and prayed for. *Panther* eventually left the remote harbor, and the crisis passed in a blur of vague, confusing diplomacy. But once again Germany had shaken Britain and the Continent to their foundations.

As the Moroccan crisis faded, Europe had to face the implications of the Balkan-Turkish war. Diplomatic observers immediately realized that the victory of Bulgaria, Serbia, and Greece over Turkey represented a grave setback for German foreign policy and German arms. Berlin had assiduously courted Constantinople for years, hoping not only for rail concessions to Baghdad that would cut across British and French imperial holdings in the Middle East but also for Turkish military support in a general European war that would surely hurl German and Russian soldiers at each other's throats. With the Turkish defeat Germany lost "the support of 700,000 Turkish bayonets, and . . . gained the hostility of 700,000 Balkan soldiers who, in case of a war between the Triple Alliance [Germany, Austria-Hungary, and Romania] and France and Russia, can create a very dangerous diversion by attacking Austria-Hungary in the south, her most vulnerable quarter." For a time German chancellor Theobald von Bethmann Hollweg hoped that despite steadily intensifying tensions between London and Berlin, German diplomacy could keep Britain neutral in any future European conflict. An Anglo-German "understanding" would mean that "France and Russia must lose the certainty that they could continue to count upon the support of England in pursuing an anti-German policy. But that was just what England would not do."[84]

In the spring of 1913 Germany's international situation deteriorated further as rumors abounded in both Berlin and Vienna that Romania could not be counted on as an ally against Russia in any future war. The effect upon the German navy and German naval strategy was catastrophic as kaiser and government rediscovered the fact that Germany was essentially and eternally a land power requiring above all an effective continental diplomacy and a superior army. The Wilhelmstrasse was learning the same lesson as Whitehall. Sea power had decided, often decisive, limits.

"Suddenly," an informed source wrote that April, "Germany has discovered that her future lies, not upon the water, but upon the land, that whilst challenging Great Britain's naval supremacy she has jeopardised not only her military supremacy but even her security."[85] Tirpitz's rationale for building a blue-water navy had been to "qualify" Germany for alliance with another great power. The fleet had been built, but the alliance had not materialized, and for good reason. Britain's supremacy at sea seemed simply too great and of too long a duration to contest. Moreover, the nineteenth-century Pax Britannica, largely enforced by the Royal Navy, had brought enormous benefits to the international community in terms of stability and trade. Instead of destabilizing the world order in Germany's favor as Tirpitz hoped, the new German navy together with Wilhelm's bellicose foreign policy had only antagonized the nation's chief rival for world power while frightening and alienating all the other powers on the Continent.

The twenty-four months between the onset of the Moroccan crisis and the spring of 1913 thus proved to be both the fault line and the turning point of early-twentieth-century history, when a rabidly ambitious Germany suddenly realized to its horror that it had pursued exactly the wrong policy and in the process had laid itself wide open not only to revilement from afar but to assault from next door. Germany had deviated, perhaps fatally, from its core competency, which was a continental army designed either for offense or for defense. Now Berlin abruptly transformed preoccupation with naval rivalry and an overseas empire into obsession with the military security of the national frontiers.

With Europe aroused, the Turkish ally routed, and the Balkans ablaze, it was essential that Germany review and revise its entire military and naval posture. Displaying his usual stunning lack of sensitivity, Tirpitz had told Bethmann Hollweg in the autumn of 1911 that the recent setback in Morocco should be counterbalanced by a supplementary naval law designed to reassert Germany's implacable will to power. The chancellor was incensed. He insisted that there had been no setback in Morocco and complained bitterly to Tirpitz's superior, the chief of the naval cabinet, because such an expression had been used. Undeterred, Tirpitz prepared a new naval bill that was introduced in the Reichstag the following spring. Designed to calm British fears of the High Seas Fleet by clearly revealing its exact size and composition, the 1912 German Naval Bill had exactly the opposite effect.

Tirpitz proposed (and the kaiser and Reichstag ultimately accepted) a modest revision of the 1908 naval law. Rather than cutting capital-ship construction from four to two hulls a year after 1911, Germany would lay down three new battleships together with two unarmored cruisers, numerous destroyers, and seventy-two submarines. According to the calculations of Archibald Hurd and Henry Castle, if German building continued at the yearly pace indicated in the 1912 law, the High Seas Fleet would eventually contain "sixty-one large armoured ships of maximum power, all of them less than twenty years old." British naval authorities admitted, however, that the latest law did not specify the character of the various large armored ships to be built but left that decision to Tirpitz's discretion. As with earlier legislation, the Reichstag could not reduce the number of new ships without repealing the entire law.[86]

Purely in terms of the Anglo-German naval-construction race, the 1912 law was less than it seemed, for a combination of domestic political and economic forces conspired in 1912 to hand Tirpitz his first legislative defeat in fourteen years. The admiral had initially wanted to sustain a construction program of at least four new battleships per annum. But with the army clamoring for more men and matériel to meet the new crises on Germany's borders caused by the Turkish defeat, the inflammation of the Balkans, and growing Anglo-French antagonism after Agadir, Tirpitz could neither expect nor demand any further significant growth of the fleet. As several scholars have emphasized, and as contemporaries suggested, Germany's naval dreams were rapidly crumbling by 1913. "From 1900 to the present time," J. Ellis Barker wrote that April, "Germany has been the pace-maker in naval armaments. . . . Largely owing to Germany's action, the naval expenditure of the world has almost doubled in the space of twelve years." Barker's accompanying statistics were striking. Germany's naval expenditure in millions of pounds sterling in 1900 was 7.9 and in 1912 23.1. Britain's in the same period was 29.5 and 45, respectively (the United States 12.8 and 26.7, Japan 6.1 and 9.7, and Russia 9.6 and 17.7). Thus, Britain was easily outspending its German antagonist—and, indeed, its naval expenditures almost matched those of Germany, the United States, Japan, and Russia combined.[87]

Yet the strain was becoming unbearable. Across the North Sea, it was worse. The cost of a forced-draft building of a major fleet had at last taken its toll on both the treasury and the Reichstag. Above all, it was essential that suddenly beleaguered Germany regain a balanced military force. When Wilhelm's ambassador incorrectly reported from London in the autumn of 1913 that the Admiralty might be considering reduction of the caliber of its heaviest guns, the kaiser "at once let out a sigh of relief." In November Wilhelm scolded Tirpitz, arguing that the fleet to be built under the 1912 naval bill "exceeded the limits of available personnel, to say nothing of the purse." The kaiser spoke of "the 'ghastly' nature of 'this screw without end'" and informed his ambassador in London that "the bow is overstrung here as in England." By 1914 "ruinous finances" had stripped the Imperial German Navy of its aura, even as the fleet grew to substantial size; the navy was "no longer the unifying force, the 'darling of the nation,'" touted by Tirpitz. The cost of Tirpitz's blunder was staggering. The German naval budget had risen from 133 million marks in 1899 to 467 million marks by 1913, with an additional sixty million marks expended on improving the Kiel Canal so that it could pass dreadnought-size warships. "Costs of battleships in the same period climbed from 21 million marks for *Kaiser Friedrich III*... to forty-five million marks for *König*."[88]

Tirpitz later expressed amazement that Britain would react so hysterically to Germany's firm commitment to build only three new battleships. But the admiral was being customarily disingenuous. What the British feared in the 1912 German Naval Law was not its construction provisions so much as the strengthening of the active fleet. Realizing that he now had to concentrate on the efficiency and response time of his navy rather than simply on its strength and size, Tirpitz seized on earlier reforms in the Royal Navy to produce a plan that would mobilize the High Seas Fleet in lockstep with the army for instant reaction to any future crises in Europe. In the current inflamed atmosphere Britain not unnaturally saw this initiative as nearly an act of war.[89]

Under the 1912 legislation, the High Seas Fleet was reorganized. In the past it had conducted summer maneuvers off Scandinavia and in the North Sea near the German coast and then retreated to winter anchorage in October to train the new round of annual recruits. With the 1912 law a new squadron of dreadnoughts and pre-dreadnoughts built around the newest and best eight battleships would remain in full commission year-round "as part of the active battle-fleet." Churchill told the House of Commons that "whereas, according to the unamended [German Naval] Law the active battle-fleet consisted of 17 battleships, 4 battle or large armoured cruisers, and 12 small cruisers; in the near future that active fleet will consist of 25 battleships, 8 battle or large armoured cruisers, and 18 smaller cruisers." Moreover, Tirpitz would expand and accelerate construction of both destroyers and submarines; of the seventy-two undersea boats, fifty-four would be kept in constant service. "Taking a general view, the effect of this Law will be that nearly four-fifths of the entire German Navy will be maintained in full permanent commission."[90]

Churchill characteristically inflated rather grossly both the current and near-future size of the German fleet. But the government and public both at home and overseas took him at his word. Observers in England and the United States were aghast. "When the present German programme is fully completed, and even without counting on its being extended," British journalist Sydney Brooks wrote in early 1912, even before the contents of the German Naval Bill were known, "Germany will have a fleet of thirty-three Dreadnoughts, a fleet, that is to say, more powerful by far than any the world has yet seen." The officers and men of the Imperial German Navy "will be admirably trained and organized" and "will have behind [them] the greatest and most powerful army in Europe."

German battleships could steam south to the Mediterranean, joining Austria-Hungary's handful of new dreadnoughts in the Adriatic to cut Britain's imperial lifeline east of Suez. More likely, the High Seas Fleet would remain concentrated in the Heligoland Bight, "capable of being launched against a foe like a single thunderbolt." The foe could be only Britain, harassed and distracted by a multitude of cares and responsibilities and just a day's steaming from the Jade bar.[91]

Britain and its allies concluded, not without reason, that the kaiser's real objective in challenging England on the high seas was to destroy British influence in continental affairs. Viscount Richard Haldane, Britain's secretary of state for war between 1905 and 1912, recalled, "The effect and the only possible effect of the building of the German Fleet was to intensify Anglo-German enmity, and to prepare the Great War," adding perceptively that "the school of von Tirpitz . . . would not be content unless they could control England's sea-power. They would have accepted a two to three" ratio in capital ships "because it would have been enough to enable them to secure allies and to break up the [Anglo-French-Russian] entente." If German diplomacy, using the navy as its blunt instrument, had shattered the Anglo-French accord, the kaiser's dream of having a free hand on the Continent might have been realized when he turned his army first against Russia, then against France. This at least was the prospect that confronted Englishmen, Frenchmen, and Russians as they uneasily huddled together in the years before 1914.[92]

What made the German initiative seem both sinister and disheartening were the efforts of His Majesty's government to find some way to slow down the naval race. When the first intimations of Tirpitz's new law had appeared at the beginning of 1912, Prime Minister Herbert Asquith dispatched Haldane to Berlin for talks, and the kaiser and his naval and military chieftains had received the British envoy with much cordiality and apparent sympathy. Tirpitz, however, soon concluded that Haldane's ostensible concessions to obtain a "holiday" in naval construction were a sham at best and a fraud at worst. Here was perfidious Albion again offering Germany the opportunity to develop a few colonies in the most worthless parts of Africa in exchange for permanent German naval inferiority of at least two to one in capital ships. Tirpitz proposed a two-to-three ratio between Germany and Britain, which Prime Minister Lloyd George had earlier suggested. Haldane politely refused, and Tirpitz concluded that the real aim of the British visit had been "the collapse of our Navy Bill."[93] The Haldane mission ended in failure.

In fact, the discussions between Haldane and the Germans had been broader than Tirpitz later indicated.

As a quid pro quo for keeping their fleet second to Britain's, the Germans demanded a promise of British neutrality in the event of war between Germany and France. This the British refused to give. Haldane returned convinced that Germany's drive for hegemony in Europe would have to be resisted sooner or later: "I thought, from my study of the German General Staff, that once the German war party had got into the saddle, it would be war not merely for the overthrow of France or Russia but for the domination of the world."[94]

Haldane was a gentle, calm man, and his obvious alarm deeply influenced the British government. Churchill ordered the last battleship home from Malta while London and Paris signed the formal naval pact that pledged British safeguard of the Channel and French concentration in the Mediterranean.

The kaiser and his chancellor were as disheartened and even frightened by the British response to the newest German naval bill as the British had been to the legislation itself. "I could not have carried, or even effectively have advocated, an abandonment of the Naval Bill," Bethmann Hollweg later wrote, "without a perceptible alteration of the general political situation." Still, he sighed, "the introduction of the Naval Bill was a mistake, as being a move that embarrassed the relaxation [of international tensions] that we had in view."[95]

Wilhelm's reaction to British opinion was extreme. By 1913 a "discernible change" had come over him; he rapidly "gravitated into isolation." After an embarrassing gaffe in 1908 he seldom spoke to the press; at the same time he ceased his frequent travels to London and St. Petersburg and came to rely solely on diplomatic and military and naval reports "selected by his staff to buttress his preconceived ideas and prejudices." Not surprisingly, the kaiser soon developed "a dangerous and simplistic 'friend-foe' mentality," so that when in 1914 Churchill again called for an Anglo-German naval holiday, he allegedly screamed, "The British surprise attack is here."[96]

With the enactment of the 1912 German Naval Law, Churchill immediately requested and received a parliamentary commitment to maintain the current 60 percent lead in dreadnought construction over Germany. His subsequent efforts to find a mutually satisfactory formula for ending the naval race went nowhere, and anxieties throughout Europe remained at a fever pitch. Churchill had come to the Admiralty with orders to further modernize the institution, and he soon appointed a new board and then established the Naval War Staff. In May 1912, in the midst of the uproar over the latest German naval bill, the staff quietly changed several centuries of British maritime policy. There were no bases on the Continent from which the Royal Navy could operate, and German sea power, particularly in the category of light combatants (including fast torpedo-carrying destroyers and submarines), had narrowed British naval superiority to a dangerous level. The staff developed a plan, quickly approved by Churchill, which called for a distant rather than close blockade of northwestern Europe in the event of war. No watch was to be maintained on the Heligoland Bight by heavy fleet units, and no coastal operations were to be undertaken by the Royal Navy until the High Seas Fleet was defeated.

Under the new scheme the Grand Fleet was based at Scapa Flow in the Orkney Islands, directly north of Scotland. Virtually "land-locked by ranges of mauve hills," Scapa encompassed "an area of sea so great that even the Grand Fleet with its innumerable dependent and satellite craft seemed almost lost in its fifty square miles." This "vast wild harbour" was deemed a perfect location from which to block the exits from the North Sea. Five hundred miles south, "a cordon of destroyers" operating out of Harwich was thrown across the Dover Straits, supported by the Admiralty's still substantial stock of pre-dreadnoughts and a cruiser force, all protected by minefields. As to civil shipping, merchandise transported under enemy flag anywhere on the seven seas was to be confiscated. Churchill subsequently observed with satisfaction that this program stood the test of war and was never substantially changed. "By this means the British Navy seized and kept the effective control of all the oceans of the world."[97]

Meanwhile, the kaiser and his admirals struggled to formulate a coherent, effective policy of their own. The diplomatic and military isolation of the German–Austro-Hungarian alliance was not as clear as it soon would be with the defection of Romania. But the tensions and crises of 1911–1912 had focused the thought of every monarch, statesman, general, and admiral on the possibility of general war. Near the end of 1912 London and Berlin were able to patch together an international conference before Serbia's demands for an outlet on the Adriatic led to outright war with Austria-Hungary. Hopes rose in the Wilhelmstrasse that London might be willing to at least tacitly guarantee the Turkish-German alliance, despite the implications for British imperial interests in the Middle East. But even as the diplomats were trying to maintain the peace, Lord Haldane told the German ambassador in London that Britain could not remain neutral if Germany attacked France, and the kaiser responded on December 8 by calling a meeting of his military and naval chieftains to ponder grand strategy. All the festering inconsistencies and uncertainties inherent in German naval strategy since the creation of the High Seas Fleet now surfaced: *Grosskrieg* (big war) versus *Kleinkrieg* (little war); *Entscheidungsschlacht* (decisive battle) versus a careful, selective wearing down of the anticipated British blockade; an essentially defensive war versus an essentially offensive war; a two-front war in the Baltic and North Seas or a concentration of power against either Russia or Britain. Even the question of submarines versus battleships as the prime instruments of German sea power received an implicit hearing.

The kaiser, as usual, had witnessed the summer's naval maneuvers and had written to the Admiralty Staff that he was firmly against a major offensive against the British fleet off the Skagerrak or Danish coast. The High Seas Fleet had to be used in the Heligoland Bight close to its bases, from which it would steam to break the enemy's anticipated close blockade of German ports.[98] But the December meeting led to a major strategic revision: the German navy would engage in all-out battle against the British fleet.

Tirpitz and the German Admiralty, together with Helmuth von Moltke, the chief of the German General Staff, submitted several reports to the kaiser, confirming what had been said and decided at the meeting. Wilhelm returned them signed and with substantial marginal notes. He now believed war was inevitable. When it would come and over what issue no one knew. But the political divisions tearing Europe apart were simply the superficial manifestations of a fundamental and irrepressible ethnic war. The conflict would be the climactic battle "between Teutons and Slavs" for the soul of humanity. The "Anglo-Saxons" would be found "on the side of the Slavs and the Gauls" as Britain, from "envy" and "hate," pursued its historic policy of suppressing legitimate German military and naval interests and objectives.[99]

The army had long and carefully prepared for a continental war. Its Schlieffen Plan would hold Russia's ponderously gathering armies off for a month to six weeks with minimal forces while the majority of the German army shot straight westward through neutral Belgium, thus bypassing French frontier fortifications. "German forces would then pivot and move directly south toward Paris, sweeping" the demoralized French armies before them. The climactic battle would be fought victoriously somewhere near the French capital, freeing the German army to turn east and deal a killing blow to the czar's forces. Lacking a similar grand strategy, Tirpitz and the Admiralty could do nothing but beg Wilhelm and Moltke to postpone considering an attack on France or a commitment to defend Austria-Hungary until at least until the summer of 1914, when the fortifications at Heligoland and the widening of the Kiel Canal would be completed. Moltke replied caustically that "the navy would never be ready for battle."[100]

Since Tirpitz and the admirals could not figure out what to do with their fleet, Wilhelm decided the matter for them. Despite the fact that the Russian navy was reviving from its drugged slumber following the crushing defeats by

Japan seven years earlier (Czar Nicholas hoped to have no fewer than eight dreadnoughts and battle cruisers together with supporting vessels operating in the Baltic by 1920),[101] the kaiser ordered his navy, ready or not, to deploy against Britain rather than Russia at the outbreak of a European war and to do so with all-out abandon. In conjunction with submarine, mine, and even dirigible attacks, the High Seas Fleet would sweep down the Channel to destroy the short British transportation and supply lines between Dover and the French ports, thus sealing off England's small army and its military depots, factories, and ports from the continental battlefields.[102]

This strategy was not only bold but also sound in light of Britain's decision (unknown, of course, to Berlin) to impose a loose blockade of the German coast and the approaches to the Baltic. The High Seas Fleet was free to erupt over the Jade bar and race down the Channel before the Royal Navy's Home Fleet, anchored hundreds of miles away at Scapa Flow and the Scottish ports, could intervene. If Britain's army could be denied access to the western front, France might well be destroyed, in which case Germany would enjoy total access to French agricultural and industrial assets, rendering meaningless any subsequent British close blockade of the Jade and Elbe estuaries and Baltic coast.

But Germany's sailors fumbled the opportunity their kaiser gave them. In the eighteen months between the end of 1912 and the crisis of July–August 1914, the Admiralty Staff failed to work out an operations plan against the expected distant blockade. Unfortunately for the German cause, Wilhelm did not become aware of this strategic failure until July 26, 1914, little more than a week before the outbreak of hostilities.[103] Confronting battle at last, German naval morale unraveled. The fleet's patent inferiority in tradition, numbers, and hitting power depressed senior flag officers who "seemed to lack the competence and confidence at sea possessed by their British contemporaries. The accusation leveled by contemporary British observers that senior German officers were happier at their desks than at sea had an element of truth in it." In the winter of 1913–1914 the German naval staff had conducted a war game, which "ended in the conclusion that a far-reaching offensive must be avoided and instead the opening phase in a war should be confined to *Kleinkrieg* which would pave the way for the *Entscheidungsschlacht*." German strategic timidity was in no way altered by intelligence information indicating that, in fact, in the event of war England would impose a distant blockade of Germany in the gap between Scotland and Norway. Thus, the navy's operational war plan of August 4, 1914, determined to whittle down the oppressively large enemy fleet through " 'offensive sorties . . . as far as the English coast' " designed to lure out and defeat inferior

British forces. One caveat was injected into this strategy of timidity. Should a favorable opportunity present itself, the enemy's Grand Fleet would be engaged "even before such an equalization of forces had been achieved."[104] It was a retreat to December 3, 1912, and represented in rough outline German naval strategy for the Great War of 1914–1918.

Across the North Sea, Britain's concerns and cares flowed together in the Royal Navy's 1913 annual fleet maneuvers. By this time, all Europe was an armed camp—a tinderbox waiting to be ignited by a single ungovernable crisis that had, mercifully, not yet appeared. Home Fleet commander Sir George Callaghan had laid out four basic mission responsibilities for his ships and sailors, the first two of which were clearly defensive in purpose: first, frustrating an enemy invasion "or serious military raids"; second, preventing the distant blockade lines against Germany (the Northern Patrolling Force) from "being broken up"; third, providing cover for transport of the British Expeditionary Force to the Continent "if such a course is decided upon"; and, finally, "bringing the enemy to battle on good occasion." In the event, an enemy "red fleet" under John Jellicoe's command landed thirty-six thousand men at Grimsby and "decamped" with the loss of but a single battleship together with some destroyers and submarines. David Beatty wrote his wife that the enemy had "done exactly what I said they would do." Later, Jellicoe was able to land a second "raiding party" on British soil. The blue fleet responded sluggishly to reports of an enemy sighting, and Callaghan with the main battleship force "never came (he is a very slow starter)" and had to be content with harrying the red fleet's weak rear forces. Even more disturbing, red-fleet submarines went on an uncontested rampage. One blue-fleet commander "was torpedoed three times in one day and is much upset. In fact," David Beatty reported to his wife, "very few ships escaped altogether," and one of the admiral's own battle cruisers, *Princess Royal,* was torpedoed leaving harbor.[105]

The Admiralty, including First Lord Winston Churchill, quickly accepted John Fisher's view that undersea craft, properly handled, could decisively affect fleet actions: torpedoes could sink battleships. Indeed, by the eve of war in 1914, advanced naval thinkers concluded they could do much more, Jellicoe insisting that submarines "can undoubtedly carry out a blockade of an enemy's coast in the old sense of the word." Since submarines (and fast torpedo-carrying destroyers) could, theoretically, destroy Britain's Grand Fleet either through blockade of its bases or on the high seas, the Royal Navy's traditional strategy of close-in blockade of enemy coasts by capital ships was no longer feasible; by the same token, British submarines *could,* again theoretically, deny an enemy fleet access to the North Sea and world ocean because they could sink any units rash enough to sortie. British officialdom reacted to this new reality in a variety of ways. Between 1912 and 1914 the Admiralty and the Cabinet (whose younger members remained obsessed with retrenchment) seriously considered reorienting naval estimates and budgets to favor small, fast, comparatively inexpensive torpedo-carrying surface craft at the expense of slow, costly battleships. What kinds of submarines ought to be built, how they would be propelled, and how they could be best employed divided Fisher and Churchill. Fisher argued that in a coming war, submarines might be gainfully employed against merchant fleets. Young Winston was appalled, as were many others. In the end, Churchill could not disenthrall himself from the romance of the big ship, fighting for and obtaining a continuation of Britain's dreadnought-construction program at a high level, despite mounting costs.[106]

And so the new navies girded for a war whose dimensions none could truly grasp. The past continued its iron hold on imaginations. As in the Age of Fighting Sail, national security and world domination would rest on great lines of battleships slugging it out at ten or twelve miles' distance until one line was outmaneuvered, gave way, and was harried to death by the other. Only the addition of fast torpedo-carrying surface ships and slow, uncertain submarines might alter the equation somewhat. One such classic battle had been fought less than a decade before, at Tsushima, and admiralties round the world confidently predicted another such battle, even mightier in scope and scale, would be fought should a great war break out among the powers. In this they were right, but Tsushima and Jutland would prove to be mere way stations on the road to even more sophisticated, and barbarous, industrial conflicts at sea.

CHAPTER 3

Rengo Kantai

AS WORLD ATTENTION focused on the Anglo-German naval race, another sea power was emerging far away across the Eurasian landmass. Old Japan was killed by sea power; modern Japan was determined to flourish with it, and eventually the Imperial Japanese Navy produced a Mahan of its own, albeit an obscure lieutenant commander whose name and works were long unknown in the West.

Commodore Matthew Perry's abrupt and frightening appearance in 1853 had been merely the first of a number of humiliations that the Japanese had had to endure as the West violated their isolated society. Soon Japan was torn by civil war as rival factions struggled to impose upon the country coherent but varied responses to the Western incursion. The old order died hard. A Jo-i or Barbarian Expelling party emerged to wage a furious campaign against the power of the shogunate, which had ostensibly betrayed the sacred national policy of seclusion. Ten years after Perry, an international squadron led by the British Far Eastern Fleet bombarded Kagoshima, the capital of the by-now dissident Satsuma clan, to avenge the murder of an Englishman by Satsuma warriors. The next year American, British, French, and Dutch warships shelled Shimonoseki in retaliation for attacks on Western merchant vessels by members of the defiant Choshu clan.

Even before this third desecration of the homeland, the larger Japanese feudal clans had laid the foundations for a national navy. Perry's visit galvanized the daimyo (hereditary noble) Shimazu of the Satsuma clan to build a modest navy of his own, including a steamer, "which was the first Japanese man-of-war designed on the European pattern." In 1857 the desperate Tokugawa shogun, sensing the impending end of his rule, invited his old friends, the Dutch, to send traders, engineers, and industrial machinery to Nagasaki for the first modern shipyard in Asia. Thus was born the great Mitsubishi Shipbuilding and Engineering Company, an enormous industrial complex that for the next eighty-five years would supply Japan with many of its best warships and aircraft. In the early 1860s French engineers began erecting the great naval dockyards at Yokosuka, and in 1866 Japanese shipbuilders launched their first steam-driven war vessel, *Chiyoda,* which weighed 138 tons. In April 1868, during the War of Restoration that would place the young emperor Meiji securely on the throne, the Aki, Chikuzen, Hizen, Kurulmi, Nagato, Satsuma, and Tosa clans combined to place six warships at the disposal of the fledgling Imperial Fleet. Thus, when the nation at last united under Meiji later that year, many of the components for a modern imperial sea service were available. Others soon followed. A small naval mission had been sent to the United States as early as 1859; by 1870 Meiji had established the Imperial Department of Defense, and a navy department followed two years later. Before long an imperial fleet of increasingly modern proportions had appeared in order to defend expanding Japanese interests (largely against China and Chinese pirates) in the Ryukyus and Formosa (Taiwan).[1]

Like their European counterparts, the Japanese ruling classes employed tradition in the service of change. Knowing that their feudal order had to industrialize and militarize or perish culturally if not politically under Western domination, the Japanese translated their objective of steadily growing industrial, financial, military, and naval power into the everyday language of "feudal and family ethics expressing ideals central to the experience" of nearly all Japanese. "With suitable interpretation to make all little loyalties lead up to one great loyalty" to the emperor and his wish to build a powerful modern state, "these ideals called up prodigies of effort and self-sacrifice."[2] Within a generation, peasant boys from remote, rural prefectures were transformed into bankers, capitalists, manufacturers, diplomats, admirals, and generals who operated on a global scale and dreamed increasingly of Japan's role as the arbiter of Far Eastern affairs.

From the beginning, Meiji Japan was aware of its fragile status in the world. The country was desperately poor. If it was to industrialize sufficiently to keep the Western barbarians from committing constant desecrations and imposing repeated humiliations, Japan had to modernize and arm. But unless and until Japan's global trading position and domestic economy grew dramatically by every way and means, the country would have to develop its power base from very narrow resources. Thus, fiscal constraints in the early years of the Meiji era kept the Japanese armed forces comparatively small. Not until 1883 did the nation's increasingly favorable economic position permit the beginnings of a truly modern fleet that was still of strikingly modest size compared to those of the distant European colonial powers. Just as fleet expansion began in earnest, Japan decided to import European models of parliamentary politics to go along with other aspects of modernity. The Satsuma clan's domination of the navy in its uncertain early years through provision of ships and men began to wane. The new professionals who began to man the fleet had to learn how to play politics and to exploit every opportunity to stimulate public opinion. This was not easy to do, for the Satsumas' long domination of the navy had stimulated jealousies and rivalries; opponents were so vociferous in their charge of naval inefficiency that for some years before the 1894–1895 war with China, "the Government had experienced considerable difficulty in getting the naval estimates passed." Only a vigorous South Seas colonization movement and growing turbulence on the nearby Asian mainland kept the momentum for naval expansion alive. "In fact," wrote one British authority on the subject, Japan "was obtaining very good value for its money all the time, but the exploits of the fleet when put to the supreme test of war were so little expected that they caused as much surprise as elation."[3]

The Imperial Japanese Navy grew, prospered, and went to war because the nation it served was surrounded by both threats and opportunities. On the one hand, the great powers, though lodged in distant Europe, possessed substantial naval forces on the Asian coast with which to threaten Nippon. China, too, though carved up into spheres of influence by the Western imperialists, maintained a central government and a relatively strong navy to go with it. Indeed, as late as 1890, "China's Northern Fleet, with its thirty warships, was larger than Japan's entire navy," and leading Japanese naval strategists entertained "deep anxieties over war with China, believing that such a course of action could result in serious"—indeed, politically, militarily, and economically "devastating"—"losses for the Japanese Navy." Moreover, Tokyo's determination to dominate the Korean peninsula in order to ward off attacks from that direction (the last such attempt to invade Japan had come from the peninsula five hundred years before) inevitably brought the country into conflict with Russia, which did not maintain a large fleet in Asian waters but whose czar coveted Manchuria and all Northeast Asia by means of expansion from the west. At the same time, the navy was one of Japan's strongest *national* institutions, and this counted greatly in a country that desperately required effective and efficient integration in all spheres and at all levels to gain and retain the strength needed to ensure continued sovereignty. Japan had no wish to be carved up into commercial spheres, as was happening to China. The navy was perhaps the chief guarantor that this would not happen. Finally, the navy was the inevitable beneficiary of that same fever for colonial expansion that also gripped the great European states in the late nineteenth century. "South Seas Consciousness" began to seep into the collective Japanese mind in the 1870s, hurried along by the vigorous Colonization Society that in many ways reflected the organization founded in Germany in 1882 to hasten naval increases, emigration of excess population, and a passion for national prestige. In Japan's case, a large, effective fleet would be needed to lead the charge into the resource-rich lands and islands of Oceania and Southeast Asia. Indeed, Japan's first naval cadets took their initial training voyages southward on Japan's first ships, visiting, and reconnoitering, Hawaii, New Zealand, Australia, New Guinea, Fiji, Samoa, Guam, and the American West Coast. When they returned, they and their officers were invited, along with "civilian adventurers," to speak and lobby before the Japanese Colonization Society and like-minded groups about promises and conditions in the South Seas. The youngsters were also encouraged to keep diaries of their travels and impressions, and upon return home these invaluable documents "were made available to newly recruited cadets and regularly used for teaching purposes at the academy."[4] Little wonder that citizens of the Pacific Islands and Australia began to wonder what Japan was up to even before its navy won its first series of victories.

The more Japan changed during the Meiji years and beyond, the more intensely it tried to remain the same. Throne and government worked assiduously to impose rigid uniformity on public thought. "'Higher scholarship,' with its fondness for debate, should be reserved for the elite few. The many, by contrast, needed careful policing." In 1890 the Imperial Rescript on education defined a population "united in loyalty and filial piety... from generation to generation." The "national way" *(kokutai)* was "infallible for all ages and true in all places." The teaching of world history had been banned ten years earlier; now the teaching of Japanese history was intensified and equated with universal history. It focused exclusively on fostering reverence for the emperor. By 1915 Japan possessed a firm public ideology that would remain until the end of World War II. The granting of universal male suffrage in 1925 was accompanied by the Police Preservation Law, whose most severe provisions could be applied against anyone who denied either the *kokutai* or "the private property system." It naturally followed that the police would systematically control "all thought that might disturb the national polity." The eternal, unchanging nature of Japanese society and history imposed a sacred duty on the emperor and his people to guide the entire world toward the higher reality that Japan enjoyed. As one university professor proclaimed in 1933, "The Japanese could only serve humanity by making Japan the strongest country" on earth. "The world can enjoy peace only when all countries reach the same level of civilization. [Japan] cannot permit such a thing as low civilization countries."[5]

Japan's forcibly renewed contact with the outside world came at just the moment when its leaders could exploit the rapid growth of advanced Western industrial technologies, leapfrogging the long, often stumbling scientific revolution that preceded them. Aggressive and influential officers within the early Meiji navy quickly grasped this fact and exploited their advantages as fully as the slender industrial base and their own bureaucratic and administrative subordination to an army pursuing its own agenda would permit.[6]

How large and efficient the emergent Imperial Japanese Navy might become, what it would do, and how it would be used were not clear to either Japanese or foreign observers for many years. By the late 1880s, however, it was known that the small but powerful Japanese fleet, largely employing British-built warships, was preparing for a struggle against China "by incessant training at sea. Special importance was attached to gunnery, torpedo work and steaming efficiency." But the Imperial Fleet possessed other, quite remarkable, attributes. "It was a single organization under the control of a central authority, and administered as such.... [T]he administration was honest and important appointments went by merit, with the result that the discipline was second to none in the world, and all ranks and ratings were animated by a high professional spirit. Training was thorough, great care and attention were devoted to the upkeep of the vessels and their armaments, and all stocks and reserves of war munitions were maintained at proper levels."[7]

Much of this was due to the Satsuma influence, and as it declined discipline in some ways degenerated into pure brutality and blind obedience. But Japan's military and naval victories over China in 1894–1895 were understandable if not predictable to a young government still uncertain of its relative military, naval, and moral strength. In the Battle of the Yalu a ten-ship Japanese cruiser squadron under Vice Admiral Count Ito completely outmaneuvered and shot to pieces a Chinese force with an equal number of larger, more heavily armed and armored battleships.[8]

The Japanese public was ecstatic. Suddenly, the brand-new *Rengo Kantai* (Combined Fleet) had gained the pride and trust of an entire people. "Ito's victory gave birth to a spirit of ambition among young Japanese to serve in the batteries and engine rooms of their fighting ships," a knowledgeable British observer wrote in 1921, "which still enables their naval authorities to pick and choose to a very large extent from among voluntary candidates for that honour." Seventy years after the battle, a Japanese naval journalist wrote that "the ideographs for *Rengo Kantai* will always stir Japanese hearts." Stories of the heroism of simple sailors raced through the country. A shell from the Chinese flagship *Ting-yuan,* "almost twice the size of any Japanese" warship present, had scored a direct hit on Admiral Ito's flagship, *Matsushima.* A fatally injured crewman, Torajiro Miura, asked a passing officer: "Sir, is *Ting-yuan* not yet sunk?" The deeply moved officer replied, "Rest easily. *Ting-yuan* has been knocked out of action." Miura smiled, cried, "We are avenged," and died. The martyred sailor, much like the later Nazi hero Horst Wessel, became the centerpiece of legend in a martial song:

> Is *Ting-yuan* not yet sunk?
> The brief remark is forever engraved
> In the heart of the people,
> The bulwark of the nation.[9]

China had chosen to concentrate on material power, Japan on the intelligence of its men behind the guns and in the engine rooms. Ito had embraced Admiral David Farragut's conviction that "the best protection for a ship was a rapid and accurate fire from her battery." Although Ito's light guns could not actually sink the heaviest Chinese battleships, they did render them immobile, and the battle seemed to demonstrate the superior value of smaller rapid-fire guns, the "quick firers" in the language of the day.[10]

If the rest of the world had paid attention to events immediately after the Battle of the Yalu, Japanese prowess in modern naval warfare might have received even greater respect. The Chinese battleships that survived took shelter in Port Arthur (Lüshun), while Ito made the mistake of escorting army transports to the "muddy shallows" of the adjacent Liao-tung (Liaodong) Peninsula. When Chinese admiral Ting saw what was happening, he raced out of port, across the Yellow Sea, and into the well-defended and mine-seeded harbor of Weihaiwei (Weihai). Having successfully seen the army ashore at Liao-tung (where it would soon invade and conquer Port Arthur), Ito quickly instituted a blockade of Weihaiwei with his heavy ships. The army "in a brilliant maneuver" sent a force of twenty thousand men supported by ten thousand field laborers marching across the Shantung promontory to fall upon Weihaiwei defensive forts from the landward side. Ito then launched a series of night attacks, hurling wave after wave of small, fast torpedo-carrying steamers into the harbor and through the minefields, where with the help of army artillery they sank or drove ashore the heavy Chinese vessels.

Although the French had developed the modern torpedo in the 1870s, no navy except Japan's had much use for fast surface torpedo boats. Three years after the battle at Weihaiwei, a Royal Navy study virtually dismissed the value of these craft, concluding that a torpedo boat under fire from a battleship had a life expectancy of no more than two minutes. But Ito and his intrepid sailors had demonstrated the worth of the torpedo boat for anyone who cared to observe. Slowly, the torpedo boat gained acceptance as an important component of the modern naval arsenal. The Sino-Japanese War as a whole and the Weihaiwei campaign in particular established a tradition of Japanese excellence in amphibious operations, surface torpedo attack, and night combat (summarized in the phrase *nikuhaku-hitchu*—"press closely, strike home") that was assiduously cultivated over the next half century, incorporated as an integral component of Japanese strategy to delay and damage an enemy battle fleet advancing through the central Pacific toward the Home Islands, and then applied with deadly effect during the World War II battles in and around the Solomon Islands.[11]

Japan's seizure of Korea and China's Liao-tung Peninsula with the strategic city of Port Arthur was immediately contested by imperial Russia, which had its own designs on the northeastern Asian coast. The ink was scarcely dry on the 1895 Treaty of Shimonoseki between Tokyo and Peking (Beijing) when the czar's government enlisted German and French support for a tripartite approach to Japan, the "Triple Intervention," in which the three powers "advised" Tokyo in the most friendly terms that Japanese acquisition of any part of the Chinese mainland would create a "permanent obstacle to peace in the Far East." Tokyo was devastated; the "Intervention" came in the midst of "boundless jubilation over the conclusion of the Treaty," and now this "sudden and cruel turn of events." According to a Japanese historian, the blundering Germans compounded the crisis by phrasing their note in such a way as to appear to threaten immediate war if the Japanese government did not acquiesce. The vice minister for foreign affairs who received the German note observed to "the perplexed German Minister" that France and Russia had "advised Japan in a friendly manner," emphasizing the cause of peace. The German hastily assured his bemused host that Berlin in no way meant to impose pressure. The Japanese responded to the tripartite demarche with perfect correctness, emphasizing the "dictates of humanity."[12] After promptly withdrawing their forces from Liao-tung in exchange for an even larger war indemnity from China, Tokyo increased its already substantial naval forces by 70 percent with an addition of "just over 234,000 tons" and doubled the size of the army in reaction to the insult. Moreover, Japan had taken both the Pescadores (Penghus) and Formosa from the defeated Chinese, and no European power dared to seriously contest these acquisitions. With its powerful garrison in Chosen (Korea), Japan now was a legitimate, authentic power in the Western Pacific–East Asian region. Its holdings directly threatened French Indochina, the Spanish (soon to be American) Philippine archipelago, as well as the German and Russian entrepôts on the northern coast of China. Given such somber realities, how should the nation continue to play its expanding role on the adjacent continent? How should it respond to the undoubted humiliation from three of Europe's greatest powers? Who were its enemies? Who were its friends? In the months and years immediately after 1895 Tokyo began to fashion some answers.

First and foremost, the Imperial Japanese Navy achieved parity with the army. Although the victories over China were a major factor, brilliant bureaucratic leadership also played a crucial role, especially the remarkable courage and persistence of a striking personality, Captain Yamamoto Gombei. Yamamoto never ceased to argue in interservice meetings and conferences that command of the seas around the Home Islands constituted not only the bedrock of national security but also the essential springboard for the expansion of Japan's interests onto the Asian continent. A single tale sums up Yamamoto's fortitude and brilliance in debate. On the eve of the Sino-Japanese War an interservice conference in Tokyo had deliberated the strategic problems of a Korean campaign. Army vice chief of staff General Kawakami Sōroku dilated at length on why the war could be settled only by a decisive land battle on the peninsula. Yamamoto, then serving as chief of the Navy Ministry's secretariat and navy representative at the meeting, suddenly intervened. Did the army have first-rate engineering units? he asked. Yes, of course, Kawakami replied, but why on earth did Yamamoto want to know? "Because, General, if the army is to get to Korea without the Imperial Japanese Navy, those engineer units are going to have to build a very long bridge."[13]

Second, the navy, with Yamamoto again at the forefront, argued successfully that Japan could never again count on victory without possessing at least some of the world's finest battleships. Yamamoto "floated his plans for a massive naval expansion on the tide of popular enthusiasm for naval glory" created by the victory over China. The navy must not "go naked into battle, sword in hand against an enemy shielded by heavy armor," as the Chinese battleships had been. Yamamoto got the imperial government to agree to a series of policies that would mark Japanese naval strategy right down to World War II. First, Japan must possess a world-class military fleet of modern battleships; four would do for a start. Eventually, as the industrial fleets of the world swelled to immense dimensions, Japanese strategists settled on the dream of an "eight-eight fleet": eight battleships and eight fast battle cruisers. Second, Japan must possess a balanced fleet, so capital ships must be surrounded by supporting cruisers and smaller vessels. And, finally, because Japan was clearly inferior to the West in terms of both industrial might and military and naval power, the battleships it did possess must be the largest, finest, and, if possible, most heavily gunned and armored war vessels in the world. Yamamoto specifically excluded Great Britain from this calculation because of London's cordial interest in Japan's future and because British yards were ready to build at least some of Japan's capital ships, though Yamamoto also laid stress on developing a national shipbuilding industry as well. The cabinet heeded the warning, and the Japanese navy began developing a modern battleship fleet. Indeed, the last of the four battleships, *Mikasa,* did prove for a time to be "among the most powerful warships afloat" when it appeared from England's Vickers shipyard in 1902.[14]

But there was grave danger in pursuing such an exuberant course, the insult of the Triple Intervention notwithstanding, and navy minister Tsugumichi Saigō, though a firm supporter of rapid fleet development, warned of the consequences. Yes, Japan could expand its naval strength dramatically. But, like its imperial cousins in far-off Berlin, it would be eternally confronted by other powers who could do the same from a dramatically larger industrial base. "If we increase our naval power," Saigō wrote at this time, "so will others. It will be endless."[15] Here was Japan's eternal, irresolvable, problem.

Finally, Japan's victory over China revolutionized the political and military situation in East Asia. Russia, Germany, and France had become China's ostensible defenders only so they could have the right to dismember and humiliate that country on their own. Russia seized Port Arthur, made it the terminus of the Trans-Siberian Railroad, and became an Asian and perhaps even a Pacific power. From its naval base and commercial entrepôt at Tsingtao, Germany continued to spread its power and culture wherever it could throughout East Asia. France remained ensconced in Indochina. Gunboats and businessmen from these three powers gathered in increasing numbers at Shanghai and the large cities along the Yangtze River.

The Americans were also a problem. In 1897 the circles of Japanese and U.S. expansionism in the Pacific intersected in Hawaii. All evidence indicates that

Japan had no desire to annex the islands but was determined to protect its sizable émigré colony in Hawaii from exploitation by the dominant American planter group. Washington, however, was determined to seize the islands and dispatched a naval squadron to Honolulu. Tokyo countered by sending a cruiser. After some tense weeks, during which Assistant Secretary of the Navy Theodore Roosevelt asked the Naval War College to prepare for a naval conflict, the Tokyo government backed away from confrontation and ordered its ship home. But the seeds had been sown for growing mutual suspicion between the two expanding sea services.[16] That suspicion would grow as the United States Navy, following its victory over Spain the following year, began to intrude upon East Asia with ever greater force and effect.

Brushing aside the legitimate hopes of rebels for a substantial measure of national independence, Washington declared Cuba a self-governing protectorate that permitted the United States unlimited rights of intervention. In the Philippines, the U.S. government simply substituted its rule for that of Spain. Whereas the Cubans reacted more or less docilely, Philippine insurrectionists under Emilio Aguinaldo waged a bitter struggle against what came to be an American garrison of more than sixty thousand men. Forty-two hundred Americans and about five times that many Filipinos died during a four-year guerilla war. Ambush was countered by burning villages and crops; torture became routine on both sides; atrocity was met with counteratrocity. The conflict generated sensation, courts-martial, prisoner-of-war issues, and growing anguish in both the islands and the United States that eerily prefigured the Vietnam years. For the first but not last time in the twentieth century the United States found itself caught up in a dehumanizing Asian campaign. Commenting on the infamous "Samar Expedition" by soldiers seeking bloody and somewhat indiscriminate revenge against insurrectionists who had massacred an army patrol, a young marine—conveniently ignoring two hundred years of mutually vicious frontier warfare with Native Americans—wrote that "subduing savages is a new thing to the American people and they *will* howl at the necessary adjuncts." But the commander of the punitive Samar raid had done only "what others have done—except that he failed to kill them all—if he had done the latter, who would have told the tale? Whatever you do; do thoroughly."[17]

The navy and its marine corps performed a wide variety of blue- and brown-water tasks all over the archipelago. Amphibious assaults were launched at Lingayen Gulf and elsewhere as the army sought to flush out the guerrilla enemy. Monitors and destroyers bombarded rebel strongholds, while shallow-draft gunboats and other craft were employed in search-and-destroy operations "upriver."

When Aguinaldo was at last captured by ruse in his mountain stronghold, he was hustled to the closest beach and taken away in the cruiser *Vicksburg*.[18]

As Kenneth Hagan has observed, the Philippine campaign, like Vietnam later, was no battleship war. Unlike Vietnam, however, the island insurgents enjoyed no adjacent sanctuary, no "impregnable base" next to the battlefields, as the Viet Cong and later North Vietnamese Army did after 1965. Aguinaldo and his people were sealed off and isolated by the United States Navy, allowing the army to encircle and gradually destroy them. The Boxer Rebellion in China during the summer of 1900 was another matter entirely. Washington dispatched major fleet units all the way from Atlantic waters to the Asian coast. President William McKinley had already sent the new first-class cruiser *Brooklyn*—Winfield S. Schley's flagship off Cuba—to Manila Bay in the autumn of 1898 together with a small contingent of lesser vessels to ensure possession of the islands in the face of an intimidating naval buildup by Germany and Britain. By 1900, the cruiser was at Shanghai, a semipermanent mother hen to a newly acquired ragtag gaggle of Yangtze River gunboats. The formerly sporadic U.S. naval presence on the coast had become permanent and soon spread a thousand miles up the river to Chungking (Chongqing). With the outbreak of the rebellion—an officially sanctioned uprising of peasants designed to drive all foreigners from China—*Brooklyn* was joined by *Oregon* (which had begun its career by "racing" eleven thousand miles from California to Key West just prior to the outbreak of the Spanish-American War) and the brand-new battleship *Kentucky*. No less than forty-two U.S. warships of all types and classes supported the international invasion of China that permitted the lifting of the siege of the Western legations at Peking. The North Atlantic Squadron had been left with only a half-dozen warships, but with the rapid collapse of the Boxers most of the American fleet steamed back to the Atlantic and Caribbean while a handful of warships reconstituted the small European Squadron.[19]

The campaigns in far-off China and the Philippines at the beginning of the twentieth century reconfirmed what the Spanish war had first demonstrated: despite the relatively short cruising range and second-rate size of its battleships and armored cruisers, the fledgling U.S. industrial navy knew how to exercise effective, and relatively rapid, power projection in moments of international tension and crisis. Even without an Isthmian canal, the United States Navy was capable of impressive global reach. The world's admiralties took notice, and none more so than that of Japan. The United States now had not only a substantial military garrison and a small fleet at Manila but also at least one small capital ship *(Brooklyn)* at Shanghai and a flotilla of Yangtze gunboats that rivaled in size and number those of any other nation plying China's rivers and policing their shores. Moreover, Tokyo could not have been pleased to read the remarks of American imperialists who noted the extreme importance that the Philippines had suddenly acquired as barracks and base for the deployment of arms, ships, and men anywhere in Asia.[20] The majority of American troops who had taken part in the international campaign against the Boxers had been temporarily withdrawn from garrison duty on Luzon and Samar. The U.S. armada that supported them was the small Philippine-based Asiatic fleet greatly enlarged. These forces, American champions of overseas commercial expansion argued, had been critical to the maintenance of Chinese political independence and economic integrity. The message was veiled but unmistakable. With Secretary of State John Hay's "Open Door Notes" of 1899 and 1900, the United States, no less than Japan, had declared itself the champion of China, and for ostensibly the same reason: to protect that unhappy nation from foreign encroachments. The U.S. military garrison and small fleet at Manila practically ensured that Tokyo and Washington were headed for serious trouble.

The Philippine insurrection and the Boxer Rebellion forced U.S. naval strategists to consider the Pacific for the first time as a vital supply and communications road that had to be kept open. After 1898 American naval architects produced battleships and escorts that matched the finest in the world in terms of size, gun power, speed, and cruising range. By the time Roosevelt ascended to the presidency nine modern battleships had been recently completed and were in service; eight others would follow in two to four years. In October 1903 the navy's permanent eleven-member General Board, created after the Spanish-American War "to devise plans which will employ our naval force to the best advantage," called for a long-range construction program to exceed that of Germany, thus keeping the United States in second place among the world's great fleets in terms of size. By 1920 America would deploy no fewer than forty-eight frontline battleships, each as well armed and well protected and with as great a steaming range as any in the world.[21]

But since the world was at general peace, no enemy navy threatened to cut the watery highway, and the ultimate financial, human, and moral cost of suppressing the Philippine rebels appalled the American people sufficiently that any further appetites for overseas expansion were put to rest. As the Philippine crisis wound down American attention once more focused on Europe. Washington's political and military establishments were as shaken by the German Naval Law of 1900 as any Briton, and in the early years of the century Germany was understandably identified as the prime enemy. Although the administration could not know of the kaiser's mad dream of shelling New York City and invading Chesapeake Bay, Berlin had already meddled in American affairs at Samoa and again at Manila. On both occasions the Germans had been turned back, but how long Wilhelm and his sailors could be contained was anyone's guess. The fact that the High Seas Fleet sailed the high seas only once before 1914 should have provided some clues, but despite the lack of German coaling stations and naval bases in the Western Hemisphere, Americans constantly worried that German colonies in South America might become the spearheads of Teutonic expansion. So in the years immediately after 1900, the United States Navy focused its attention on the waters close to home. But Tokyo had no way of knowing when or if U.S. naval policy might again shift decisively to the far Pacific.

Japan thus entered the new century a volatile, uncertain, and somewhat embittered young power. Despite or perhaps because of its stunning victory over China, it believed that it was despised and condescended to by most in the West, and in many ways it was. But sophisticated opinion makers in Britain, and in the United States beyond the rabidly intolerant West Coast, wanted to think the best about Japan. For many years the contradictory attitudes of mutual contempt and admiration expressed by both Japanese and Westerners kept their relationship in a tense and often strange balance.

During the earliest years of the twentieth century, Japanese diplomats and intellectuals fluent in English flooded Western periodicals and publishing houses with books and manuscripts that sought to explain their nation and its own sense of manifest destiny to a bemused and uneasy West. In 1902 an American-educated diplomat, T. Iyenaga, wrote an essay complaining that his country's "thirty years of peaceful progress in civilization—the sweeping reforms, political, social, legal, educational, and economic, accomplished in the three decades of the Meiji"—had "availed but little to raise the estimation of 'heathen Japan' in the eyes of Christendom." Japan's demand to be treated as an equal with the other "civilized powers" of the earth after its war with China "was met by thinly veiled, if not open, derision."[22]

Perry's crude gunboat diplomacy was a humiliation that sensitive Japanese could neither forget nor overcome. "The American would not be denied," one Japanese writer recalled as late as 1906.

> Encouraged in his conviction that insolence was the only virtue which impressed the Asiatic mind, the American commodore outraged the sensitive patriotism of the Nippon people far beyond words. From the way he handled his ships and the guns upon them, you would have said that a

dignified officer of the great nation had come all those thousands of miles over the seas that he might treat a childish people to a country show. . . . He was pitiless. Of the internal troubles of the Shogun and his government, the stranger knew nothing. . . . However that mattered little. Nothing succeeds, after all, quite so well as success. A profoundly frustrated people soon overthrew the Shogunate, restored the emperor, and set out to battle the Americans and the rest of the West on their own terms.[23]

More than three decades of forced-draft modernization and immersion in the folkways of Western civilization had convinced the Japanese of some hard truths:

> It is Japan's firm conviction that the modern nations, although sending forth missionaries by the thousands to foreign lands to preach the gospel of peace and holding now and then such conferences as that of The Hague, are at heart militant and aggressive. She believes, consequently, that in order to hold her position among them a proper military equipment is necessary; and she is thus driven to arm herself with the efficient weapons of modern warfare.[24]

The boorish, thrusting behavior of the European powers in China and the rest of East Asia had clearly revealed Japan's own destiny: it had to dominate the region, curb Western activities and appetites, and serve as Asia's spokesman and interpreter to the rest of the world. Marquis Ito, who had signed the Sino-Japanese Treaty, later gently but unmistakably warned a New York City banquet audience that "we are the only people in the Orient who properly understand the import and significance of the two civilizations," Western and Asiatic.[25]

Ito readily acknowledged that China was still the heart and soul of Asia. The world's oldest civilization had endured even when Egypt, Greece, and Rome had fallen, and Europe had struggled through its own dark ages before surging upward once more to eventually dominate the earth. But China was now irredeemably corrupt, the minds of its Mandarins "completely stunted by antiquated philosophy, ethics, and literature." Its ancient glory could not be tarnished or destroyed by thoughtless Western greed. Japan would defend and protect its Asian neighbor regardless of the cost. Tokyo had only peaceful intentions, but those intentions had limits. Russia, in particular, needed to "confine herself to her proper sphere of action in the Pacific borderlands."[26]

In 1905 the artist, archeologist, and cultural activist Okakura-Kakuzo penned a little book, *The Awakening of Japan*. The country's sudden development, he wrote, remained more or less an enigma to the rest of the world. Japan was viewed as a nation of exotic and disturbing paradoxes, a "country of flowers and ironclads, of dashing heroism and delicate tea-cups—the strange border-land where quaint shadows cross each other in the twilight of the New and Old World.... We are both the cherished child of modern progress and a dread resurrection of heathendom—the Yellow Peril itself!"

Japan, Kakuzo insisted, must be viewed in its proper context. Immensely grateful to the West for what it had taught, Japanese still regarded Asia "as the true source of our inspiration." For centuries, Japan, no less than China or India (the great centers of Far Eastern civilization), had been enveloped in lethargy; "the Night of Asia" had enveloped "all spontaneity within its mysterious fold." Intellectual activity and social progress had been stifled in an atmosphere of apathy. Asia's decadence had begun in the thirteenth century with the Mongol conquest that had "crush[ed] the life of Indian and Chinese culture." Six hundred years later, new Mongols in the form and person of Western gunboats, missionaries, and merchants fastened a fresh reign of imperialism upon the peoples of the East for whom "the earth is no longer filled with that peace which" formerly "pillowed their contentment. If the guilty conscience of some European nations has conjured up the spectre of the Yellow Peril," Kakuzo added, "may not the suffering soul of Asia wail over the realities of the White Disaster?"

To the peoples of India, China, and Japan, Kakuzo continued, Western idealism was seen as nothing more than soulless materialism; Western propaganda on behalf of universal brotherhood was utterly devoid of true spiritual content. Yet despite their many bitter resentments, the peoples of the East represented no Yellow Peril. How could they? India, China, and Japan had never been expansionist. Western fears of Asian aggression were not only unfounded but absurd and ridiculous. Japan had been isolated for centuries. China had historically been the victim, not the perpetrator, of invasion. Japan had gone to war with China in 1894–1895 merely to preserve Chosen as an essential buffer against future assaults from the Continent—especially from the Russians who now inhabited the lands of those barbarians who centuries before had brought night to Asia. And what had happened? "The kindly intervention of the Triple Coalition... was but a farce, for thereby Russia gained Port Arthur, Germany Tsing-tao, and France a tighter grip on Yunnan."[27] Kakuzo's argument may well have triggered in the minds of many of his readers an association of Japanese policy with the historic British inclination to seek alliance with the enemies of any power that controlled the Low Countries across the narrow Channel that separated England from Europe.

It was in this context that Yamamoto Gombei, now a vice admiral and navy minister, along with his protégé, Satō Tetsutarō, began to seriously consider the country's regional and world position.[28] In an October 1899 memorial to the throne, Yamamoto amplified Japanese naval strategy. The Home Islands could be preserved from assault only by attacking a prospective enemy as far as possible from Japanese shores. For this reason Japan had to possess not only a large, efficient blue-water battleship navy but also one that would be the primary, most powerful component of national defense. For the next two years the admiral's memorial formed the basis of heated but inconclusive debate at the throne, in the Japanese Diet, and in the press. Having studied Mahan, Yamamoto realized that he needed a sound historical basis for his assertions and turned to young Satō, a graduate of the Naval Staff College currently in the Naval Affairs Bureau, to provide it. Yamamoto sent Satō to Britain and the United States to immerse himself for eighteen months in the writings of Western naval historians. By late 1901 Satō was back in Japan and the next year completed a brief treatise, *On Imperial Defense,* that was widely disseminated in naval and military circles after approval by the emperor. Satō confined his argument to supporting Yamamoto's assertions that Japan could defend itself only by winning a victory as far out as possible on the sea approaches to the Home Islands and that strengthening the navy should take precedence over all other strategies.

Yamamoto and Satō's initial efforts raised more questions than they answered and caused an uproar within government and military circles. Had not the war with China proved that Japan's destiny lay on the adjacent Asian continent? Japan had wrung from Peking substantial concessions for itself and the Western colonial powers and in the process had gained the admiration and increasing support of the world's mightiest sea power. Britain and Japan were island nations strategically placed to shape if not dominate the affairs of adjacent continents. Both feared Russia as an expansionist power, threatening British interests in India and the Near East and Japanese interests in northeastern Asia. Not only did the Japanese navy owe its expertise to British advisers, but during the Sino-Japanese War, British merchant marine officers also commanded and staffed many of the transports that carried Japanese army units to their successful invasions of Chosen and Manchuria. When Count Ito and his entourage arrived at Chefoo (Yantai) in 1895 to exchange peace-treaty ratifications with their Chinese counterparts, only Admiral of the Fleet Edward Seymour, commander in chief of the British China Squadron, deigned to exchange a formal salute; French, German, and Russian vessels in the harbor insulted the Japanese by remaining mute. Realizing that another war on the Asian coast probably could not be avoided, Tokyo immediately contracted with British shipyards to stock the Japanese navy with numerous warships of the latest design—from first-class battleships to thirty-knot turbine-powered destroyers. When these ships reached Tokyo Bay, Japanese designers went over them from stem to stern, preparing for the day when Japan would begin building its own modern ships.

The outbreak of the Boer War just four years after Japan's defeat of China revealed to the lords of Whitehall just how isolated and disliked the English had become within the international community. It was time to search for friends not only in Europe but beyond as well. The Royal Navy had long before lost its desire to tutor Japan; it wished to engage the country as a partner. The wary Japanese were willing to accept such an arrangement as long as it was in their national interest.

In 1902 London and Tokyo signed a firm treaty of alliance. With Britain on Japan's side, it seemed reasonable that Japan's chief enemies would be China, Germany, and especially Russia, the three countries most likely to thwart Japanese ambitions in China and northeastern Asia. If so, the navy's role would be to control the Sea of Japan and support the army in whatever campaigns it might wage on the Chinese coast and up the Yangtze and Yellow Rivers, not to expand into the Pacific. The rebuff to Japanese interests in Hawaii suggested that there was little hope of permanently projecting Nippon's naval power east of the international dateline in any case.

Was the navy also to be an arm of national expansion, carrying the Japanese flag to the Pacific Islands or, more attractively, southward toward Western imperial holdings in Indochina, the Philippines, Malaya, and Indonesia? If so, the alliance with Britain would be disrupted, and Nippon might face the combined weight and wrath of the entire Western community. In anticipation of such a possibility, Japan's orders of ships and matériel from England and other foreign countries began to diminish after 1905. "Just as she gave up the employment of foreign advisors in the 'nineties, as soon as she felt herself in a position to dispense with their services," a foreign observer wrote in 1928, "so now, for some years past, [Japan] has been virtually independent of foreign ship-building yards for the construction of her warships."[29] Assuming that a major Pacific war could not be avoided, how large did the navy have to be to ensure victory against aroused Western imperial powers? Satō promptly set to work on a much longer and more thoughtful presentation. Long before Satō finished, the Russo-Japanese War had again transformed the fortunes and ambitions of the Imperial Japanese Navy.

From 1895 onward, Russia seemed to frustrate Japan at every turn. As part of the international settlement reached after suppression of the Boxer Rebellion,

Russia agreed to remove its troops from Manchuria. It never did so, and as the century turned, St. Petersburg incautiously began meddling in the affairs of Chosen. Tokyo proposed a conference to settle comprehensively spheres of influence in northeastern Asia. Negotiations begun in the late summer of 1903 quickly deadlocked over the status of northern China and Manchuria.

Neither side wanted war, the sailors in particular. Yamamoto, now navy minister, was especially fearful. A naval conflict with the admittedly small Russian Far Eastern Fleet at Port Arthur might cost Japan half its warships. Japan could not afford such a defeat. And suppose Nippon lost the entire war? The heavy indemnities that a victorious Russian court would demand at the peace table might well send Japan spinning back into the dark ages financially and industrially, prey once again to those predatory Western powers (including the United States) happily enjoying the fruits of their commercial dominance of China. Across the Eurasian landmass, Russia's seamen were no happier with the prospect of war. Port Arthur had been occupied only since 1898, and its fortifications and fleet facilities were primitive. Coordination in naval and military matters with far-off St. Petersburg was practically nonexistent, and when, in 1902, the Headquarters Staff asked about naval operational plans in the event of war with Japan, Vice Admiral Aleiff, commander in chief of Far Eastern forces, cabled that "he had no such plan," and the matter was dropped. Moreover, Russia's admirals were as fearful of the Japanese as their Japanese counterparts were of them. At a staff conference in Port Arthur in the spring of 1903 among local naval officials and the commanders of a newly arrived squadron, agreement was quickly reached on the superiority of the Japanese fleet. Plans to base the new squadron at a basin more suitable to its needs were scrapped because of fears of a Japanese naval blockade. Under the circumstances, both St. Petersburg and Port Arthur agreed that "it was madness for Russia to go to war at all."[30]

Unfortunately for those in St. Petersburg and Port Arthur, Vice Admiral Tōgō Heihachirō was about to take the question out of their hands. On February 6, 1904, Japan broke off diplomatic relations even as Russia foolishly moved 20,000 troops into Korea. Two evenings later, Tōgō arrived off Port Arthur with the main part of the Japanese fleet and immediately sent his destroyers into the harbor on a daring night torpedo attack against the Russian battleship-cruiser force anchored in the outer roadstead.[31] Since war had not been formally declared, the Russian ships were brilliantly lit. Racing in, the Japanese small ships fired their torpedoes and sped away before the Russians knew what was happening. Two battleships and a cruiser were hit, and although flooding was controlled and the ships got under way toward the inner harbor, the battleships became grounded at the entrance, blocking the channel to the rest of the squadron. Tōgō moved in the next day to destroy the blockaded enemy with his heavy guns, but shore batteries drove him off. At the same moment, a Japanese cruiser-destroyer force entered Inchon harbor in Korea and forced a Russian cruiser and gunboat to scuttle themselves to avoid capture. A week later, with the two countries now formally at war, a Japanese invasion force went ashore at Inchon under the guns of Tōgō's covering battleships and soon drove out the Russian forces.

Tōgō then moved back to Port Arthur and began a lengthy siege in which both sides laid minefields and elements of the Japanese battle fleet made inconclusive forays to bombard the port. The admiral's strategy reflected how much the new navies of the industrial age were borrowing liberally from each other's thoughts and doctrines. If Satō Tetsutarō and Yamamoto Gombei were the preeminent Japanese politico-naval theorists of the time, Akiyama Saneyuki was the leading tactician. An 1890 graduate of the Japanese naval academy who eventually rose to the rank of vice admiral before retirement in 1918, Akiyama in his younger years was dispatched on several missions to the West. In 1898 he appeared in the United States to gather what information he could about American naval planning and behavior. He insinuated himself into naval and military circles and was able to observe firsthand the blockade of the Spanish fleet at Santiago and its subsequent destruction. Later he traveled in Europe and was struck by the vulnerability of the French naval base at Toulon to siege from the surrounding heights. Returning home, he wrote his impressions and conclusions in a lengthy report, which soon landed him a position at the Naval Staff College in Tokyo, where he began drafting plans for a campaign against Port Arthur.[32]

For two months Tōgō besieged the largely immobile enemy fleet at Port Arthur, while the Russians managed to refloat the battleships *Czarevich* and *Pallada* and towed them into the inner harbor for repair and eventual return to service. Only once did the Russians stir, and then their spirited vice admiral, Stepan Makarov, was killed on his battleship when it went down chasing a Japanese mining force. Thereafter the czar's sailors sank into gloom and inaction. Meanwhile, Japanese forces landed on the Liao-tung Peninsula and began moving down toward Port Arthur.

The world's navies were still in the pre-dreadnought era, and Russia was rated the world's third- or fourth-largest sea power; Japan was no better than sixth. Japan possessed six modern battleships, each of which had been welcomed eagerly as it steamed up Tokyo Bay fresh from British building yards; Russia had fifteen, ranging from modern to obsolete. It also had thirty-eight destroyers to Japan's twenty-one. The Japanese did possess more seagoing torpedo boats and twenty-five cruisers to Russia's nineteen. Russia, however, was economically more self-sufficient, although not any more industrially advanced, and was nominally allied with France, still the largest creditor nation in continental Europe. But Japan, a distinctly regional power, could immediately concentrate its forces in the theater of operations; Russia, a largely land- and ice-locked power sprawling well over half the Eurasian landmass, could not. Most of the czarist navy was in the Baltic; a smaller squadron was confined to the Black Sea by the provisions in the Treaty of London of 1870, which closed the Dardanelles to foreign passage. The bulk of the Far Eastern Fleet was at Port Arthur. The Japanese by this time had built "four major naval bases and eleven large commercial docking and repair establishments in their home islands."[33]

These were the circumstances and conditions under which Russia's military and naval staff officers began drafting war plans. Admiral Zinovi Rozhestvenski, chief of the navy's Headquarters Staff, argued that "our object is not to wipe out the Japanese, but only to annex Korea [Chosen] to our possessions." Although this could theoretically be accomplished by a land campaign from Manchuria, it was evident to others within the navy that sea power had become the decisive element of the war. Japan's successful invasion of Korea under Tōgō's guns was sufficient to prove the point. As it slowly developed in the first weeks of conflict, "the whole Russian war plan hung on the ability to dispute the command of the Yellow Sea; without speedy reinforcements, the damaged Port Arthur squadron was unequal to the task."[34]

Naval reinforcements were under way to Port Arthur, but the czar and his circle concluded that they would come to grief trying to either break or evade the Japanese blockade. Better to let Admiral Virenius's squadron of a single battleship, two cruisers, and seven destroyers stand off hundreds of miles and wait for the big reinforcement, the entire Baltic Fleet. Critics would later fault this judgment. The Japanese navy was not up to full strength. The diplomatic crisis that had prompted the Port Arthur attack had come too quickly to get the entire fleet out of the repair yards. Had Virenius sought either direct action against Tōgō's less than full-strength fleet or evasion and a successful entry into Port Arthur, Russia's naval situation might have improved dramatically. If the Japanese had been fought, their forces might have been gravely weakened by the time the Baltic Fleet appeared; had Virenius stolen into Port Arthur, his formidable force, in conjunction with the Baltic Fleet, might have placed Tōgō's force in a real vise.

The navy that the czar's sailors confronted at Port Arthur and later at Tsushima had come a long way in the decade since the Battle of the Yalu. Japan was always one of the most avid seekers of industrial naval knowledge. Its fledgling sailors had employed as tutors the Royal Navy whose guns leveling Kagoshima in 1863 did more than anything else to shame the great clans into a quest for technological and political modernity. One of the first initiatives undertaken after the Meiji Restoration was to send the country's most promising young warriors and scholars abroad to immerse themselves in the workings of the new industrial-financial-corporate order that had revolutionized the West. In February 1871 seven young cadets went to England for several years to study naval affairs and technology. Among a second group of students sent several years later was Tōgō Heihachirō, who learned gunnery on a Royal Navy training ship. He remained in Britain for seven years and actually served for a time in Her Majesty's fleet. Tōgō concluded his highly successful tour by supervising construction of a number of modern Japanese warships in British yards. As the first seven cadets set sail for the West, their superiors established a naval college in Tokyo directed by a British mission consisting of both gunnery and engineering officers. The curriculum was modeled after that of the British Gunnery School, the first two directors of the college were British officers, and the teaching staff consisted of both officers and petty-officer specialists from the Royal Navy. By 1895 most of the mission had departed, and in 1908 the college, now staffed almost entirely by Japanese instructors, was transferred to the island of Eta Jima and renamed the Japanese Naval Academy.[35]

As Satsuma's influence declined and the service leaped in popularity after 1895, appointments to the academy became available "to any young man of good family who can negotiate the very severe entrance examination." Eminent naval writer Fred T. Jane observed in 1904 that the emphasis on "good family" in fact meant wealth. "Theoretically, the Imperial Japanese Navy is a democratic institution; actually, it is no more so than the British Army. All classes are eligible for commissions, but owing to the low rate of pay, only those with some private means care much to become officers." Cadets entered the academy between the ages of sixteen and nineteen after a "severe competition" in which an average of five applicants vied for each slot. The young men pursued a rigorous three-year curriculum of naval and physical sciences with large doses of history, foreign languages, and philosophy. "The percentage of civilian instructors was relatively high as they taught all subjects not inherently naval. It was considered a great honor by officers to be ordered [to Eta Jima] as instructors, and as a result the duty was much sought after."[36] Classroom work was followed by a year's voyage aboard one of the several training cruisers, after which the cadets were spread throughout the growing fleet. Upon reaching sublieutenant's rank, they became eligible to specialize in a one-year specialty course in gunnery, navigation, torpedoes, or staff work. Even before the academy had settled in at Eta Jima, the ambitious British instructor corps had insisted upon the establishment of a midcareer training course for their charges that "would continue formal professional development into an officer's senior years." In 1888, the Japanese Naval Staff College opened its doors in Tokyo.[37]

Drawing upon a pool of thousands of youngsters with maritime experience, the officer corps of the Imperial Japanese Navy certainly seemed impressive. As early as 1894 a knowledgeable American observer wrote that Japanese ships "are kept in exceptionally good condition in every respect, and their officers are considered . . . more able" than those in the Chinese navy, with whom they were about to wage war. Japanese enlisted sailors, "with a natural aptitude for the sea, are in excellent training and discipline."[38]

But appearances masked ultimately crippling weaknesses. From the day it opened the naval academy was a hellhole of mindless discipline and abuse. First-year men were routinely beaten by upperclassmen for the slightest deviation from rigid rules. Tameichi Hara, who entered in 1918 and later commanded a destroyer, recalled:

> After a few months of such treatment the newcomers became sheeplike in their obedience. Every man's face bore evidence of the brutality we endured. My ear trouble [from being constantly cuffed and boxed] became chronic, and I suffer from it to this day. . . . Certain of my seniors were sadistic brutes. They took singular delight in terrorizing freshmen. To this day I feel a revulsion at seeing these men, even though we have since shared the labors and miseries of war, and the same luck in surviving it.

Occasionally, a reform-minded superintendent tried to mitigate the harshness, but his tour of duty was soon completed and he was rotated out before accomplishing much. As a result the spirit of the officer corps was one of blind devotion to emperor, duty, and orders.[39]

Jane noted that "such god" as the Japanese naval officer had "is the navy to which he belongs." A blind devotion to emperor and the Nelsonian tradition bred hardness and moral coarseness. "If people don't like being killed, why do they fight?" a Japanese officer had remarked when discussing war. "Death in battle he views as we view ordinary death in our beds," Jane added. The English-man discerned beneath this swaggering machoism an underlying hysteria, an unhealthy impatience, that would prove destructive in the climactic battles of a later world war. "They are," he wrote of his subjects, "in a way a discontented lot of men as a whole, despite all their fatalism, their enthusiasm," and even "their joviality. Every civilian officer [that is, members of the medical, paymaster, and construction corps] fumes over to himself that he is not an executive [a line officer]; every lieutenant curses the time that must pass before he is a lieutenant-commander, and so on all through. Wherever they are in the professions, they want to be better and higher."[40]

Seventeen years later, naval journalist Hector C. Bywater noted that although the typical Japanese officer was neither the superman nor the exalted superpa-triot of Western caricature, his "patriotism does undoubtedly take the form of a religion, and [his] devotion to duty is very marked." Jane added that the Japanese idea of "working at their profession" meant the exclusion of literally all else within and beyond the naval sphere. When asked about the possible whereabouts of a visiting officer, for example, the naval attaché at the Japanese Embassy in London replied that he could not know because such information was not his responsibility. "The proportion of those" naval officers "who are casual is very small," Jane concluded. Both captains and ensigns spent their "free" time poring over Mahan "with halma-pieces [grain stalks or stems] on sheets of paper to work out the tactics."[41]

A German naval officer in Tokyo just before World War I observed that whereas once Japanese naval education had been "primitive and based upon faulty principles," it was "now very sound, very thorough, very practical. Almost as much importance is attached to the study of naval history as with us." Both junior and senior officers exhibited a fanaticism that their British counterparts might have airily described as "overly keen." The Japanese were "sober, diligent, and enthusiastic for their profession. They are astonishingly self-confident, but whether this readiness to attempt the impossible is a characteristic of the class whence they spring, or whether it is deliberately inculcated by their teachers, I am unable to determine." The German officer was told that the Japanese could easily defeat the German, French, and American navies and could "hold their own" against the British. "As I have said, their confidence knows no bounds."[42]

In such a system there was little room for innovative thought. On the eve of the Russo-Japanese War, Hesibo Tikowara, a Japanese destroyer captain, chastised himself for thinking about political matters. "I must keep my mouth shut.... [I]t would be better to spend our time drilling our men, and instilling obedience into them, so that the vessels confided to our care may always be in the highest state of efficiency." The creation of the staff college eased the problem somewhat by forcing the best minds in the service to keep abreast of foreign developments and to develop strategic capabilities of their own. But strategic and tactical doctrines, created and modified in the crucible of battles against China and Russia, were seldom if ever discussed or altered as a result of day-to-day activities and the experiences of junior and midlevel officers.[43]

Thus, although talented staff officers such as Minoro Genda of Pearl Harbor and Midway fame occasionally appeared in times of crisis, the kind of give-and-take dialogue between superiors and subordinates that is essential for steady, ongoing professional development at all levels of a military or naval establishment was almost unknown. Japan relied for victory at sea on a mere handful of brilliant tacticians and strategists like Count Ito, Yamamoto Gombei, Satō Tetsuturō, Akiyama Saneyuki, Tōgō, and later Yamamoto Isoroku, who either created or, in Yamamoto Isoroku's case, could transcend basic naval doctrine. But when individual brilliance faltered, as it invariably does occasionally, Japan suffered accordingly. The web society that had so thoroughly transformed itself from a feudal order to a military-industrial complex in two generations was severely hobbled by its own outmoded, destructive traditions and values.

Purely technical education, however, did not suffer in such an environment, and the Japanese navy trained its enlisted men to a surprisingly high level. By World War I it was nearly an all-volunteer force.[44] As socially stigmatized as their Western counterparts, Japan's bluejackets were assumed to have been "drawn chiefly from the lowest social stratum." But this was not true. Many had previously worked in respectable, essential jobs in the fisheries and whaling fleets of the northern islands. About one-quarter of the enlisted men were conscripts, but this was the result of a conscious decision to obtain men from the inland provinces and thereby spread the navy's influence throughout the nation. Youths between eighteen and twenty enlisted for six years; draftees served for three years but had to spend an additional seven years in the frontline reserves. "Except for a very brief spell of preliminary instruction in shore establishments, the naval recruit spends all his time on shipboard, in accordance with the sound Japanese view that the proper school for a seaman is the sea-going ship." After 1900 special places were made for midcareer warrant and petty officers at the gunnery and torpedo schools with the stipulation that they would serve for an additional three years. Once back in the fleet these men were given important positions aboard ship. Jane observed that not only did Japanese enlisted men replicate their officers' temperament in many ways ("the bravest sailors have been educated from early youth upward into a disregard for death") they also shared their superiors' passion for advancement and self-improvement: "Like their officers, their ideas of dissipation centre around learning something."

Both Jane and Bywater agreed that Japan's seamen were generally "a fine body of men, very amenable to discipline under good officers, but liable," in Bywater's words, "to get out of hand if treated with harshness or injustice." Unfortunately, harshness and injustice were what most Japanese sailors experienced from unsympathetic superiors, and this rendered them increasingly turbulent and unruly. Jane noted that shipboard drinking was increasing within the imperial fleet by 1904, and although it was "rarely a cause for trouble, . . . a drunken Japanese is a nasty customer." The Englishman added that Japanese sailors frequently brawled ashore with their bigger but slower Russian counterparts and usually gave as good as they got. Tameichi Hara recalled that life as an enlisted recruit in the Imperial Japanese Navy was "miserable." There was an old saying that " 'navy castes are made up of officers, NCOs, cattle (meaning enlisted men), and lastly, cadets.' " He remembered that right up to the end in 1945 "Japanese warships were never built with any idea of comfort for their occupants. They had no regular sleeping quarters for enlisted men or cadets," and every night both sailors and officer trainees spread their "hammocks in any available space to sleep. Meals consisted of rice and barley with some canned fish or meat."

Saburo Sakai, who enlisted in 1933 as a sixteen year old, later observed that "it is still difficult, if not altogether impossible, for Americans and other Westerners to appreciate the harshness of the discipline under which we then lived in the Navy." Training-station petty officers were bitter men in their thirties who could not expect further promotions. Saburo called them "sadistic brutes of the worst sort" who behaved like "absolute tyrants in their own right." Recruits were beaten viciously and often for the most minor infractions. If a man passed out from the heavy blows, he was revived with a bucket of cold water, whereupon the beatings continued. If a victim groaned or cried out in his bunk after such punishment, "to a man every recruit in the outfit would be kicked or dragged from his cot to receive the full course." The six-month basic training "made human cattle of every one of us. We never dared to question orders, to doubt authority, to do anything but immediately carry out all the commands of our superiors. We were automatons who obeyed without thinking." Saburo had assumed that the awful regimen would cease once he joined the fleet, but conditions aboard the battle cruiser *Kirishima* were, if possible, even worse than ashore. The desperate youngster began studying furiously during his one free hour a day so he could gain admission to the Navy Gunners School. Once he was back in the fleet as a gunner's mate striker, conditions began to improve, and when he finally made third-class petty officer he began to be treated and to feel like a human being. He had been in the navy well over a year.[45]

With such terrible conditions, mutinies had not been unknown during the turbulent, uncertain early years of the Japanese navy. As a result the best commanders and division officers—of whom, Captain Tameichi Hara emphasized, there were always far too few—learned to employ the basic tenets of the web society to instill and maintain discipline. Shortly after the triumphant war with Russia a high-ranking Japanese officer said that his sailors would do anything for their ships and their officers, "provided that you scrupulously observe four rules: first, feed them well, preferably on a Western dietary; secondly, treat them with politeness and consideration; thirdly, do not encourage them to read the newspapers, least of all the gutter journals of Tokyo and Osaka; and, fourthly, drill into them the fact that the Navy has nothing to do with politics, but exists for the glory of Japan."[46]

The web society expressed itself in the Japanese navy in various ways. Young seamen were not only physically abused but also emotionally manipulated. In the 1930s a Japanese commander told U.S. naval attaché Ellis Zacharias how he disciplined his men. If a sailor appeared before him for a serious offense, the commander would say that he himself had not instilled a proper sense of discipline and integrity in his crew and that he was ashamed of his failing. To atone he would spend his next leave aboard ship, reading and thinking of ways to improve himself as a commanding officer. The mortified sailor, realizing that he had caused his superior to lose face, would then do the only thing he could to atone for *his* shame: kill himself. The ship's company would thus have a double lesson in the need for self-control and humility.[47]

In 1904 the average Japanese naval officer, unlike Minister Yamamoto, had little respect for Russian prowess. The Russians were good fighters, but unlike their opponents they had little practical experience in modern land or naval warfare, "and their ships, with a few exceptions, are not worth much." Destroyer skipper Hesibo Tikowara and his colleagues were appalled by the reports of spies in Port Arthur that the Russians did not conduct maneuvers at sea, did not have gunnery drills, and failed to maintain their formidable arsenal. "There are goodness knows how many torpedoes, quite neglected. For months they have not been inspected by either officers or engineers." The Japanese were quite proud of their own torpedoes and had developed "a new explosive called shimose that was more powerful than guncotton." When a *shimose* shell exploded

on impact, it blew its casing "into dozens of deadly metal fragments" and produced huge clouds of smoke designed to "incapacitate those not killed by the
blast." *Shimose* would work perfectly in battle.[48]

With Port Arthur under Tōgō's blockade and threatened by the Japanese
army coming down the Liao-tung Peninsula, St. Petersburg at last decided to
dispatch the Baltic Fleet under Rozhestvenski on an eighteen thousand–mile
voyage to the Far East, and this initiative gave Rear Admiral Vilgelm Vitgeft,
Makarov's successor as head of the Russian Far Eastern Fleet at Port Arthur,
some badly needed options. If the Japanese army could be held on the peninsula
for several months, Tōgō could become caught between Vitgeft's battleships
coming out of Port Arthur and the arriving Baltic Fleet. Alternatively, Vitgeft
could sortie before the Baltic Fleet arrived and deal Tōgō such a blow that the
Japanese would be disastrously weakened before Rozhestvenski's forces appeared.
For weeks Vitgeft—and the government at St. Petersburg—dithered. At one
point two of Tōgō's battleships struck mines and sank, decisively changing
the ratio of blockaders to blockaded in the Russians' favor. But Vitgeft refused
to sortie.

Finally, with the Japanese army approaching the city, the czar ordered Vitgeft
to race his ships up to the more modern protected port of Vladivostok. At dawn
on August 10, 1904, Vitgeft sailed with his six battleships, four cruisers, and
eight destroyers. Alert Japanese scouts soon picked him up and began shadowing.
Radio was used for the first time to summon Tōgō's main force to the fight, and
the admiral ordered every Japanese unit in the area to join the chase.[49]

Although outnumbered in ships, Tōgō retained superiority in number of
heavy-caliber guns and speed. But he prudently chose to cross the Russian T
three times at long range, hoping to turn Vitgeft from his line of advance. Tōgō
swung too far on the third crossing and lost time ensuring that his flagship would
remain at the head of the column; Vitgeft seized the opportunity, shook the
Japanese off, and raced for the Korea Strait. Tōgō refused to try to cross behind
the Russian column, fearing that his force could be beaten up by the guns of
Vitgeft's cruisers in the rear, allowing the Russian battleships in the van to
steam unmolested. Instead, the Japanese commander swung his fleet south,
then north again, trying to catch up with Vitgeft. "There ensued an afternoon-
long battle of the boilers that was also a race with the sun." Finally, near dusk,
Tōgō's vessels pulled abeam of the Russians and opened fire, but Tōgō again refused to close, and it seemed for many long moments that the Russian gunners
were getting the best of their enemies. Then a twelve-inch shell shattered the
bridge of the battleship *Czarevich,* killing Vitgeft and every member of his staff,

and another shell burst on the conning tower, jamming the steering gear. The suddenly leaderless Russian fleet promptly fell into confusion.

Tōgō prepared to close in for the kill but then backed off at nightfall, fearing a Russian torpedo attack in the dark. Most of the Russian fleet—five battleships, a cruiser, and three destroyers—raced back to Port Arthur, while a relief force of four cruisers steaming down from Vladivostok ran afoul of an equal Japanese force and was mauled; two ships sank, and the other two scurried back to port. Tōgō has been severely criticized for excessive caution against Vitgeft, but this was the first real fight between large forces of modern warships. Indeed, it was the biggest naval battle since Trafalgar. Tōgō was smart enough to realize that the existence of modern long-range guns of unprecedented power, together with torpedoes, made the kind of hull-to-hull hammering of sailing days extremely hazardous. As it was, the Russian Port Arthur fleet never came out again.

The Japanese army moved desperately to neutralize it by capturing the city before the Baltic Fleet arrived. Using human-wave assaults that cost them sixty thousand men, the Japanese reached the heights overlooking Port Arthur in early December. The panicked Russians practically dismantled their blockaded fleet; its heavy guns, along with most of their crews, were taken ashore and used to defend the city. By the time Rozhestvenski arrived months later the Russian Far Eastern Fleet was no more.

The defeat of Rozhestvenski's ships by Tōgō and the Japanese navy at the Battle of Tsushima climaxed one of the most mournful tales in maritime history, a story of a cruise literally into hell.[50] Rozhestvenski was an extraordinarily able man, fiery, committed, skillful at cutting through red tape and obtaining the best officers for his command. He and his subordinates harbored unbridled contempt for the Japanese. But Rozhestvenski quickly discovered what would be common knowledge after the war: the czar's government was incredibly corrupt and inefficient. Preparations for sailing to the Far East that should have taken days or a few weeks consumed several months. Moreover, the Russian navy lagged far behind its sister services in the acquisition and training of acceptable personnel. The majority of Rozhestvenski's sailors were short-term, ill-trained conscripts. And his ships, although ostensibly modern and splendid looking, proved inferior.

Moreover, His Majesty's government in London would ensure that Rozhestvenski would have bad press. Colonel A. C. Repington, military correspondent of *The Times* in 1904–1905, let slip in the preface to the publication of his wartime articles that "every one whose duty it was to comment on these great events in the British press was bound, from first to last, to keep before his eyes the terms of the Anglo-Japanese Alliance of 1902, and to write nothing which might directly or indirectly serve the cause of Russia, or injure that of Japan." Thus Repington attributed the Japanese sneak attack on Port Arthur "to the masculine decision of the Mikado and his advisers," adding, "Far from thinking the Japanese attack on the night of February 8, two full days after the announcement of the intention to take action, was an exception or a deviation from tradition and precedent, we should rather count ourselves fortunate if our enemy, in the next naval war we have to wage, does not strike two days before blazoning forth his intention instead of two days after." Japanese naval officials thirty-seven years later may have recalled those words with interest.[51]

The Baltic Fleet that finally left Libau on October 14, 1904, constituted four new twelve-inch-gun battleships, three smaller battleships (one new one with ten-inch guns and two older types carrying twelve-inch main batteries), three old heavy cruisers, four new light cruisers, seven destroyers, and nine auxiliaries. The battleships would slightly outgun Tōgō's fewer but powerful vessels, but the old cruisers were no match for Japan's eight splendid new vessels. And Russian advantage in heavy ordnance was offset by Japanese superiority in speed and "quick firers."[52] Under normal conditions Rozhestvenski and his men would have a stiff fight on their hands. But by the time they reached the Far East after eight months of alternate steaming and lying much too long in hot, fetid foreign harbors, conditions were no longer normal.

The spectacular eleven thousand–mile cruise of the U.S. battleship *Oregon* from California to Cuba during the Spanish-American War had seemed to prove conclusively that modern steam and steel battleships were capable of very long-range cruising if foreign coaling stations were available or if they were accompanied by a sufficient number of colliers. But almost as soon as the Russian ships left the Baltic, engines began breaking down, and although the engines were repaired, the fleet's rate of advance fell dramatically.

Throughout the long voyage east, Rozhestvenski and his men, together with the government at St. Petersburg, were convinced, not without reason, that Britain was actively aiding Japan. After all, British yards were building Japanese battleships; might they not be building torpedo boats as well? And would not these torpedo boats find the passing Russian fleet too good a target to pass up? Just two years before, London and Tokyo had concluded a formal alliance that many interpreted as an effort "to contain the empire of the tsar within continental Eurasia." What other mischief might the perfidious Britons be brewing? Even before Rozhestvenski's fleet left port, "agents reported that the Japanese, backed by the British, were preparing an ambush on Russia's doorstep—in the

Baltic Sea." At the beginning of the war an alarmed Russian Admiralty warned its ships in the Red Sea of the possibility of attack by "Anglo-Japanese torpedo boats," even as British warships based at Suez were preventing Russian cruisers there from stopping the flow of seaborne war contraband to Japan.[53]

On the night of October 21, 1904, while steaming through the North Sea, Russian lookouts sighted small vessels, which they immediately concluded were Japanese torpedo boats. The Russian fleet opened up on what were actually British fishing vessels peaceably going about their business on the rich fishing grounds around Dogger Bank. Before the folly ended battleships and cruisers were firing on each other as well. In the melee several fishing boats were sunk. Britain was predictably outraged: Colonel Repington harrumphed in *The Times* that the onus of proof that this was not a deliberate act of war rested solely with Rozhestvenski. "On the most charitable hypothesis," Repington added, "the Baltic squadron has proved itself to be irresponsible, and as such, a public danger." Cunard and north German Lloyd passenger steamers should keep a sharp lookout. In fact, units of the Royal Navy chased after the Russians and subsequently imposed a virtual blockade of Rozhestvenski's ships in the Spanish port of Vigo for a time, then shadowed the Baltic Fleet all the way to Gibraltar. Later, cruisers from the Royal Navy's Far Eastern station took pleasure in following Rozhestvenski and reporting his whereabouts to the world.[54] The czar was humiliated by the Dogger Bank incident and to ensure his fleet's passage east was forced to accept a commission of inquiry.

Slowly, week by week, month by month, halting here and there for news or to await paltry reinforcements, the Baltic Fleet crawled down the coast of Europe, split up at Gibraltar, either went through the Mediterranean or down to the Cape, met up again at the island of Nossi-Bé off Madagascar, where it refitted and coaled, then moved with agonizing slowness across the steamy Indian Ocean and up the South China Sea, clumsily coaling from accompanying colliers whenever necessary. All the while, Japanese forces moved ever closer to capturing Port Arthur. Throughout their melancholy passage, Rozhestvenski and his men were dogged by repeated rumors that Tōgō and the Japanese navy were somewhere about, ready to pounce. The British, too, were worried by one tale that apparently was born in the mind and mouth of the Japanese foreign minister: "Torpedo boats might attack Rozhestvenski in the Indian Ocean." Whitehall became alarmed. "An attack near Singapore would have been terribly embarrassing for His Majesty's Government."[55] In the event, no such wild incident occurred, and by April 1905 Rozhestvenski's fleet had reached Cam Ranh Bay in French Indochina for a brief stop. Morale had already collapsed. There was no mail at Nossi-Bé or Indochina (the Russian Admiralty did not think it necessary to concern itself with such trivia), but the fall of Port Arthur to the Japanese army had become general knowledge. Moreover, according to sources within the Russian fleet, Rozhestvenski had already rather gone to pieces, and in the process lost the respect and trust of his men. "The commander of the fleet never left" the flagship *Suvoroff* "except to administer reprimands," one Russian sailor remembered. Sitting in an armchair on his bridge, Rozhestvenski allegedly "passed his days and often his nights, keeping watch on the movements of the units, studying their positions and having their signals interpreted." If a ship got out of line, the admiral "completely lost control," leaping out of his armchair, "shouting furiously. Sometimes he flung his cap on the deck, whereupon one of his officers would pick it up and hold it reverently as if it were a holy relic" while "panic swept across the bridge." Rozhestvenski screamed, "Signal that idiot a reprimand." Only when the miscreant replied, admitting his "blunder," did the admiral calm down. During maneuvers, Rozhestvenski supposedly "would suddenly clench his fists and shout at the top of his voice, 'Where are you going, you foul bitch? Where in the hell are you going?'"[56] "Foul bitch" seemed his expletive of choice.

The fall of Port Arthur ostensibly deprived the Baltic Fleet of any reason for its seemingly never-ending voyage. Hopes for the defeat of the Japanese fleet, dominance of the Yellow Sea, and the consequent sealing off of Korean ports from Japanese reenforcement—permitting Russian counterattack and reoccupation—were swept away. But what else could Rozhestvenski do other than push on? To sail back fifteen thousand miles to the Baltic was plainly impossible. The fleet had long since reached a point of no return. Moreover, British press sources claimed that the mood in St. Petersburg remained hopeful that "a successful naval action with Admiral Tōgō will at once bring the whole military edifice of the Japanese to the ground with a crash, and . . . the Russian army will then have nothing to do than pick up the pieces." When sailors heard that they were pressing on, their response was simple and sober: "Food for the fishes— that's all we're good for now, comrade."[57] Tokyo, with the tacit support of the still-infuriated British Admiralty, repeatedly protested the coaling of enemy vessels in French colonial ports, and Paris duly insisted that the Russians leave Cam Ranh Bay. By late May Rozhestvenski's force rounded the eastern side of Formosa, out of the frequented trade routes, and headed north for Vladivostok. Off the Ryukyus on May 23 the Russians coaled for the last time and set course for the Korea Strait and Tsushima Island; there at last Tōgō found them.

Because of the surrender of Port Arthur and the collapse of the Trans-Siberian Railroad under the weight of troop and matériel movements from Europe, Vladivostok was desperately short of supplies. Rozhestvenski thus had to keep his colliers with him and also carry large supplies of coal on his open decks. "He had . . . at the same time to solve the problems of combat, flight, and convoy protection," and the extra weight not only reduced the speed of his ships but also lowered their freeboards to such an extent that the armor belts designed to protect hulls at the waterline were forced beneath the surface, while many of the antitorpedo sponsons and gun ports were virtually at water level, "and thus unworkable in heavy seas."[58] Moreover, because of the essential auxiliaries Rozhestvenski's battle fleet could make no more than ten knots.

Tōgō had entrusted strategic planning of the battle to Akiyama Saneyuki who, after weighing various considerations and options open to the Russian fleet commander, correctly surmised that Rozhestvenski would make for the Korean Strait and Vladivostok. Tōgō situated auxiliary merchant cruisers to cover the approaches to the strait, and at dawn on May 27, 1905, one of them made contact with the enemy fleet near Tsushima Island and promptly radioed its position to Tōgō's forces at Masampo (Masan) on the southeastern coast of Korea. Two hours later Tōgō was at sea. His plan of battle, worked out with Akiyama, was similar to that employed against Vitgeft the previous August. Japan's sixteen-knot battle fleet of four modern battleships, eight cruisers, and numerous torpedo boats would attempt to "scissors" the enemy force in a series of engagements, steaming back and forth at long range across Rozhestvenski's line of advance in a kind of "articulated barrier" to turn back the Russian fleet, while light-cruiser divisions would harass the colliers and their escort ships. At nightfall the Japanese heavy vessels would fall back, allowing the torpedo boats to assault the enemy in the darkness, and the next morning the heavy ships would steam back into the battle zone to finish off the confused, damaged enemy. "The pattern would be repeated until the Russian fleet was annihilated."[59]

Rozhestvenski's own various maneuvers to protect his slow-moving auxiliaries and keep his ships together eventually forced Tōgō to change course from a sweep ahead of the still-reforming Russian battle line to one that would take him down the port bow of the enemy on an opposite course. At the "crucial and dangerous moment" when Rozhestvenski was still reshuffling his ships into a single column," Tōgō's main battle fleet, headed by the flagship *Mikasa*, appeared on the horizon "as a long, steady line of gray hulls and towering superstructures, beneath a streaming cloud of black smoke."[60] As the Japanese bore down on the Russians, signal flags shot up from Tōgō's bridge, bearing messages that were quintessentially both Japanese and Nelsonian: "The enemy has been sighted; the Combined Fleet is moving in to annihilate him. The waves are high but the day is clear. . . . The rise or fall of the nation is at stake in this battle; all hands are exhorted to do their utmost."[61] For the next twenty-four hours they did just that.

Tōgō proved himself a seaman not only of Nelsonian pretensions but also of Nelsonian capabilities. Against the blundering Russian line he maneuvered his fleet like a light-cavalry force attacking a wagon train, constantly harassing and outmaneuvering the confused if determined foe. He used any stratagem that the immediate situation required to close and remain close to the enemy on his own terms. Quickly realizing that a passing exchange of broadsides would be indecisive and enable Rozhestvenski to escape as Vitgeft had done, Tōgō chose a move so incredible that men on both sides gasped in astonishment. Signaling "follow me," he turned toward the enemy, then continued around to the opposite course, reversing his ships in succession in order to retain his own position at the head of his fleet. This sixteen-minute "countermarch" briefly gave the Russians a gigantic stationary target.

But Tōgō believed that Rozhestvenski, who had been unable to get his battle line into a single column, could not exploit the opportunity. He was right. Indeed, the Japanese maneuver threw the Russians into complete disorder, leaving each of their ships a separate tempting target for Japanese gunners, who were masterful. Tōgō's fleet completed its maneuver and headed directly toward the Russian van, guns blazing. As the big naval rifles thundered and the seas heaved, Tōgō drew his racing ships ahead of the Russians and, maintaining fourteen knots, gradually came right in an effort to cross Rozhestvenski's T. The Russian, steaming at barely nine knots, countered by giving way to the right. But Tōgō was able to retain the lead, and his fleet poured a mass of firepower directly into the front of the Russian column.

Russian gunnery improved briefly as the battle raged, and delayed-action fuses allowed Russian shells to penetrate deeply into the Japanese ships before exploding, causing terrible damage. But the highly explosive Japanese shells, although perhaps not as deadly, were more demoralizing because they burst on impact, shattering superstructures, causing huge paint fires, and driving Russian gunners from their weapons with clouds of smoke. As scores of Russian sailors milled about, blinded and choking on their decks, they were cut down by deadly shrapnel. Near three o'clock the flagship *Suvoroff* lost control and sheared to the right, out of the battle line, with one funnel and a mast shot down, its upper works a shambles, and Rozhestvenski lying on the bridge with a serious head wound. Exploding shells on the waterline soon brought *Osliabya* down by the head as foaming seas entered its hull. Rapidly flooding, the big ship rolled over to port, hung on its beam ends for a few moments, and then sank, carrying six hundred of its eight hundred–man crew to the bottom. It was "the first modern battleship to be sunk entirely by gunfire."[62]

What remained of the leaderless Russian fleet tried vainly to maintain course for Vladivostok, but the Japanese smelled blood. They foiled every attempt by the enemy to come to the correct course (023), using their superior speed to sweep back and forth across the Russian line of advance. Soon the Russians were forced to come to starboard through two complete clockwise circles to avoid the deadly barrage. There was still fight left in the czar's fleet, however, and after suffering some hits Tōgō disengaged and ordered his destroyers in for a torpedo attack. They failed utterly, and Tōgō, seeking another engagement with his heavy ships, mistook fire on the horizon for the Russian battle fleet when it was actually his light cruisers dueling with the Russian vessels guarding the auxiliaries. Detaching several of his ships to help with this operation, Tōgō again raced northwest after the main enemy units and shortly before six o'clock caught up with the Russians off his port bow. He closed quickly to engage before dark but found himself and his gunners staring directly into the setting sun and outnumbered ten to four. Tōgō quickly altered course to the right to come parallel with the Russians, thereby shifting the light away from the Japanese and silhouetting the enemy against the afterglow. Massed Japanese fire concentrated first on *Alexander III,* which was now at the head of the Russian line. Shell after shell blew up on its decks or on its hull at or near the waterline. The Russian battleship, reduced to a flaming wreck, fell out of line, capsized, and went down. As darkness finally came, the merciless Japanese shifted to *Borodino* and set it ablaze, giving Tōgō's range finders an easy target. At 7:20 *Borodino* blew up, capsized, floated bottom up for a few moments, and disappeared beneath the waves. The Russian line broke and headed southwest, while Tōgō sailed off with his battleships and again sent in his light forces against the Russians from all directions. *Suvoroff* finally sank but not before Rozhestvenski was rescued by one of his own destroyers, which itself was captured by the enemy. Japanese light forces sank two more Russian battleships, torpedoing them to death in the dark. Two cruisers were so heavily damaged that their crews scuttled them to avoid capture. At dawn on May 28 Tōgō was informed that the remnants of the Russian fleet were sixty miles south, and by nine thirty he found them: the battleships *Orel* and *Nicholas I,* two coastal-defense ironclads, and a cruiser. Tōgō opened fire; the Russian response was a tablecloth raised as a white flag on *Nicholas I.* The battle of Tsushima was over. Never again in the twentieth century would an admiral or captain surrender a capital ship.

Tōgō and his sailors had destroyed the world's third- or fourth-largest sea power through superior tactics, seamanship, and gunnery.[63] The triumph at Tsushima reverberated throughout the international community. "If the victory of the Japanese was foreseen as probable by the best available naval opinion," Colonel Repington wrote with evident shock in *The Times,* "we were certainly not led to expect that such an example would be made of the Russian armada in so short a time, and least of all that this result would be obtained practically without loss to the Japanese."[64] Russia could no longer be considered a sea power, and perhaps it was not now a major world power. Who would want such blunderers and incompetents as allies? Certainly, the pressure was off both Britain on the Indian frontier and Germany in the Baltic. Germany and its proposed Berlin-to-Baghdad railroad now replaced Russia as Britain's chief rival in the Middle East, which was becoming important as the major source of fuel oil for the Royal Navy.

The battle produced other incalculable results. First, Tsushima caused Japan to go as mad with navalism as any Western sea power—a development that the emperor's proud sailors exploited to the hilt. The returning fleet visited port after port in triumph, parading itself before throngs delirious with love and pride. On October 23, "the navy choreographed the most impressive naval review in Japan's history." At least 150,000 Japanese crowded the docks and shoreline around Yokohama to view this extravaganza, including a "meticulously" handpicked group of dignitaries. Navy publicists carefully arranged the lines of warships in such a way as to demonstrate to the maximum Japan's newfound sea power. To drive the point home, the riddled remains of those Russian warships that had survived and been captured were also paraded. Following the review, "politicians, civic groups, and wealthy industrialists" vied with one another in lavishly entertaining Tōgō and his triumphant men; the press went wild over the fleet, "channeling popular support and gratitude for the navy into material benefits" like "bluejacket's entertainment funds" and garden parties. Tōgō himself soon led a strident crusade for naval expansion, and Minister Yamamoto exploited the excitement further by organizing warship launches and grand fleet maneuvers as festive holidays open to the public. Great naval reviews like those across the Eurasian landmass at Portsmouth or Kiel or Kronshtadt now became routine. In 1908 the emperor himself attended a "Grand Naval Maneuver" off Kobe by 124 warships displacing more than 400,000 tons. After strenuous lobbying by sailors, press, and public, May 27 was declared Navy Day, and great fleet reviews like those of 1908 were held in Tokyo Bay in 1911 and 1912. As in the West, cards and postcards depicting the nation's great warships were issued, historical exhibitions about the navy's brief life were developed, and statues and shrines were established. Naval officers themselves "tapped into an expanding popular-fiction market to further sell naval expansion to a mass audience." Japanese authors produced their own war fantasies, and most of those from abroad were translated into Japanese. In 1913 Mizuno Hironori of the Navy Department's publicity section, under an assumed name, published a highly popular novel called *The Next Battle,* depicting in "imaginative and depressing" prose a future Japanese-American war.[65]

Japan's rampant navalism reflected another emerging element in world affairs, what Maurice Low characterized in 1908 as Asia's "thrill of race pride."[66] The Imperial Japanese Navy now represented the core symbol of a Rising Sun on the march, uniting an isolated, chronically poor, and overworked nation behind the fatally potent notions of power, expansion, and destiny that it hoped to sell to fellow Asians.

European capitals reacted with fear and loathing. Low noted, "That earlier bugbear, the 'Yellow Peril,' is being revived and is again the subject of discussion." According to another observer, the French foreign office, shockingly ignorant of both history and geography, privately expressed fears that the Japanese would lunge at Vladivostok, "'the only port and naval base on the shores of the Pacific Ocean which hitherto have been in possession of a European power.'" Conveniently ignoring the existence of British Hong Kong and Singapore, and the Western Treaty Ports farther north, the French proceeded to predict that in a few years the entire commerce of the Far East would be in the hands of those two upstart powers, Japan and the United States.[67]

Europe's diplomats ignored the fact that Tōgō's triumph had been a victory for Britain. His Majesty's government had consistently and conspicuously supported its new ally throughout the war, aided, of course, by Russian stupidity in the North Sea. For a while London had quietly toyed with declaring war on Russia as a result of Rozhestvenski's assault on the British fishing fleet and had joined Tokyo's protests to Paris regarding the Baltic Fleet's layovers in several French harbors. The emperor and his government were duly appreciative and invited the British China Squadron to Tokyo to participate in ceremonies commemorating the peace, including a great naval review. On one occasion all British officers and men who could be spared left their ships at Yokosuka and went to Tokyo, where their Japanese counterparts feted them with a wild,

drunken beer party in Hibiya Park. In February 1906 Prince Arthur of Con-
naught and other British dignitaries traveled to Tokyo to present the emperor
with the hallowed British Order of the Garter, and Emperor Meiji honored his
distinguished English visitor with an unprecedented appearance at the railroad
station to greet him in person.

Beyond that, Tsushima reconfirmed to Britons' satisfaction, at least, the
superiority of their naval establishment. Tōgō after all had won with British
ships, British armament, and British training. "Just as Germany, by the agency
of Meckel and others, has been instrumental in shaping and sharpening the
Japanese army as a weapon of war," Colonel Repington wrote not long after
Tsushima, "so British seamen and British constructors have been responsible in
large measure for the excellence of the Japanese navy." Tōgō's battle tactics bore
the impress of Nelson: "The battle-worthiness of the ships is a tribute to the
efficiency of British yards, while the havoc wrought by guns made in England
appears to justify us in the belief that we can hold our own with the best."[68] It
was the same message that Archibald Hurd was trying to spread in the same circles and echoed Jacky Fisher's cocksureness at its worst. Only Jutland, a decade
away, would shake such assumptions.

Some Americans also welcomed Japan's triumph. The long-delayed but inevitable struggle between Europe and "the remaining nations of the Far East" had
finally materialized, and the right side had won. A resurgent Japan was leading
the ostensibly "effete" and "decadent" East toward youth and virility. Thanks to
Japan and its heroic sailors, Asia was "better able to demand and secure fair
treatment from even the greatest powers of the world, every year." In the recent
war Russia had stood as "the typical aggressor and marauder of Europe," whereas
Japan was "the self-constituted champion and defender of the inalienable and
self-evident rights of the governments upon the Asiatic coasts of the Pacific."
Japan was "defending the independence and territorial integrity of her neighbor
[China] as necessary to the ultimate protection of her own. . . . There will be no
occasion to fear or mention a 'Yellow Peril,' if the governments of Europe recognize [the] issues determined by the war, accept them in good faith, and govern
themselves accordingly."[69] Japan's status as the preeminent power in Asia seemed
ensured. It was not to be.

A keen student of international politics, Theodore Roosevelt instantly grasped
the implications of Tsushima. It was in no one's interest to let Japan have its
way in Asia. On the other hand, neither Japan nor Russia could be allowed to
become so weakened as to upset the balance of power on the Eurasian landmass.
Roosevelt sincerely admired the "wonderful" Japanese. "They are quite as

remarkable industrially as in warfare," he wrote British diplomat Cecil Spring Rice soon after the war. "I believe that Japan will take its place as a great civilized power of a formidable type."[70] But at the Portsmouth Peace Conference that he convened in order to resolve the knotty problem of ending the Russo-Japanese War, TR was determined to impose a settlement that would not destroy Russia as a world power, and this meant the inevitable frustration of Japanese ambitions. When the results of the conference were announced, riots broke out in Tokyo and the few American shops were stoned.

Within weeks, the San Francisco School Board issued an insulting order clearly aimed at Japanese immigrant children: "The Trustees shall have the power to exclude children of filthy or vicious habits . . . [or suffering] from contagious or infectious diseases, and also to establish separate schools for Indian children and for children of Mongolian or Chinese descent."[71] The Japanese fleet promptly put to sea for maneuvers off the Bonin Islands under battle conditions. A serious war scare swept over both nations. Lloyds of London offered even money that there would be a Pacific war within the year. Roosevelt tried to defuse the situation by publicly excoriating California officials and forcing the San Francisco School Board to back down in exchange for a curtailment of Japanese immigration to the U.S. mainland. Japanese officials and intellectuals were not mollified, however, and when anti-Oriental riots broke out on the West Coast, their bitterness deepened. The United States seemed determined to thwart and humiliate Japan at every turn, just as it had in Perry's day.

Self-righteous and fearful Americans—of which there were many in the comfortable years leading to World War I—refused to back down. They indulged in paranoid race-baiting with relish. "The Government of Japan does not wish to lose citizens," Harold Ridgely wrote in 1913. "It desires to maintain colonies in foreign countries and to draft soldiers from them when needed." All along the West Coast, good Americans were being displaced from their property by nefarious "agents" working for Japanese farmers. Smith, Jones, and Anderson would purchase adjoining farms, "and it is not until later that Mr. Hashihashi is found to be the real owner. Then the rents are raised, or the occupants are requested to move and are supplanted by a yellow man's colony." Japan had already "overrun" Hawaii in this way and was seeking to dilute good, old-fashioned American racial stock through intermarriage and race assimilation. But "the yellow canary and the white pigeon do not mate together. . . . They have different habits, eat different food, fly differently and live in different nests." Such views, proponents insisted, constituted not racial prejudice, but simple fact. Japan was on the march and had to be watched; in 1913 Japanese allegedly owned or leased more than 190,000 acres of the best land in California and another unnamed state and had purchased all the property around a critical power plant for the ostensible purpose of raising strawberries. Japanese military and naval expenditures had increased "out of all proportion to the size of the nation. . . . Russia was caught off guard and defeated; Korea was unprepared and vanquished; China was forced to give up valuable territory because Japan wished to increase her possessions. Are the Japanese unfriendly toward us?" Ridgely asked. "Perhaps not, but it is always wise to maintain an efficient navy."[72]

CHAPTER 4

The Boast of the Red, White, and Blue

AS THE U.S. NAVY further honed its skills in the decade after its victory over Spain, one characteristic began to distinguish it from every other sea service; its concept of command. British, Japanese, German, French, Italian, and Russian naval officers assumed that rule over other men was a God-given right. So for a long time did too many of their American counterparts. Just managing a rapidly developing industrial fleet placed a premium on tradition. In the twenty-four years between 1884 when America's first steam-driven, steel-clad "protected cruisers" came into service and 1908, "the authorized strength of the enlisted force . . . increased a staggering 523%" to 44,500 men. As late as 1900, Edward L. Beach, now a junior lieutenant, was assigned to one of the navy's last sailing vessels and on a voyage to England discovered how gratuitously brutal life could be in a fast-disappearing age. The navy still operated under a "capricious and petty system of justice" in which a "liberal dose of double irons as a means of punishment" still prevailed and liberty ashore was rarely granted, even though ships spent most of their time in harbor. Beach's captain was a martinet who abused and browbeat his officers, brooked no opposition no matter how mild or modest, and allowed his more ruthless subordinates, both officers and petty officers, to literally trample over the youngest and most inexperienced seamen aboard. When a boatswain-mate-of-the-watch did just that, injuring several boys in the process, Beach brought the man up on charges only to receive his captain's bitter condemnation. The lieutenant was told to withdraw his report;

he refused and got a tongue-lashing on proper naval etiquette and discipline for his troubles. The captain (whom Beach never identified) knew that his superiors in the naval hierarchy would support him. But Beach and his skipper also knew that orders that were given with the expectation of obedience had to be proper, and if not, the giver, rather than the recipient, was liable. In the event, the captain did not pursue a vendetta for fear that the incident might get out to his eternal professional discredit.

His insistence on a basic standard of human conduct marked Beach as a man of the future, not the past. Slowly over the first decade of the new century, younger officers came to appreciate that unreflective cogs and automatons, "mere intelligent machines," could not be flogged or beaten to efficiency. Increasingly complex steam and steel ships required far more of their crews than that. Moreover, the spirit of rising nationalism that swept the country in the years just before and after the war with Spain induced the Navy Department "to 'Americanize' the enlisted force," restricting enlistment to citizens and aliens "who had declared their intention to become citizens." The open American political culture with its emphasis on individual rights guaranteed that the more barbaric punishments and restrictions of the eighteenth- and nineteenth-century sailing navy would not long endure. Parents could and did write their congressmen and senators whenever sonny wrote home of outrageous and mindless discipline. When that failed to evoke change, increasing numbers of unhappy sailors, who felt they had been betrayed by smooth-talking recruiters, simply deserted. All of these developments, largely absent in the European and Japanese navies, forced the officer corps to accept a different standard of conduct and discipline toward their men, despite a stubborn discrimination against enlisted men in the civilian world that was as instinctive and cruel as in any reactionary European monarchy.[1]

"It is clear," Rear Admiral William S. Sims told the graduating class of the Naval War College in 1922, "that it is the duty of each officer to make himself, and those whom it is his privilege to command, as efficient as possible in training and military character. It has been well said that 'the soul of the army is the mind of the individual.' The same applies, of course, to the navy." Twenty-one years later, in the midst of the most devastating war in history, American naval officers were advised to "make sure that you are loyal to your men. Look out for them. Be jealous, for them, of their rights and privileges. If you show them in many little ways that their welfare is your concern, that you are always thinking of ways to better their lot, you will find that they will *give* you a loyalty which you could never *command*." Naval historian John Hattendorf has glimpsed the profound implications of such a bedrock professional perspective. In the twentieth-century United States Navy as in no other sea service, "strategy became more than just the physical distribution of fleets." It also "involved an understanding of the capabilities and limitations of men as well as the machines with which they worked and lived." Such a spirit would eventually propel the U.S. Navy to global supremacy.[2]

There was, of course, a single devastating exception that existed for all but the last few years of the first half of the twentieth century. The United States was a blatantly racist, rigidly segregated society. The 1896 Supreme Court decision *Plessy v. Ferguson* officially confirmed and ratified the fact. African Americans were utterly excluded from the mainstream of the armed services, and the navy was widely regarded as the most conservative—the most aristocratic—of all the branches.

It had not always been so. African Americans had been recruited in small numbers throughout the early nineteenth century and during the Civil War; desperate manpower needs together with the moral imperative of the Union caused the navy not only to substantially enhance its number of African American enlistees but also to integrate them widely throughout the fleets that blockaded Confederate shores and broke Rebel control of the lower Mississippi. By 1870, however, "the number of black petty officers dwindled to a handful ... and members of the race began gravitating from assignments that required seamen skills to those usually performed by landsmen, like cooking and cleaning up or waiting on officers." As Jim Crow came to rigidly define race relations in the last decades of the nineteenth century, the navy embraced beliefs common in civil life that African Americans were unable to comprehend the complexities and intricacies of modern industrial life; specifically, they could not master the advanced technologies of steam, steel, and electricity that were transforming the fleet. This was, of course, a rationale for resolving a larger problem: white antipathy. "Since white recruits often objected to serving alongside blacks, the Navy decided to segregate the races." In 1893 it formally established the rate of messman (later redesignated steward's mate) and sought to shunt all African American recruits into the role of servants and housekeepers for the white officer class afloat and ashore. "A few African-Americans retained the ratings they had earned before Jim Crow took hold in the Navy." One of them, Fireman Second Class Robert Penn, won a Congressional Medal of Honor in 1898 for responding heroically to a potentially disastrous fire-room accident aboard *Iowa* off Santiago. Another, "Dick" Turpin, survived the *Maine* explosion, served in boiler rooms and gun turrets aboard gunboats and cruisers for the next decade, and in 1917 was made chief petty officer. In the 1920s the navy sent Chief Turpin around the country on recruitment drives, but only to attract white sailors.

African Americans were never welcome. Recruitment oscillated according to the needs of the service. As it expanded prior to and during World War I a limited number of blacks were enlisted, largely to share the mess duties with Filipinos and Guamanians. Postwar enlistment of African Americans was suspended in August 1919. In the 1930s as the fleet began another slow expansion and Washington prepared the Philippines for an early independence that was to be deferred by World War II, African Americans were again carefully recruited as servants for the officer class. In that role they remained rigidly subordinated and segregated both ashore and afloat and were the frequent subject of white shipmates' contempt and dislike. As late as June 1940, "only 4,007 African Americans served in the Navy." It would require the stark national emergency created by Pearl Harbor to at last dissolve unyielding traditions.[3]

Annapolis had been founded in 1845 to prepare midshipmen for a rigorous career with a hard four-year professional course.[4] From the beginning discipline was strict but usually applied intelligently. There was a severe outbreak of hazing in the years just before and after the Civil War, and at first authorities were overwhelmed and then overreacted. But by 1900 a reasonable balance had been struck, and rules and punishment seldom degenerated into the kind of capriciousness that, if not curbed, eventually destroys all human relationships. The academy had been perceived both as a place to prepare members for the naval way of life and as "a college similar to any other great undergraduate institution." The midshipman was to "be developed to the end that he will become a valuable citizen of his country, both in domestic and foreign circles." Indeed, Annapolis has always been proud that its graduates receive a bachelor of science degree, and many who have subsequently left the service for some reason have easily found civilian employment.

At the end of the nineteenth century, the U.S. Navy made a decision that saved it much subsequent grief and imparted a unified spirit to the service not widely found elsewhere: engineering officers would enjoy the same status and privileges as their brothers in line positions. Even in the Age of Sail, American naval officers with technical specialties had insisted on equal rank and perquisites and had generally won them. The decisive importance of steam power during the Civil War seemed to guarantee the emerging engineers the same rights, but a reaction set in soon after 1871 when Annapolis was run on the same sort of two-track system found in Germany and elsewhere. The emergence of the new steam navy made such a division untenable in the minds of farsighted sailors. In 1899 engineers and line officers were amalgamated, the two-track system at Annapolis disappeared, and courses in steam engineering were brought into the curriculum.[5] The triumph of the engineers in gaining equal status provided both the incentive and the rationale for later aviators to demand and obtain the same thing.

The Annapolis curriculum has always been demanding. As at Eta Jima, much of the teaching of nonnaval subjects at Annapolis has been the responsibility of civilian instructors. By World War I midshipmen had required classes in leadership, seamanship, navigation, ordnance and gunnery, marine engineering, mathematics, chemistry, physics, electricity, English, history, government, economics, and public speaking. After 1920 an aviation course was added. The only electives were in foreign languages, in which a midshipman could choose German, Spanish, Russian, Italian, French, or Portuguese. Unlike their British and German counterparts, the American midshipmen spent comparatively little time at sea during their academy years; cruises were confined to the summer months. A solid grounding in theoretical knowledge preceded experience. Because of this penchant for intellectualizing naval life and action, reform-minded officers and civilian instructors who were determined to advance the navy's professional and scientific knowledge in 1873 established the U.S. Naval Institute on the academy grounds. In 1884 Commodore Stephen B. Luce convinced the U.S. secretary of the navy, William Henry Hunt, to open a naval war college in Newport, Rhode Island, so midlevel and senior officers could study and shape modern strategy and tactics.[6]

The establishment of the U.S. Naval Institute and Naval War College demonstrated that the U.S. Navy was undoubtedly the most progressive and least-hidebound sea service in the world when the twentieth century began. But America's naval destiny was not at all obvious on the eve of the war with Spain or, indeed, for many years thereafter.

For all its potential strengths, the officer corps was demoralized. It should occasion little surprise that, for all its progressive attitudes toward leadership, Annapolis was home to the sons of what critic Peter Karsten has labeled "the nation's business and political elite of their age."[7] The generally high social position enjoyed by midshipmen entering Annapolis at the beginning of the twentieth century ensured that most if not all harbored serious professional ambitions. But promotion was based strictly on seniority and was extremely slow. When a new personnel law was finally enacted in 1899, "many ensigns up to 11 years in grade, and lieutenants of 22 and more years seniority were promoted." In these mournful circumstances, few officers could be expected to maintain a consistently high professional interest, and it was to their lasting credit—and a reflection of the intrinsic fascination of their profession—that such a large proportion in fact did so. Still, the system was a scandal, and all knew it. Reform was imperative, and by 1916 the navy had developed a system based on commanding-officer fitness reports; examining, promotion, and retirement boards; and in extreme cases military courts. It was probably the fairest method that could be devised, although one critic caustically characterized it as "election, rejection, and selection."[8]

The slow pace of reform ensured a certain snobbish and hidebound attitude among many Annapolis graduates who vigorously fought efforts to enlarge the size and background of the officer corps by permitting enlisted men to seek commissions. Not until 1901 were provisions made to appoint up to a half-dozen warrant officers a year to the rank of ensign, and only then if there were vacancies to fill after the commissioning of all academy graduates. Thirteen years later, Woodrow Wilson's aggressively democratic secretary of the navy, Josephus Daniels, shepherded legislation through Congress providing for the selection of as many as fifteen enlisted men per year for admission to Annapolis, and thereafter the number gradually grew. Some writers have also criticized the Annapolis men for an excessive adherence to traditional warships and warship designs in the face of new realities such as the torpedo and the limited width of the Panama Canal that would in the future clearly circumscribe the historically dominant role of the battleship.[9]

Nonetheless, the gradual reform of the promotion system reflected a wider movement for progress that paralleled the changes instituted by Jacky Fisher in the Royal Navy. Between 1901 and 1909 William S. Sims, Bradley A. Fiske, Homer Clark Poundstone, and a handful of others successfully agitated for major improvements in gunnery and ship design (though within the traditional battleship framework). Sims, the leader of the faction, had met both Percy Scott and John Jellicoe while on duty in Hong Kong at the turn of the century. Enthusiastically supported by Teddy Roosevelt, Sims and Fiske became the Scotts and Jellicoes of the U.S. Navy, while Poundstone was the driving force behind the all-big-gun battleships *Michigan* and *South Carolina,* which slightly preceded *Dreadnought.* Sims in particular applied Scott's continuous-aim firing techniques, exploited new developments in fire control, and devised technologies of his own. By the end of the Roosevelt administration American naval gunnery was probably equal if not superior to that of Great Britain because of the perfection of such instruments as range clocks and range-deflection transmitters.[10]

The training of enlisted personnel was as advanced as that of the officer corps. As the navy reached its nadir in the mid-1870s, Commodore Luce initiated a layered system of professional education for seamen that is still being used. Recruits, who generally enlisted at eighteen or nineteen for four to six years, first went to station ships for basic indoctrination before transferring to training vessels to learn gunnery and seamanship. In the 1890s the navy acquired property at Newport, Rhode Island, and on Yerba Buena Island in San Francisco Bay for land-based training stations (although these facilities were not formally established for some years); later the service added stations at San Diego and Great Lakes, north of Chicago. As it slowly evolved in the last decades of the nineteenth century and the first decades of the twentieth, training for American sailors consisted of three stages: initial instruction on a station ship, a cruise on one of the vessels of the training squadron, and then assignment to one of the ships of the fleet until the apprentice reached his twenty-first birthday, at which time he could reenlist or be mustered out.[11]

The spread-eagle patriotism that swept across the United States in the aftermath of the Spanish-American War stimulated a demand to man the navy with American citizens. During the Civil War the service had been filled with foreigners and newly arrived immigrants. Twenty years later the naval hierarchy began to search diligently not only in eastern cities but also in the towns and hamlets of the Midwest for intelligent boys of "native stock" to serve on the handful of steam and steel vessels that constituted the new fleet. Like their colleagues in the Japanese naval hierarchy, America's admirals and navy secretaries wanted to spread the message and attractiveness of sea power to the most obscure corners of the nation. They also undoubtedly wanted to develop and maintain a navy composed largely of "native stock" at a time when immigrants from southern and eastern Europe were flooding the country. To induce enlistment by teenagers from respectable homes, the service promised to instruct apprentices in "the elements of English education, alternating with practical seamanship and other professional occupations designed to prepare them for sailors in the Navy."[12] In practice "English education" was subordinated to the demands of marlinespike seamanship, but the young men did find themselves in a clearly defined professional atmosphere. The navy also established advanced training programs for especially promising petty officers during their second enlistments. Classes for gunners and artisans began at the Naval Gun Factory in Washington, D.C., and somewhat later training courses in diving, electricity, and torpedoes were instituted at the Torpedo Station in Newport. When the electrician's rating was established in 1898, new schools started in Boston and New York and on

Mare Island north of San Francisco, and in 1902 a new artificer's school opened
in Norfolk. So important had engineering rates become by this time that the
navy instituted special pay grades to attract and retain high-quality personnel.

Out in the fleet imaginative commanding officers set up their own regimens.
The war with Spain revealed again that modern naval gunnery was extremely
tricky and difficult to master. While British commanders were ordering their
officers to throw practice shells overboard to avoid shooting them at targets,
thus dirtying the white decks of His Majesty's ships with shell smoke, their
American counterparts began a practical course for gunners aboard the monitor
Amphritrite. It was so successful that a school for firemen was soon organized
aboard the cruiser *Cincinnati*. In 1909 Roosevelt could boast that his sailors
were no longer the bluff, jolly, illiterate, profane marlinespike seamen of old
but instead a new breed of "sea mechanics," masters of the most advanced military technology in the world. Their officers generally treated them that way, realizing that there was an art to disciplining intelligent, well-trained young
products of a society not far removed from its raw frontier beginnings and
prizing personal independence over almost every other virtue.[13]

But the modern American navy had an Achilles' heel. The innovative, progressive society that produced superior officers and enlisted recruits thwarted
the growth of professionalism based on long-term service. American boys who
had been enticed to "join the navy and see the world" did not take instinctively
or even kindly to the essential demands of naval discipline. Most sailors chose to
get out of the service at the end of their first "hitch," leaving only a handful of
increasingly well-trained enlisted men to run the lower decks and all the machinery. The U.S. Navy was thus chronically undermanned—and was erroneously
believed to be undertrained and underdisciplined as well—throughout the first
four decades of the twentieth century, and its combat capabilities were always
in question.[14]

With the growth of Japanese and European naval power during the first
years of the century, the United States was confronted with a stark either-or situation. It could build a two-ocean navy that would require a fleet at least as large
as that of Great Britain, or it could seize control of either the Isthmus of Panama
or Nicaragua and build a canal that would allow the shuffling of fleet units between one ocean and the other during times of tensions or conflict. But as
Theodore Roosevelt and Alfred Thayer Mahan both recognized, an Isthmian
canal itself demanded a large navy; otherwise, as Roosevelt said, the "building of
the canal would be merely giving hostage to any power of superior strength."

Mahan added that a canal would be a strategic asset only if the U.S. Navy had indisputable command over both its Caribbean and its eastern Pacific approaches.[15]

Construction of the Panama Canal inevitably tied the American fleet to the Caribbean and adjacent Atlantic waters. But the 1907 crisis with Tokyo over the harsh treatment of Japanese immigrants on the West Coast caused many in Washington to share the feelings of those on the other side of the Pacific: a Japanese-American conflict might well be inevitable, even welcome.

Nonetheless, American naval officials did little or nothing about it. As transpacific tensions boiled up early in the year, Roosevelt asked the navy if it was developing plans to prosecute a war against Japan. George Dewey, head of the General Board, assured Roosevelt that such planning was under way, but this was not true. Ever since the 1897 incident with Japan over Hawaii, the Naval War College staff and then the General Board itself had intermittently pondered the possibility and nature of a Far Eastern war, but neither had developed realistic scenarios or studies. Given America's preoccupation with the German navy and the Open Door in China, initial thinking involved fanciful conflicts between coalitions of imperial powers for control of Asia. For a time there was loose, rather melodramatic, talk, and apparently some planning, among board members, usually led by Rear Admiral Henry C. Taylor, "Dewey's right-hand man," of an Anglo-U.S.-Japanese alliance against Europe's continental powers (Germany, France, and Russia). Field officers such as Rear Admiral Frederick Rogers, who commanded the Asia Station, responded unenthusiastically. The most that America's small Asiatic Squadron of thirteen cruisers and destroyers could be expected to accomplish in any Asian war against the European powers was destruction of the French fleet at Cam Ranh Bay before steaming north to assist the Japanese and British in a blockade of Russian and German ports.[16]

When the Joint Army-Navy Board was established in 1903, army planners immediately demolished Taylor's fantasies. The navy "scripts" were "nonsensical." Given its small military as opposed to naval resources, the United States should concentrate on defending the Western Hemisphere and the Panama Canal.[17] But such maunderings did provide the Naval War College staff with several working hypotheses about a future Asia-Pacific war. It would be primarily naval in orientation; it would have to be fought off the Asian, not the American, coast; it would climax with a single decisive battle like Santiago or Tsushima; and the U.S. Navy would therefore require substantial support facilities in the Philippines to sustain operations, including one or more large dry docks with accompanying machine and repair shops, a major supply depot, oil or coaling stations, and barracks.

As Japanese-American tensions eased, planners at the Naval War College be-gan drafting rough suggestions about a war between the forces of Blue (United States) and Orange (Japan), but the exercise soon flagged.[18] Four years later war-college president Raymond Rogers reinvigorated the staff, and the planning process was finally concluded. His strategists "predicted that eventually Japan would shift its tactics from gradual economic encroachment to open aggression" in Asia, which "would require a 'call for action' in support of the Open Door. In the best of circumstances, one or more allies would rally to the cause and check Japan in a continental war in which threats to U.S. possessions would be mere diversions, the role of the Blue navy was minor and of the Blue army nil." Rogers and his colleagues also explored another possibility. Japan could try to break out into the Pacific, destroying the "containment" that the European powers and the United States exerted on the island nation. In this scenario Japanese fleet units would move against the Philippines, Guam, perhaps even Hawaii. The Blue fleet would have to fight the Orange enemy alone and impose a rigor-ous blockade on the Home Islands to force Tokyo to disgorge its imperial hold-ings in Manchuria. Thus, even as Satō Tetsutarō and his colleagues were artic-ulating powerful reasons for an inevitable war with the United States, American naval planners were creating their own "credible rationale" for such a conflict.

Rogers's remarkably farsighted description struck sensitive chords in Washing-ton. It was too close to reality, and the recommendation that the United States seek European allies to pin down substantial Japanese forces in a conventional war on the Asian mainland was "inflammatory" to those who cherished tradi-tional American isolation from Europe. Dewey ordered the Naval War College staff to stop meddling in affairs that were essentially the prerogatives of diplomats and foreign-policy experts. Thereafter, planning for a Japanese war was always uncoupled from a defense of the Open Door in China and elsewhere on the Asian mainland. But the idea of a "Blue-Orange" conflict itself had been firmly planted and had developed momentum in the imaginations of those responsible for formulating American naval policy. In 1914 the General Board finally adopted the broad thesis of a war arising from Orange intent to expel Blue from the western Pacific. War was an increasing probability, the board argued, "because the Japanese national character was greedy, combative, overweening, and scornful of American power."

The General Board thus embraced the illusion, however carefully phrased, of the Yellow Peril. That specter had become a staple of American popular thought after the Russo-Japanese War. In May and June 1907 the *New York Times* and *Colliers* published serials describing a conflict with Japan fought around the Philippines and Hawaii. The same year the translation of a German novel titled *Banzai* appeared in the United States. It depicted a war in which the Japanese navy, using secret weapons, destroyed the U.S. fleet in a mid-Pacific battle lasting little more than thirty minutes, after which Japan invaded and seized California.[19]

Two years later Homer Lea, a short, nondescript former Stanford University student, published *The Valor of Ignorance*. Echoing Roosevelt's philosophy, Lea's book was about the perils of military and naval weakness. He dedicated his work to Secretary of State Elihu Root, who was busy arranging a series of treaty agreements with Japan, and he secured an enthusiastic endorsement from Lieutenant General Adna R. Chaffee, former chief of staff of the U.S. Army. The novel differed from other jeremiads in one significant sense: Lea was no racist. His checkered career included several years as military adviser to Sun Yat-sen, who was then in exile awaiting the fall of China's corrupt Manchu dynasty. Lea depicted the Japanese as highly intelligent, valorous, and resourceful warriors on land and at sea. He wanted no war with them.

Lea argued that a sudden Japanese assault on the United States would inevitably follow California's vicious racial policies and that it would happen soon, before the Panama Canal was completed. The American battleship fleet would be in the Atlantic, at least two months' steaming from San Francisco. The American army, centered in California but pitifully small ever since the Civil War and ten years away from its "splendid little war" against Europe's worst soldiers, would be no match for Japan's one hundred thousand troops recently seasoned in battle on the heights of Port Arthur. The Imperial Japanese Navy would brush aside the few small American warships on the Pacific Coast. The Imperial Japanese Army would simultaneously storm the San Francisco and Marin peninsulas. American troops, bottled up in the Presidio, would be unable to stop Japanese guns from reducing San Francisco to rubble, causing general panic that would dwarf the hysteria after the 1906 earthquake.

> The inevitable consummation that follows the [Japanese] investment of San Francisco becomes apparent in the utter helplessness of the Republic. In the entire nation is not another regiment of regular troops; no generals, no corporals. Not months, but years, must elapse before armies equal to the Japanese are able to pass in parade. These must then make their way over deserts such as no armies have ever heretofore crossed; scale the intrenched and stupendous heights [that is, the Sierras] that form the redoubts of the

desert moats; attempting, in the valor of their ignorance, the militarily impossible; turning mountain-gorges into the ossuaries of their dead, and
burdening the desert winds with the spirits of their slain. The repulsed
and distracted forces to scatter, as heretofore, dissension throughout the
Union, brood rebellions, class and sectional insurrections, until this heterogeneous Republic, in its principles, shall disintegrate, and again into the
palm of re-established monarchy pay the toll of its vanity and its scorn.[20]

Conservatives throughout the country agreed with Lea's description of a militarily weak, politically fragile republic. Appomattox, less than a half century in
the past, remained a living shame to the many thousands of vanquished who
still revered the cause. Could the South be considered loyal if the Union was
again imperiled? The industrial strikes of the nineties were still fresh in people's
minds, and the International Workers of the World, a revolutionary labor union
of considerable force and influence, continued to agitate openly and effectively
throughout western mining and timber camps. Finally, several million immigrants, officially designated "aliens," continued to pour onto American shores
each year. If the Pacific Coast was detached by a Japanese occupation, no one
could predict how badly the rippling effect might tear the nation apart.

Roosevelt undoubtedly read or knew about most of the alarmist tales about
Japan that were swirling around the country. Certainly, they conformed generally
with Taylor's scenarios and the quiet work by naval planners to devise a plausible
rationale for a Blue-Orange war. The rising tide of American concern about
Japanese intentions and capabilities after 1906 thus closely paralleled British
hysteria over Wilhelm's High Seas Fleet. The Panama Canal was still years from
completion, and American bases in Hawaii, the Philippines, and the island
holdings in between were either rudimentary or nonexistent. The only way the
United States could demonstrate its power in the Pacific was to send the fleet
there. But when word came from Washington that the battle fleet would soon
leave the Atlantic, all the old fears of being left undefended resurfaced in the
East Coast press and legislative halls. Editorial writers up and down the seaboard
concocted doomsday scenarios of American battleships being dashed to pieces
on far-off rocky coasts or sabotaged by foreign agents in Latin or Asian ports
while German or even British naval bombardment reduced Boston, New York,
and Philadelphia to rubble and the White House became the headquarters of
European invaders.[21]

Roosevelt decided to trump his domestic critics. He would not only send
the fleet to the Pacific to awe Japan; he would also immediately bring it back to

the Atlantic via the Indian Ocean and Suez to act as sentry against possible German machinations. American battleships would thus make the most spectacular around-the-world voyage ever undertaken. The U.S. Navy would demonstrate a previously unimaginable global reach. The idea had been in the president's mind as soon as Zinovi Rozhestvenski had been defeated at Tsushima. "Unquestionably a main object was to impress Japan with our power so that she would not be tempted to make trouble."[22] But visits to Latin American ports on both oceans could also strengthen hemispheric solidarity and send a message to Berlin. Moreover, a successful cruise far exceeding in length and hardship the earlier dramatic dashes of *Oregon* around South America and *Brooklyn* from New York to Manila would demonstrate beyond question U.S. superiority in navigation, engineering, communication, vessel and crew stamina, and fleet maneuvering. The cost and duration of such a voyage would reveal the imperative need to complete the Panama Canal, whose construction according to constitutional law had to be refinanced every two years by a new Congress. And finally, a world cruise would stimulate increased national pride in the navy as the changeover to expensive dreadnoughts made public support for naval spending essential.

Later, Roosevelt would write that dispatching the American battle fleet round the world "was the most important service that I rendered to peace. . . . I had become convinced that for many reasons it was essential that we should have it clearly understood, by our own people especially, but also by other peoples, that the Pacific was as much our home waters as the Atlantic, and that our fleet could and would at will pass from one to the other of the two great oceans." Not only would the voyage benefit the navy and arouse popular interest in the service, but also it "would make foreign nations accept as a matter of course that our fleet should from time to time be gathered in the Pacific, just as from time to time it was gathered in the Atlantic, and that its presence in one ocean was no more to be accepted as a mark of hostility to any Asiatic power than its presence in the Atlantic was to be accepted as a mark of hostility to any European power. I determined on the move without consulting the Cabinet," Roosevelt continued, "precisely as I took Panama without consulting the Cabinet. A council of war never fights, and in a crisis the duty of a leader is to lead and not to take refuge behind the generally timid wisdom of a multitude of councillors." Roosevelt claimed that "neither the English nor the German authorities believed it possible to take a fleet of great battleships round the world. They did not believe that their own fleets could perform the feat, and still less did they believe that the American fleet could. I made up my mind that it was time to have a show down in the matter."[23] If the United States Navy was incapable of roaming the global sea-lanes, American foreign policy would have to be dramatically reshaped.

In the weeks between the formal announcement of the voyage and the departure of ships, Roosevelt slowly became aware of the enormous implications of his decision. Like a great magnet swimming through forty-six thousand miles of ocean, America's sixteen battleships would attract all the tensions, animosities, excitements, and yearnings of a profoundly unsettled world. Roosevelt worked day and night to control the impending enterprise. Officers were warned that anxieties about the ability of their ships and men to complete such a voyage could never be expressed. Only the most jingoistic journalists—unreflective friends of the administration and the navy—were allowed to make the trip and report on its progress. A small "train" of colliers and supply ships was dispatched to key ports throughout the world to replenish the fleet as it passed by. Roosevelt and others repeatedly assured Ambassador Baron Kogoro Takahira that the American naval demonstration was not directed at Japan. President and ambassador exchanged many notes, in which each informed the other that a fleet visit to Tokyo Bay could be considered only an act of friendship, not intimidation. When an unexpected message arrived in the midst of the battle fleet's voyage from the aging empress dowager in Peking inviting the battleships to visit China for a joint naval review that would symbolically reinforce the concept of the Open Door, Roosevelt quickly capitulated to Takahira's insistence that fleet commander Admiral Charles S. Sperry administer a subtle but unmistakable insult. Only a handful of American ships would be detached for a China visit, while most of the fleet would sail from Tokyo to Manila Bay.

On December 16, 1907, America's sixteen newly refurbished pre-dreadnought battleships steamed majestically down Hampton Roads and out into the Atlantic. They were initially commanded by Admiral Robert "Fighting Bob" Evans, who because of exhaustion would unexpectedly turn his command over to Sperry once the fleet reached California. The white hulls and buff upper works gleamed in the pale early-winter sunlight. Roosevelt proudly led them out of the Roads on the presidential yacht *Mayflower*. As the long column reached the ocean, *Mayflower* swung aside, and each battleship passed with a twenty-one-gun salute and bands playing before wheeling southward toward Brazil and the distant fog-shrouded Strait of Magellan. Just before departure Dr. Lee De Forest visited each ship, adjusting his new wireless communications systems while confidently spreading the word that signal flags would someday be obsolete.[24]

Nowhere along its route would this Great White Fleet be viewed with indifference. Over the next sixteen months, as Evans's and Sperry's ships passed by, Peru, Australia, China, and Turkey would resent the U.S. Navy for not going to war on their behalf. When Yankee sailors brawled in Rio, Sydney, and Brest, relations with the host countries were briefly strained. Greece became "battleship-mad" as a consequence of the American fleet's visit, and a handful of other small naval powers such as Argentina and Austria-Hungary decided that they simply had to have a battleship or two for the sake of national prestige.

But American audacity reverberated most among the great naval powers. Within days of the fleet's departure from Norfolk, Roosevelt's rudimentary diplomatic and military intelligence agencies began receiving shards of information from European dinner tables and drawing rooms: A Japanese diplomat tipsy on too much champagne told listeners in St. Petersburg that the Rising Sun would soon be flying over Hawaii and the Philippines, and after that who could tell where else in Asia and the Pacific the Japanese flag might be raised? British naval officers were openly stating that the odds were five to four in favor of a Japanese-American war once the American fleet reached the Pacific. Whitehall "dreaded the day when the bull would enter the china shop" of international naval politics, probably forcing Britain to choose between its alliance with Japan and its growing desire for American power to restrain Germany. Canadian prime minister Wilfrid Laurier predicted that the Royal and Imperial Japanese Navies would unite "in the northern Pacific against a common enemy," and everyone knew to which "common enemy" he referred.[25] If a war between Japan and the United States materialized, Laurier and his people fully expected an American invasion since Roosevelt had promised to take Canada if Britain supported Japan.

Kaiser Wilhelm, delighted at having an opportunity to further discomfort and destabilize his Anglo-French antagonists (and their Russian ally), promptly wrote the president, offering "the friendly help of all German vessels wherever the touring battleships might encounter them."[26] Roosevelt, evidently unaware of the German navy's recent plans to wage a terror campaign against East Coast cities, responded by soliciting Alfred von Tirpitz's opinion of the world cruise. The German naval chief during an informal visit to the United States urged the president not to hesitate in dispatching the fleet but privately predicted that a Japanese-American conflict in the Pacific was a near certainty. Wilhelm next offered Sperry's battleships access to Germany's handful of brand-new coaling facilities along the Asia-to-Europe sea-lanes and all the resources of the Wilhelmstrasse's excellent espionage system. He publicly pledged to send a German army to North America to help the United States in any possible attacks from Canada or Mexico during the many months when the American battle fleet was on the other side of the world. Roosevelt seemed blissfully unaware of the implications of the German actions. As the U.S. fleet neared the Strait of Magellan, Ambassador Speck von Sternburg replaced his French counterpart as the president's favorite tennis partner. Some sources claimed that Wilhelm's ambassador and the president spent long hours poring over world maps on the Oval Office desk, trying to determine the likeliest spots where a future world war might begin.

Near midnight on February 7, 1908, the Great White Fleet raised anchor at Sandy Point off the little city of Punta Arenas, Chile, halfway through the Magellan Strait, and started threading its way westward through the narrow, twisting, squally channel leading to the open ocean. One knowledgeable European observer immediately began to define for the American establishment the precise implications and dimensions of the new world it had created by dispatching its fleet to Pacific waters.[27] His perspective, sharply different from that of the American president, doubtless reflected much informed opinion in Britain and on the Continent, as events immediately following the Great War of 1914–1918 would reveal.

Roosevelt's America was "a great nation in the very crisis of a vast political transition," wrote Sydney Brooks. For three hundred years, first as a collection of Crown colonies and then as a vibrant young country, it had been a creature of Europe. Throughout decades of willful national isolationism during the nineteenth century, New England, New York, and Washington, D.C., had been portals through which European immigrants, culture, and political influence continued to pass. Now all was changing. The menace of an Atlantic war had "been dissipated." The expulsion of Spain from Cuba and the Caribbean removed the last "possible source of conflict between the United States and any European Power." Roosevelt's 1904 corollary to the Monroe Doctrine provided a convenient framework for resolving outstanding European-American problems in the New World. "Indeed, the development of the Monroe Doctrine from now onwards is far more likely to be concerned with the relations between the United States and South America than with the relations between the United States and Europe."[28]

America's destiny now lay in the West. Since 1898 Washington had "strewn the Pacific with stepping-stones from Hawaii to the Philippines." The United States had built up an export trade with the Far East estimated at roughly $150 million per year; it had landed an army on Chinese territory to help stifle the Boxers; it had "been drawn, willy-nilly, into the vortex" of Far Eastern affairs.[29]

Indeed, in the decade since the Spanish-American War Washington had helped shape those affairs, especially with its own policy of the Open Door.

The voyage of the Great White Fleet was thus based on no passing, aimless, or provocative whim but on the shifting imperatives of national power. The Anglo-Japanese alliance and the growing preoccupation of the Royal Navy with Wilhelm's High Seas Fleet and the protection of home waters had forced Americans to adopt an "imperial consciousness," to realize that the nation was a world power fronting two oceans and that the safety of its Pacific "back-door" had to be ensured. The country's destiny was clear: a Panama Canal would be built; the fleet would remain in or would soon be transferred to the Pacific; relations with Japan, China, and the rest of Asia would soon dominate popular thought and diplomatic strategy; and the emergence of the kaiser's High Seas Fleet in the Atlantic would eventually force the United States to build a two-ocean navy and become the world's second-greatest sea power.[30]

Speculations soon became facts as Sperry's battleships began the southern and western Pacific portion of the cruise. Sailing southwest from San Francisco, the Great White Fleet headed for Australasia. New Zealand prime minister Joseph Ward had worked hard to arrange its visit to Auckland "as leverage to gain a more active say in decision-making related to Britain's defense of its empire." Roosevelt and Root had reasons of their own for agreeing to the stop: "The time will surely come," the secretary wrote, "although probably after our day, when it will be important for the United States to have all ports friendly and all causes of sympathy alive in the Pacific." Roosevelt went one step further: the fleet visits to Auckland and several Australian ports were designed to show Britain that its Pacific colonies "are white man's country."[31]

Observers quickly grasped both Roosevelt's point and its implications. "Australia is a part of the British Empire, an empire that is linked to Japan by a treaty offensive and defensive," Maurice Low wrote soon after the fleet's departure from Sydney. "But if there is any place on the face of the globe where the Japanese are more bitterly disliked than on the island continent, it is not known." Since Australia's inception its citizens had resolved that white supremacy would be the law of the land and that Asian immigration could not be allowed. A continent of enormous opportunities, it suffered from a paucity of labor, and certain potentially profitable industries, such as sugar growing and processing, remained severely undeveloped because white men simply would not work in them. The nation was now virtually defenseless because the Anglo-Japanese alliance had permitted Britain to send most of its Pacific fleet back to home waters to confront the Germans. "The coming of the most powerful fleet the Australians have ever seen gave them a feeling that in time of peril they might find succor from friends rather than from their own family." Low stated the Australian case baldly:

> The inhabitants of British Oceanica [*sic*] have watched the growing friction between the United States and Japan with keen interest and sympathy, for they have much at stake. The world believes that the time is coming when the struggle for the mastery of the Pacific will bring the United States and Japan into conflict, and on the issue of that conflict is bound up Australia's future. If the Saxon triumphs and the United States makes the Pacific an American lake, which is the dream of more than one American statesman, Australia has nothing to fear; but if Japan is victorious, if the rising sun mounts ever higher, Australia is at the mercy of Nippon, and a white man's Australia is a memory only.[32]

Sperry and his men thus had to do little more than show themselves and their mostly obsolete war machines in the harbors of Australasia to practically detach that area from the British Empire. The American sailors behaved themselves in New Zealand, which greeted them with triumphal arches and the first state banquet ever held in that country. Sperry's officers were "impressed with the strong anti-Asiatic feeling" of their hosts, and as the Great White Fleet disappeared over the South Pacific horizon, a longtime Auckland resident sent them on their way with this doggerel: "Stars and Stripes, if you please, / Protect us from the Japanese."[33]

The seamen's riot in Sydney was largely offset by the determined goodwill of both the hosts and Sperry's officers, along with the appearance of several of their wives, who somehow contrived to follow the fleet during much of its Pacific cruise. As the American battleships finally set course northwest toward Tokyo Bay in the autumn of 1908, all of the risks and possibilities inherent in the voyage coalesced, and all its implications for global stability and instability were revealed. Former Japanese prime minister Count Shigenobu Ōkuma told the *New York Times*: "I do not know what meaning the expansion of the American navy implies, but from the speeches of the President we can gather that it is made against Japan. . . . America has no enemy at present, and it would be thoughtless policy for America purposely to make an enemy by inflaming public opinion in Japan."[34]

Tokyo assumed that humiliated Russia was still scheming with Roosevelt to make trouble for Japan, as it had at Portsmouth three years earlier. Germany, waiting to pounce on England, was actively fomenting friction between Japan and the United States. Once that friction burst into flame, as it surely would, Japan would almost certainly ask Britain for assistance. With most of the Royal Navy sailing eastward, the German High Seas Fleet could run wild whenever it chose. Such speculations had been given apparent credence late the previous spring: as Sperry's battlewagons prepared to leave San Francisco for the transpacific cruise, the kaiser suddenly ordered the majority of his navy into the Atlantic toward the Azores. Europe was astonished. Never before had Wilhelm allowed the High Seas Fleet to venture beyond the Norwegian coast. Was a general world war imminent, pitting Britain, Japan, and perhaps France and even Russia against the United States and Germany? Nothing came of the German move, and within weeks the High Seas Fleet was back at its anchorages. But given the inflamed world opinion, global peace might not be preserved unless Sperry and his sailors behaved with the utmost restraint and circumspection while in Japan.

They did so. Tokyo had ordered the Imperial Japanese Navy to conduct maneuvers north of Luzon, directly across Sperry's course, but nature intervened decisively with a terrible storm, which scattered both fleets and caused the Japanese to speculate that the American ships might have been sunk or badly damaged. A day after the fleet's scheduled arrival wireless operators on Honshu picked up signals from Sperry's battleships, which appeared the next day steaming up Tokyo Bay, where they were quickly joined at anchor by obsolete vessels of the host navy ostentatiously serving as "brother" ships.

During the next week the Japanese were punctilious, sumptuous hosts. Although there were no drunken beer parties in Hibiya Park such as had occurred when His Majesty's sailors had visited two years before, the Americans were nonetheless royally entertained and were, in turn, always on their best behavior. Festivities were undoubtedly influenced by the reappearance of the determinedly gracious American wives. In an age of civility and decorum, who would wish to initiate inflammatory conversations with ladies present? Nonetheless, Roosevelt was so jittery about his fleet's impending presence in the harbor of a putative enemy that he wrote Sperry on the eve of the visit to Tokyo Bay, directing that no enlisted men be allowed ashore. Sperry promptly wrote back that "anything less than a great pageant, with all the trimmings, might be considered by the Japanese as 'equivalent to a declaration of war.'" But Sperry had also prudently contacted Japanese authorities and obtained their approval of bluejacket liberty in Tokyo before writing the president. Eventually, 150 of Sperry's most trusted

"'first-class men whose records show no evidence of previous indulgence in in-
toxicating liquor'" were ordered to attend the first grand garden party, and
after that the success of the visit was ensured.[35]

On October 25, 1908, the Great White Fleet sailed out of Tokyo Bay with
missions accomplished by both sides. The evident sincerity and intensity of
Japanese hospitality had deeply touched most officers and sailors, but a minority
remained suspicious. Some officers spread stories they had heard that Japanese
enthusiasm had been a fraud, a mechanical effort organized by the government
and imposed on docile, hypocritical people and that the frenzied cheering, torch-
light parades, and children's songs had been produced by imperial command.[36]

If the cruise of the Great White Fleet did nothing else, it demonstrated decisively how completely the new cult of navalism had intensified many of the
ills and tensions of an increasingly unstable world. The huge, growing battle
fleets of Britain, Germany, Japan, the United States, and to a lesser extent France,
Austria-Hungary, and Italy now dominated international thought and calculation
and set the tone and pace of antagonistic national policies.

But the voyage also marked a definite milestone in U.S. naval development.
In the words of Admiral Sperry, the sixteen first-class pre-dreadnoughts of the
Atlantic Fleet and their supporting ships had displayed to a bemused world
"our greatest show on Earth" as they cruised smoothly, routinely, around the
world ocean for fourteen months from Norfolk to Japan and back again. An
entire generation of young officers and sailors had seen the world for the first
time and had gotten a taste not only of its enormous, always varied ocean but of
the complexity and danger of its politics as well. Two midshipmen fresh from
Annapolis—Bill Halsey and Ray Spruance—sailed with the Great White Fleet.
The journey must have broadened their horizons and sensibilities far beyond
those of the average Western or Japanese officer of the time. Their experiences
undoubtedly contributed to the breadth of view, intuitive strategic and technical
grasp of naval affairs, and comfort in handling big fleets and thousands of men
over large distances and long periods of time that these men demonstrated so
brilliantly thirty-five years later.[37]

Sperry finally brought his ships home on February 22, 1909, after four
months of steaming down the China Sea, across the Indian Ocean, through Suez,
and across the Mediterranean and the Atlantic, punctuated by the inevitable
port calls, "pageants," and banquets. The impression of American sea power
was only slightly spoiled by the fact that it was expressed purely in terms of pre-
dreadnoughts. None of the sixteen American vessels could match the brand-

new "all-big-gun" battleships and battle cruisers that were beginning to dominate King Edward's and Kaiser Wilhelm's navies. But the world knew that the Americans were completing their own dreadnoughts. They would be seen again in European waters with the right kinds of ships. Meanwhile, the hulls of Sperry's pre-dreadnoughts still gleamed white as they hove into view off Hampton Roads, and the salutes were snapped out with appropriate crispness as the sixteen ships again steamed past the man who had sent them on their epic voyage. The vessels anchored, and the barges began darting between them and *Mayflower*, bearing Sperry and his captains to a formal audience with the president. It was Teddy Roosevelt's last hurrah as chief executive. As he told the officers and enlisted men of his beloved navy, they composed "the first battle fleet that has ever circumnavigated the globe. Those who perform the feat again can but follow in your footsteps."[38]

Roosevelt's legion of friends and supporters saw in the navy he had largely willed into being the very essence of his leadership and of the nation's newfound glory. His administration "will be ranked among the greatest in our national life," a Chicago editorialist wrote, not because the country had built a huge fleet — though it had — and not because its wealth had grown exponentially in the seven-plus years of Roosevelt's stewardship, though that was a deeply satisfying fact as well. Roosevelt's administration "has been great because it embodied and expressed the new spirit in our democracy. . . . No President was ever more thoroughly the mouthpiece of the entire country. Jackson and Lincoln embodied sectional ideals. Mr. Roosevelt has spoken for the united country." The editor left it to a young professor at the University of Chicago to articulate exactly what Roosevelt's spirit of national unity and purpose meant in the realm of international affairs. The promise of greater freedom to the peoples of Cuba had been fulfilled; outstanding boundary issues with Britain and Canada had been resolved. "A commercial treaty with China and a cordial arrangement with Japan have strengthened our position in the Orient." Much of this was due to the navy whose powerful fleet had carried the flag around the world and whose "cordial welcome in many harbors has brought satisfaction to a people always proud of their battle-ships. The traditional policy of peace and friendship with all nations, entangling alliances with none, has gained strength by wise diplomacy."

Although some voices continued to cry out against "imperialism," "the overwhelming tide of public opinion has accepted the views of national duty and responsibility held by the administration. The development of a great navy and the increased efficiency of a larger army than formerly was deemed necessary, have been supported likewise by a people on the whole pleased with the 'speak softly, carry a big stick' theory of their chief magistrate."[39]

As the Great White Fleet at last reached home, far across the Pacific, Satō Tetsutarō finally completed his nearly nine hundred–page project titled *On the History of Imperial Defense*. Despite the disconcerting if temporary appearance of another powerful American fleet in home waters, Japan remained the un-challenged maritime power in the western Pacific and a significant colonial power in East Asia. The question of which direction its ambitious expansionist appetites should take was now acute. Much of Satō's opaque treatise justified points that had been rendered moot by the smashing naval triumph at Tsushima. But other aspects of his work invited profound controversy and reflected linger-ing problems. Satō argued that the navy was the essential component of Japan's national defense establishment. No enemy's army could threaten Japan if it could not land on Japanese shores. Since enemy navies were the prime threat to Japan, the best way to deal with them would be strike them a crippling blow in their home waters. Tōgō Heihachirō had shown the way with his preemptive night strike at Port Arthur in 1904. Thus, thirty-three years before Pearl Harbor, Satō was "confirming and prefiguring a central strategy of the Japanese Navy."[40] But who was Japan's enemy? Certainly not Britain. Russia had disappeared for the moment. French and German home waters were half a world away, and neither Paris nor Berlin had dispatched substantial naval units to the Far East.

This left only the United States. But Hawaii had not yet been developed as an advance base, and the U.S. Far East Squadron at Manila was as small as the European detachments farther north in China. Moreover, the Russo-Japanese War had given Japan substantial interests and property on the Asian mainland. Was not the navy's role to support the army and Japanese business circles in holding and perhaps expanding this foothold? Satō's claim that Japan's only policy was one of oceanic defense both undercut and ignored these new realities.

Fully aware that he had boxed himself into a problem, Satō took up an argu-ment being advocated by a growing number of colleagues in the naval establish-ment: Japan should consider a policy of "southern advance." He remained de-liberately vague on this point, but he had at least lent his considerable and growing stature to the idea of imperial expansion beyond northeastern Asia.

Expansion southward toward the riches of the Philippines, Malaya, and the East Indies would, of course, bring Japan into direct conflict with every other imperial power. Expansion into the islands of the mid-Pacific would directly threaten the American lifeline from the West Coast to the Philippines via Hawaii,

Midway, and Guam. In the years immediately after the war with Russia it became clear that Japan could safely advance only in northeastern Asia and only in a narrow, incremental way. In 1910 Satō returned to the Naval Staff College, where he helped initiate the "golden age" of Japanese naval thought. Together with tactical genius Akiyama Saneyuki and torpedo tactician Suzuki Kantarō, Satō "developed a body of naval doctrine that influenced a whole generation of naval officers."[41] Refusing to tie the navy to the army's limited perspectives, he emphasized the need for focused, sweeping naval planning. Japan could and eventually had to expand its influence over all of the Far East. Germany and the United States were the only other world powers with the motive and capacity to deny Japan its destiny, and of the two the United States was much the more likely opponent. Three basic, tightly interrelated concepts flowed naturally from this assumption: first, that an eventual Japanese-American showdown for mastery of the Pacific would involve a colossal midocean battle between big-gunned big ships far from Japanese shores; second (following extensive research by Satō and Akiyama), that a strongly maintained 70 percent standard of naval strength in relation to the Americans would give Japan more than a fighting chance to reach its objective; and third, that construction of an "eight-eight" fleet of superior battleships and battle cruisers would sustain the 70 percent power ratio.

Satō and Akiyama were aware that advanced gunnery technologies and the dreadnought battleship had rapidly increased both naval power and range. A modern battle fleet, unlike its predecessors in the Age of Sail, could by superior maneuvering and anticipation wipe out an inferior foe without suffering any losses whatsoever. Even when "both sides could aim their fire accurately, there would be 'an expanding cumulative advantage for the larger force.'"[42] But the two men were also acutely aware that world conditions for the foreseeable future strongly favored Japan *as a regional power*. Japan had no interest in and no real capacity to shape European affairs. At the same time persistent tensions in both Europe and Latin America forced the United States to maintain most of its fleet in the Atlantic. If Japan could maintain 70 percent parity with the United States, then it would always enjoy at least a seven-to-five power ratio over the Americans in the Pacific, and probably more like seven to two or three. This assumption was substantially modified but not wholly abandoned after the completion of the Panama Canal in 1914. It would still require many weeks to muster the entire U.S. battle fleet in the central Pacific in case of a national emergency. In the interim Japan could run wild, particularly if America's Pacific squadron could be dealt that surprise "crippling blow" in its home waters that

Satō had emphasized in his writings. In short, the U.S. Navy, because of its two-ocean commitment, could be defeated by an inferior Japanese battle fleet. To that end Satō and Akiyama insisted that Japan could and must build big, fast, heavily gunned battleships and battle cruisers that were qualitatively superior to those of any other nation. Satō's young students Yamamoto Isoroku, Yamaguchi Tamon, Nagano Osami, and Yonai Mitsumasa, all destined to lead Japanese battle fleets in World War II, listened attentively.

In the United States, satisfaction over the achievement of the world cruise—an undeniably remarkable feat of professional seamanship—was clouded by realization that the U.S. Navy, now number two or three in size, was not ready for war. Henry Reuterdahl ignited concern with his 1908 article in *McClure's* describing the many problems in U.S. warship design and naval administration. The man behind the article was undoubtedly Roosevelt's young naval aide William Sims, then a mere lieutenant. Although the article caused scarcely a ripple in public opinion, it rocked the Navy Department and led to a Senate investigation, which the defenders of existing navy yards and shipbuilding practices managed to stifle. Commander Albert Lenoir Key would not keep quiet, however, and after inspecting the new dreadnought *North Dakota* in dry dock, he reported to Roosevelt five areas in which the ship's design seemed faulty. The president, already interested in expanding battleship main batteries to fourteen inches, promptly called a conference at the Naval War College that went nowhere; TR persisted. The Moody and Swift Commissions he established introduced a number of badly needed reforms in ship construction, yard efficiency, department reorganization, and modern cost-accounting techniques. William Taft's secretary of the navy, George von Lengerke Meyer, carried on the move for reform. Following British (and soon German) practices, he maintained reserve flotillas of out-of-commission vessels on both coasts. The Atlantic Fleet remained the preeminent force, consisting of twenty-six battleships (most still pre-dreadnoughts) and a flagship. Four battleships were sent to the yards every three months for upkeep and repair, "leaving seventeen vessels practically on a war basis."[43]

While Sims and his fellow reformers pressed for badly needed changes in the fleet, the staff of the Naval War College was proceeding with a revolution of its own. Closer contacts with the Army War College at Carlisle Barracks, Pennsylvania, had convinced the faculty to adopt new war-game techniques, including estimates of situation and a more standardized form of issuing orders. They now viewed war as a science to be studied much as law or medicine and brought junior as well as senior officers to Newport, where all were immersed in a common curriculum emphasizing the latest advances in military and naval thinking. "The implications were profound. Where formerly seniors commanded and juniors obeyed without question, now the full range of what was involved in any given strategic or tactical situation could be known and understood by all." Discipline and courtesy remained, but blind obedience was replaced by intelligent execution.[44]

The introduction of this "applicatory system" was another example of the witting and unwitting flow of ideas around the international naval community during the first two decades of the century. By this time the *United States Naval Institute Proceedings,* with articles on the latest advances in U.S. technology and doctrine, was circulating worldwide. At the same time the German navy was developing the concept of situation estimates and the formulation of written fleet orders to promote maximum efficiency in both training and combat. This applicatory system had been discovered by Akiyama Saneyuki, during his travels through Europe at the close of the nineteenth century. After returning to Japan, Akiyama had promptly incorporated the system into the training course at the Japanese naval college in Tokyo. Even as Japanese-American tensions reached an unprecedented level in 1907–1908, Akiyama passed the concept on to his good friend Commander Frank Marble, the American naval attaché. Marble subsequently returned to Newport and began lecturing on the concept of written fleet orders that would include an overall clearly articulated strategy along with tactical doctrines that could be flexibly employed. One analyst has suggested that Akiyama shared his thoughts with Marble (including detailed information about Japanese strategy and tactics during the recent war with Russia) because of gratitude for being allowed to participate in war gaming and tabletop map exercises when he had passed through Newport a decade before. Whatever his motives, Akiyama apparently invited Marble to join in a war game at the Japanese naval college that recapitulated the combat off Port Arthur and at Tsushima, and the American received the Japanese naval staff's internal documents about combat operations during the recent conflict, which he promptly translated and took home with him.[45] In the United States the applicatory system eventually filtered down to classrooms through textbooks and example during the wartime emergency of 1917–1918, thus ensuring that the enormous expansion of the nation's naval leadership would be accomplished with maximum professionalism and continuity.

Meanwhile, Roosevelt stressed the need for more battleships and a Mahanist concentration of force. Taft continued the dreadnought-construction program.

By 1914 the United States had built or authorized fifteen new ships including such eventually famous vessels as *Utah, Wyoming, Florida, Arkansas, Texas, New York, Oklahoma, Nevada, Pennsylvania,* and *Arizona.* The two presidents allowed themselves to become as battleship mad as the Greeks, and Congress followed. While the German and Japanese navies were building at a ratio of three cruisers to two British vessels and Britain at a ratio of two dreadnoughts for every one comparable German vessel, the U.S. Navy between 1900 and 1914 built thirty battleships and ten armored cruisers but only six true cruisers. A big-ship frenzy seized the country, leading to a badly imbalanced fleet of capital ships with few supporting vessels to scout and screen. As early as 1900 Senator Henry Cabot Lodge, the leading Mahanist in Congress, pressed for a twenty thousand–ton battleship and dreamed of a forty thousand–ton vessel. "The great purpose of the American Navy and of the American policy," he told his colleagues, "is to have ships that are better... than any other ships in the world."[46] Lodge, no less than Japanese and earlier British naval planners, had become bewitched by the chimera of the supership.

Despite its flaws, the United States Navy continued to be an active, powerful, and influential presence in Atlantic waters in the brief years between its return from the world cruise and the outbreak of war in 1914. In December 1910 Taft sent sixteen of the twenty-six battleships then composing the Atlantic Fleet to French and British ports including some of the first of many planned dreadnoughts. When the fleet reached Portsmouth just before Christmas, William Sims, known to the British press as the U.S. counterpart to Percy Scott and John Jellicoe, was nominated official spokesman. At London's famous Guildhall he used every rhetorical flourish in virtually pledging an Anglo-American naval alliance. "There is a strong blood-tie between our two peoples," he assured a mesmerized audience. The U.S. fleet had literally been all over the world in the past several years and had been entertained royally. But there was something official and formal about all the exhausting pageants and lengthy welcoming speeches. They had been arranged and given, after all, by foreigners, who were incapable of conveying "to our minds quite the same impression that has been made by the English people." The United States was still an Anglo-Saxon country, Sims maintained, and it was natural for the officers and men coming ashore to look up grandparents, uncles, and aunts who still lived in the old country or to seek out the old neighborhoods where their parents had been born. Beneath the common Anglo-Saxon surface of amity and sentiment was a stronger feeling still, "a sort of undefined defensive sentiment." Sims added, "I wish to express an opinion on this subject which is entirely personal, and it is this—if the time ever comes when the British Empire is seriously menaced by an external enemy, it is my opinion that you may count upon every man, every dollar, and every drop of blood of your kindred across the seas."[47]

Taft later "mildly reprimanded" Sims for his "incursion into politics," which understandably angered the large Irish and German American populations in the United States. But Washington never repudiated Sims or asked him to retract or modify his statement, and the U.S. correspondent for *The Times* of London later assured readers that Sims "'was the voice of the American Navy.'"[48]

The following summer, around the time of the Moroccan crisis, a division of battleships visited Kiel for fleet week, then steamed on to various Russian and Scandinavian Baltic ports. Wilson in one of his first orders sent a large part of the battle force to the Mediterranean for another prolonged voyage, which was quickly curtailed by growing troubles in Mexico. The U.S. Navy between 1903 and 1913 thus exceeded any other sea service in the extent of its long-distance cruising.[49] It was and remained a force that could not be ignored.

So in the quarter century prior to 1914, naval mania came to define an age. More and more huge industrial war castles foamed through the waves of the world ocean. Philosophers provided them with missions and justifications; their ambitious, jealous, monarchical owners loved them and yearned to display them as talismans of personal power. The modern steam and steel battleship "is a greater example of power than anything else existing," an American admiral exulted. "It could whip an army of a million men ... knock down all the buildings in New York, smash all the cars, break down all the bridges and sink all the shipping."[50]

Cartoonists portrayed Theodore Roosevelt in short pants, dragging warships on a string through puddles or launching them in a bathtub. Wilhelm openly referred to his battleships as his "darlings" and "could not bear to think of any of them disfigured or sunk." Russians referred to their "'Holy Fleets,'" and an American described the dreadnought battleship as "'the noblest work of man.'" To Admiral George Dewey and the American Naval Board, the battleship became, in Robert L. O'Connell's felicitous phrase, a "sacred vessel." All efforts to modify enthusiasm for the unwieldy behemoths by emphasizing the potential destructive power of torpedoes carried by fast destroyers and the newfangled submarine or the potential of fast "battle cruisers" were rejected as anathema by American naval authorities steeped in the tradition of the stout hulls and cannon of the Age of Fighting Sail. Ironically, the U.S. Navy would embrace the battle cruiser as perfect for distant operations in the far Pacific at just the point that several were blowing up spectacularly in the North Sea. In the event, none were ever built prior to World War II when two of eight proposed "large cruisers" of thirty-three knots mounting nine twelve-inch guns saw short but sharp action at the end of the Pacific conflict.

Ship models were the rage in stores on both sides of the Atlantic and on Tokyo's Ginza; the naval war game, "a form of chess with tiny ships for pawns and queens," was advertised for years in British magazines. English boys and girls adopted battleships and armored cruisers while their parents snapped up penny postcards of this or that leviathan. As in Japan, popular novels and boys' adventure stories abounded, filled with handsome young naval officers sinking enemy ships single-handedly or heroically jamming their bodies into shell or torpedo holes below the waterlines of their gravely damaged vessels. "Erskine Childers, John Buchan, and E. Phillips Oppenheim wrote mystery stories about battleships, and in the *Strand Magazine* Sherlock Holmes grew increasingly occupied with plots to steal British naval secrets."[51] Governments and newspapers continually published competitive naval statistics, and enraptured citizens pondered their nations' places in the pecking order of world sea power.

But in these early years of industrial shipbuilding it was difficult to rate navies precisely. Ships that all could agree were "battleships" or perhaps "armored cruisers" varied considerably in length and width, speed, gun size, armor, and range. In a careful assessment of international naval strength two late-twentieth-century scholars concluded that in 1898 Britain possessed twenty-nine steel-clad big-gun battleships; France had fourteen, Russia six, Germany and the United States four each, and Japan three. But a contemporary evaluation gave much higher relative numbers for nearly all the powers.[52] However they were rated, the industrial navies grew yearly thereafter, ultimately reaching enormous proportions. Each battleship was attended by one or more large "armored" or smaller "protected" cruisers plus a multitude of gunboats, dispatch boats, torpedo boats–cum–torpedo boat destroyers–cum destroyers, and monitors. By 1910 or so, lesser navies like those of Italy and Austria-Hungary, although possessing relatively few battleships, could still muster a large number of cruisers and destroyers.

Powerful navy leagues already existed in Germany, Britain, and the United States. "Little publicity was given their most important members—Krupp, Armstrong, Vickers, Morgan, Schwab, DuPont, Frick, and other makers of steel and weapons." Instead, the spotlight was deliberately shone on naval heroes like George Dewey and Winfield Schley, "who made speeches and appeared in the pageants." And pageantry there was. The enormous success of the Spithead naval review in 1897 prompted Europe's monarchs and other ambitious heads of state, like Theodore Roosevelt, to include naval reviews as part of the deliberate effort at displaying the pomp and circumstance of their ambitious, pushy nations. The Japanese, of course, needed to look no further than Tsushima for justification, though except when the Americans came to call in 1908, their remote location restricted lavish reviews to their own fleet.[53]

Historian Robert A. Hart has drawn an indelible portrait of an era when warships ruled the public imagination. Each year between 1900 and 1914, Kronshtadt, Kiel, Toulon, Portsmouth, and eventually Norfolk were the scenes of great naval fetes. The rows of battleships and cruisers—their hulls painted black, white, or blue, their turrets and upper works a contrasting light brown— stretched longer and longer as navies continued their seemingly irresistible growth. Each review included regattas, balls, banquets, toasts, and speeches by hosts and guests. "Once a year was not enough by 1907, when each of the parade grounds was the scene of three or four gala reviews during the summer alone. When foreign navies sent regrets, having made commitments elsewhere, one simply put his own fleet through its paces once again."[54]

Review days were always declared local public holidays, and spectators arrived at the harbor early in the morning. The lucky few who found some high ground could look toward the bay over a sea of straw hats, parasols, and vendors' booths selling lemonade and popcorn balls. Soon black smudges appeared on the morning horizon, and within moments the long line of visiting battleships could be seen approaching at high speed so that their plow-shaped bows

> could turn up water in a way that always pleased the crowds. More slowly, and in perfectly measured formations, they entered the harbor through swarms of sailboats and steam runabouts to find moorings beside the vessels of the host navy. Anchors splashed in unison. Together, the fleets were a city of metal castles, swaying from the recoil of salutes and partly obscured by coal and powder smoke. Here and there the sun would flash upon gilt prows, brass railings, band instruments, and admirals' uniforms. With jealousy or pride, the spectators compared the two fleets.[55]

At some point the royal or presidential yacht appeared; inevitably, the splendid vessel was wreathed in white and gold. Slowly, it steamed down the line of warships, whose blue- or white-jacketed crews lined the rails and gave lusty cheers as the distant figures of the monarch and queen or president and his lady indolently waved back. At noon and dusk ships' bands came on the quarterdeck to serenade the throngs ashore with sprightly airs.

But when the test of war came at last to Europe, how would ambitious monarchs, prime ministers, and admiralties use these increasingly powerful products of industrialism? *Could* they use them? How truly professional at war were the officers and seamen of these great fleets? And if they were not, how quickly could they be made so? Peacetime planning and strategizing were one thing, but as civilian-turned-soldier Ralph Ingersoll would rightly emphasize in a later war and another context, the battle is always the payoff.[56] Once the guns began to speak, would battleship navies prove to have been essentially agents of peacetime intimidation, or could they be, as their champions constantly boasted, the supreme instruments of war? How effective were the administrative, industrial, and political establishments that supported them? These questions had hung in the balance for nearly twenty years when the crisis of August 1914 abruptly thrust them to the forefront of international calculation.

Alfred Thayer Mahan, sketched in 1894 shortly before receiving honors at both Oxford and Cambridge Universities. (U.S. Naval Historical Center, NH 48058)

Admiral of the Fleet Tōgō Heihachirō, Imperial Japanese Navy. Photo taken at New York Navy Yard, August 15, 1912. (U.S. Naval Historical Center, NR&L(M) 1018)

Admiral of the Fleet Sir John "Jacky" Fisher, first sea lord of the Admiralty, 1904–1910, 1914–1915. (U.S. Naval Historical Center, NR&L(M) 23490)

Admiral Viscount Sir John Jellicoe of Scapa, commander in chief of the British Grand Fleet, 1914–1916, first sea lord of the Admiralty, 1916–1918. (U.S. Naval Historical Center, NR&L(M) 699)

Admiral Sir David Beatty, commander of the Battle Cruiser Squadron, Grand Fleet, 1914–1916, commander in chief of the British Grand Fleet, 1916–1918. (U.S. Naval Historical Center, NH 372)

Vice Admiral Reinhard Scheer, commander of the German High Seas Fleet, 1916–1918. (U.S. Naval Historical Center, NR&L(M) 15591)

USS *Iowa* under way during the North Atlantic Fleet Review of 1905.
(U.S. Naval Historical Center, NH 60248a)

HMS *Dreadnought*. (U.S. Naval Historical Center, NH 63596)

USS *Connecticut* leads the Great White Fleet out of Hampton Roads, Virginia, in December 1907 at the start of the round-the-world cruise. (U.S. Naval Historical Center, NH 100349)

President Theodore Roosevelt addressing officers and enlisted men aboard USS *Connecticut* at Hampton Roads, Virginia, February 22, 1909, after the cruise around the world of the Great White Fleet. (U.S. Naval Historical Center, NH 1836)

German armored cruisers *Scharnhorst* and *Gneisenau* lead Vice Admiral Maximilian Graf von Spee's cruiser squadron out of Valparaiso, Chile, November 3 or 4, 1914, after the Battle of Coronel. Steaming around Cape Horn, they were destroyed off the Falklands shortly thereafter. (U.S. Naval Historical Center, NH 59638)

170

Jutland: The British battle cruiser *Indefatigable* races into battle, May 31, 1916, its main battery trained to starboard. Note the smoke and deepening murk of a North Sea late-spring afternoon. (U.S. Naval Historical Center, NH 50152)

Jutland: The German battleship *Oldenberg* fires its main batteries, May 31, 1916. (U.S. Naval Historical Center, NH 92629)

Jutland: The British battle cruiser *Invincible* photographed at the very start of the cataclysmic magazine explosion that destroyed the ship in an instant, May 31, 1916. (U.S. Naval Historical Center, NH 354)

Jutland: All that remains visible of HMS *Invincible* three minutes after the explosion. A battleship of the Grand Fleet can be seen through the haze and smoke of battle. (U.S. Naval Historical Center, NH 349)

The German battle cruiser *Seydlitz* steams into Scapa Flow for internment, November 21, 1918. (U.S. Naval Historical Center, NH 89511)

CHAPTER 5

Rush to Conflict

AFTER 1912 international naval tensions began to slowly ease, though Winston Churchill never quite relaxed his guard. If war did come and Britain decided after all to impose a close naval blockade on Germany, staging bases would be needed somewhere on the Continent. As he struggled to protect the necessary funds for maintaining the pace of British naval construction, Churchill ordered staff planners to consider seizing beachheads on the coasts of Holland, Denmark, or the Scandinavian countries as bases for British cruiser and destroyer forces, even if it involved a flagrant violation of neutral rights. He even considered raids against now heavily defended Heligoland or up the Elbe. As one critic observed, such thinking reflected a temperament and personality that "did not come near to understanding the dangers and complexities of amphibious operations, the most hazardous undertakings of war, nor the need for large quantities of specialized equipment and a high degree of training on the part of the men of all services committed to their execution."[1]

Despite such ill-considered pugnacity, no developments in the international climate of 1913 and early 1914 inspired fear of an impending catastrophe. The Balkans remained at war, but few people and statesmen bothered to worry much about the consequences. Which great power, after all, would be willing to go to war for or against Serbia or the new nation of Albania? As for immediate concerns, the Germans had not secretly built any dreadnoughts after all, and apparently Alfred von Tirpitz did not intend to build more than the three battleships and other war vessels indicated in the most recent German Naval Law.

It was during this palmy time that young Brian Schofield joined the Royal Navy's Home Fleet. Years earlier, all of thirteen or so, he was interviewed for a

naval career by none other than the Great Man himself, and after Jacky Fisher
and his board expressed satisfaction, the youngster went off for four years' training
at Dartmouth, followed by six months in a training cruiser. He reported aboard
the lithe, powerful seventeen thousand–ton battle cruiser *Indomitable* in May
1913. Captain Francis W. "Cuts" Kennedy, so named for "the generous doses
of corporal punishment he was reputed to have handed out to young offenders
in command of the last of the old training brigs," was a strict disciplinarian and
"as full of energy as a boiling kettle." When Kennedy first encountered Schofield
and his fellow "snotties" (cadets), the captain kept the trembling youngsters
waiting for long moments as he finished some correspondence, then abruptly
swung about and announced that the reason the boys were aboard the battle
cruiser could be summed up in one word: "war." Life for the snotties in the
cramped gun room featured a wine steward named Cessar who combined a
haughty demeanor with a fiery temper, treated all the youngsters "with an air of
condescension well suited to a priest of Bacchus," and treated any order for
beer instead of wine as beneath contempt. When called upon by the senior
midshipman to entertain, Cessar's demeanor changed at once. "The curtains at
the end of the mess would part dramatically to reveal the little man. Gone was
the haughty look. Now his eyes had a merry twinkle. With arms folded as if for a
jig, he would start to dance, his coat tails flapping and fat short legs keeping time
with the music provided by a paymaster midshipman on the gunroom piano."
When word came that *Indomitable* was heading for the Mediterranean, contracts were awarded to various Maltese relatives of the gun-room messman and
canteen manager "for the privilege of doing our laundry when we should arrive
on station."

Nonetheless, there might be other jobs that Malta's native population might
find aboard the big battle cruiser, and so when *Indomitable* entered the Grand
Harbor, decks crammed with sailors and yardarms with flags, "an indescribable
clamour arose from the floating populace gathered to greet us. . . . [O]n this fine
October afternoon as the bugler sounded the 'G' at which signal the booms
swung out and the gangways were lowered with clockwork precision . . . dozens
of dghaisas surged forward" to converge on the big ship.

Over the next nine months, young Schofield obtained an unforgettable
"glimpse of the old Europe of the nineteenth century" as it was about to pass
from the scene. "Turkey held sway down the Palestinian coast, Egypt was under
British tutelage, and the aged Emperor Franz Josef still sat on the throne of the
Austro-Hungarian empire." In November the battle cruiser called at Alexandria,

and Schofield visited Cairo and the Pyramids. Lord Kitchener gave a ball for the fleet "and omitted to remove his sword so that officers had to dance" with the ladies with swords on, "much to their partners' discomfort, until an aide-de-camp summoned up enough courage to acquaint the great man, who did not dance, of the trouble he was causing his guests."

After winter months spent largely at Malta, Britain's bastion at the strategically critical point where the eastern and western Mediterranean basins joined, the battle cruiser went up the Adriatic to Venice, Trieste, and Pula and visits with the Austrian navy. It was late spring 1914 now, and more balls, dances, and luncheons awaited Britain's maritime ambassadors of power and goodwill. *Indomitable*'s gun-room cadets and midshipmen traded visits with their "chummy ship," an Austrian battleship. The young officers engaged in a delightful round of mutual visits, never dreaming that just a few short weeks separated them from bitter enmity and even death.[2]

That summer, for the first time in nineteen years, a British battle squadron visited Kiel during fleet week. At the same time the German ambassador in London, Prince Karl Max Lichnowsky, led Alfred von Tirpitz to believe that "England had agreed to the present German rate of shipbuilding; a war about our fleet or our trade was now out of the question; our relations were satisfactory, and *rapprochement* was growing."[3]

Tirpitz was entertaining the British ambassador and some Royal Navy officers on board the German flagship at Kiel when the news came that a young Serbian nationalist had murdered the Austrian heir apparent, Archduke Ferdinand, and his wife, Sophie, in the streets of Sarajevo. Early the next morning the British quietly raised anchor on schedule and sailed away.

The crisis, when it came after five weeks of tense jockeying and maneuvering among the powers, proved unstoppable. In the now fully mature railroad age, even rumors, hints, and whispers of full mobilization by any one of the powers panicked all the others into reaction. As each great power mobilized to protect its frontiers and armies from sudden, unprovoked assault, the German army found itself bound by the imperatives of the Schlieffen Plan to attack in the West in order to forestall national disaster, and the peoples of Europe, with near-universal expressions of relief and even joy, finally fell into the general war that had been long anticipated with mingled dread and curiosity. For the moment all the terrible strains that racked European life were drowned in a wave of public emotion. The fatherland was in peril! That was not the supreme consideration; it was the only consideration. Fleets raced to battle stations, armies to the field. Civil societies of long-standing and rich accomplishment were transformed at a stroke into garrison states. A seventy-five-year age of unparalleled barbarism and terror was about to begin.

In 1914 kings and commoners embraced violence for the simplest of reasons: they thought it would serve a useful purpose. The nature of that purpose varied with different nationalities, but everyone shared a common assumption: war would make things different and therefore better. Not far beneath the glittering surface of early-twentieth-century Western life lurked a deep malaise. The material progress of the industrial age had taken humanity only so far and in the process had created dreadful tensions between peoples, among nations, and within societies. For the comfortable classes no less than for the restless masses who confronted them with an unappeasable yearning for security and respectability, everyday experience had become unbearable. European men—and women—demanded something more profound, more exciting, from life. They wanted a resolution of all the outstanding differences and problems that industrialism had created. War, they thought, was the perfect solution, and the vast throngs who gathered in the streets and churches of London, Berlin, St. Petersburg, and Paris embraced it with literally a religious fervor.

For ninety-nine years there had been general peace in Europe, broken only briefly in the Crimea in 1855–1856 and in France fifteen years later; no one could imagine what bloody, incessant, inconclusive combat between industrial armies and navies would mean. Monarchs, statesmen, and diplomats had flirted with disaster for nearly two decades. Behind the Krüger telegram, the Moroccan crises, the unrelenting naval races, and the constant emergencies in the Balkans were fiery, frustrated personalities, eager to do something, to force an issue, to cut a figure, to make a statement, to resolve unbearable dilemmas or tensions, to shape history. And when the specter of Moloch appeared before their suddenly opened and terrified eyes and they faced either retreat or catastrophe, Wilhelm, Nicholas, George, and Franz Josef discovered that they were captives to the juggernauts they had so blithely created, prisoners of the mutual jealousies and fears they had so assiduously cultivated or so carelessly allowed to mature.

Those juggernauts and emotions had been created largely by the strident naval rivalries that had shaped international politics during the previous quarter century. After 1890 sea power in its broadest sense and numerous manifestations had transformed the world scene. It had become the chief symbol and expression of unbridled industrialism, the emblem of national greatness. Sea power had entered into every calculation of national advantage or reverse. Huge ships with terrible names like *Dreadnought, Lion,* and *Invincible,* even *Titanic,* were examples of the cutting edge of a new industrial civilization characterized by steady advances in technology and engineering. The possession of sea power sustained the British and French empires; the loss of sea power marked the decline and eventual or immediate fall of their Russian and Spanish counterparts. The imperatives of sea power drove the restless newcomers on the global stage—Germany, Japan, and the United States—to create overseas empires. Navies absorbed and reflected the internal stresses of the nations they served, and naval power and warfare were perceived as the ultimate solutions to bitter ethnic and national hatreds. By itself the German fleet became the focal point of an increasingly restive and irritable European political system.

Yet as crisis followed crisis and nerves approached the breaking point, sea power imploded. The warships that flew the White and Imperial Ensigns and the Stars and Stripes were recalled to home waters, from which the Rising Sun had seldom strayed. All the impressive advances in naval architecture and power had merely made ships and guns bigger and stronger but only marginally increased the reach of fleets. The navies of 1914 were still highly visible, short in range of hitting power, and above all one-dimensional. They had not yet truly reached the skies or plumbed the ocean depths. To find and destroy each other, strategists believed, merely required movement and maneuvers in the narrow seas off northwestern Europe or the Caribbean.

But what kind of movement or maneuvers was never clearly defined. Filson Young who attached himself to David Beatty's Battle Cruiser Squadron at the outbreak of war recalled in 1921 that "of the three great naval reputations made in the war—those of Beatty, [Reginald] Tyrwhitt [commanding the Harwich Force] and [Roger] Keyes [commander of submarines]—none of them was a Fisher man." When Beatty first took his battle cruisers and supporting ships to sea in the spring of 1913 for training, "he found that there were no instructions from the Admiralty as to what it was to be trained for, no policy formed as to the nature of its employment in the Fleet. . . . There could be no clearer example of the deplorable lack of a Staff, a mere thinking department." The Royal Navy, like its counterpart across the North Sea, thus lacked "the most formidable weapon of all," a "collecting, coordinating brain." On the eve of war, Winston Churchill would send John Jellicoe and the Grand Fleet to Scapa Flow in the Orkney Islands, well away (five hundred miles) from any surprise lunge by the High Seas Fleet. Simultaneously, he dispatched the battle cruisers to Cromarty Firth on Scotland's east coast as a rapid-response force (the battle cruisers would soon be moved farther south to Rosyth to protect Britain's east coast towns from raids by Franz von Hipper's battle cruisers). Over the early months of the war Jellicoe and Beatty would sketch a broad scheme for a great naval action in which the two British battle fleets would rendezvous in the middle of the North Sea in the event of a German breakout, with the battle cruisers then to be employed as bait and lure and the Grand Fleet the trap.[4]

Beyond that, British naval tactics and strategy did not go. Navies had not fought enough to know themselves. The belief that sea power both defined and controlled national destinies had become an article of faith, but that faith had only been tested off the Yalu and at Manila Bay, Santiago, and Tsushima. In 1914 the mighty fleets were far larger and stronger than those that had battled off the coasts of China, Cuba, the Philippines, and Japan. They remained cutlasses of unknown quality.

CHAPTER 6

Standoff, 1914–1915

OVER ALL THE FORCES that shaped the Great War lay the realities of British sea power and Germany's persistent unwillingness to challenge it directly. However poorly or imperfectly employed throughout the Great War, however exhausted and demoralized it eventually became, the Royal Navy (with later help from its American ally) guaranteed the steady reinforcement and resupply of the western front and imposed upon the German war effort a slow and distant but inexorable strangulation through blockade. Berlin's response was to keep the *Hochseeflotte* in port (with the occasional and inconclusive exception of Franz von Hipper's battle cruisers) until 1916, while dispatching a single capital ship from the western Mediterranean to the Porte with almost unlimited consequences for the subsequent course of Russian and east European history. As stalemate gripped the western battlefields and the great fleet action off Jutland proved inconclusive, the kaiser and his desperate advisers resorted to unrestricted submarine warfare. This decision drew the United States into the coalition against the Central powers, sealing their fate and leading to permanent and profound changes in the balance of international power. The use and misuse of naval power thus defined not only the contours and outcome of World War I but much of subsequent twentieth-century history as well.

Could the kaiser's expensive, "pretty toys" have disrupted British strategy at any point? The answer must be a qualified yes. Had the kaiser and his high command held true to their sketchy plans of December 1912 to send the High Seas Fleet with U-boats and airplanes rushing into the North Sea and down the Channel in aggressive support of the Schlieffen Plan, World War I would probably have ended with a German victory in six weeks. (It would also have initiated years in advance of actuality three-dimensional war at sea.) With the Belgian and French battlefields sealed off from critical British reinforcement, the Germans would have had to deal with only a French army in almost perpetual, headlong retreat. That army would have been further weakened and demoralized if the small but powerful German Mediterranean squadron (the new eleven-inch-gun battle cruiser *Goeben* and light cruiser *Breslau*) had moved to cut the convoy lanes from Algeria carrying essential supplies and reenforcements for the western front rather than fleeing superior but ineptly led British forces and escaping to Constantinople. To be sure, the Allied navies would have eventually destroyed their numerically inferior German enemy in both the Channel and the Mediterranean. But Jutland suggests that the Royal Navy might have suffered grievous, perhaps irretrievable, damage in the process. And if Admiral Friedrich von Ingenohl could have initially raced his substantial surface forces down the North Sea past John Jellicoe's big ships at Scapa Flow five hundred miles from the German coast (it is doubtful David Beatty's battle cruisers at Cromarty Firth would have steamed out independently against the entire High Seas Fleet), he would have initially confronted a British Channel fleet that comprised only eighteen pre-dreadnoughts of significantly inferior speed, strength, and gun power, plus Commodore Reginald Tyrwhitt's Harwich Force of destroyers and light cruisers.

Could the Germans have slipped past the Grand Fleet during the first days or even weeks of the war? Winston Churchill thought so, and he was haunted by both the possibility and its consequences. On October 27, 1914, the first lord of the Admiralty propounded a series of sixteen questions on steps to be taken in the event of a German invasion of Great Britain. During the course of elaborating those questions, Churchill, or one of his analysts, observed, "If the Channel Fleet were destroyed by the High Seas Fleet without our Grand Fleet giving any assistance, the effect on public opinion would be disastrous." But "the only position from which the Grand Fleet can ensure engaging the High Seas Fleet before it engages the Channel Fleet is in the middle of the North Sea." And "it [the Grand Fleet] cannot always be there, and while there it is subject to loss by submarine and mine."[1]

There was thus every likelihood that von Ingenohl could have sailed safely down the North Sea, destroyed the Channel Fleet and Harwich Force, then run wild for at least a day destroying transport and cargo ships and shooting up supply and embarkation ports before Jellicoe and his sailors could rush down from Scapa Flow and Cromarty Firth to a fatally belated rescue.

Indeed, the Grand Fleet might have been neutralized for much longer than a day if, as Churchill suggested, German U-boat, aircraft, and light surface forces had been coordinated in a carefully orchestrated offensive. Shortly after the war it became clear that Jellicoe was fearful that German submarines could successfully attack his ships both at anchor and at sea. The admiral's fears were the direct result of those last prewar fleet maneuvers in 1913 in which big "overseas" submarines were deemed to have sunk 40 percent of the Grand Fleet's capital ships. Jellicoe wrote soon after, "So far as the North Sea and Great Britain and Germany are concerned, these vessels [submarines] can remain in positions off any hostile port for a week or more, and they go far to deny the use of German ports to German ships and similarly British ports to British ships, except at great risk to the surface vessel."[2]

Those risks were first dramatized just days after the war broke out when several U-boats scattered three British dreadnoughts conducting firing practice off Scapa Flow. None of the big ships was hit, and several U-boats subsequently failed to reach home, but on September 2, U-21 torpedoed and sank the small British scout cruiser *Pathfinder* off the Firth of Forth with the loss of 259 of its 360 crewmen. Word of the sinking did not apparently shake the Admiralty, but the loss of three twelve thousand–ton cruisers, *Aboukir, Hogue,* and *Cressey,* to Kapitänleutnant Otto Weddigen's U-9 three weeks later understandably "panicked" the British naval high command. More than fourteen hundred Tars, some of them quite young, perished in the three vessels "named for famous British victories on land and sea."[3] Days later, the brand-new "superdreadnought" *Audacious* succumbed to a mine off the Irish coast. In these early days of modern naval warfare, admiralties were incapable of differentiating, nor, indeed, did they much care, what kind of undersea weapon had destroyed one of their capital ships.

Nor could they do much about it. "There was no organized hunting for submarines," Filson Young recalled not long after the war, "because we had not got the light craft to hunt with." Neither had the Royal Navy developed an effective depth charge; indeed, it did not begin work on such invaluable and terrifying if often inaccurate weapons until three months after the sensational autumn sinkings. Finally, the British had no real mining capability, and when the navy began a development program, the prototypes "turned out to be more dangerous to us than to the enemy."[4]

Following the sinking of the three enemy cruisers, U-boats concentrated largely on the British fleet until imposition of the counterblockade against British merchant shipping five months later. Jellicoe's sailors responded to the submarine threat with "bouts of nerves and sudden bolts like a horse that hears the rustle of a snake." Twice during the first month of the war, the Grand Fleet raced out of Scapa Flow after erroneous reports of enemy submarines in the anchorage (the sightings were probably of seals). On one occasion in October the fleet steamed to Loch Ewe on the west coast of Scotland to escape the ostensible U-boat threat to Scapa. At another time the same month Jellicoe took his ships to Lough Swilly on the northern coast of Ireland, "leaving the North Sea free to the Germans had they known it. . . . If the Germans had launched a naval offensive at this time, it might have obtained startling results." Indeed, when the Admiralty ordered the fleet back to Scapa Flow from Swilly, Jellicoe personally countermanded the order, taking his ships out into the Atlantic west of Galway Bay for some time, "thus placing two islands and a couple of seas between himself and the enemy."[5] Beatty was furious, and wrote plaintively to Churchill at the Admiralty:

> The situation as it is, we have no place to lay our heads. . . . We have been running hard now since the 28th July; small defects are creeping up which we haven't time to take in hand. 48 hours is our spell in harbour with steam ready to move at 4 hours notice, coaling on an average 1400 tons a time, night defence stations. The men can stand it, but the machines can't, and we must have a place where we can stop for from four to five days every now and then to give the engineers a chance.

With the submarine menace defined in the terms it was, "Such a place does not exist." The wartime Royal Navy harbormaster at Scapa Flow later implicitly criticized Jellicoe for timidity if not cowardice in his response to the enemy submarine menace. "Of course there never was a German submarine in Scapa," Captain D. J. Munro scoffed a decade and a half after the war. "None during the whole war achieved the terrors of the passage." One U-boat was destroyed in the outer approaches to the anchorage in late November 1914, but not until the final hours of the war did another German submarine, manned entirely by officers, perish at the harbor entrance in a desperate suicide mission to preserve German naval honor. Despite the patent inability of the German U-boats to assault Scapa, "the mere apprehension of submarines attacking the sleeping ships on which all else reposed, was sufficient in the winter of 1914 to destroy that sense of security which every Fleet demands when in its own harbors."[6]

However long it might have taken the Grand Fleet to meet its marauding enemy in the Channel, the great naval battle that followed would have further ensured that no British troops or supplies could cross the narrow straits between Dover-Harwich and the French and Belgian ports. A Channel choked with flaming, sinking ships, dead sailors, and desperate men fighting to the last shell, bullet, torpedo, and hull would have been no place for cargo ships or transports to travel. Thus, for days and perhaps weeks no British armies could have appeared on German flanks or fronts to fatally slow down General Alexander von Kluck's huge sweep, as in fact they did at Mons and Le Cateau. Alone, encircled on land and sea, beyond all help, with Russian armies still completing mobilization a thousand miles away, France could only have surrendered. Britain, its navy probably victorious but certainly battered and perhaps in ruins, could never have considered an invasion to reconquer the Continent alone. A British blockade of the Continent would have meant little with the mineral- and grain-rich areas of France (and undoubtedly the Ukraine eventually) held by the Germans. Italy would have had to reconsider its neutrality and rejoin the Central powers. The United States, with its large German and Irish American populations, would never have contested a German triumph, especially since Berlin would never have needed to initiate submarine warfare.

Certainly, the world expected the German navy to move quickly and vigorously against its opponents. The *New York Times* headline for August 5, 1914, read: "ENGLAND DECLARES WAR ON GERMANY; BRITISH SHIP SUNK; FRENCH SHIPS DEFEAT GERMAN, BELGIUM ATTACKED; 17,000,000 MEN ENGAGED IN GREAT WAR OF EIGHT NATIONS; GREAT ENGLISH AND GERMAN NAVIES ABOUT TO GRAPPLE..." The accompanying article stated, "The German fleet is concentrated for the defense of the Kiel Canal. Its destruction will be the first object of the British fleet....As was anticipated, Germany's first naval effort was to deal a heavy blow to the Russians in the Baltic, but as yet there is insufficient evidence that it succeeded or that the Russian fleet was rendered powerless." In fact, the Imperial German Navy made no move in the Baltic, or anywhere else.

Why the Germans did not seize their opportunity continued to baffle British sailors long after the war. The leading historian of British naval intelligence in that era has written that "both the Royal Navy and the public felt certain that a major clash between the two Fleets would occur within a few weeks, and that it would result in a second Trafalgar and so end the war." Jellicoe spoke for the entire Royal Navy when he wrote in 1919 that everyone assumed that the Germans would try to disrupt the transportation of the British Expeditionary Force to France. Von Ingenohl's failure to make at least some attempt in this direction showed a lack of enterprise which surprised me, as I think it surprised most naval officers. Our main Fleet was based, as he must have been aware, far away to the northward, and if he had timed an attack on the cross-Channel traffic for a period during which he reckoned that the Grand Fleet, or at least the destroyers, were returning to the base to fuel, he would have stood a good chance of making the attack and returning to his base before that Fleet could intervene.[7]

Admiral Reinhard Scheer, High Seas Fleet commander at Jutland, later blamed the army and civil authorities for not "adopting a fresh joint plan of operations" at the outbreak of war, or sooner. Had the two services cooperated in acquiring for the High Seas Fleet that portion of the French coast "which commanded the Dover-Calais line," England's cross-Channel transportation line, "as well as the trade routes to the Thames, would have been seriously threatened." But Scheer suggested that officials in Berlin and at Army Headquarters totally misjudged the ultimately decisive "influence of England's sea power on the course of the war."[8]

Certainly, planners and strategists in Berlin and Wilhelmshaven too easily dismissed the possibilities of German sea power. The last prewar operational directive issued on July 30, 1914, reconfirmed conclusions reached at the end of the previous winter's war games calling for a progressive whittling down of the British fleet with a series of attacks against anticipated British patrol and blockade forces in the Heligoland Bight "by ruthless mining and, if possible, also by a submarine offensive close to the English coast." Such a war of attrition, one could hope, would result in "a levelling out of the strength" of the two navies, after which Germany could seek an *Entscheidungsschlacht* (decisive battle) somewhere in the North Sea. *Kleinkrieg* would thus lead to *Grosskrieg*. Chancellor Theobald von Bethmann Hollweg approved the plan on August 6, just forty-eight hours after declaration of a state of war between Germany and England and at the moment when the German army began its westward drive with the Battle of the Frontiers. The operational directive did not address the issue of disrupting Britain's transportation and communications lines to France. That was left to a later document apparently drafted several days or perhaps even weeks after the German offensive failed, as a transparent excuse for the navy having done nothing.[9]

The authors of "German Notes on Transportation of the BEF [British Expeditionary Forces]" argued that "the German [that is, Heligoland] Bight would be watched or blockaded with special strictness" by the British fleet "in order to cover the transports" carrying the British army to France. The best way to thwart this strategy was to take "counter-measures against the blockade" as an

> effective means of threatening and thus delaying the transport of British troops. The more frequently and emphatically we take the offensive against the British blockade, the more insecure the enemy will feel and the more difficult it will be for him to decide to permit the transports to sail. Shall we require to damage the transports themselves we should do so chiefly by submarine operations and by mining the routes and entrances to the ports of embarkation and disembarkation.

German naval planners explicitly excluded employing the kaiser's precious dreadnoughts and battle cruisers in the effort. "Should we risk our Fleet for this purpose we should only succeed at best in delaying the transports and not in actually damaging them." With the British Grand Fleet lurking off the Bight in close blockade, any attempted advance southward by German capital ships "would be reported to the enemy in sufficient time for the transports to be able to reach safe harbours, their route being short in comparison to that of our Fleet."

German strategists believed England incapable of transporting its army to France quickly. The Ocean Transport Department of the Imperial Navy Office calculated that British embarkation could not take place for at least a dozen days and perhaps longer after the first mobilization orders went out "and ... disembarkation in Belgian and French ports could not end before the 15th and 16th day" after the commencement of hostilities. "Up to 7th August," the document continued, "reports on the transport of British troops were uncertain and meagre." However, that day German naval intelligence learned from sources in Holland "that the transport of advance parties was to begin that same day and that embarkation of the whole [British] Expeditionary Force would be proceeded with immediately afterwards."

The Kaiser quickly dispatched a message to the High Seas Fleet:

> Transport of the British Expeditionary Force is in progress, probably to Zeebrugge, Ostend, Dunkirk, Calais. British Naval Forces have been pushed forward to positions between the Netherlands-Belgian and the English coasts covering attacks from the North Sea. The 1st [Grand] Fleet is in the North Sea, presumably ready for action. The [enemy] covering forces [in the Channel] offer a good objective for our light forces and minelayers. His Majesty recommends an advance with destroyers, minelayers and

particularly submarines. The method of carrying out the above instructions will depend on the chances of success offered by weather conditions and other circumstances.

Fair enough. Wilhelm apparently was consistent after all. He would wage daring *Grosskrieg* against British sea power, albeit with light forces. But then he threw the entire opportunity away by insisting in the last paragraph of his cable that no heavy units of the High Seas Fleet should accompany and cover the light units, to say nothing of themselves being employed directly against British shipping and embarkation ports. Staff planners at Naval Headquarters promptly—and rightly—concluded that "without the support of the Fleet [that is, the capital ships] it was hardly possible for destroyers and minelayers to penetrate into the Channel during these short moonlight nights and to get near the enemy's transports or even their covering forces."

But the planners, of course, committed a gross error of their own. They never questioned, much less tested, their assumption that Jellicoe and most of Britain's Grand Fleet were in fact lurking on Germany's doorstep, just off the Heligoland Bight. The most cursory investigation by submarine, airplane, or zeppelin would have revealed an empty ocean through which the High Seas Fleet could have sailed down the Channel with impunity to destroy the British transportation line to the battlefields of France. Thus did the German Navy lose its supreme opportunity to influence decisively the course of world affairs. The kaiser's order was never implemented. No light unit or element of the High Seas Fleet stirred from harbor. In the end, Wilhelm—and those who served him—loved their big ships more than victory. Millions of German marks had been spent on what Admiral Hugo von Pohl, second wartime commander of the High Seas Fleet, dismissed as a mere *Paradeflotte* to bolster Wilhelm's *Prestigepolitik.*

Powerful lessons lurk in the unwillingness of the High Seas Fleet to move against British embarkation ports and risk battle with the Royal Navy in the earliest days of the war. Like the Japanese twenty-seven years later, German naval planners could not bring themselves to do the one thing that had to be done if the German surface fleet was to be any sort of creditable resource. To influence in any significant degree a grand conflict at its inception, the High Seas Fleet had to be employed with daring and imagination. "*L'audace!*" General Patton states in the quasi-factual film biography *Toujours l'audace!* Britain's Special Air Services proclaims, "Who Dares Wins." To win the war, the German

Court and Admiralty of 1914 had to act on those principles, and in failing to do so they eventually lost everything.

Helmuth von Moltke had long known of the hesitance of the High Seas Fleet and the kaiser, and so he never considered the possibility of extensive naval support on his seaward flank as he and his generals prepared for a victorious thirty-six- to forty-day battle under the provisions of the Schlieffen Plan. This oversight cost Germany the war. Not only did the small but competent British army of "old contemptibles" swiftly transported to France harry and bloody the oncoming German right flank from Mons onward, but the pressure of British presence or absence at any given moment also helped to fatally shape German troop movements as the enemy chased Charles-Louis-Marie Lanrezac's French army south and east of Paris. And finally, the rush of BEF units into the gap between Karl von Bülow's Second Army and Kluck's First Army decided the climactic Battle of the Marne in favor of the Anglo-French allies.[10] Meanwhile, Belgian troops in the fortress at Antwerp far to the rear continued to hold out throughout the German offensive, something they could not have done had a German fleet controlled the Channel. "The fact that [the Germans'] rapid advance to the south-west left a flank dangerously open on the Belgian coast was appreciated by no one more clearly than Churchill." Not until the end of September, after the German offensive had been repulsed at the Marne, was the first lord of the Admiralty allowed to dispatch several hastily collected, mostly poorly trained brigades of marines and naval volunteers to reinforce the Antwerp garrison. "Churchill's view of the strategic opportunity offered by a landing on the exposed German flank is fully confirmed by our later knowledge of the German High Command's nervousness about the possible consequences of such a move."[11]

Regrettably, the "meagre strength" of the British riposte guaranteed no more than a delay in Antwerp's surrender, and the public believed that Churchill's flamboyant offer to take command of all troops in the besieged fortress transformed an important military opportunity into a farce.[12] Young Winston was widely ridiculed, even in the navy, and his prestige, already weakened by earlier budget battles, was further eroded. Antwerp finally fell on October 10, and the remnants of the Belgian army withdrew down the coast to France. If the cabinet and War Department had possessed another two or three divisions of seasoned troops and deployed them to the enemy flank in Belgium, the Germans could have been in serious trouble after as well as long before the Marne, with incalculable impact on the war.

Even so, the presence of determined, hard-fighting British allies on their flanks and, at the Marne, in their midst restored French resolve. When the German armies, exhausted, hungry, and at the end of their endurance, reached the Marne, it was their generals, Moltke, Bülow, Kluck, and the others, who broke and ordered retreat to the Aisne to save their overextended soldiers. Thereafter, both sides engaged in a "race to the sea" and its precious ports until a line of barbed-wire trenches extended from the Channel to the Swiss border, where they would remain for four awful years. Moltke bluntly told Wilhelm: "'Your Majesty! We have lost the War!'" Admiral Henning von Holtzendorff added that the collapse of Germany's grand plan to end the war in the West had now exposed the country "to the perils of a war of exhaustion—with Britain exercising complete Command of the Sea."[13] A blockade, whether close or distant, would eventually strangle Germany's economic life.

If the British themselves had been more aggressive, the war might have taken yet another turn, one that would have probably concluded hostilities quickly, though on what basis is impossible to say. Jacky Fisher possessed the audacity to see what the British fleet might be able to accomplish in the few years remaining before defensive airpower became a formidable component of battle. From the opening hours of war, Fisher begged and pleaded for an early amphibious assault against the German Pomeranian coast and a blitzkrieg rush to Berlin, just ninety miles away. The first sea lord assured his civilian superiors that the navy could be relied upon to safely transport the army up the North Sea, through the Skagerrak and Kattegat, into the Baltic, and onto the low, sandy beaches of north Germany. But the navy would require "huge amphibian monsters, ploughing their way in thousands like huge hippopotami," and small draft, heavily gunned support vessels like his beloved battle cruisers.[14] While the Royal Navy of 1914 did not possess the requisite thousand amphibian monsters, it could have found suitable assault ships, quickly converted from Britain's enormous merchant marine. But as noted in connection with Churchill's 1913 speculations on possible wartime raids against the Dutch, Danish, or Scandinavian coast, the Admiralty instinctively recoiled from any idea of amphibious operations, which were deemed of daunting complexity. As in Berlin, no one in authority in London, not even the audacious Churchill, was willing to conceive of bold naval operations at the opening of hostilities, especially since Britain had committed the bulk of its army to a western front in Flanders and France as far back as the 1904 Anglo-French staff talks. Had a huge naval amphibious force somehow been scraped together and appeared in the northern North Sea in the days just after declaration of war, it would certainly have provoked the High Seas Fleet to come out and fight, and if the kaiser's navy had been shattered, Wilhelm might well have been induced to immediately sue for peace. On the other hand, the small British Expeditionary Force (the British army sent only six divisions to France in 1914) might well have come-a-cropper against the 850,000 Landsturm troopers that Berlin presumably could still muster to defend Pomerania. Churchill and the government were wise to ignore the pleas of their boldest sailor.[15]

While the High Seas Fleet did not come out of its lair in 1914, other elements of the German navy generated a substantial literature of dashing exploits. Surface forces and raiders like Vice Admiral Maximilian Graf von Spee's squadron—*Emden, Karlsruhe, Cap Trafalgar,* and somewhat later a handful of armed merchant cruisers—kept the Royal Navy busy.[16] But however spectacularly it was reported, the German surface-raider war on the world ocean never significantly disrupted either British trade or, even more important, the transportation of Canadian forces to Europe and Anzac (Australian and New Zealand Army Corps) units to the Mediterranean. After early alarms and frustrations that deeply angered the English people, the Royal Navy quickly swept the first generation of the kaiser's surface raiders from the seas, and by early December 1914 British seaborne commerce was again proceeding unmolested. Britain had lost only 215,000 tons of merchant shipping.[17] Thereafter, only a handful of determined German raider captains were able to sift quietly through Britain's distant blockade to assault commerce, and many of these were discovered by the radio interceptors and code breakers of the British Admiralty's famous Room 40. Only *Möwe* of 1915 and 1917 and *Wolf* and *Seeadler* in the later year evaded Royal Navy hunters long enough to create some havoc. Even at the height of their careers the Royal Navy considered them "no more than an irritant."[18]

At the outbreak of war the German Far East Squadron was away from Tsingtao, and von Spee, knowing that base would soon fall to the Japanese, began a long voyage home. The British Admiralty ordered the Far Eastern Fleet under Admiral Thomas Jerram to first concentrate at Hong Kong, thereby forfeiting any chance that the Royal Navy might bring the Germans to early battle.[19] Von Spee's force of two large armored cruisers and supporting vessels was hurried on its way by a Japanese naval task force, which hunted for the Germans diligently but ineffectively. Thereafter von Spee created much fear but little havoc until his task force reached South American waters. Berlin ordered two independently steaming light cruisers, *Leipzig* and *Dresden,* to engage in raiding actions before joining von Spee, and for several weeks *Leipzig* paralyzed British and French shipping from Vancouver to Panama. Soon after the two ships joined von Spee off Coronel Bay, Chile, the small German fleet destroyed a cluster of under-gunned, undermanned, obsolete British cruisers under Rear Admiral Christopher Cradock. It was the Royal Navy's first defeat in one hundred years.

Then the German squadron headed for the Falklands, misled by British intel-ligence into believing that it could seize essential coal supplies there before units of the Royal Navy arrived. But two of Britain's finest battle cruisers, racing eight thousand miles down the Atlantic, got to Port Stanley hours before von Spee arrived and obliterated the German force in a series of daylong engagements off the Falklands. *Inflexible* and *Invincible* between them expended 1,174 twelve-inch rounds in destroying the German's squadron, suggesting both poor British fire control and continuing flaws in the heavy armor–piercing shells, which often broke up upon contact with German armor plate rather than ripping through it to create internal havoc. Britannia remained mistress of the seas, but the margin of superiority was closer than anyone had imagined.[20]

Only one German ship, the battle cruiser *Goeben,* had a major impact on the early days of the war.[21] When hostilities commenced, Rear Admiral Wilhelm Souchon was coaling his ship and the cruiser *Breslau* at Messina on the north-eastern coast of Sicily. Souchon had conceived a bold, intelligent plan. Theoret-ically, no single British or French warship in the Mediterranean could match *Goeben* in speed and power except three British battle cruisers then in the area. But the Allies did not know that *Goeben* had leaky boiler tubes, which limited its speed to twenty-two and a half knots. Souchon, in turn, did not know that one of the British heavy ships, *Indomitable,* "was in very foul condition" and that her sister, *Indefatigable,* suffered from serious machinery breakdowns.[22]

Souchon reckoned that the three rather new dreadnoughts of the Austrian navy could stand up to any warships that Britain possessed in the Mediterranean as long as they were not bottled up by superior forces in the Adriatic. The kaiser's government hoped that Italy remained an active ally. Surely, the Austrians could sail out of the Adriatic to keep the English—and French—preoccupied long enough for Souchon to take his two powerful ships on a sweep to the west to disrupt transportation and communication lines between France and its North African possessions. At least the two German ships could avoid enemy forces until the Austrians could deal with them.

If the German Admiralty had allowed Souchon to carry out his bold plan the results might have been catastrophic for the Allies. Much of the professional French army, including the foreign legion, was in North Africa. If Souchon could have kept them from the western front during the first critical weeks of the war, German fortunes and world history might have been different. But Berlin soon had other ideas for the squadron.

The political situation in the Mediterranean during the last days of peace in July and early August 1914 was decidedly unsettled. Turkey's commitments were unclear. The Austrian fleet upon which Souchon counted for assistance was contemplating a move to Constantinople. Vienna and Berlin hoped the presence of the Austrian navy at the Porte would lure Turkey to the Austro-German side and allow the Austrians to mount naval operations out of a more secure site than in the Adriatic, where the main base at Pula was subject to bombardment and imminent assault from nearby Serbian-held territory. Austria's handful of battleships, dispatched to the Black Sea, could also raise havoc with Russian land and naval forces there. Rome was known to be wavering toward neutrality instead of maintaining its diplomatic commitments to Berlin and Vienna. London and Paris did not wish to antagonize Italy with its large army and modest fleet. In the last hours of peace the Austrian government finally realized that Constantinople did not possess the facilities necessary to support even a modest naval force, and the Austro-German connection with Turkey threatened to collapse. Just hours after the outbreak of war Italy formally declared its neutrality, and the Austrian Admiralty decided it had to keep the fleet in the northern Adriatic while Italy's final status in the war was clarified. If the Germans were going to lure Turkey to the Austro-German side, they would have to find means other than Austrian sea power to do so. The kaiser's diplomats quickly turned their attention to *Goeben* and *Breslau.*

Completing his coaling at Messina, Souchon sailed southward at best speed to the Algerian coast, which he reached in the few hours between the French and British declarations of war against Germany. *Goeben* shot up Philippeville (Skikda), and *Breslau* bombarded Bône (Annaba). French shore batteries responded, and the Germans withdrew, but Paris and French North Africa were devastated. Fear of a German return spread along the coast.

That afternoon, limping back to Messina to top off his ship's bunkers, Souchon received formal orders from Berlin to proceed immediately to Constantinople. The Wilhelmstrasse and the Porte had just signed a formal alliance; the two German warships would be the talisman of German commitment to Turkey and also the agents of as much mischief as possible against the Russians in the Black Sea. Of course, Souchon could expect no direct or diversionary help from the Austrian navy in his dash to the east. As Souchon considered his new orders, *Goeben* and *Breslau* happened across *Indefatigable* and *Indomitable* sailing on an opposite course. "Strictly speaking, we should have saluted the German Admiral's flag," Brian Schofield later wrote, "but as the smoke of our saluting guns might have been mistaken for opening fire, as an entry in my log book records, 'we loaded all guns but kept them trained fore and aft.'" No gunfire was exchanged because the formal state of war between Britain and Germany was still some hours away, although both sides knew the other would not back down. The two British ships swung about and at maximum speed began chasing the Germans, who escaped thanks to heroic efforts by the stokers and engineers of *Goeben* and *Breslau*.[23]

Souchon was soon back in Messina but was told that since Italy had declared its neutrality, he could remain only twenty-four hours. Learning that the Austrians would not come out of the Adriatic to help him and that the Turks had hesitated in granting him permission to enter the Dardanelles, Souchon gambled that German diplomacy could ease his way, and he took off running—leaky boilers and all—for the Porte.

Vice Admiral Archibald Berkeley Milne, commander in chief of the British Mediterranean Fleet and known to the navy as "Arky Barky," was apparently a rather dim bulb.[24] Churchill sent him ambiguous instructions, which further addled his wits. He was told that the first priority was to protect the French convoys from North Africa, but with three powerful battle cruisers it might also be possible to bring *Goeben* to battle. Milne decided these orders meant that he should engage Souchon only if *Goeben* and *Breslau* moved against the French convoys. Pursuing this interpretation, he broke off his watch over Souchon's ships at Messina and moved his battle cruisers west of Sicily after Souchon's return to Messina and then sent *Indomitable* to coal not at Malta, where it might have been able to stop Souchon's race eastward in tandem with a British force cruising off Corfu, but to Bizerte on the African coast. The two British battle cruisers taking station off Pantelleria could catch Souchon only if they received enough warning that the Germans were leaving port. Milne clearly believed Souchon would come west from Messina to attack the French transports. What he did not know, and what neither the French nor his own admiralty told him, was that after Souchon's bombardment of Philippeville and Bône all convoys between Algeria and Marseilles-Toulon had been cancelled and there was nothing either to protect or to attack.

Goeben and *Breslau* left Messina on the evening of August 6. They were cleared for action, their bands were playing, and Souchon had left his final will and testament behind with Italian authorities. He fully expected to encounter at least two of Milne's battle cruisers as he left the Gulf of Messina and Italian territorial waters. Instead, he found an empty sea. Poor Milne was still dithering far behind him. Now only Rear Admiral E. C. T. Troubridge, sailing off Corfu with the best remaining units of the British Mediterranean Squadron, could stop the Germans. Troubridge had four armored cruisers with 9.2-inch and 7.5-inch guns along with a handful of escorts. Presumably, their engines were in reasonable working order, allowing them some maneuvering room against their crippled German foe. After receiving word that Souchon was at sea with *Goeben* and *Breslau,* Troubridge moved to intercept. But his flag captain, Fawcett Wray, argued that standing orders against engaging superior forces precluded jousting with *Goeben*'s ten 11-inch guns. Although Troubridge's ships greatly outnumbered the German force, which would have to split its main battery fire among at least four powerful vessels, this superiority apparently did not impress either the British flag captain or the admiral. Troubridge accepted Wray's reasoning and decided to stay back and wait for Milne's battle cruisers to catch up. By that time, however, Souchon had an insurmountable lead. The Germans briefly engaged in a long-range running battle with a lone British cruiser but had no trouble reaching the Dardanelles, where, after a brief hesitation, they were allowed in, and the Turkish forts were ordered to fire on any pursuing British vessels that might appear.

Goeben was soon anchored off Constantinople, "carrying with her for the peoples of the East and Middle East," Churchill later observed, "more slaughter, more misery and more ruin than has ever before been borne within the compass of a ship." At the end of October the battle cruiser, now under the Turkish flag but still manned by its German crew including Souchon, entered the Black Sea and conducted a raid against Russian shipping and installations that included shelling the city of Sebastopol. Until that point Russia and Turkey had not been at war, and St. Petersburg desperately wished to avoid a conflict with another enemy that would open one more huge war front and strain the country's resources to the breaking point. The *Goeben* raid, however, settled the issue and led to unimagined consequences, which Barbara W. Tuchman memorably recalled. Russia fell into conflict with Turkey, and

> the red edges of war spread over another half of the world. Turkey's neighbors, Bulgaria, Rumania, Italy, and Greece, were eventually drawn in. Thereafter, with its exit to the Mediterranean closed, Russia was left dependent on Archangel, icebound half the year, and on Vladivostok, 8,000 miles from the battlefront. With the Black Sea closed, its exports dropped by 98 per cent and imports by 95 per cent. The cutting off of Russia with all its consequences, the vain and sanguinary tragedy of Gallipoli, the diversion

of Allied strength in the campaigns of Mesopotamia, Suez, and Palestine, the ultimate breakup of the Ottoman Empire, the subsequent history of the Middle East, followed from the voyage of the *Goeben*.[25]

Never before and only once again (with *Bismarck*) would a single ship dramatize the potentially limitless influence and effect of sea power.

While *Goeben* and *Breslau* raced to the Porte, von Spee's squadron pounded Cradock to pieces off Coronel, and the German offensive died at the Marne, the High Seas Fleet lay at anchor. On August 28 a British force of submarines, destroyers, and light cruisers covered by several of Beatty's battle cruisers burst into the Heligoland Bight, shot up the German patrols, sank three cruisers and a patrol craft, killed an admiral and twelve hundred others, and captured Tirpitz's son before getting away with a few damaged ships. Though the British were fortunate that audacity trumped poor planning and coordination, Wilhelm became hysterical, telling von Ingenohl that he "feared that the fleet might engage a superior enemy. . . . In his anxiety to preserve the fleet, he wished you to wire for his consent before entering a decisive action."[26]

By midautumn 1914 rumors began to swirl around the lower decks of the High Seas Fleet: von Ingenohl had an English mistress and was therefore unwilling to fight the Limeys; the kaiser and his admirals were afraid of risking the big ships. Doggerel began appearing on Wilhelmshaven walls:

> Lieb' Vaterland, magst ruhig sein,
> Die Flotte Schläfft im Hafen ein.
>
> (Dear Fatherland, rest in peace,
> The fleet lies sleeping in port.)

Officers and men began to believe they were wasting their time; worst of all, the navy began to lose its status as the darling of the people.[27] Across the North Sea, Jellicoe recovered his nerve despite the submarine menace, and he dispatched both his Grand Fleet and Beatty's battle-cruiser squadron at Cromarty Firth (and later Rosyth) out on frequent sweeps of the North Sea. "The real trouble about the war," wrote Filson Young about life aboard Beatty's flagship *Lion*, "the thing that robbed it of joy and excitement, was the continued absence of the enemy. Hardly anyone in the fleet had seen a German since war had been declared and only a few had seen a German ship." Young wrote eloquently about the tedium, ennui, and growing sense of unreality that gripped the Royal Navy in those early months when "the King's ships" were often at sea. "The enemy began to grow unreal, chimerical. Was there an enemy after all?"[28]

In Berlin von Ingenohl and his admirals completely misread the situation. They insisted that "the existence of our Fleet, ready to strike at any moment, has hitherto kept the enemy away from the North Sea and Baltic coasts and made it possible to maintain our trade with neutral countries in the Baltic." And having assumed protection of the German coasts, the fleet had freed up troops for use in the fields of both the eastern and the western fronts. Seeking battle with the Royal Navy under these circumstances would be the height of folly. Even a successful battle would not destroy the numerical superiority of the British fleet, which could be expected to initiate "pressure" on the Baltic and North Sea coasts, prejudicially influencing neutral opinion. "The Fleet must therefore be held back and avoid actions which might lead to heavy losses."[29]

But Berlin was as aware as Wilhelmshaven of declining morale, and the Admiralty introduced two caveats: favorable opportunities to damage the enemy severely should not be missed, and *there is nothing to be said against an attempt to use the big cruisers* [that is, Rear Admiral Franz von Hipper's battle cruisers] *in the North Sea to damage the enemy.*"[30] Hipper and his captains immediately set out to implement a *Kleinkrieg-Grosskrieg* scenario. In November and December 1914 his battle cruisers mounted raids against Britain's east coast ports of Yarmouth, Scarborough, Hartlepool, and Whitby in support of mine-laying operations. In January 1915 they went after the British patrols that were protecting the fishing fleet near Dogger Bank. The objective of all three operations was to lure part of the British fleet to destructive battle and thus progressively whittle down the disparity between the two navies.

The Germans did not know that the enemy after the first raid of November 1914 had a priceless intelligence advantage. Aided by incredible good luck and a steadfast Russian ally, the Royal Navy by the end of 1914 had acquired all of the three principal German naval wireless codes along with gridded charts of the Baltic, the North Sea, and the Heligoland Bight, "by which the position of German and enemy forces was indicated when making situation reports." Wireless telegraphy was still a very new technology in 1914 and one restricted to electric signals. Voice transmission lay in the future. Nonetheless, nearly every medium- and large-size naval vessel in the world possessed a "radio shack" for the transmission and reception of unclassified and secret messages, and commanders at anchor or at sea could communicate directly with their admiralties. The new technology thus revolutionized both naval and land warfare, permitting distant governments to have formerly undreamed of command and control over battlefields ashore and at sea. Top-secret naval, military, and diplomatic wireless messages had to be encoded, of course, and successful coding techniques could be traced back to ancient times. Incredibly, however, before the war neither Britain nor Germany had developed any capabilities to intercept and "read" (that is, decrypt) encoded enemy signals. The Russians had created an army intelligence office, but as the Battles of Tannenberg and Lemberg would prove, it was so incompetent that it could not encode all of its own signals. Only Japan (in 1904) and France (in 1912) had established *cabinets noir* dedicated to the exploitation of wireless intelligence.[31]

With the German codebooks in hand, however, the British Admiralty immediately established Room 40, under command of the legendary commander William Reginald "Blinker" Hall, to intercept and translate enemy signals. By midcentury intercepts of enemy messages and orders transmitted to one's own forces in electronic code would be known collectively as C3I—or See Cube Eye—command, communications, control, and intelligence. By the end of the century advances in electronic and video intelligence would expand the acronym to C3ISR—command, communications, control, surveillance, and reconnaissance.[32] But in 1914–1915 few admiralties or commanders had adequately absorbed the implications of the new technology either as an aid to themselves or as a possible windfall to the enemy if security was compromised. Consequently, although those ashore often had some idea not only when the enemy might sail but also where, those afloat were seldom if ever given the big picture or, indeed, became well trained themselves in ways and means to tease it out.

As in World War II, German authorities in 1914–1918 frequently wondered whether the enemy was reading their messages. They changed their codes and keys frequently, and during the war, Churchill recalled, "it was only occasionally and for fitful periods that we were able to penetrate them."[33] But Berlin never fully succumbed to suspicion, believing that British fishing vessels operating in and around Dogger Bank were posing as neutral Dutch to report whatever German fleet maneuvers occurred in the North Sea. So at key moments London was more or less aware of German plans and purposes at sea and passed more or less what was known to the fleet. Thus, when German ships crossed the Jade bar on two occasions in December 1914 and January 1915, the British steamed to meet them.

Little went right for either side. In the first of the three operations the Germans badly shot up Yarmouth, laid a minefield (which claimed a British submarine), repulsed light naval units defending the area, and skipped home before Beatty's battle cruisers could catch them. But German ship handling and operations scheduling between minelayers and battle cruisers left much to be desired.

The next operation in December 1914 was designed to catch Beatty and any other British units in a vise between von Ingenohl, with much of the High Seas Fleet, and Hipper, whose battle cruisers would lure the enemy to sea by bombarding Scarborough and several other Yorkshire port towns.[34] But the British responded by sending out not only Beatty's battle cruisers (including the three that had returned from the Mediterranean once *Goeben* and *Breslau* had escaped to Constantinople) but also the five new *Queen Elizabeth*–class fast battleships with their fifteen-inch guns under the command of Vice Admiral George Warrender. Not knowing the exact location of the German force, its composition, or its plans, the British planned their own rendezvous in what turned out to be the middle of von Ingenohl's fleet. The two destroyer screens brushed each other in the murk and fog of a late North Sea winter night, and von Ingenohl promptly turned and ran, leaving Hipper, who was about to bombard Scarborough, in the lurch. Beatty and Warrender gleefully took off after von Ingenohl only to be jerked back westward on learning of Hipper's assault on the Yorkshire coast.

Although von Ingenohl had escaped, there was still an opportunity to catch and kill Hipper and his big ships. Beatty knew the North Sea minefields and therefore could guess the route Hipper would have to take to return to Germany. Soon Beatty's light-cruiser screen under Commodore William E. Goodenough in *Southampton* picked up Hipper's advance units and began shadowing them. But with funnel smoke swirling around in the rain and gloom, Beatty became concerned that his own force might be attacked by torpedo-carrying German light units once the battle was joined. He wanted those cruisers not shadowing Hipper to return to a position from which they could repel an enemy torpedo attack. He sent out a badly phrased message by searchlight toward the cruiser *Birmingham,* ordering it to resume station with the battle cruisers. Unfortunately, the searchlight beam was broad enough to be picked up as well by Goodenough in *Southampton* who promptly broke off contact with Hipper and hastened to rejoin Beatty's column.[35] The cruiser *Stralsund,* which had spotted Goodenough charging down on the German screen, immediately warned Hipper of the enemy's presence, and the German commander swerved his battle cruisers onto a new course, which the British never guessed. By nightfall the entire German fleet, dodging the British minefields, was back in the Elbe, and both sides wrote and spoke bitterly of missed opportunities. Tirpitz was understandably infuriated: "Ingenohl," he wrote, "had the fate of Germany in the palm of his hand. I boil with inward emotion whenever I think of it." Jellicoe's comment ("The escape of the enemy's force was most disappointing, seeing that our own squadrons were in a very favourable position for intercepting the raiders") was one of the mildest British responses recorded.[36]

A month later, in January 1915, the Germans decided to go to sea again. The Admiralty in Berlin rightly guessed that the two battle cruisers that had defeated von Spee off the Falklands were still steaming homeward. Now was the time to strike before *Invincible* and *Inflexible* returned. Moreover, von Ingenohl believed that the British fishing steamers in the North Sea were a real threat to the High Seas Fleet. If not removed, they could reveal German strength and movement, thus further restricting German operational alternatives.[37] Some of the first naval aerial reconnaissance of the war, conducted by zeppelins, had revealed enemy fishing vessels, augmented by British light units, patrolling the Dogger Bank area.

Wilhelm reluctantly agreed to another operation by fast surface forces despite the risk of battle with the bulk of the Grand Fleet. Von Ingenohl promptly ordered Hipper to make a battle-cruiser sweep of Dogger Bank with cruiser and destroyer screens "to observe the nature of the enemy's patrol work and attack his light forces." At dusk on January 23, 1915, Hipper again took his ships over the Jade bar. Unfortunately, the battle cruiser *Von der Tann* was refitting, so Hipper had to fill the gap with Germany's oldest (1911), weakest (twelve 8.2-inch guns), and slowest (twenty-four knots) big ship, the armored cruiser *Blücher*. But *Blücher*'s guns matched the 12-inchers of the bigger ships in range, and its speed was only a knot or two slower. As Hipper's biographer emphasized, taking *Blücher* along was a justifiable risk.[38]

Room 40 picked up enough information to conclude that "four German battle cruisers, six light cruisers and 22 destroyers will sail this evening to scout on Dogger Bank, probably returning to-morrow evening." Orders for part of the Grand Fleet to sail went out by landline to avoid any possible German suspicion that the enemy might be aroused. Beatty's three available battle cruisers plus the two under Rear Admiral Archibald G. Moore weighed anchor in their new base at Rosyth ("eight hours nearer the enemy") just minutes after Hipper's departure. They were to be joined thirty miles north of Dogger Bank by Goodenough's first light-cruiser squadron from Scapa Flow and Commodore Reginald Tyrwhitt's destroyer force from Harwich at 0700 the next morning. After a night of steaming German and British screens once more brushed against each other, at 0720, just before dawn.[39]

Thinking that he had merely contacted the British light naval patrol, Hipper raced in for the kill, but within minutes *Stralsund* reported heavy smoke bearing north-northwest, indicating the presence of enemy capital ships. Hipper believed that such a large force could only be the advance guard of the entire Grand Fleet, and he immediately broke off and turned his squadron back toward the Bight. But *Blücher* could make only twenty-three knots through the heavy seas, and the British were literally pouring on the coal and oil, racing toward the astonished, dismayed Hipper at twenty-six to twenty-seven knots. High on *Lion*'s compass platform, Beatty and his staff stood exulting in a chase at speeds never before attained in naval warfare and anticipating the first salvoes between dreadnoughts. Aboard *Indomitable*, young midshipman Brian Schofield heard action sound at 0845. "I grabbed my notebook and pencil and rushed up on deck and clambered into my turret. Test loading gear—everything correct—then up on top of the turret to look round. Off the starboard bow, four battle cruisers, *Lion, Tiger, Princess Royal* and *New Zealand* cleaving the water at full speed. On our port bow the distant smoke of light cruisers, ahead the black and heavy smoke of the enemy in full retreat followed by three light cruisers leading a host of destroyers." *Indomitable* failed to keep pace. But gradually the British came within heavy-gun range of the fleeing Germans, and at twenty thousand yards *Lion* opened fire on *Blücher* at the rear of the German column as Beatty and his staff briefly descended into the battle cruiser's conning tower before returning to the compass platform with its unparalleled view of the action.[40]

For the first time smoke played a major role in naval combat; this had not been a factor about which Lord Nelson had needed to worry. Initially, Hipper's range finders and gunners were blinded as they struggled to fight off the fast-closing enemy. But as the British came within range of Hipper's column, smoke began to obscure his ships from British gunners. Nonetheless, both sides found the range and in a running battle began to pound each other. An eleven-inch shell damaged *Lion*, as Beatty, eager to destroy the entire enemy column, signaled his small fleet to engage corresponding ships in the German line. But battle cruiser *Tiger*'s captain erroneously believed that *Indomitable* was in action with *Blücher*, when it actually was still out of range. *Tiger* thus joined *Lion* in concentrating fire on Hipper's flagship *Seydlitz*, which left the battle cruiser *Moltke* undisturbed to concentrate its batteries on *Lion*. To compound the error, *Tiger*'s gunners, peering through the heavy smoke spewing from guns and funnels, mistook the *Lion*'s fall of shot for their own and thought they had found the range on *Seydlitz*, when in fact they were overshooting by nearly three thousand yards. Nonetheless, *Lion* did land a devastating salvo on *Seydlitz*, destroying both its after turrets, one by detonation, the other with an explosion when the flash fire created by the detonation raced unimpeded through a connecting ammunition chamber whose doors had been left open to allow passage of shells and powder. Only the less volatile German cordite and powder bags saved the ship from being blown up, and on return to port the German Naval Command immediately ordered that all magazine doors be firmly secured during battle, a precaution the British did not think to take.

Meanwhile, Moore's flagship, the battle cruiser *New Zealand*, began pounding *Blücher* to pieces, and when *Indomitable* finally appeared, Beatty ordered that battle cruiser to concentrate on *Blücher*, leaving *New Zealand* free to fire on Hipper's three remaining battle cruisers.

> Flash, flash, flash—bang, bang, bang, the battle raged. . . . At 10:31 the enemy altered to port and so did we and that brought my turret into action against the *Blücher*. In and out recoiled the guns as we pounded the enemy. "Left gun ready," shouts someone and another 850 lbs of explosive goes hurtling toward the enemy. At about 10:45 a Zeppelin joined the action and dropped a bomb about 20 yards on our starboard bow with a bang like a gun going off; however soon after it fell prey to the guns of a light cruiser.[41]

Unfortunately, *Seydlitz* was beating up on *Lion* by this time, and as *Blücher* fell back toward the advancing British column in flames, *Lion* was slowed to fifteen knots by heavy shell hits on and below the waterline (with its open magazine doors, the battle cruiser was saved from a destructive explosion only because the fire in its "A" turret was easily contained due to the small quantity of ammunition in its turret lobby). Suddenly, the British were distracted by a U-boat scare: lookouts on several ships claimed positively that they had spotted periscope wakes, although in fact no U-boats were within sixty miles of Dogger Bank.[42] Beatty ordered an evasive turn to the northeast, which took the British battle line across the German wake at nearly a right angle with the flaming *Blücher* nearby and the rest of the German ships fleeing toward Heligoland as fast as their stokers could shovel.

As *Lion* fell back, Beatty, seeing his control of the battle slipping away, frantically ordered his battle-cruiser captains to "engage the enemy's rear." He intended that the British fleet resume its chase of Hipper. But in all the noise and excitement *Lion's* signalmen had not lowered the flags calling for the earlier course change, and a confused Moore, now in command, though far astern of the lead battle cruisers *Tiger* and *Princess Royal*, thought that the two signals in conjunction meant that the entire British line was to focus on the hapless *Blücher*, which it did. Moore was also misled by a bogus signal from the German Admiralty, further garbled by his staff during retransmission, that the entire High

Seas Fleet was preparing to "come out" to Hipper's rescue. Beatty, "horrified" at the sudden abandonment of the chase, promptly ordered a destroyer to come alongside the damaged *Lion*, and he raced off in it to rally his battle line.[43] But by the time Beatty arrived *Blücher* was sinking and Hipper was disappearing over the horizon. Beatty climbed aboard *Princess Royal* and resumed the chase, but he soon realized he could not catch the Germans before they reached the Bight, the protection of their own minefields, and the guns of the Heligoland fortress. He turned back to Rosyth with *Indomitable* towing *Lion*. Once again a substantial part of the German fleet had escaped because of human error and incompetence in the Royal Navy. Moreover, German gunnery had clearly been superior to that of the British: Hipper's retreating ships had scored fourteen hits on *Lion* and *Tiger* with only three hits scored on them.[44]

"The disappointment of that day is more than I can bear to think of," Beatty wrote. "Everybody thinks it was a great success, when in reality it was a terrible failure," very possibly due in part to poor coordination between the two battle-cruiser commanders, Beatty and Moore, for which Beatty, as overall commander, must share the bulk of the blame.[45] But the public knew nothing about a victory lost because of carelessness. Motion-picture cameramen had been aboard Beatty's big ships and had recorded the awful death of *Blücher*, capsizing in cold, heaving seas, its guns trained uselessly toward the heavens while the doomed crew scrambled like ants over the upturned, rapidly sinking hull. Britain had downed a (small) enemy capital ship and driven the Hun back to skulk in his harbor again. That was all that mattered.

The Germans thought so too. "Profound depression" gripped the High Seas Fleet and the Admiralty in Berlin. A "thoroughly inept" operation met a deserved fate. Von Ingenohl and several of his key staff were sacked, and the kaiser concluded that the entire war at sea should now be borne by mines and submarines. By the end of 1914 the U-boat had already proved that it could disrupt fleets and destroy warships; undoubtedly, it could destroy large numbers of unescorted merchantmen as well.[46] Just two weeks after Dogger Bank, Berlin announced the establishment of its own war zone around the British Isles. This counterblockade, which the High Seas Fleet had been unable to achieve either through battle or simply by swinging around its anchor chains at Wilhelmshaven and Cuxhaven, the submarine would now try to enforce through terror.

Britain's blockade of Germany (initially undertaken by old small cruisers, soon found to be unfit to battle the frequently towering seas between Scotland and Norway, and then by large armed merchant cruisers) has never received much attention except as an important factor in ever shifting Anglo-American relations between 1914 and 1917. The most recent and authoritative naval history of the Great War devotes only seven pages to the enterprise.[47] Yet there is no doubt that the blockade was intended to be Britain's supreme expression of sea power. Bottling up the High Seas Fleet would allow the northern patrol and Royal Navy units in the Channel to suppress enemy and neutral shipping, ultimately starving Germany to death in terms of both food and munitions.

To accomplish this objective Britain's maritime lawyers stretched the meaning of contraband to the limit and squeezed the rights of neutral shipping to the vanishing point, allowing the king's sailors to flagrantly and repeatedly violate prewar international law embodied in the 1909 Declaration of London. That declaration specifically favored land powers by excluding not only food but also raw materials from the list of prohibited contraband. As the world's mightiest sea power, Britain never accepted the declaration for obvious reasons. As a continental power, Germany announced its adherence to the declaration early in the war for equally obvious reasons, as did the United States, the wealthiest and most economically powerful neutral on the North Atlantic rim. The blockade immediately strained Anglo-American relations over such issues as the neutral status of American-owned ships formerly under German registry, the arming of British merchantmen and their appearance in American ports, the detention of U.S. steamers by British warships, and Germany's right to wage unrestricted submarine warfare. President Woodrow Wilson's response to the British blockade was often characterized, in the words of his chief biographer, by "immaturity and inherent confusion."[48] Was the blockade worth the severe strains it created in Anglo-American relations? Did it work? The answer is an unqualified affirmative.

The first British Order in Council was issued on August 4, 1914, and the contraband list conformed essentially to that set forth in the Declaration of London. Subsequent orders issued in September and October 1914, however, made "severe inroads" into the "free list" of articles generally assumed to be beyond seizure by a blockading nation.[49] These included foodstuffs and raw materials critical to the German war effort. On November 5, 1914, with its northern patrol finally in place, Britain announced a broad "military area" on the approaches to Europe within which *all* civilian ships, without exception, would be stopped, boarded, searched thoroughly, and, if necessary, seized.[50] The blockade proved a humiliating ordeal, especially for those nations like the United States seeking to defend neutral rights. Wilson was tempted to break off relations with London on several occasions, and those in the U.S. government and Navy with long memories would fashion later postwar policies accordingly, much to Britain's detriment.

Britain's blockade extended from the Arctic Circle to the Brittany peninsula and westward into the Atlantic to the eastern coast of Iceland. When Germany announced its own counterblockade by submarine in February 1915, it included the British Isles and the continental coast from southern Norway to Brittany, an area that encompassed the effective reach of the 1914–1918 U-boat. Within this "war zone" all enemy vessels would be destroyed without warning, and neutral vessels would be in grave danger because of British misuse of neutral flags.[51] As British naval historian Antony Preston has observed, the German gamble might have paid off "if the neutral countries could have been persuaded" by the success of Berlin's counterblockade "to forbid their ships to trade with the Allies." But the effectiveness of the British blockade against Germany meant that neutral shipping companies could exchange goods only with Britain and France, "as there was not enough trade with other countries to keep everyone in business. It was a fact of life which had brought Napoleon's Continental System crashing in ruins" little more than a century before.[52]

On March 11, 1915, the British responded to the German counterblockade by issuing the most sweeping Orders in Council of the war. They declared not only a virtual blockade of all German ports (exercised from a distance, of course) but also the intention to stifle all indirect seaborne commerce to and from Germany through adjacent neutral territory. By carefully articulating and applying the doctrine of continuous voyage, "the British were successful in stopping the greater part of Germany's overseas trade." This latter provision could not truly be enforced at sea; it required the cooperation of the neutral states on Germany's borders, that is, the Netherlands and the Scandinavian countries. But once again British sea power proved to be decisive. Britannia ruled the waves. If neutral states wished to maintain their non-German overseas trade, they had no choice: either bend to England's will or face the possibility of being indicted as a cobelligerent by the arrogant, high-handed lords of London. His Majesty's government quickly obtained agreements with the most important of the European neutrals, and the ruthless strangulation of Germany's overseas trade continued.[53]

In the three years between November 1914 and November 1917 the Royal Navy's armed merchant cruisers on northern patrol intercepted nearly 13,000 vessels, 1,816 of which they seized and sent into English or Scottish harbors under armed guard. An additional 2,039 vessels voluntarily sailed into British examination ports, and 642 vessels managed to escape the blockade net. Britain lost 7 armed merchant cruisers to submarines; 1 was sunk in action with the armed German merchant raider *Grief,* and 2 sank in heavy weather.[54]

The several patrol lines "were arranged so that a reasonable attempt could be made to intercept all approaching ships. The preliminary line was west of the Hebrides, based on St. Kilda and extending northwestwards towards Iceland. This was backed up by other patrol lines, one extending north of the Shetlands, one based on the Faeroe Islands and a third in the waters north of the Faeroes." In late January 1915, Admiral Dudley De Chair, commanding the Tenth Cruiser Squadron, sailed out to the patrol lines from his headquarters on the Clyde River at Liverpool. Over the next six weeks he recorded the routine work of the squadron: ships on patrol, ships coming off patrol, ships refueling ("coaling") at Loch Ewe on the west coast of Scotland. The merchant cruisers spent hours "chasing" various vessels or dodging mines that intelligence reported were laid either by enemy trawlers or by freighters flying neutral flags. Armed parties were sent aboard various cargo and passenger ships to find either nothing, some contraband, or in one instance several passengers traveling under assumed names who "were probably German Reservists." All suspicious ships were sailed under armed guard into Kirkwall (a mile from the Scapa Flow anchorage) or another one of the various small ports in the Orkneys or northern Scotland. In these early months of the war, some neutral skippers remained eager to cooperate with British authorities. When his vessel was boarded on Sunday, February 14, 1915, the captain of the Norwegian sailing ship *Olav* "stated that he felt sure the cargo, which was bran, was intended for Germany. There were three Germans among the crew." Whenever enemy minelayers were reported in the area, De Chair sent his merchant cruisers on sweeps in an attempt to find them, though few were successful. Breakdowns were more frequent than anyone liked. On February 25, for example, De Chair detached HMS *Colmbella* "to proceed to Liverpool . . . relative to her unsatisfactory loading and bad steering." HMS *Calix* had to repair its "W/T" (wireless telegraph, or radio) while under way in "severe weather," and was soon sent back to the Clyde to refill its coal bunkers. Eighteen months later, in the high of summer of 1916, De Chair's successor, Vice Admiral Reginald Tupper, undertook an inspection cruise of his own with the Tenth Squadron. Although weather conditions were much improved, the security situation had deteriorated markedly. While neutral ships now reported numerous U-boat sightings round the north coast of Scotland and between the Faeroes and Norwegian coast, neutral skippers were proving far less cooperative. On August 19, for example, "*Almanzora* reported that the American Auxiliary Schooner *Speewell* bound East with fish had been intercepted in the neighbourhood of Lagnaes by the armed trawler *Saxon* and sent in to" the Irish port of "Lerwick with an armed guard. She had no Consular Certificate and refused to sign a guarantee."[55]

Postwar Britons were convinced that the blockade had worked. First Sea Lord Eric Geddes claimed that after 1916 every cry from the Central powers for an armistice contained a plea to lift the blockade. German spokesmen claimed otherwise. In January 1917 the head of the German War Food Office said:

> There is absolutely no question of our ability to pull through. Despite the blockade and the practically complete stoppage of our imports, despite the partial failures of some of our own crops last year, we have enough food. We do not pretend that it is all that we should like to have. There are numerous things which we enjoy, but they are not necessary. We eat them with pleasure when we have them. But we do not starve without them, nor do we lose health and vigor for the lack of them.... I tell you there is absolutely no question of starvation for the German people.[56]

For many years, the German bureaucrat's assertion found broad acceptance. As late as 1960, the international military historian Lynn Montross wrote that although the British blockade caused 1917 to be known as the "Turnip Year" in Germany, "Teutonic self-pity exaggerated the privations, but there can be no doubt that the national diet was monotonous even if sufficient." In fact, the blockade did work but only after a prolonged period and in tandem with Teutonic blundering. Onerous as the British Orders in Council were, European neutrals found ways to work with them, if not around them. The Netherlands government, for example, and its businesspeople decided to place all their import business into the hands of a trust that "negotiated with the Allied governments over the issue of trade.... In various guises," the resulting agreements "became the pattern for other neutrals," including the Danes, Norwegians, and Icelanders. Later in the war, the British developed the idea of the "Navicert" or "Letter of Assurance" to ensure that while no agricultural contraband reached Germany, sufficient food supplies were guaranteed to the neutral nations. At the point of ships' loading, either in the United States, another Western Hemispheric port, or elsewhere, a document was issued by local British inspectors declaring that the goods being shipped "were as stated, that they were consigned to acceptable recipients, and were within the [food] ration for the particular destination country." Although the inspectors were invariably thorough and their inspections tedious, time was actually saved, for "by telegraphing copies of manifests with Navicert numbers, to the Contraband Committee" in Great Britain, "a ship would be assured of rapid consideration, and perhaps even of an undisturbed passage.... The beauty of the system," a recent analyst has concluded, "lay in the fact that all these measures...were actually by and large operated by the neutrals themselves."[57]

Despite the blockade, German soldiers at the front remained well equipped and well provisioned, as industrialists found acceptable substitutes to cover the severe shortage of manganese. Invention of ersatz wool and leather products also meant that both the civilian population and the troops were reasonably well clothed.

But from the beginning of the war, civilian food supply was a problem, at once created and compounded by gross bureaucratic insensitivity and incompetence. Although the Anglo-French Somme offensive of summer 1916 proved disastrous for the Allied cause, it did impress the Germans with Britain's determination to commit all its resources to victory. The next month Germany embarked on the Hindenburg program of enormous expansion in munitions production at the expense of the rest of the national economy. This resulted in a "chronic neglect" of agriculture: men, horses, and fuel were taken from the land to serve the needs of the army or the war factories.[58] By the fall of 1916 there were severe shortages of meat, milk, and bread on the home front. That year's crop was poor not only because of a disastrous agricultural policy but also because of persistently bad summer weather throughout the country. The comfortable classes somehow managed to maintain their supplies, but the middle and lower classes suffered increasingly, although communal kitchens throughout Germany fed the poor better than they could have fed themselves.

The winter of 1916–1917 brought outright calamity. A freezing autumn brought failure of the potato crop, and Germans found little more than turnips to eat. Albert Speer recalled that as a twelve-year-old youngster from a wealthy urban family with no relatives in the countryside who could send food, he "gradually consumed...in secret...a whole bag of stone-hard dog biscuits left over from peacetime." Letters to the front and the fleet described civilian pain, and the resentment of Wilhelm's sailors, swinging forlornly around anchor chains in Kiel and Wilhelmshaven, turned to fury when they realized that not only were the fat cats at home somehow managing to eat well but so were their own officers, who were served from separate kitchens. As enlisted rations were cut and cut again and enlisted pay disappeared, the officers continued to live and eat well. "Insisting on their privileges and determined to maintain their superiority over the men, the officers allowed a revolutionary situation to arise in the fleet by their stubborn maintenance of unequal rations." By the spring of 1917, after only two and a half years of war, the British blockade had created a crisis in German morale on both the home front and in the High Seas Fleet. This was a remarkable achievement considering that "it took ten years of blockade and the disastrous campaign in Russia to defeat Napoleon after Trafalgar."[59]

No one in 1914 anticipated a long war; no one in 1915 wished to endure one. At Christmas 1914 Churchill wrote Prime Minister Herbert Asquith asking could "the power of the Navy" not "be brought more directly to bear upon the enemy?" With his quick mind the first lord saw an emerging and potentially eternal stalemate in the West, and concluded that "if the fronts or centres of armies" in the "decisive theatre" of action could not be broken, "their flanks should be turned. If these flanks rest on the seas, the maneuvers to turn them must be amphibious and dependent on sea power. . . . The least-guarded strategic points should be selected for attack, not those most strongly guarded." Churchill had happily supported Fisher's call for a campaign in the Baltic, where a modest British submarine offensive in conjunction with the Russians was going nowhere while the Germans easily shuffled their major fleet units back and forth between Wilhelmshaven and Kiel as the needs of the eastern front required. An invasion of Schleswig-Holstein would neutralize the Kiel Canal, bring Denmark in on the Allied side, and prepare the way for an Anglo-Russian amphibious operation that would land the czar's armies only ninety miles from Berlin. When this proposal elicited little enthusiasm, the focus of interest shifted to the Belgian coast. Perhaps the Royal Navy could support an assault on the German trench lines at the mouth of the Yser River. If successful, the operation could be progressively broadened to roll up the entire enemy trench system on the western front, north to south. But the Admiralty quickly squelched the idea: its "light ships" could not stand up to German coastal artillery, while the battleships "could not be risked in such confined waters." Undeterred, Churchill next suggested a dramatic operation at the other end of Europe as an alternative to "sending our armies to chew barbed wire in Flanders."[60]

Shortly after the outbreak of war, Turkish leader Enver Pasha sent an army south toward British-dominated Egypt. Several months later, he launched a major invasion of the Caucasus. Both operations rapidly came to grief, but Czar Nicholas and his generals became alarmed. The Turks might be inept, but they seemed determined, and despite their dramatic decline as a world power in the nineteenth century they still retained a fearsome reputation as warriors. If not checked, Turkey posed a clear and present danger not only to southern

Russia but also to British interests in the Middle East, which included the Suez Canal as well as the oil-rich Persian Gulf from which the Royal Navy derived an increasing amount of its fuel supply. When Nicholas begged his British cousin King George V and France for a "military diversion" in the eastern Mediterranean, the Western Allies responded with alacrity. Churchill quickly took up the argument that an "amphibious enterprise to strike down Turkey" would not only remove grievous pressure on Russia's southern flank but also "influence and rally the Balkans." This was a critical point, for Italy, territorially avaricious but militarily weak, was on the verge of completing its swing from tepid prewar association with the Central powers to outright alliance with Russia and the West. Together with a revivified Serbia, Italy could form a strong southern front that would tie down a substantial portion of the Austro-Hungarian army while completing the ring of steel around Germany and Austria. An "amphibious enterprise" against the Turks might well do more than that, Churchill concluded. Dismissing Admiralty fears for the fate of the battle fleet in restricted waters, he insisted that if the Gallipoli Peninsula dominating the narrow Dardanelles could be seized "with an adequate army by an amphibious surprise attack," an Anglo-French fleet could be "passed" into the adjacent Sea of Marmara to besiege and take Constantinople, thereby exposing Turkey to "a fatal stroke." With the Turks subdued, a direct all-weather supply line to Russia became available as well as a back door for the direct invasion of Austria-Hungary up the Danube corridor. Ultimately, Germany itself could be threatened.[61]

Throughout his life Churchill displayed a weakness for subordinating military realities to political fancies. Twenty-eight years after Gallipoli he would press for the main Allied assault against Germany to be made not across the beaches of northwest Europe but in the Adriatic, supposedly the "soft underbelly of Europe," with the decisive thrust to follow through the Ljubljana gap to Vienna and on to Berlin. Anyone who has been to Ljubljana knows that the town lies in a perfect defensive position: a handful of well-armed divisions could hold the heights against the road corridors below for months, if not forever. Europe's soft underbelly was in fact embedded with sharp bones and protected by tough skin with the most vicious teeth.

So it was at Gallipoli. A small force could easily defend forever the rocky, mountainous peninsula, lying athwart the Dardanelles, if an invading enemy tipped its hand soon enough. Minefields in the waters supported by heavy artillery on the adjacent heights could make the strait a death trap for an assaulting navy. Churchill waved these objections aside. Good administration and intelligent staff work might have saved the first lord from folly, but neither existed within the British Admiralty.

In the age of Nelson a commander at sea had operated from sketchy hand-written orders from Whitehall and when battle loomed might call his captains to the flagship for a brief tactical discussion. This had become a useless model for waging effective war between huge, powerful, fast-moving steel battle fleets. It was even less effective when a modern navy sought to project power ashore against a well-informed, well-entrenched enemy. The applicatory system developed by the Germans and slowly being incorporated in the U.S. and Japanese war colleges was useless in the absence of well-conceived doctrines and a competent staff willing to apply them consistently.

Churchill had been dispatched to the navy with orders to create such a staff. He had done so, but three years later it "was not functioning properly," in large part because unimaginative sea lords regarded staff work "with distrust, not to say contempt." Moreover, Churchill and Fisher were men of "passions and enthusiasm"; each was used to exercising much authority and having his own way. They recognized the qualities in each other and retained a firm but always wary friendship. But the pressure of their partnership had to explode somewhere, and subordinates were often victimized by the whimsical wrath of their superiors. It was rash and often professionally suicidal to speak out against them or their plans. Vice Admiral Frederick C. D. Sturdee, chief of staff at the outbreak of war, compounded the problem. He was supposed to possess keen strategic abilities and insights but was actually wedded to the belief that Britain's capital ships were invulnerable, despite serving most of his career as a torpedo specialist and having long exposure to the emerging submarine service. Moreover, Sturdee was a pompous fool who "'would never listen to anyone else's opinion.'" Captain Herbert Richmond, who himself "tended to overreact in frustration," complained that Sturdee's sense of self-importance led to an aura of impenetrable secrecy in which no one "'is allowed to know what great issues are in contemplation. The result is that no one can help.'" After three months of war Sturdee was removed and sent to the Falklands to redeem himself by killing von Spee, but after his departure the war-plans staff at the Admiralty never stood up to Churchill or to Fisher who indulged in schemes and vendettas that continually distracted both Admiralty planners and the fleet throughout the Dardanelles campaign.[62]

The divided, fractious Admiralty was confronted throughout the war by a public that always wondered: "Where is our navy?" By dispatching its professional

army to the Continent (and later raising another and far larger army of conscripts) Britain had embraced both a maritime and a continental strategy. The
navy could enforce the former, but by the end of 1914 it could only assist the
latter by helping to open up a second front. Churchill was determined to do so,
and on January 13, 1915, heeding cries for help from St. Petersburg, the cabinet approved the Dardanelles campaign.[63]

Whether Gallipoli could have been captured by a secretly mounted and rapidly
executed amphibious assault is a moot point; Churchill had already concluded
that a naval assault on its own could succeed in pushing past the peninsula and
into the Sea of Marmara. British battleships would soon be shelling Constantinople, forcing the city to surrender, firing the Balkans with insurrection that
would require the withdrawal of thousands of hard-pressed German troops
from both the eastern and western fronts, and opening an all-year supply route
to the Russian ally through the Black Sea. "The fact that success seemed possible
without commitment of substantial bodies of troops made the project seem
attractive" at a time when the casualty figures from the stalemate in the West
were rising daily.

The army and many in the navy were skeptical of the fleet's ability to force
the Dardanelles by itself. Months before the outbreak of war, naval and military
experts had emphasized "the futility of sea attack alone" in reducing enemy
fortifications ashore. Both at Santiago in 1898 and at Port Arthur six years
later, armies had had to be landed together with long-range heavy-siege guns to
bring about the surrender of fortified land positions.[64] Others in Britain's Senior
Service were excited by the challenge and convinced it could work. One of the
most vociferous champions of Gallipoli from start to finish was dashing young
Roger Keyes, commander of submarines at the outbreak of the war who sought
and was awarded the job of naval chief of staff just as Gallipoli was getting under
way. "We are all desperately jealous & frightfully interested in your doings,"
Commodore Tyrwhitt, commander of the Harwich Force, wrote Keyes at the
time of his appointment. "I can imagine you, perfectly happy & without a
care. I honestly think you have a much bigger thing on than you had as Com
[S] & I am sure you will enjoy it all a hundred times more." But as a powerful
force of British dreadnoughts and pre-dreadnoughts (including units sent from
home waters) gathered off the Adriatic island of Lemnos, Colonel Maurice
Hankey, secretary to the British War Council, warned colleagues that everyone
in the Admiralty, "from Lord Fisher downwards," who knew of the coming operation "believes that the Navy cannot take the Dardanelles position without
troops."[65] They were right. Efficient in defense against a High Seas Fleet of

equal composition but inferior strength, undeniably adept at blockading, the Royal Navy proved unable to project its power ashore.

Despite widespread misgivings in London, the French decided to make a modest contribution to the operation in order to dramatize and advance their own substantial imperial interests in the area. Paris despatched four pre-dreadnoughts and a number of cruisers and destroyers to the Aegean. If the British were successful, France's postwar imperial interests in the Near East would not be compromised; if the operation failed, the heavy preponderance of British forces would guarantee that England would receive by far the greater share of humiliation.

Vice Admiral Sackville Carden, commander of the Anglo-French fleet, began bombarding the small Turkish forts at the mouth of the Dardanelles on February 19, 1915, but stopped until February 25 because of bad weather. If the Turks had not learned of British designs before, they had now, and Carden and the weather gave them ample opportunity to respond by establishing nearly impregnable defensive positions. By March 1 Carden's ships had pushed one-third of the way up the Dardanelles, reaching the first Turkish minefields at Kephez. But there the operation was stopped dead as concealed, mobile Turkish batteries prevented the battleships from effectively supporting the minesweeping operations. It quickly became clear that the effectiveness of flat-trajectory guns on land targets had been overestimated, "whereas the difficulties of spotting and fire control" from the ships had been grossly underestimated.[66] Caught in a stalemate, Rear Admiral John de Robeck, who relieved the exhausted Carden on March 11, nonetheless continued to send optimistic messages back to London about the progress of the campaign, despite his initial misgivings about the entire operation. His attitude was buoyed by the always enthusiastic but not always thoughtful Roger Keyes who noted privately the "extraordinary preparations the Germans [sic] have made to prevent a landing—they must have spent thousands. Searchlights of the most modern and powerful description. One was mounted on a motor car." Still, Keyes remained buoyant at this early stage in the operations, adding, "Pity we have to destroy all the booty."[67] At the Dardanelles, as later in Vietnam, the prosecutors of an increasingly dubious enterprise stubbornly claimed to see a light at the end of the tunnel.

But London had already decided that only an amphibious assault on Gallipoli could force the Dardanelles. An army was sent to hastily built quarters on Lemnos. Numerous Anzac units that had reached Egypt quickly followed British troops to the island. Soon there were eighty-one thousand Allied troops jammed onto the island, and chaos quickly degenerated into tragedy. Disease swept the camps (celebrated poet Rupert Brooke was one of the earliest fatalities), while to the north de Robeck found it impossible to push his battleships past the Kephez minefields even though he made desperate attempts at nighttime sweeping. Three Allied pre-dreadnoughts blundered onto a secret Turkish minefield near shore and were sunk, and the battle cruiser *Inflexible* was badly damaged. Despite considerable gallantry the battleships and minesweepers had failed, although Churchill and especially Keyes always insisted that just one more effort by de Robeck could have succeeded.

Embracing folly rather than courting wisdom, London determined to press on. Orders went out to General Ian Hamilton on Lemnos to land his forces on the Turkish shore and on Gallipoli. An amphibious expedition was hastily and chaotically mounted, and British troops managed to push ashore at Cape Helles on the southern tip of Gallipoli, while the Anzacs mistakenly landed on a narrow beach farther up the peninsula. A smaller French force invaded the Asiatic shore of the Dardanelles as a diversion. Within hours, the Anzac position became desperate. Rapidly recovering their nerve, Turkish gunners on the heights above began to pour down a withering barrage on the Anzac beach. Aboard the pre-dreadnought *London,* part of the offshore fire-support gun line, young midshipman Charles Drage noted, "Although the Turks had guns on both flanks, they couldn't actually see Anzac beach and so see how accurate their fire was. They could have blown us off the beach altogether." *London* and her two pre-dreadnought sisters moved in close to the beach and returned fire, but that evening the Anzac commander lost his nerve. The incessant enemy barrage had driven his troops back to the last ditch, and he signaled the fleet: they must be taken off. Young Drage and several other midshipmen were ordered to man small boats and soon found themselves being towed in the battleships' wakes toward the beach. An awed Drage later wrote that the midnight black sky "over the shore was simply white with shrapnel bursts." But Vice Admiral Cecil F. Thursby refused to evacuate, and the mighty new dreadnought *Queen Elizabeth,* lead vessel of a five-ship class of fast battleships that would see active duty in both world wars, arrived at dawn and drove the Turk gunners back with its own devastating counterfire. The Anzacs were saved, but only for further ordeals.[68]

Slowly, agonizingly, over the first few weeks, British and Anzac forces pushed up the cliffs from their landing beaches at or near Cape Helles and managed to establish trench lines on the heights. But there the exhausted, bloodied troops were stymied by determined Turkish forces. The Germans soon dispatched a handful of submarines to assist the Turks. The U-boats managed to sink two other British pre-dreadnoughts supporting the ongoing operation, and thereafter these undersea craft waged always irritating if not spectacularly successful war throughout the Mediterranean. At the same time the British sent submarines to Lemnos and then into the mine-laden Dardanelles. A handful of incredibly brave—or foolhardy—British submarine skippers managed to sneak through the Turkish defenses and into the Sea of Marmara, where they eventually sank two old Turkish pre-dreadnoughts and more than forty other vessels before being re-called at the end of 1915. All won Victoria Crosses, one of them posthumously.[69]

On August 8 British forces made a fresh landing at Suvla (Anafarta) Bay far-ther up the peninsula in order to move in behind and outflank the well-entrenched Turkish defensive line near Cape Helles. Twenty-eight years later, at Anzio, Allied forces would try the same tactic to gain the same end. In both in-stances the attacks failed for lack of rapid and resolute advance against a momen-tarily stunned foe (indeed, the Gallipoli and Italian campaigns of 1915 and 1943 respectively bear similarities that are nothing short of haunting). Both of-fensives quickly bogged down amid heavy casualties.

For months British and Anzac troops huddled in their trenches on the various beaches and heights of Gallipoli, as the steadfast Turks waged a textbook war of defense, preventing the various "shallow and static enclave[s]" from coalescing into a single powerful force. Gallipoli proved to be as costly and stalemated a trench war as the western front. With no end in sight, Keyes returned to London to beg for one more naval assault. He convinced the head of the Imperial General Staff, Lord Kitchener, who decided to go out to Gallipoli and see for himself what could be done to break the stalemate. Keyes later wrote sadly to a colleague that when Kitchener left England, "he told me he was determined never to agree to the evacuation of the [Gallipoli] Peninsula and if it was forced on him he would be the last man to leave!" But once on the spot, Kitchener was surrounded by "'the Egyptian limpets' as they were called," men who insisted that any large Middle Eastern force must defend Egypt rather than make an impossible assault on Turkey itself. When Keyes went to Kitchener to plead for continuation of the offensive to clear Gallipoli of the enemy, the old man replied: "I have seen the place, you can't possibly do it." He had wired the Admiralty twice to get their views, Kitchener added, "and had heard nothing in return." Moreover, the generals on the spot were beginning to turn against the campaign. When Keyes sought to stiffen their resolve, "they both talk[ed] of a loss of 50,000 men and much material, and say that sentiment cannot be allowed to interfere with 'higher Military Strategy.' General Sir Charles Monro and his colleagues were now obsessed with the idea that the only place to fight the Germans is in Flanders or France, that men employed elsewhere are being wasted." On November 22

Kitchener cabled London recommending the evacuation of Suvla and Anzac beaches, with the retention of a foothold at Cape Helles. The War Committee decided instead to wrap up the whole campaign and evacuate completely. Keyes still refused to give up, and when de Robeck went back to England, exhausted in mind and body, the determined young man successfully pressed his case on de Robeck's successor, Rear Admiral Rosslyn Wemyss. But when the two approached Monro with cables from London (Churchill?) opposing the evacuation and proposing one more naval assault to force the straits with the army held in reserve to exploit whatever advances might be made, the general continued to evoke "higher Military Strategy." The Hun must be confronted and broken in France. "He said even if we open the Straits and appear off Constantinople and reduce it, what then? It isn't going to win the war in France." Keyes's insistence that abandonment of the campaign would throw Britain's Middle Eastern forces back to Egypt with great loss of prestige in the Near East and Balkans failed to move the army chief. Keyes was overruled, and the British and Anzacs evacuated Suvla and Anzac beaches by small boat on the night of December 19–20 and Cape Helles eight days later. Together, British, French, and Anzac forces lost 265,000 men. The British "29th Division had lost its strength twice over, while the New Zealanders, of whom 8,566 served on the peninsula, recorded 14,720 casualties, including wounded who returned two and three times." The Australians lost two-thirds of their troops.[70]

In their withdrawal, the British and Anzacs demonstrated either marvelous capability or experienced incredibly good luck, for their Turkish hosts let them go without firing a shot. In World War I, as in World War II, the British proved that although they were frequently inept as seaborne invaders, they were masters of seaborne withdrawal.[71]

The Anglo-French effort of 1915 to knock Turkey out of the war was a disaster, and it cost Churchill his cherished job. But it did not in and of itself directly threaten continued British supremacy on the world ocean or significantly weaken the Allied war effort on the strategically crucial western front. Even if the campaign had succeeded, it would not have materially affected the Austro-German war effort. Without delving deeply into the melancholy debate over Gallipoli, the conclusions of British historian Stephen Roskill seem, on balance, irrefutable. Churchill failed to consult his war planners or to ask for staff assessments of a campaign against the Dardanelles. Nor did he honestly represent the reservations of his "top sailors" to the War Council. Churchill not only exaggerated the effects of naval gunfire—and especially British naval gunfire with its weak heavy shells—against either fixed or mobile shore batteries but also committed "the really colossal blunder" of assuming that naval operations alone could force the Dardanelles and thus bring the Turks, and perhaps the Germans and Austrians, to the surrender table. Even if the Anglo-French fleet carrying the expeditionary force with it had been able to force the Dardanelles, it did not possess either the manpower (until much too late) or the resources to control a city of more than one million inhabitants while fighting off an inevitable Turco-German-Austrian counteroffensive waged along strong interior lines of communication.[72]

But the real disaster of the Dardanelles campaign, as Roskill observed, was that "it not only threw serious doubts on our competence to plan and conduct war operations efficiently but it revealed for the first time that, despite the splendid qualities of its fighting men, the greatest empire of the day might prove to be built on a foundation of sand."[73]

In retrospect, Gallipoli can certainly be understood as the first major instance in the twentieth century in which the armed forces of a nominally non-Western country frustrated a Western imperial power. The later humiliation of British, French, Dutch, and U.S. forces in the Far East by the Japanese juggernaut of 1942 and the crushing setback of advancing Anglo-American United Nations troops by the Chinese army in Korea in November–December 1950 completed the process of destroying Third World deference and respect for the ostensible moral and material superiority of the West. By 1955, at the very latest, the age of empire was over.

CHAPTER 7

Jutland

THROUGHOUT THE SPRING of 1916 Reinhard Scheer sent Franz von Hipper's battle cruisers on raids against the English coast. They bombarded Lowestoft and Yarmouth again, causing panic along the East Anglian coast. Winston Churchill and the cabinet promised that no more raids would be allowed, but John Jellicoe guessed what Scheer was really up to. He warned David Beatty that the Germans might be about to decoy the independent British battle-cruiser force into a hopeless conflict. To Beatty's many critics, then and now, Jellicoe's warning seemed most appropriate. Beatty was rash and lacked specialist training in gunnery, signals, or torpedoes. "He was a protégé of Mr. Churchill," wrote Commander John Irving, and thus prized by a "gladiator-conscious public" for "the panâche they desperately required" after nearly two years of bloody, frustrating, stalemated warfare.[1]

Scheer grew bolder. To lure Beatty and perhaps other squadron commanders, Hipper's big ships would have to bombard a town closer to the enemy's battle-cruiser anchorage at Cromarty Firth. Scheer planned a raid on Sunderland on May 17, but damage to the battleship *Seydlitz* postponed the operation nearly two weeks to the twenty-ninth. Then he set sail.

Jutland might have been the first three-dimensional naval conflict in history if Scheer's desire to lure part of the Grand Fleet into a submarine trap had worked or if U-boats below and zeppelins above had been able to provide the High Seas Fleet with the intelligence it needed.[2] Certainly, the British Admiralty was confident of its intelligence sources. Room 40 had now learned to intercept and decode a large number of enemy transmissions. So adept had Blinker Hall's

people become by this time that Whitehall was convinced that no German vessel could move without London, and thus Scapa Flow, learning of it.

On the other hand, Germany owned the skies over the North Sea, thus providing Scheer with a major intelligence source of his own whenever the gods of
weather permitted. Friedrich von Ingenohl and Hipper fully appreciated the
long-range reconnaissance capabilities that Count von Zeppelin's lighter-than-air
ships provided. One of them, L-5, had hovered helplessly over *Blücher* at Dogger
Bank, witnessing the armored cruiser's agonizing demise. Another, as Brian
Schofield noted, nearly bombed the battle cruiser *Indomitable*. Upon taking
command, Scheer quickly concluded that airships accompanying fleet units
could provide "security" against surprise by superior forces.[3]

During the early months of the war, however, the Royal Naval Air Service
(RNAS) was "the most aggressive air arm of any nation" as its seaplanes and
land-based "aeroplanes" mounted dusk and dawn patrols over the North Sea
from several harbors and airfields in East Anglia looking for surfaced enemy
U-boats or advancing enemy fleet units. However, frequent murk and clouds,
short hours of winter daylight, and an unwillingness or inability to patrol during
morning and afternoon hours greatly reduced the effectiveness of the patrols.
Seaplanes proved more promising as attack weapons, and the zeppelin sheds
and bases across the North Sea quickly became the focus of their attention.
One aviation expert has recently insisted that the RNAS antizeppelin campaign
of World War I rather than the Battle of the Coral Sea in 1942 or the assault on
the Italian naval base at Taranto in 1940 marked the beginning of aerial "strike
warfare" from the sea. Early on Christmas morning 1914 nine of the earliest
and crudest seaplanes ever built were lowered into the North Sea from their
"carriers," HMS *Empress, Engadine,* and *Riviera,* at a position twelve miles north
of Heligoland for a raid on Cuxhaven. The three ships were covered by cruisers
and destroyers of Commodore Reginald Tyrwhitt's "Harwich Force." Each aircraft carried an observer and three bombs. "The raid was actually a failure,"
Empress's captain, F. W. Bowhill, wrote, "due to low cloud and thick fog inshore."
Only seven planes actually took off: three returned. The crews of three others
were picked up by submarine, "while the seventh landed safely alongside a
Dutch trawler." *Empress* itself was attacked by two German seaplanes and one
zeppelin. The zeppelin "numbered L6 . . . dropped her bombs from the central
car; the bombs apparently being lowered through a hole in the centre of this
car." In retaliation Captain Bowhill promptly issued rifles to his crew who blazed
away at the attacking aircraft and dirigible with enthusiasm and possibly some

result, though none fatal. But Bowhill concluded that "a Zeppelin attack can be beaten off by continuous rifle fire, particularly so when at such close range." Angered by the pesky zeppelin, Bowhill at last turned to his single "12 pounder" gun to fire eight shots at the German craft. "One, I think, went very close as she sheered right off and did not worry me again." So ended what Admiral Hezlet has characterized as "the first carrier strike in history," which might also go down as the first attack against "carriers" by enemy aircraft.[4]

Britain employed seaplanes during the Dardenelles campaign. The tender *Ark Royal* was sent from the North Sea to the eastern Mediterranean with a half-dozen aircraft to provide scouting and gunfire-observation support to the fleet. The results were mixed. Tethered balloons functioned much better in spotting fall of shot, though later seaplanes and land-based airplanes were instrumental in finding and providing the gunfire observations that destroyed the German commerce raider *Koenigsberg* holed up in an East African river. In August 1915, as the Gallipoli campaign moved toward its unhappy climax, British seaplanes engaged in aggressive bombing attacks against Turkish communications, and a Short 184 aircraft from the fast seaplane carrier *Ben-my-Chree* staggered into the skies with the world's first aerial torpedo and launched it from an altitude of just fifteen feet. The tiny fourteen-inch missile managed to strike a five thousand–ton Turkish supply vessel that had grounded after being torpedoed by a British submarine. Naval aviation had now completed all the tasks of which it would ever be capable (a few aerial "dogfights" had already taken place in the earlier raids against the German zeppelin sheds in Europe). The only job remaining was to elaborate technologies and techniques.[5]

But that proved to be a daunting assignment. Although seaplanes had achieved some success in Africa and at the Dardenelles, they were terribly crude and fragile, proving consistently inoperable in even moderate seas and often frustrated by bad weather. After nearly two years of war, the RNAS and the British Admiralty began to look at true aircraft *carriers* with flight decks for launching and landing conventional planes as the optimum solution to deploying at sea the increasingly promising medium of airpower.[6]

By this time, the zeppelins' main strategic role as an instrument of terror had been firmly fixed. German airships first bombed London in August 1915, even as Royal Navy seaplanes continued futile attacks against their sheds and bases. Nor were British pilots able to effectively intercept the zeppelins either on their way to or returning from raids. When Churchill left the Admiralty late in the year he took with him much of the enthusiasm for sea-air operations in general and sea-based attacks on enemy zeppelin sheds in particular. But with the assaults against English cities creating a measure of public panic, the Royal Navy had no choice but to continue attempting to bomb enemy airship bases.

As Scheer elaborated plans in May 1916 to lure a portion of the Grand Fleet to its doom, British planners hit upon a new stratagem. For the next raid against the zeppelin bases, why not bring the Royal Navy's seaplane tenders right up to the High Seas Fleet's front door by placing them off the island of Sylt? Surely, the Germans would respond with at least a portion of their fleet, and Jellicoe's battleships waiting just over the horizon could pounce. Scheer never took the bait. During the course of a raid that should have lured the Germans, only three of eleven British fliers managed to get airborne from alongside their sea-plane tenders, and the only one who got over the enemy coast bombed the wrong facility. The zeppelin raids continued, and Scheer stayed in port.

Undiscouraged, Jellicoe turned to other ways and means to force the High Seas Fleet to come out and fight. He planned a major surface operation for the first days of June built around a light-cruiser raid in the Kattegat and a major British naval demonstration in the Skagerrak employing Beatty's battle cruisers. Using Beatty's ships as bait, Jellicoe and the main part of the Grand Fleet would lie to the northwest and race down against Scheer's battleships as soon as they appeared against the battle cruisers.

Thus, both sides by the spring of 1916 were eager for a major fleet action. Planners on either side of the North Sea had elaborated much the same scenario involving battle cruisers as bait and lure. But Scheer's reliance on zeppelins and submarines proved fatal. The long-planned raid on Sunderland had been post-poned because bad weather prevented adequate aerial reconnaissance over the North Sea, and by the time it could be rescheduled German submarines had been on patrol so long off Scapa Flow and the Firth of Forth that they were about to be recalled. Scheer hastily devised yet another plan. Before the U-boats were forced to withdraw, he would send Hipper north up the coast of Jutland with the bulk of the High Seas Fleet following some fifty miles behind. Beatty and perhaps some of the Grand Fleet at Scapa might well take the bait and race after Hipper. The German submarine patrol off the English coast and Scapa Flow would spot and perhaps ambush these units. If not, zeppelin reconnaissance over the Dogger Bank area and farther north would pick up British ship move-ments, providing Scheer and the submarine commanders precious information on which to plan an ambush either by U-boat or by surface units.

But the usual cloudy, foggy North Sea weather, with its few moments and patches of light and sun, defeated the zeppelins, while the German submarine line was robbed of any potential usefulness by mechanical troubles, poor visibility,

slow speed, and enemy destroyer screens. Although some U-boats spotted elements of the Grand Fleet departing from Scapa Flow and Rosyth, their commanders never grasped the fact that the entire Royal Navy was going to sea, thus
depriving Scheer of invaluable intelligence.

The initiative, therefore, fell to the British with their superior signal-intercept
and decoding capabilities. But Room 40 also failed. Because its analysts did not
realize that Scheer had decided to change his radio identification code when he
went to sea (the High Seas Fleet had not been out of its anchorage as a unit in
more than a year and had never steamed under Scheer's command), the Admiralty, Jellicoe, and Beatty were promptly informed of some German ship movements but received only vague, misleading details. Thus, as the entire Royal Navy
steamed out of Scapa Flow, Harwich, and Cromarty Firth near midnight on
May 30, 1916, several hours before Hipper's five battle cruisers began crossing the
Jade Bar, Jellicoe had no idea that the whole German battleship fleet, sixteen splendid dreadnoughts and six pre-dreadnoughts, along with eleven light cruisers and
sixty-one destroyers, was on Hipper's heels. At sea hours later the two British commanders continued to receive false or fragmentary information from Room 40.

Shortly before 1300 the following afternoon, as Beatty's battle cruisers steamed
toward their rendezvous with Jellicoe's main fleet units, both men were handed
a dispatch from the Admiralty sent less than a half hour before: "No definite
news of enemy. They made all preparations for sailing this morning. It was
thought Fleet had sailed but directional wireless places flagship *[Friedrich der
Grosse]* at Jade at 11:10 GMT. Apparently they have been unable to carry out
air reconnaissance which has delayed them." As John Irving observed, this rather
blasé message removed any sense of urgency regarding the need either to seek
out the German force or to effect a rendezvous of Grand Fleet units so the entire
weight of British sea power could be brought to bear against whatever enemy
units might be found. The dispatch also encouraged a false sense of security,
which lent a nearly fatal hesitancy to the actions of Jellicoe and especially Beatty
throughout the coming hours.[7]

The two commanders might have known the truth if their own air reconnaissance had been more effective. Beatty had with him the seaplane tender
Engadine. When he first encountered Hipper's squadron at midafternoon, he
immediately ordered the ship to launch a broader search. One of *Engadine's* four
aircraft managed to get aloft and apparently spotted through the low clouds at
least part of Scheer's fleet behind Hipper. But when the sighting report reached
Engadine the searchlight attempt to relay the information to Beatty on *Lion* was

garbled. Shortly thereafter, mechanical problems forced the seaplane to land, and heavy seas prevented further launches. *Engadine's* slow speed caused it to fall behind the rest of Beatty's forces, and the tide of battle quickly swept well beyond the little ship and its crude, flimsy aircraft. Because commanders were unable to obtain essential intelligence, the two fleets would have the full-scale clash that neither side truly wanted.

If Tsushima resembled an Indian attack on a slow-moving wagon train, Jutland approximated a classic infantry-artillery battle like Antietam or Gettysburg, with ignorant armies slowly coming onto the field piecemeal and groping for an enemy that neither expected to encounter when they did. Beatty sailed from Rosyth not only with his usual complement of six battle cruisers but also with four brand-new, fast fifteen-inch-gun battleships of the *Queen Elizabeth* class, the apex of early-twentieth-century British battleship design. The four vessels were designated the Fifth Battle Squadron, under Vice Admiral Hugh Evan-Thomas who also enjoyed the usual assortment of screening and scouting cruisers and destroyers. Jellicoe had with him from both Scapa Flow and Moray Firth twenty-four dreadnoughts, three battle cruisers under Rear Admiral Horace Hood, and a large number of light cruisers, armored cruisers, flotilla leaders, and destroyers.

The British Fleet in the North Sea on the last day of May 1916 was a sight of blundering industrial might never before seen on the world ocean. As dawn touched the murky waters and turned dark to light gray, observers on the decks and bridges of the big ships saw their fellow leviathans take shape in columns on either side, five or more in all. "'As far as you could see, looking over the bows, there would be ships going down over the horizon. And as far as you could see astern, more ships. And each side to port and starboard would be cruisers and destroyers, really a breathtaking sight.'" Glimpsed from afar coming over the horizon, the vast armada appeared first as column after column after column of black smoke. Then the warships big and small passed in parade moment after moment after moment, seventy-eight small, feisty destroyers capable of making thirty-five miles an hour, then the eight big armored cruisers together with twenty-six "light" sisters and at last the twenty-eight dreadnought battleships and nine battle cruisers; all of Britain's seaborne might, ready it would seem, to replicate Nelson and win a war.[8]

Beatty and Jellicoe were to rendezvous at roughly midafternoon in the middle of the upper North Sea unless Beatty came across Hipper first, which he did shortly after 1400 hours. Unlike Dogger Bank, the German and British screens might have missed each other completely if both had not caught sight of a small Danish steamer between them and found each other when they went over to investigate.

After the usual prolonged, confused period of suspicion and identification, Beatty, with his six battle cruisers and four fast battleships, went racing off to meet what he rightly guessed was Hipper's inferior fleet. But, as always with Beatty, discipline in the handling of orders and signals was faulty, and confused maneuvering instructions from the flagship *Lion* caused Evan-Thomas's battleship squadron to momentarily fall far behind the battle cruisers. When the British and German fleets finally encountered one another at 1535, German luck, range finding, and shooting proved to be better than those of their enemy and German hulls more stout. Beatty's force was silhouetted by the sun in the western sky, appearing "crisply" in German range finders. The gunnery officer in *Derfflinger* later wrote, "'Suddenly my periscope revealed some big ships. Black monsters; six tall, broad-beamed giants steaming in two columns'" of threes.[9] Beatty's force suffered from a lapse in firing discipline so that for many minutes the British ships, with bigger, longer range guns, closed without shooting, handing the initiative to Hipper's gunners until at last the captain of *Lion* opened fire on his own initiative and the other five battle cruisers swiftly followed. Suddenly, thousands of throats went dry—many for the last time—as men glimpsed the first muzzle flashes of the enemy's great guns through the gloom. When the duel began, Beatty's gun directors concentrated their shooting in such a way that *Derfflinger* was left alone for some time, free to fire on whichever enemy ship or ships she wished.

For a while the two squadrons of battle cruisers blazed away, both sides obtaining wounding hits on the other. Beatty's gunners drove one of Hipper's escorting cruisers, *Wiesbaden*, under the waves and pounded two others close to death. But the Germans were hitting too, and at 1604 three 11-inch shells from Germany's oldest battle cruiser, *Von der Tann*, struck *Indefatigable* near its forward turret. Suddenly, thousands of astonished British and German seamen witnessed a sight no one had ever seen before. A nearly six hundred–foot piece of modern machinery foaming through the seas, crammed with humming engines, blazing guns, electric lights, food, ammunition, tables, chairs, bunks, hammocks, and nearly eleven hundred men, abruptly vaporized into nothingness in one horrendous thunderclap of an explosion. Shortly thereafter, the battle cruiser *Queen Mary* was hit. Aboard her sister ship, *New Zealand*, a spotting officer saw a small cloud of what appeared to be coal dust erupt from where the vessel was struck, and then the entire ship disappeared in "a terrible yellow flame" and heavy, dense smoke. When *Tiger* came abreast of the wreck, its propellers still slowly revolving and men crawling out of the top of the after turret, there was another huge explosion. "The most noticeable thing was the masses and masses of paper which were blown into the air as the after portion exploded. Great masses of iron were thrown into the air and things were falling into the sea around us."[10] Many a Tar, convinced that no British ship could be destroyed in such a manner, cheered the handful of poor devils struggling in the water, convinced that the destroyed vessel and its sailors were the enemy.

Flagship *Lion,* too, was hit repeatedly, and a serious fire began that forced a flooding of the magazines to save the ship. Beatty may well have been shaken, although he tried not to show it. As fire and smoke settled over the shattered remains of *Queen Mary,* the admiral turned to his flag captain and uttered the immortal complaint: "Something's wrong with our bloody ships today." He had signaled the still-distant Jellicoe at 1545 that he was in heavy combat with the German battle cruisers, and Jellicoe sped up to come to Beatty's defense. But when Evan-Thomas hurried to the scene, fortunes changed. The battleship boys could shoot more rapidly and accurately than their cousins in the battle cruisers, and Hipper's ships began to take a terrible beating.

The conflict that naval enthusiasts had been dreaming of for a half century had finally materialized. As the two lines of warships continued to pound away at each other, Beatty and Hipper unloosed their light forces for close-in attacks. Small ships darted forth at express-train speed to meet in a wild melee in the watery no-man's-land between the battle lines. Overhead, the air shook with the thunder and concussion of the huge naval rifles, while the 3- and 4.7-inch cannons of the small boys barked and torpedoes hit the water everywhere. Slim gray hulls twisted through seas heaving with towering fountains as 11-, 12-, 13.5-, and 15-inch shells hit the sea and detonated. Occasionally, there would be a terrible scream of suddenly torn metal as a torpedo or a shell found its mark and a German or British destroyer slowed to a halt, smoke pouring from its innards, bows or sterns already awash. As the big ships were hit, turrets erupted in flames, steam lines burst, decks were torn apart, and upper works and hulls became wrecks and tombs for hundreds of men.

Slowly, with infinite care, Hipper drew the unsuspecting Beatty and Evan-Thomas toward Scheer's main force, leaving Jellicoe and most of the Grand Fleet fifty miles to the north, steaming hard to catch up and, as the fleet commander

would later write, totally confused as to "the true position of our battle-cruisers
and of the enemy's advanced forces."

> The earlier reports from the *Galatea* between 2:20 p.m. and 3:40 p.m.
> referred to German light vessels, but reports from the *Nottingham* at 3:24
> p.m. and from the *Galatea* at 3:25 p.m. indicated that other vessels might
> be present. In a signal timed 3:35 p.m. Sir David Beatty in the *Lion* re-
> ported having sighted five German battle-cruisers, with destroyers, and
> gave his own position at Lat. 56° 53'N., Long. 5°33'E. and the bearing of
> the enemy as N.E.... Ten minutes later... the *Lion's* position was given as
> Lat 56°53'N., Long. 5°33'E., giving a distance travelled in 10 minutes of
> 3 miles, or a speed of 18 knots on a course E. by S. ¼ S. Signal 1530, inter-
> cepted in the *Iron Duke,* had stated the speed of the Battle-Cruiser Fleet as
> 25 knots an hour and the course as east. In signal 1550 in which Sir David
> Beatty reported that he was engaging the enemy the *Lion's* position was
> given as Lat. 56°53'N., Long. 5°31'E., showing a movement of 1¼ miles
> to the westward in the 5 minutes elapsing since the previous report.[11]

Commodore William E. Goodenough, Beatty's light-cruiser screen captain,
first glimpsed Scheer's battle fleet through the uncertain light of a cloudy, misty
day made more hazy by heavy funnel and gunpowder smoke. The commodore
bravely held course in order to determine the size and composition of the enemy
squadrons. Soon he radioed an accurate report to Beatty, who, as supreme scout
commander, correctly maintained his own course until he could confirm his
subordinate's sighting. Then Beatty and Goodenough turned and ran. But once
again Beatty's signal gang blundered, garbling the retreat message on the *Lion's*
yardarm, and precious minutes were lost before Evan-Thomas got the word.

Whereas Hipper had once been in danger from a superior British force
(gravely weakened by Evan-Thomas's inability to reach the battle scene on time),
so now Beatty was in trouble. But just as Hipper had drawn his unsuspecting
adversary onto the German fleet, so now the British battle-cruiser commander
was about to return the favor. Whatever sins of omission or commission both
men may have committed that day, Beatty and Hipper used their battle cruisers
as they were intended to be used: as scouts, bait, and lure.

Knowing that Scheer's main force was coming up rapidly behind him, Hipper
raced after Beatty's battle cruisers while Evan-Thomas's battleships sniped
viciously at the advancing German column from the rear of the retreating
British line. It was after 1730 by this time, and with course changes the light
began to shift, favoring the British. The Germans coming up from the south-

west were now silhouetted against the slowly declining sun, whereas the British, racing north and eastward, were moving in murk and haze. Gun directors aboard Hipper's ships could frequently discern the enemy only by his muzzle flashes.

Although Beatty had lost two of his big ships, British gunnery, especially that of Evan-Thomas's battleships, continued to fearfully maul the German battle cruisers. *Von der Tann* was so badly battered that it literally became gunless; its entire main battery was knocked out, and it remained in the line merely to mislead the enemy into thinking it was still intact. *Lützow, Derfflinger,* and *Seydlitz* were badly damaged. But the Royal Navy was on the run, and to the exultant Germans this was a chance that could not be missed. Hipper's men gave as good as they got, and the battleships *Malaya* and *Warspite* took a pounding as they retreated toward the safety of Jellicoe's guns.

Jellicoe was coming up fast. But in the thick haze of the North Sea afternoon and the excitement of battle, with no messages from Beatty for more than forty minutes and mist, cloud, and funnel smoke providing "very baffling light," Jellicoe was never certain at any time before contact occurred exactly where the enemy was or its size and composition.[12] At 1755, hearing heavy but unexplained gunfire ahead, Jellicoe plaintively signaled the leading ship in his starboard-wing division: "What can you see?" Five minutes later he received a reply from *Marlborough:* "Our battle cruisers bearing SSW (189°) steering east (77°). *Lion* leading ship." Not until visual contact was made soon after with the entire High Seas Fleet was Jellicoe fully aware that Scheer was present as well as Hipper and that the moment had finally arrived for decisive combat.[13]

As soon as he had received word of Beatty's initial contact with Hipper, Jellicoe had dispatched Hood with his three battle cruisers to help. Riding *Invincible*, Hood left the Grand Fleet column at 1605 but did not reach the combat area until shortly after 1800. He was coming in at an oblique angle from the north and east because of uncertainty about Beatty's exact position, which was determined only when four of Hipper's scout cruisers ambushed, shot up, and almost sank the cruiser *Chester*, screening ahead of Hood's forces. Around 1820 Hood's three ships and their escorts finally came into visual range of the approaching enemy. The British opened up on the advancing Germans as Jellicoe's main line trailed just behind. Spotting the three new British battle cruisers ahead, Hipper immediately guessed that the entire Grand Fleet was at sea and close by. He fell back on the head of Scheer's column as the Germans opened fire on the oncoming British units and were themselves struck by heavy gunfire from *Invincible* and its mates. *Invincible* was hitting hard with its big guns when at 1832 it was

struck by a heavy shell in the "Q" turret, which blew the roof off and caused
a flash fire that "shot down to the magazines" and tore the entire 17,250-ton,
567-foot hull to pieces in a matter of seconds. Although the figures vary slightly,
at least 1,021 men, including Hood, perished instantly. Only *Indomitable* now
remained of this three-ship class, the first battle cruisers ever built.[14]

But now Jellicoe was on the scene, about to ambush the still-unsuspecting
Scheer. Since Beatty had been completely silent on the German position, Jellicoe
was not sure how to deploy for battle. The commander in chief had placed his
twenty-four dreadnoughts in a cruising formation of six divisions of four ships
each, in line abreast, that covered five miles of ocean. He would have to deploy for
battle, on either his port or his starboard column, depending on his estimation
of which direction the enemy would appear.[15] The deployment of the battleships would consume fifteen to twenty minutes, and if Jellicoe guessed wrong,
his fleet could be completely at the mercy of an inferior enemy.

Nor did Beatty enlighten him. As the dashing battle-cruiser commander
forced his ships between the Germans advancing from the southwest and the
Grand Fleet swinging around to the northeast, he steamed right across Jellicoe's
bow. To his chief's anxious query about the enemy's precise course and whereabouts, Beatty replied with a laconic enemy-position report. Making the situation worse, Beatty brought his ships into Jellicoe's formation on an angle, indicating that he believed the Grand Fleet commander was about to form a single
line to starboard, or to the west, which would have allowed Scheer either to
wage battle on very favorable tactical terms or to practically steam right on past
and escape. Beatty compounded his felony. "The whole British Battle Fleet
was not able to get into action during this period," Jellicoe would later write
with understandable irritation, "several ships, particularly those in the 2nd Battle
Squadron at the van, being unable to see any of the German ships and others
having their fire temporarily masked by their own ships. In each case this was
due to the passage between the opposing battle fleets of our battle cruisers" and
supporting vessels.[16]

Jellicoe, however, guessed right. Seeing *Lion* coming up fast from the southwest, he ordered a deployment to port, that is, to the east. This threw the British
battle line into confusion for many minutes as ships and squadrons struggled to
get into position. The situation was complicated when the helm jammed aboard
Warspite of Evan-Thomas's division, sending that damaged battleship into several complete turns. At this moment Rear Admiral Robert Arbuthnot, commanding two old armored cruisers screening ahead of Jellicoe, spotted Scheer's

main fleet and created a momentary diversion by recklessly throwing his ships at the enemy. Both were smothered by heavy-caliber gunfire. The flagship *Defiance* blew up and sank with all hands, and the badly damaged *Warrior* limped away.

Meanwhile, German attention was briefly distracted by *Warspite*'s ordeal. The battleship soon regained sufficient maneuverability to escape the area, and as Jellicoe's ships gradually moved into the proper battle line, it was clear that the Grand Fleet commander had achieved a near-miraculous solution: he had crossed Scheer's T. Indeed, with his many more heavy ships he had done more: he had created an arc across Scheer's bows that extended from the port to starboard flanks of the advancing German line. The Grand Fleet could now use the majority of its heavy guns in repeated broadsides against the enemy, whereas the advancing Germans could employ only their forward guns against the British. Moreover, Jellicoe was east of Scheer, not only cutting off the Germans' line of retreat to the Bight but also placing the High Seas Fleet in the light of the afterglow while the British remained in the dusk of the dying day. It seemed that the climactic moment of the battleship era had come.

Perhaps it had already passed. Jellicoe later came to believe that the passage of Beatty's battle cruisers through his formation, the necessity to sort out his battle formation, the smoke from funnel and cordite fumes, and the murk and mist of a dying northern afternoon all conspired ("had the undoubted effect") to "save the van of the German Battle Fleet and their battle-cruisers from a concentration of fire which might well have proved disastrous to them."[17]

Nonetheless, for many long moments, Scheer was unaware of the terrible trap into which he was steaming; the limits of the human eye, even when aided by telescopic enhancement, precluded understanding. Enemy forces had appeared piecemeal in front of him; he was growing uneasy about his distance from home base and somewhat weary of the chase. Having sunk three British capital ships, he could congratulate himself on a major victory. Suddenly, he was handed a dispatch from the commander of one of his destroyer flotillas. Survivors picked up from an enemy destroyer sunk earlier stated that at least sixty big enemy ships were in the vicinity, including twenty dreadnoughts. Before he could properly digest the news, the entire horizon ahead of the German fleet erupted in a line of gun flashes. Completely lacking the kind of advance intelligence information available to Jellicoe and Beatty, Scheer experienced a sudden, "stupendous" shock. The plight he abruptly confronted was summed up in the German official history of the battle:

His bases were some hundred and fifty miles away, his fleet was faced by a more numerous enemy and, thanks to the presence of the German II Squadron [of pre-dreadnoughts], he was woefully inferior in speed to his opponents. To turn his fleet at once towards home would have meant the inevitable loss of his slower ships and grave danger to the whole fleet if it stayed behind in an attempt to support them. The only chance appeared to be to keep the British Fleet at a distance during the few remaining hours of daylight and then use the darkness for escape.[18]

For ten minutes between 1830 and 1840 enemy gunfire mercilessly pounded the main part of the German High Seas Fleet, while Scheer, as blinded by mist, murk, and smoke as his enemy counterpart, struggled to understand the situation.[19] Another Trafalgar seemed in the making. But it was not to be. The weak penetrating power of British shells undoubtedly saved several of Scheer's ships, including the comparatively well-armored battle cruisers, from total destruction, though three of them suffered heavy structural damage forward as they approached the British line. The resultant flooding was so extensive that *Lützow* sank on the way home, *Seydlitz* reached port in a virtual sinking condition (though it was repaired), and *Derfflinger* was in the yards being rebuilt until mid-autumn. Most important, the struggle seemed just as confusing and uncertain from the British side as from Scheer's bridge. Admiral Thomas Jerram, who had come home from the Far East to command a battleship squadron within the Grand Fleet, wrote in his after-action report to Jellicoe that "it was impossible to gather any general idea of the action, only momentarily glimpses of the enemy being obtained." Jerram complained that visibility on his bridge and in the fire-control stations was "hampered" by the hazy atmosphere, by "what I imagine to have been cordite fumes from the battle cruisers after they passed us, and from other cruisers engaged on the bow," and by funnel gases "from small craft ahead, and, for a considerable time by dense smoke from" the cruiser *Duke of Edinburgh* "who was unable to draw clear."[20]

The half-dozen and more battle reports from Jerram's subordinate commanders aboard the battleships and cruisers of the Second Battle Squadron echoed his own sense of confusion. Even as they followed Jellicoe in crossing Scheer's T, they did not seem to realize the situation. They complained that their bridges were wreathed in smoke and haze. Only a handful of gunnery officers high in the foretops of one or two ships obtained a reasonably clear view of the scene. Otherwise, only one or two of the leading enemy vessels (most often the battle cruiser *Derfflinger*) were sighted visually. As the enemy began steaming into British gun sights partially obscured by smoke and haze, neighboring vessels or aggressively handled escort destroyers and cruisers suddenly "cut off" fire from one battleship or another by getting in the way of the target.[21]

Once they gathered their wits, Scheer and his captains reacted with a brilliant act of seamanship that confirmed the professional competence of a very young service. Realizing that he had been literally corralled, the German admiral at 1836 ordered a *Gefechtskehrtwendung* ("battle about-turn"), which meant a 180-degree (16-point) change of course to flee the trap. What made the maneuver both extraordinarily difficult and extraordinarily swift was that it began with the *last* ship in line turning first and the first, that is, Scheer's flagship, turning last. The High Seas Fleet had not practiced this maneuver often, but Scheer had confidence in his captains and they in him. Despite some confusion, twenty-two German battleships and their escorts pirouetted gracefully and fled, their images "disappear[ing] instantly and mysteriously from the British range-takers' field of vision as the smoke and gathering dusk of a misty evening enclosed them."[22] The British battleship captains who witnessed the maneuver watched dumbly, continuing to fire at the escaping foe as ordered and never reporting Scheer's sudden exit. Not until the Germans were out of range did Jellicoe realize that the trap had never been fully sprung.

But the British still held the initiative. The badly mauled German forces had been forced to steam to the west, away from the Bight; the Grand Fleet remained in a very advantageous blocking position. Jellicoe reduced speed to seventeen knots and headed east and then south to keep himself and his fleet between Scheer and home. Fully aware of his predicament, Scheer made the second of his battle turns directly back into the trap, risking having his T crossed for a second time in order to throw Jellicoe off balance and give his British adversary something to think about.

Arthur J. Marder, the leading authority on the early-twentieth-century Royal Navy, has suggested that Scheer was actually trying to break through to the north into the Skagerrak and the Baltic and misjudged Jellicoe's position. John Keegan agrees. Certainly, misjudgment of speed and position in the murk would be easy to do, especially when burdened as the Germans were with no less than a half-dozen comparatively slow and weak *Deutschland*-class pre-dreadnoughts.[23] Whatever the reasons, Scheer stuck his head into the lion's mouth one more time, and Jellicoe bit—hard. Indeed, the British bit so hard that the Germans simply could not stand the chewing. With only their forward guns able to bear on the British line, the Germans could see the enemy only by his gun flashes, which ringed the horizon around the High Seas Fleet. Once more the sea erupted in foam and cordite as British shells landed all around the kaiser's ships, large and small. Once again tortured metal screamed as gun turrets were blown apart and decks were torn to pieces. Men who could not hear above the din of constantly firing and exploding shells were abruptly scalded to death by steam, seared to death by flash fires, or simply disintegrated inside shell bursts.

Within minutes Scheer, quietly frantic, ordered a suicide charge by Hipper's battle cruisers to mask another *Gefechtskehrtwendung.* Hipper was actually on board a destroyer by this time, for his flagship, *Lützow,* had been so badly damaged in earlier action with Evan-Thomas and Hood that it was slowly sinking. The remaining four battle cruisers began their death ride with their commander watching from afar through tremendous "shot, splinter and shell." As the badly wrecked (for the second time) battle cruisers prepared to perish, their tiny colleagues saved them. Scheer ordered another destroyer attack against Jellicoe. Although the German torpedoes did not find their marks, the enemy, in conformity with existing doctrine, turned away long enough for Scheer and the limping battle cruisers to crawl out of range to the west and into the deepening night.[24] "It was unfortunate that I was ignorant of [their] formation at this time, and indeed at any period of the engagement," Jellicoe later wrote, adding that only an earlier message from *Southampton* had provided any clue that the enemy was "in single line ahead, but subsequent movements might well have modified this formation, and as I had never seen more than three or four ships at a time from the *Iron Duke* it was quite impossible to gauge the situation from my own knowledge."[25]

For Jellicoe and the Grand Fleet it had been a punishing afternoon. Beatty and the battle cruisers had not acquitted themselves particularly well. Three battle cruisers had blown up, and others, especially *Lion,* had incurred serious damage to their upper works, wireless, searchlights, and other communication gear. *Warspite* was almost lost because of crippled steering gear. *Malaya* had been badly damaged. All in all Beatty's showing was, in Jellicoe's carefully measured phrase, "unpalatable."[26] A dispassionate British Tar might have characterized it as a bloody balls-up. Beatty and his men, together with Room 40, had been particularly remiss in carrying out the essential tasks of command, communications, control, and intelligence (C3I in later parlance). Signaling had been especially abysmal. Beyond that, Beatty's sailors had been outshot and outmaneuvered. A decidedly inferior German force had defeated Beatty's battle cruisers and Evan-Thomas's battleships. But however imperfectly, Beatty *had* brought the German High Seas Fleet to Jellicoe's doorstep, which was exactly what the battle cruisers were meant to do. And the German battle line had been very roughly handled in the process. *Lützow* was slowly sinking, *Seydlitz* was in danger of going under, and *Von der Tann* was absolutely destroyed as a gun platform. Once Jellicoe had sprung the trap on Scheer, the German fleet commander had inexplicably come back for a further drubbing until his destroyers and their torpedoes saved him. Tomorrow promised to be another day of triumphant combat that could destroy the High Seas Fleet forever.

And then Jellicoe and his captains let their advantage slip away. Serenely confident of his own abilities to trap Scheer, but having a total lack of confidence in Room 40, which had let him down so badly regarding Scheer's whereabouts at the beginning of the day, Jellicoe allowed Scheer to duck in behind the Grand Fleet's main force during the night and race for home. "Since well before midnight, an almost impenetrable veil of 'unawareness' had thus enveloped the British fleet: its warp was the abysmal failure of the Admiralty to pass on to the Commander-in-Chief *all* the material information in its possession; its woof, the absence of reports from the commanding officers of those British ships which had seen and identified enemy units."[27]

Once again the British completely failed to understand or exploit C3I, and Jellicoe stubbornly refused to listen to the evidence of his own ears. In a wild night at sea, lit by strange gun flashes and probing searchlights, the light screening forces in the rear of the Grand Fleet made contact with and sporadically fought the determined German force of pre-dreadnoughts and lighter craft masking Scheer's escape. "Strange vessels" were sighted, Beatty observed in his formal dispatch, "and it [was] much to be regretted" that no one took steps to identify them. Gunfire from the occasional skirmishes between British and German destroyers and light cruisers could clearly be heard aboard Jellicoe's flagship *Iron Duke*. British destroyers delivered an admirably executed attack that sank the pre-dreadnought *Pommern*. But in the end carelessness and ignorance allowed Scheer and his "anxiety-stricken" sailors to push through the thin British line at the rear of Jellicoe's main body.[28]

Captain Anselan Stirling, who commanded the northern destroyer screen that kept in longest contact with the enemy and sank *Pommern* in the process, sent several messages to Jellicoe's flagship, but they were incompletely logged or routinely suppressed, considered of no importance. Stubbornly poor visibility compounded the confusion. Jerram wrote in his after-action report to Jellicoe that about 2100, "I negatived an attack with Whitehead torpedoes ordered by "CAROLINE" as I was certain the vessels seen on our starboard beam were our own battle-cruisers. The Navigating Officer of my Flagship, who has just come from the battle-cruiser fleet, was also certain that they were ours and saw them sufficiently clearly to give their approximate course which I reported to you."

Caroline continued to stubbornly importune the flagship, and "shortly afterwards" a reluctant Jerram ordered its captain to attack "if he was quite certain they were enemy ships, as he was in a better position to see them than I was." But, Jerram added, he was not certain if an attack had in fact been made, an observation that itself reflects the dismal state of communications within the Grand Fleet.[29]

It was especially unfortunate that information from Room 40 reporting on an intercepted message from a German destroyer giving the course and position of Scheer's rearmost battleship reached Jellicoe at 2223. Since the position was wrong (probably due to an error on the part of navigators aboard the German ship), Jellicoe ignored the implication. Although he could hear gunfire from the tail of his long column steaming south, the fleet commander also paid no attention to a signal sent from Room 40 at 2241, indicating that Scheer had been ordered home and was heading for Horns Reef off the southern coast of the Jutland peninsula. It took nearly an hour for the message to reach *Iron Duke,* and by that time Jellicoe chose to believe the cruiser *Birmingham* that "placed battle-cruisers at 11:30 p.m. some 30 miles nearly right astern of the *Iron Duke,* but slightly on her starboard quarter. These vessels were obviously not our own battle-cruisers and must therefore be German." The Operations Division of the Admiralty inexplicably sat on a later intercept that absolutely confirmed German plans to return to the Jade via Horns Reef. Jellicoe's reward for his and others' repeated follies came the next morning: an empty sea and the realization that the enemy had disappeared through its mine-swept channels toward home.[30]

Captain Donald Macintyre has imagined Jellicoe, Beatty, and Scheer in Valhalla, forever replaying the battle, forever arguing about who won. Historians, too, will always ponder that question, sifting through the evidence from several hundred ships' logs and the official battle histories on both sides. But in light of all we now know about the social dynamics of the two navies and the world in which they functioned, the real question is how it was possible that tolerably trained but abominably treated enlisted men and warrant officers on both sides fought as well as they did for their arrogant, distant, often incompetent officers. The answer, of course, is that despite all the unhappiness and degradation that plagued the lower classes of the industrial world at the beginning of the twentieth century, despite all the attention paid then and now to the radical agitators and movements of the time, almost all of the masses remained touchingly faithful to king or emperor and country. The men who shot the guns and fired the torpedoes at Dogger Bank, and Jutland, like those who went over the top to certain death at Vimy Ridge and the Somme, bore out the observation of Italian writer Guglielmo Ferrero that the industrial peoples of 1913 were more, not less, conservative than their largely agrarian grandparents had been.[31] Privation or hazard alone could not radicalize such folk; only defeat would rouse them to fury.

As for Jutland itself, the outcome is clear enough. Scheer achieved a tactical victory; he killed more enemy ships and sailors than did his British opponents. If the High Seas Fleet had immediately ventured out again to fight, the Royal Navy would have been a slightly weaker opponent. In the aftermath of battle this appeared a sufficient triumph. As the battered German fleet limped across the Jade Bar to safety (battleship *Ostfriesland* hit a mine offshore, while the slowly sinking *Seydlitz* grounded on Horns Reef), a vastly relieved Scheer ordered champagne served on the flagship's bridge. Within hours an "orgy of victory celebrations" broke out across Germany, culminating in a Reichstag vote of another substantial appropriation to continue the war. A week later, the American ambassador in Berlin reported rumors sweeping the city "that by September preparations will be finished and that the Suez Canal will be cannonaded, bombed, and mined so that it will dry up, and then [Britain's] Indian-Afghan troubles will begin." Heavy work was obviously expected of the *Hochseeflotte*![32] But Jellicoe in fact won the strategic prize—indeed, a number of prizes.

First, the Grand Fleet remained intact and seemed ready to fight. Twenty-four hours after the Royal Navy returned to Scapa and the Scottish firths, Jellicoe proudly cabled Churchill that all the ships had steam up again and were ready for sea at four hours' notice. The public had expected nothing less. Six months before, naval correspondent Archibald Hurd had visited the Grand Fleet in its Scapa Flow anchorage and had rhapsodized over "its youthfulness, its mobility, its size, and the extent of the influence which it is exerting." All the chaps from Jellicoe on down were keen. "The Grand Fleet, in all its strength, is manned by men with the sea instinct, who make the sea their profession instead of their naval service being a mere three years' interlude," as in Germany. "Our ships are even younger than the officers and men. That is a complete reversal of the conditions which existed during the Trafalgar period. The ships which fought at Trafalgar were, in the main, old ships. There is not a vessel in the Grand Fleet half the age of Nelson's flagship when she went into action. . . . The ships that count most have been built during the past ten years." One would always have to understand such conditions when confronted with the inevitable question: "'Will there ever be a battle in the North Sea on a grand scale?'" The disproportion of British to German strength materially, morally, professionally, and technically,

Hurd maintained, was such that victory for the Grand Fleet could be safely assumed.[33] The public thus expected at least another Trafalgar, and for the briefest moment believed that it might have gotten one.

Second, the Royal Navy after Jutland as before remained the linchpin of the Allied cause. Had the German surface fleet been able to roam at will after June 1, 1916, it would have broken Britain's naval blockade, intensifying the subsequent German U-boat campaign immeasurably as Scheer's heavy ships and cruisers hunted down the last British destroyers and "Q" ships that posed a danger to the German undersea arm. Britain would have starved within the year if not sooner. And in the interim the British coasts would have been wide open to invasion. Jutland maintained the status quo. Whether at Scapa and in the Scottish firths or conducting periodic sweeps through the North Sea, the Grand Fleet allowed the Allies to sustain a cruel pressure on their continental enemies.

Third, the German fleet was more gravely weakened by Jutland than its numerically larger adversary. Although all except two *(Lützow* and *Pommern)* of the stouter German dreadnoughts and pre-dreadnoughts managed to reach port, many were in a near-sinking condition and required many months of repair, which Germany simply could not afford in its increasingly desperate situation. Scheer remained as willing as Jellicoe to put to sea again after Jutland, but his heart may not have been in it. In his formal report to Wilhelm, he observed somberly that "it may be possible for us to inflict appreciable damage on the enemy, but there can be no doubt that even the most favorable issue of a battle on the high seas will not compel England to make peace in this war. The disadvantages of our geographical position, compared with that of the Island Empire and her great material superiority, cannot be compensated for by our fleet." Only resumption of the earlier program of unrestricted submarine warfare, Scheer concluded, offered Germany hope of victory.[34]

In fact, appearances were deceiving. If the High Seas Fleet did not win the Battle of Jutland, it nonetheless demoralized the Royal Navy and the British people. In the aftermath Scheer and the German court both overestimated the material and moral superiority of the Royal Navy and underestimated their own formidable capabilities. These facts, obscure at the time, first came into play several months later when Scheer led another attack by the High Seas Fleet toward the port of Sunderland. Once again British reaction was so ineffective that the Germans were able to approach within sixty miles of the English coast before turning away.

Scheer's general objective in the Sunderland raid of August 1916 remained the same: to vigorously employ the air, surface, and subsurface resources at his disposal to ambush and destroy a substantial portion of the enemy fleet while suffering comparatively few casualties. The High Seas Fleet would sail relying on a scouting line of zeppelins in the North Sea to warn of an enemy approach. Once the enemy was sighted, units of the High Seas Fleet would lure all or a portion of the British heavy surface units across a U-boat ambush line, then cut off and attack a portion of the surviving forces with overwhelming strength, thus defeating in detail a significant portion of the enemy fleet and whittling the Royal Navy down to manageable proportions. The plan failed largely because Room 40 was alert, and Jellicoe put to sea in search of Scheer before the German zeppelin scouting line was in place. Under clearer summer skies, German airmen were nonetheless able to spot and shadow the Grand Fleet's heavy units and reported their locations and courses to Scheer, whose intelligence staff misinterpreted much of the information they received. At one point the unsuspecting High Seas Fleet was only thirty miles from advance units of the entire Grand Fleet, and Scheer was saved only by an erroneous report from one of his zeppelins that a British force coming up from Harwich contained one or two battleships. This was exactly what Scheer had been looking for, and he turned southeast to attack, thus swerving away from Jellicoe and a Grand Fleet that had no idea where he was, as the Royal Navy's seaplanes aboard *Engadine* were once again totally ineffective. In the event, Scheer never made contact with the oncoming Harwich Force of cruisers and destroyers, and both fleets returned to port disappointed. Scheer was especially critical of his zeppelin scouts, though in fact they performed quite creditably.[35]

Indeed, the German navy as a whole performed better. The Royal Navy's response to Scheer's latest—and, as it would prove, last—serious sortie revealed once again those flaws in the British fleet and naval establishment that had been so pitilessly revealed at Dogger Bank and Jutland. Several days after the incident, Commodore Reginald Tyrwhitt, commander of the Harwich Force since the outbreak of the war, wrote Jellicoe apologetically: "I am afraid we failed you on Saturday and I am kicking myself for not standing on for another hour instead of turning at 12:45 p.m. I imagine I should have sighted the Germans if I had. It will probably seem inexplicable to you, but I had not the slightest idea where you were until I received your message ordering Captain D. (4) to meet you at 3 p.m. I did not even *know* you were out, although I felt sure you were." Such crippling lapses in coordination and communication between the Grand Fleet and the Harwich Force were compounded by the German scouts. "I did not completely realize how completely we were in the hands of the Zepps.," Tyrwhitt admitted, "who were always with us and no doubt reported all our movements." Moreover, "I also never credited the Germans with daring to proceed so far to the westward, and feared that possibly they had steered S.W. and were going back by way of Terschelling. Then the first W/T directional position of the Germans from Cleethorpes *must* have been incorrect." This experienced commander had thus been completely flummoxed by Jellicoe, by erroneous intelligence, and, not least, by the German navy.[36]

The High Seas Fleet commander planned another foray in September that had to be called off because of bad weather. The next month fleet elements made a sortie to attack any British shipping found east of Dogger Bank; British light forces in the area torpedoed one German cruiser. Foul weather kept Jellicoe in port, but the Germans had to return home when heavy seas forced the destroyer screen to fall back.[37] Thereafter, the High Seas Fleet scarcely moved at all.

If it had, it would have confronted a Grand Fleet steeped in ever deepening gloom. After Jutland the Royal Navy and the British people constantly wondered how good were the sailors and how strong the ships. Jellicoe stimulated public disillusion by refusing to issue an immediate laudatory account of the battle. The Germans were thus able to steal a propaganda march, and as accounts and results began to dribble out it appeared that at best the Grand Fleet had blundered into an inconclusive standoff that looked suspiciously like the terrible, bloody stalemate on the Continent, which would culminate in the senseless slaughter at the Somme. An impatient people had expected the navy to do as it had always done: rescue the nation from disaster. They forgot, as did experts like Hurd, that the successful exercise of sea power against a strong opponent is invariably a long, tedious process. Thus, as historian Correlli Barnett has acidly observed, Jutland "was a curious 'victory' in that for forty years a controversy was to rage as to who was principally to blame for it."[38]

At Rosyth dockside workers jeered and booed the weary, battle-scarred sailors of *Lion* as the damaged battle cruiser limped in for repairs. Jack Tar reacted angrily. Every damaged warship on both sides had suffered hideously. The last major clash of dreadnoughts "had inflicted appalling human damage," a British surgeon recalled. Hundreds of "dreadful cases . . . that cannot be written about" lay in the sick bays aboard the British and German battleships, battle cruisers, and smaller vessels.[39] The common British seaman and his mates, of whom more than four thousand lay at the bottom the North Sea, had fought hard and bravely; their reward was condemnation as cowards and shirkers. A bitter rift developed between the public and the Royal Navy that never completely healed before the onset of another world war. Britain, too, would experience a naval mutiny. The crisis did not come until 1931, but who can say that one of the origins of Invergordon was not the poisonous atmosphere created by Jutland?

Marder has argued that the vigorous reforms in strategy, tactics, and matériel undertaken by the Admiralty and fleet commanders immediately after the battle "increased the efficiency of the Grand Fleet to a degree that would not have been thought possible before Jutland and which, indeed, would not have been possible but for Jutland." He concluded that if the Germans had risked another pitched battle at sea within a year, the Royal Navy would have beaten them decisively.[40]

Jellicoe clearly did not think so. In the weeks following the battle in the North Sea, he found fault with everything in the navy: gunnery, ordnance, signaling, and perhaps most important basic ship construction. The Fifth Battle Squadron composed of the fastest and newest battleships could neither keep up effectively with Beatty nor outrun Hipper's battle cruisers "when they are in range." Obviously, the penetrating power of British shells was much weaker than those of the Germans. The enemy battle cruisers had been hit and hit hard. Yet none had blown to smithereens as had three of their British counterparts. Shells had been seen to strike enemy turrets, fires had been seen to start, yet the enemy did not blow up. Clearly, something was wrong both with British shells and with Beatty's "big cats." In July, following study of the preliminary battle reports, the Admiralty directed that in the event heavy enemy surface forces should conduct coastal raids, Beatty's battle cruisers should not seek to engage them alone "while the Battle Fleet is too far off to support him." Not surprisingly, Beatty wrote Jellicoe a stinging letter. "That Their Lordships, after practically two years of war, find it necessary to lay down very definitely a rule which must restrict officers very considerably in the exercise of their judgement leads me to suppose that there is some motive which is not apparent to me." Despite Beatty's spirited defense of his tactics, his men, and his ships, there was no motive beyond common sense. Jellicoe quietly supported his superiors, observing that his battle-cruiser commander's "difficulties" were "very much enhanced by the fact that he is based so much further south than is his supporting force," adding the devastating observation that "Sir David Beatty overstates the excess speed of the 5th Battle Squadron over the enemy's 3rd Squadron." The Admiralty's judgment and orders stood.[41]

In September, three months before he left the fleet to become first sea lord, Jellicoe told the Admiralty that "our future fleet policy is largely dependent upon whether the Government is prepared to face the fact that the Fleet cannot prevent bombardment of coast towns on the east coast or interfere with the early stages of a landing on the part of the enemy, particularly in northern waters." If Jellicoe was right, Britain had practically lost command of the seas—or at least absolute command. Shortly thereafter, the Grand Fleet briefly moved from Scapa Flow south to Rosyth to better cover the east coast from German naval raids. That was not enough for Jellicoe.

Once ensconced at the Admiralty, with the German submarine menace reaching its climax, Jellicoe stated flatly what he had earlier suggested. In a memorandum to First Lord of the Admiralty Eric Geddes near the end of April 1917, with the Americans just in the war, Jellicoe wrote of the necessity to make clear to His Majesty's government "the very serious nature of the naval position. . . . The real fact of the matter is this: We are carrying on this war . . . as if we had the absolute command of the sea. We have not—and have not had for many months . . . or anything approaching." The Grand Fleet remained "absolute masters of the situation as far as surface ships are concerned," but in the aggregate, practical German control of the skies above the North Sea together with the rapidly growing enemy submarine offensive had stretched the Royal Navy beyond its breaking point. There were simply too few resources to cover too many commitments. Naval policy had to be changed and reshaped "to conform with the fact that we have neither the undisputed command of the sea nor even a reasonable measure of this command." The escorting of transport ships bringing admittedly essential foreign labor to British mills and factories had to be curtailed, as did the escort of hospital ships.[42]

Britain's loss of command did not imply that mastery had shifted to Germany. But by the spring of 1917 Germany clearly ruled the skies above the North Sea and the depths beneath it, their submarine campaign now extending into the Irish Sea and out into the eastern Atlantic as well. Had Scheer, or someone else, taken the High Seas Fleet out once more in strength, perhaps, as so many feared, seeking to roust and destroy a convoy or two coming in from the United States, the Royal Navy might well have broken. But the German Court and Admiralty, long bedeviled by the lack of a coherent strategy at sea, allowed the chance to slip. While conditions at home seriously deteriorated under the blockade, the great ships of the ironically named *Hochseeflotte* that might have broken it swung uselessly around their anchor chains at Wilhelmshaven and Kiel.

The kaiser's sailors finally began to wilt and grow sullen. Despite Hipper's dash and competence and Scheer's brilliance, the German navy had been defeated. It had met the enemy and after a few brief, exhilarating exchanges had rushed back to port. Everything wrong with the High Seas Fleet—its lack of a strategic purpose, its inferiority in numbers if not matériel to the British adversary, its inability or unwillingness to contribute directly to a desperate war effort, and above all the dreadful, overbearing arrogance and insensitivity of its officers with their aristocratic pretensions and their need to inflict an "increasingly unbearable harassment" on the enlisted ranks—doomed a once promising sea service. The German navy had always been a political tool of an autocratic court, its feudal retainers, and their lackeys in the industrial management classes. Neither its sponsors nor its leaders ever perceived the High Seas Fleet as a professional force closely integrated into a functioning national security system. The navy paid the inevitable price for such neglect. As weeks and months passed with little or no action the best officers and men were drafted for the rapidly growing submarine service. Those sailors who remained on the big ships began to loathe their superiors and regarded the desire of captains and lieutenants to continue the war "as an unscrupulous attempt to perpetuate their privileges and to exploit them."[43]

In August 1917 what was essentially a wildcat strike by a handful of hungry, unpaid sailors on the dreadnought *Prinzregent Luitpold* was interpreted as mutiny by the lords of discipline. Ten men were hanged. Two months later operations on the Baltic coast in support of the German army advancing into Russia gave the kaiser's discontented sailors brief employment, and in November 1917 the battle cruisers briefly encountered Jellicoe's battleships off Heligoland before racing back to harbor. But there were no more great fleet actions, although several German destroyer flotillas were subsequently transferred to Belgian ports, where they undertook sporadic, occasionally successful raids in conjunction with the U-boats against the Dover Patrol guarding the sea-lanes to France.

In the final year of war the High Seas Fleet steadily deteriorated in harbor. Scheer was able to take it to sea one last time in April 1918, cruising uneventfully as far north as the lower tip of Norway, while the Royal Navy, now back at Scapa Flow and substantially reenforced by a division of U.S. battleships, remained blissfully unaware. But lower-deck morale had reached rock bottom in Scheer's navy as the German army finally retreated in October and November 1918. When the admirals revolted against the newly installed peace party and tried to take the fleet to sea on one last suicide mission, the sailors had had enough and staged a full-fledged mutiny of their own that finally destroyed the High Seas Fleet as a fighting unit and permanently sullied the name and memory of the kaiser's navy. The fault, however, lay not with desperate sailors but with their corrupt, self-serving leaders.[44]

The old Royal Navy of swagger and dash was gone, too, and with it the simple-minded belief that tradition and bulldog courage were all that were needed to win a war at sea. Jacky Fisher and his youthful colleagues had exerted all their efforts to reform the navy; they had only partly succeeded. Beyond the tin-clad battle cruisers, the faulty shells, and the inexcusable failures in command, communications, and control lay a terrible void in creative, innovative thinking. Jellicoe was not a great commander, though he was doubtless a member of that much rarer breed, the incorruptibly honest man. No later than the spring of 1917 he saw to what low state his beloved fleet had sunk and grasped the implications. Others more or less did, too.

In January 1918 young Andrew Cunningham came home from three years in the Mediterranean to temporarily command the Grand Fleet destroyer *Ophelia*. "I was not a bit impressed by her appearance," he wrote years later. The ship was "dirty," the men "slack and slovenly." He discovered that the entire destroyer fleet was "in a state of staleness with their officers and men in the last stage of boredom." Most of the ships had just moved from Scapa to Rosyth, and while in the Orkneys the men found little to do ashore. Frequent patrols at sea were often conducted in "vile weather." Jellicoe's and Beatty's depot ships treated their destroyer charges as a nuisance, not a responsibility. The result was a gradual but definite decline in morale. "Each destroyer worked her own routine, and I noticed that in harbour some of them did not turn to until well after 9 a.m."[45]

When Beatty replaced Jellicoe as first sea lord late in 1917, he maintained the drumbeat of alarm. In a typical memorandum to the Admiralty on January 9, 1918, he claimed that the paper strength of his navy considerably exceeded its real power. There was a chronic deficiency in destroyers for U-boat hunting, convoy duty, and fleet screening. Suitably powerful armor-piercing heavy shells for the battleships and battle cruisers would not be available until the summer of 1918. "Only the *Lion, Princess Royal,* and *Tiger* were fit to be in the line" against Hipper's six battle cruisers. Thus, Beatty continued, it was impossible for the Grand Fleet to both defeat the enemy and control communications and transport in the North Sea. Since protection of overseas trade was the supreme consideration, "the deduction to be drawn is that the correct strategy of the Grand Fleet is no longer to endeavor to bring the enemy to action at any cost but rather to contain him in his bases until the general situation becomes more favorable to us. This does not mean that action should be avoided if conditions favor us, or that our role should be passive and purely defensive."[46] Despite his caveats, Beatty's memorandum read like a 1914 German position paper on the uses of the High Seas Fleet. Both the first lord and the first sea lord emphatically endorsed the document as an accurate reflection and summation of Admiralty policy.[47]

In the months and years after Jutland the knives came out in the open throughout the Royal Navy; most of them were wielded by Beatty. When he took over the Grand Fleet from Jellicoe in November 1916, Jerram was peremptorily told to haul down his flag and get out of Scapa Flow. No victim of a modern corporate restructuring had his professional head removed more expeditiously or brutally than the commander of the Second Battle Squadron. The reason did not become fully clear to the public until 1924 when the *Harper Report,* commissioned by the Admiralty in 1920 but initially quashed by Beatty, at last became public. According to Commander Harper, Beatty made a signal at 1947 hours on the evening of May 31 to Jellicoe to ask that the van of the Battle Fleet, that is, *King George V* leading the Second Battle Squadron, follow the battle cruisers in "cut[ting] off the whole of the enemy's battle fleet." Jellicoe's flagship, *Iron Duke,* received the message at 1954. Six minutes later Jellicoe ordered a course change to the west (presumably to follow Beatty in accordance with the latter's wishes) and told Beatty he had done so. At 2014 the fleet commander gave orders for *King George V* to follow the battle cruisers. But Jerram did not reply for another thirty minutes, then at 2045 reported that the battle cruisers were not in sight to follow. Beatty's apparent plan to trap the entire *Hochseeflotte* by leading elements of the Grand Fleet with the rest of Jellicoe's force steaming up rapidly in support was thus foiled. However, as critics noted, it did not matter at 2014 whether Jerram and the van of the Grand Fleet followed Beatty since Scheer had, for all practical purposes, escaped. But Beatty was determined from the morning following the battle to have poor Jerram sacked. In the words of his most recent defender, "Beatty's achievement in drawing the High Seas Fleet into the killing ground in front of Jellicoe's 240 heavy guns, in spite of devastating setbacks, was a tribute to his leadership, single-mindedness and stamina, but to have the enemy escape at the last moment, like Houdini, was, in Beatty's own words, 'gall and wormwood.'" Jerram never got another command, though he put in repeatedly for one. Admiralty officials urged him to retire, which in 1918 he did.[48]

Jerram was not the only such casualty of Jutland. Commander Harper was savagely critical of Beatty for neglecting to give Jellicoe frequent and precise information about the enemy's position and for failing to inflict damage "on a

greatly inferior enemy owing to incorrect disposition of his ships," that is, Evan-
Thomas's accompanying Fifth Battle Squadron. All this could be attributed to
both faulty signaling and poor gunnery. Ralph Seymour, Beatty's wartime flag
captain responsible for signals and a longtime personal friend and supporter of
the dashing battle-cruiser commander, found himself in the middle. Beatty
turned on the unhappy officer as soon as Harper's report reached the public,
openly charging that Seymour's faulty handling of signals in the battle-cruiser
fleet throughout the war had cost the Royal Navy no less than "three battles."
Brokenhearted, Seymour committed suicide.[49]

Beatty got his own Admiralty report written in 1922, but it was so outra-
geously biased that it never saw the light of day. Harper's report, which appeared
two years later as *The Admiralty Narrative of Jutland,* castigated Evan-Thomas
as much as Beatty for not following the battle cruisers more closely so as to be
able to lend the full weight of four fast, modern fifteen-inch-gunned battleships
to the British line of battle. But, of course, the commander of the Fifth Battle
Squadron could argue just as vociferously as anyone that the fault was really
Seymour's because of faulty signaling. Churchill's *World Crisis,* appearing in
1927, defended Beatty and castigated Jellicoe so roundly that one critic, C. F. G.
Masterman, writing in the London *Sunday Express,* spoke of "the full-in-the-
limelight, slap-dash Society's darling . . . contrasted with an assumed timid admiral hiding up in Scapa Flow; enclosing his ships in cotton wool."[50] All could
have been forgiven if Jellicoe and Beatty had been able to engage Scheer on the
morning of June 1, 1916. By that time, however, the German fleet commander
was serving champagne on the bridge of his flagship entering port, ostensibly
to celebrate a great victory against overwhelming odds, but in reality, one sus-
pects, to celebrate getting home at all. Andrew Gordon, the most recent student
of Jutland, condemns Jellicoe as a rigid by-the-book man who did not lose an
empire in an afternoon, but did not gain a victory, either. "Jellicoe's desire for
control and centralization caused his command style to be . . . signals oriented."
The movements of a vast fleet could be regulated only by "a ceaseless stream of
signals from the flagship," and as Jellicoe himself later admitted, "'in the smoke,
confusion, and uncertainty of battle the process was far too elaborate.'" But
Gordon reserves his major criticism for the latter stages of the battle. Jellicoe's
system, according to Gordon, really broke down during the night of May 31–
June 1, when the admiral's senior officers at the rear of the Grand Fleet failed to
adequately inform him of the possibility that the actions then occurring might
well mean that Scheer had cut in behind the British and was on the point of es-

caping. Such criticisms are not new. They first emerged more than sixty years ago as the British Admiralty continued its struggle to understand exactly what had happened at Jutland two decades before. Jellicoe had already said that he had practiced the Grand Fleet over and over again to respond to a possible *Gefechtskehrtwendung* by the enemy and had concluded that there was no effective antidote to turn-away tactics short of interposing his superior fleet between the enemy and the German ports. He actually achieved his objective at Jutland without realizing it. "We are often told," Sir Hubert Russell wrote in 1935, that the [British] tactics employed at Jutland were wrong; that they were out of date and too 'rigid.' We are never told what else Adm. Jellicoe could have done" either to respond to Scheer's turn-away tactics or to effectively fight the German commander at night once Scheer had begun to slip in behind the Grand Fleet. Certainly, Jellicoe should have listened both to what Room 40 was telling him and to the evidence of his and others' ears. But as Russell concluded, "The battle was too vast, too unwieldy, for one centralized control. So long as there was centralized control"—and what alternative was there?—"there was bound to be 'rigidity.'"[51]

It is, in fact, unjust to castigate Jellicoe and Beatty—and Scheer as well (though the latter steams through the fountains of criticism as a rather brilliant seaman)—without understanding their terrible burdens. A major world conflict had not occurred since the Age of Fighting Sail a century and more before. The three commanders themselves and nearly all of their immediate subordinates had first gone to sea at the end of the sailing era and had absorbed its ethos and mystique. Their professional training in modern industrial warfare at sea had been limited, narrow, and fitful. Like Captain Edward J. Smith of *Titanic,* another veteran of the sailing age, they simply did not realize the awesome yet fragile power at their command. There were no manuals on how to wage war with huge, fast steel battleships, and the sword bearers of 1914–1918 had to write their own books—often from the perspective and experience of their own failures, their own sins of omission and commission.

Modern technology had given them strange, frightening new killing machines to command; irresponsible politicians had burdened them with too many such monsters; science and industry had not yet fashioned the tools—powerful directional radio and telegraphy, advanced aerial reconnaissance, and radar—needed to use such fleets with intelligence and imagination. Above all, the naval commanders of the Great War were of a generation that still clung to monarchy and imbibed the feudal ethos. Naval battles were fought and told in terms of military campaigns: Battle cruisers were compared to fast, powerful cavalry units meant to scout ahead and skirmish with the approaching enemy's battle line, whose battleships resembled the armored knights of the Middle Ages, riding to war for God, king, and right. Cruisers and destroyers were the pickets of the fleet, and when battle became hot and furious they became the sharpshooters, archers, or point men who went ahead to disrupt the enemy line as best they could. "Throughout," Marder has written of Jutland, "I have . . . borne in mind how little those concerned in the battle really knew of what was going on."[52] This was true of every major surface action fought during the Great War, a fact that should humble anyone who blithely tries to fix blame and responsibility for follies and tragedies that were inherent in the events themselves.

Yet Marder himself remained restless and dissatisfied with his first cut at understanding the enormous, beguiling complexities of Jutland, and so, in 1978, he took a second shot at telling the story and reaching conclusions. He at last identified the chief villain on Britain's side as "centralization. . . . Everything was, in truth, centralized in the flagship. The tendency was to do nothing without an order from the C.-in-C [Jellicoe]. Except for avoiding torpedoes whose tracks had been sighted, little initiative was left for squadron and division leaders." Lack of "independent divisional training and practices," one of Jellicoe's subordinates later wrote, led ineluctably to lost opportunities. The "centralisation principle that reigned supreme in the Navy" led to "a mass of signals . . . to alter course so many points, to steer such and such a course, to go so many revolutions or take up such and such a bearing" that simply overwhelmed the comprehension and tactical grasp of men immersed in the immediate imperatives of combat. Even if it is conceded that there were few times in the epic battle when such shortcomings affected the overall outcome, Marder concluded in his reconsideration that "the lesson of Jutland is clear enough. It is the unwisdom of the C.-in-C. maneuvering a big fleet in battle and allowing little initiative to subordinates." A big fleet eager to take the offensive, Marder added, quoting yet another dissatisfied British naval officer, "*must* have leaders on the wings who will seize every opportunity." Scheer's sailors "did not need the lesson." The German commander expected his chief subordinates to use their own initiative "in forwarding the C.-in-C.'s intentions without waiting for orders, and at Jutland they did just that," avoiding defeat where outright victory was impossible.[53]

The grand follies and ambiguities of Jutland—and, indeed, Dogger Bank— together with the recriminations that followed obscured the salient point of the Great War at sea: Britain's sometimes precarious maintenance of the blockade of Germany. There was no point during the Battle of Jutland when the German battle fleet could glimpse victory; therefore, the blockade of its homeland was never shaken. That blockade progressively weakened the German war effort and sapped civilian morale to the point where food riots broke out in Berlin in October 1918, even as the army began to break in the West after four years of remarkable effort. The outbreak of violence among a people at war and habituated to obey had a profound and perhaps decisive effect on a government at war habituated to obedience. Three weeks later, a hungry, if not semistarving, Germany surrendered.

The last word on Jutland—and, indeed, on the Royal Navy's entire effort during World War I—properly belongs to those who were there. On October 28, 1929, the day before the New York Stock Exchange collapsed, sending the world careening into a new crisis that would lead to yet another world war, Admiral Ernle Chatfield, commander in chief of the British Atlantic Fleet, addressed his senior officers aboard the flagship *Nelson* following annual autumn maneuvers. During the course of his remarks, he observed, "Before 1914 we had many years of peace and, in peace time, conflicting ideas prevail because your weapons cannot be properly tested under fire."

> Consequently in 1914 some held a big ship action should be fought at 9,000 yards and our battle practices were based on this range; others imagined 15,000 or greater range were probable. The war showed the latter to be more correct but it was then too late to alter our material. Our rangefinders were too small; our armour was not placed to the best advantage; our shells had not been designed for oblique impact; our sights had not been graduated for long enough ranges and elevations; our torpedoes did not run far enough.[54]

Germany did not relent after Jutland. It simply turned to the submarine to terrorize Britain's sailors and people. Scheer's August 1916 sweep through the North Sea turned Jellicoe's long-standing unease and fear about the U-boat menace "into a virtual obsession." A torpedo narrowly missed the flagship *Iron Duke* as it steamed ahead of the fleet to pick the admiral up off the Firth of Forth. Then a cruiser was sunk near the Farne Islands, and Jellicoe ordered a two-hour about-turn for the whole fleet. As the Grand Fleet turned for home after learning of Scheer's move southwestward toward the light units steaming up from Harwich, it was subject to repeated alarms and attacks from enemy submarines, one of which sank another cruiser. "For Jellicoe this sweep proved the last straw. Backed up by Beatty, he insisted that the Grand Fleet must avoid going further south than latitude 55°30'North (the Farne Islands) and farther east than longitude 4° East unless it had sufficient destroyers: only if the need were very pressing should this rule be broken."[55]

But whereas the Grand Fleet might avoid the U-boats, Allied merchantmen enjoyed no such luxury. With one blow delivered on an early May afternoon in 1915, Germany introduced a brand-new element to humanity's wars at sea— blatant terror. England could survive only by calling desperately upon its former subjects across the Atlantic for help.

CHAPTER 8

Terror at Sea, 1915–1918

The Submarine and Its Consequences

EARLY ON THE CALM, sunny afternoon of May 7, 1915, a little boy stood gazing out to sea next to the lighthouse at the Old Head of Kinsale on the southern coast of Ireland. Centered in his vision was the most magnificent sight he had ever beheld. A huge ocean liner, its four orange funnels belching smoke, its black hull cleaving the water, its gleaming white upper works standing in stark contrast to the bright-blue sea all around, was rapidly steaming toward him. As he watched, the majestic ship made a graceful turn into the broad Saint George's Channel and then was suddenly shaken by two explosions on its starboard side. As the shocked child watched, the vessel lurched sharply but never stopped despite the rapid flooding of its forward engine rooms. Once its stem was awash, momentum drove the bow quickly downward as the hull twisted more and more to starboard. Hundreds of frantic people rushed onto the decks to crawl up or leap off its upper works into a swelling sea littered with falling debris from the dying monster. When the bow hit bottom three hundred feet beneath the surface, the hull rose to an impossible angle until the stern sank slowly back into the water. The ship disappeared "with an unearthly, keening moan as the air was forced from her hulk." The chilly waters were full of the dead, the dying, and the desperate. Seventy-nine years later an old man named George Henderson vividly described what he had seen that day to maritime explorer and historian Robert Ballard. He would never forget it. Neither would the world.[1]

Lusitania had been ambushed, and 1,200 people (some accounts say 1,198, others 1,201), including at least 128 Americans, had been murdered by a new weapon of war, the submarine. Nine months of battle on the western front had not yet completely hardened modern man and woman to the horrors of industrial combat. Only a few had begun to understand that the machine gun, barbed wire, and poison gas were the harbingers of a new form of total war that would eventually engulf civilians and homes as well as soldiers and ships. The first zeppelin raids against England had occurred just a month before *Lusitania* made its last voyage, and the bombing of London was still some months in the future. But Winston Churchill was sure that these "enormous bladder[s] of combustible and explosive gas would prove to be easily destructible," and he was eventually proved right.[2] The stealthy killing of a huge passenger ship on a bright spring afternoon was on an altogether different level; it was, in fact, the first act of calculated wartime terror in the twentieth century by one "civilized" nation against the helpless peoples of another. After the sinking of *Lusitania*, humanity's road to Rotterdam, Coventry, Dresden, and Hiroshima was clear and straight.

Over the years, and particularly as immediate memories of the atrocity faded, several silly books appeared, the authors claiming either that the Germans were correct in sinking a ship they believed had been converted to an armed merchant cruiser or that they had been led to commit the massacre by devilishly cunning British statesmen like young Churchill, who had somehow lured *Lusitania* to the U-boat's torpedo tubes in order to create an international incident that would bring the United States into the war.[3] Since Kapitänleutnant Walter Schwieger had launched only one torpedo from his U-20 toward *Lusitania* and most survivors distinctly saw or heard two explosions, credence was given to German insistence that the liner had been carrying illegal contraband, probably heavy-artillery shells, that had exploded after the torpedo's detonation. Not until Ballard carefully examined the wreck nearly eighty years later, after reviewing records of the sinking, was there conclusive proof that the second and fatal explosion was caused by the ignition of coal dust in the nearly empty bunkers along the starboard side of the ship.[4]

Knowledgeable historians, however, would not have needed Ballard's evidence. The contraband that *Lusitania* carried (rifles, small arms, and 4.2 million cartridges) was equivalent to only about ten tons of explosives, certainly not enough to cause a major detonation if ignited by an initial explosion. As for the insistence that Churchill had deliberately lured *Lusitania* into Schwieger's periscope sight, anyone minimally knowledgeable of maritime history would know that navigation in 1915 remained comparatively crude and shipping schedules were far from precise. There was no way that Schwieger could have been enticed to the precise ambush point at precisely the right moment to accurately launch his torpedo. Haphazardly cruising in a known shipping lane, anxious to expend his few remaining torpedoes and go home, Schwieger came upon *Lusitania* (which had changed course in response to an Admiralty submarine warning) at the worst possible time.

Diana Preston, a cool and clearheaded scholar, has recently revisited the incident and concluded, "There is no evidence that the Admiralty deliberately lured the *Lusitania* into the path of a submarine." There would have been only one motive for such a despicable act: to entice the United States into the war on Britain's side. But as Preston points out, the war was still in its earliest stage, and no responsible official in His Majesty's government wanted to give the moralistic Woodrow Wilson an opportunity to meddle either in the conflict or in peace negotiations. Moreover, the Americans were doing just fine as arms suppliers to Britain. That was quite enough for Whitehall and Downing Street. But were Churchill and his senior sailors guilty of negligence by failing to keep the huge liner out of harm's way? Here Preston is more cautious. Schwieger had stalked *Lusitania* before. As recently as the previous March he had slipped into Liverpool Bay in hopes of sinking the great ship. Moreover, his current orders, and those of his fellow U-boat skippers, were to sink British troop transports on their way to France. The British Admiralty was at least vaguely aware of U-boat policy, and in the past *Lusitania* and other passenger and troop ships had either been provided with destroyer escorts or been kept in port when enemy U-boat sightings had occurred. Why had *Lusitania* been allowed to run unescorted on this occasion, especially since the Germans had issued a flat warning against sailing on the liner just before its departure from New York? Preston reaches two compelling conclusions. First, the Admiralty "believed that the Germans probably could not sink the *Lusitania*, and that even if they could, they would not." International reaction against them would be too great. Second, the British Admiralty was fatally distracted at this moment by another matter of seemingly transcendent importance—the deteriorating situation at the Dardenelles. Jacky Fisher and Churchill feared that such a large portion of the Royal Navy had been sent to Gallipoli as to fatally compromise John Jellicoe's ability to defeat the German High Seas Fleet should it sortie. Indeed, Churchill had rushed off to Paris on the eve of *Lusitania*'s death in an effort to bring Italy into the war on the Allied side, thereby relieving Anglo-French pressure to carry on the Gallipoli campaign alone.[5]

Britons, of course, saw the tragedy as an unadulterated atrocity. Schwieger could have surfaced, ordered off all the passengers—including the comparatively few Canadian troops traveling in civilian clothes—and then sunk *Lusitania* if he believed it was carrying contraband. There were no enemy destroyers within miles, and if one had suddenly appeared Schwieger could have torpedoed the big liner and submerged, pleading wartime imperatives. Instead, he chose to bushwhack the ship from a safe position beneath the waves. It is a compelling argument, and one is forced to agree with Preston that "by firing without warning Schwieger and those who dispatched him were guilty by the standards of 1915 of 'willful murder.'"[6] The only justification Germany could produce was that *Lusitania* had become the fast, armed merchant cruiser that it had been designed to be and that the British deliberately placed in harm's way more than a thousand civilian lives to carry out their nefarious scheme. But then two questions arise: How did the Admiralty plan to use such a warship largely filled with innocent passengers? And why, after many months of transatlantic service, had not one passenger complained of seeing any guns aboard or remarked about gun drills?

The Germans nonetheless insisted that Schwieger and the crew of U-20 were heroes for sinking what the kaiser and his officials insisted was a British warship carrying both munitions and Canadian troops that had been warned of its possible fate before it sailed. Wilhelm proclaimed a national holiday and ordered a medallion to be struck commemorating the event, which he labeled "'a great triumph for German sea power.'" The Allied peoples and neutral governments were sickened and outraged. Archibald Hurd summed up the prevailing sentiment:

> The youngest navy in Europe, whose supreme officer until recently was an honorary Admiral of the Fleet in the British service, and professed his respect for British naval traditions, has reverted to the most ancient, repellent, and irreparable crimes of war. . . . The moral sense of the world shows a distinct tendency to become benumbed and dull owing to the repeated shocks, on a continually rising scale, received since Germany inaugurated her reign of terror at sea by laying mines [that is, mines and torpedoes] in the pathway of peaceful commerce, contrary to her pledged word.

Land warfare had frequently degenerated into barbarism in the past, but "sailors, even more than soldiers, perhaps have always admitted that there are certain acts which are inexcusable, even in the height of war, when the passions of combatants are excited and their moral judgment tends to lose its balance."

German U-boat attacks against peaceful British fishing fleets in the Channel and now on merchant ships, along with bombardment by German battle cruisers and smaller vessels of undefended English coastal towns like Scarborough and Whitby, revealed a previously unsuspected brutality in "the Hun" that soiled the entire human race.[7]

The U.S. public was equally outraged. The sinking of *Lusitania* convinced a majority still rather early in the war that national interests as well as sympathies lay with the Allies, not the Germans.[8] That commitment would be strained from time to time by the ferocity of the British blockade, and by the arrogant behavior of British statesmen and officials, who hid mounting fright that the war might be lost behind a facade of determined effrontery. But after May 1915 Germany never regained a place of affection or honor in most American hearts.

Theodore Roosevelt pronounced the sinking an act of piracy on a larger scale of murder "than old-time pirates ever practiced." Secretary of State Robert Lansing, who, along with President Wilson and most of the people of the United States, still wanted to remain neutral, nonetheless confided to his diary that the *Lusitania* episode dramatized the essential evil of the German government. A German triumph in Europe "would mean the overthrow of democracy in the world" and "the turning back of the hands of human progress two centuries." Rushing back from England just after the liner perished, the president's most trusted adviser, Colonel Edward M. House, persuaded his chief "not to conduct a milk-and-water war, but to put . . . all the energy of our nation into it, so that Europe might remember for a century what it meant to provoke a peaceful nation into war." The president replied that "he had never been sure that we ought not to take part in the conflict and, if it seemed evident that Germany and her militaristic ideas were to win, the obligation upon us was greater than ever." Several months later, as Wilson continued to argue inconclusively with Berlin over the nature and responsibility of the tragedy, he instructed his secretaries of war and the navy to draw up plans for the "full development" of the country's fighting forces, including "a consistent and progressive development of the Navy" as the "great defensive arm of the nation." To a people personally untouched by war for a half century, the issue seemed painfully obvious. As the editor of an eastern journal wrote: "The submarine is a comparatively new weapon. It can only be used in accordance with established principles of international law. Those principles must not be altered to make destruction and murder still easier than they have been. If the submarines cannot act without violating binding laws, they must cease to act. They can only be tolerated if they are willing to accept the indispensable restrictions."[9]

Given such adherence to traditional principles of naval combat, Germany's case—strategic and tactical, if not moral—for pursuing unrestricted submarine warfare had scant chance of being recognized, much less accepted. Traditional rules of "cruiser warfare" demanded that a marauder carefully ensure the safety of passengers and crew before sinking enemy passenger and cargo ships. Innocent civilians had to be permitted to escape in well-provisioned lifeboats and given, if possible, correct courses to the nearest landfall. Conformity to such rules meant that submarines either had to surface to conduct attacks against enemy merchantmen or had to surface immediately after such attacks to render the necessary assistance.

German U-boat commanders swiftly discovered, however, that surfaced submarines with their thin hulls and small deck guns (originally most U-boat carried no deck armament) were extremely vulnerable to sinking by the same ships they were trying to destroy. A determined merchant captain had an excellent chance of ramming a surfaced submarine to death before the U-boat could fully disable his ship either by gunfire or by torpedo. When the Admiralty began arming British merchantmen soon after the outbreak of war (which traditional rules of war at sea allowed), German submarines became even more vulnerable. By 1915 the Royal Navy went so far as to fly neutral flags on some of its own armed merchant cruisers, which they dubbed "Q ships," so that when a German submarine surfaced to investigate it was suddenly smothered in heavy gunfire.[10] To insist under these circumstances that the submarine surrender its unique capability to strike suddenly and devastatingly from beneath the sea was, the Germans argued, asking too much from a desperate nation struggling to survive an assault on two fronts while suffering from hunger and want. British merchant ships, usually sailing without any protection whatsoever, were ridiculously easy prey for the U-boats, and if enough of those ships could be sunk quickly, Britain would be driven from the war and peace would soon reign. No one could ask a country fighting for its life to holster its one winning weapon.

And it very nearly was a winning weapon. In the years of enormous technological change leading up to 1914, Britain's "naval elite" focused (as would the Japanese High Command little more than a quarter century later) on maintaining command of the seas through a superior and triumphant battle line, which would, it was firmly believed, resolve all subsidiary problems, including the protection of global trade. Britain's naval bureaucracy never considered that a war with Germany would for the first time ever pit "two, non-self-sufficient industrial economies . . . against one another in a struggle where the exploitation of economic vulnerabilities was to prove every bit as crucial as any military prowess." Nor did they understand prior to 1915 the enormous potentiality of the U-boat as a commerce raider, fixated as they were on the 1913 naval exercises in which submarines sank or neutralized a sizable portion of the British battle line. Even the comparatively farsighted and innovative Jacky Fisher "seemed unable to recognize that [submarine] depredations on the trading route," whether within or beyond the bounds of traditional international law, "could seriously threaten even a power of Great Britain's magnitude." His assistant deputy of naval operations, Herbert Richmond, wrote very early on in the war, "The submarine has the smallest value of any naval vessel for the direct attack upon trade. She does not carry a crew that is capable of taking charge of a prize, she cannot remove passengers and other persons if she wishes to sink one."[11] Seldom in modern naval history has such an appreciation been so devastatingly wrong.

But in an age not quite yet ready to embrace war as a series of "most ancient, repellent, and irresponsible crimes," Britain—and Woodrow Wilson and his countrymen—continued to hold the moral upper hand.[12] And for good reason. As the first effective stealth weapons ever employed at sea, submarines, properly employed, were legitimate weapons of war. They could surely be used against enemy warships large and small. And in the context of international law, they could also properly destroy enemy freighters and cargo ships carrying weapons of war from neutral or allied nations to the home country or to continental ports for direct delivery to the battlefronts.

Passenger ships, however, were an entirely different proposition. Troop transports were fair game, and any civilians traveling on them assumed all risk. But there can be absolutely no justification for destroying commercial passenger liners. Germany's elated public reaction to the sinking of *Lusitania* was at once inexcusable and reprehensible, conveying to U-boat commanders the explicit message that destruction of noncombatant women and their children was politically if not morally sanctioned. Four months after *Lusitania* went down, another German submarine, U-24, lurked off Kinsale. Having just properly stopped the British steamer *Durnsley*, permitting the crew to take to lifeboats before planting destructive charges in the hull, Captain Rudolph Schneider caught sight of another, larger, steamer approaching. He quickly identified it as a passenger vessel, but "as I had been shot at by a large steamer" earlier in the week, "I decided to attack this one from under water." One torpedo was enough to send the White Star liner *Arabic* beneath the waves with the death of forty-four civilians, two or three of whom were Americans. That same day, Schwieger and U-20 torpedoed and sank the British passenger liner *Hesperian* off Fastnet with the loss of thirty-two civilians, none of them American. Kaiser Wilhelm barely avoided a complete rupture in relations with the United States by sacking his naval chief and issuing firm orders in council against attacking any and all passenger vessels.

But Schneider's callousness reflected the cruel and reckless course that Germany was prepared to follow at sea if it became desperate enough.[13] The following November no less than three British hospital ships—all clearly marked with bright white paint and broad red crosses on their hulls—were sunk almost simultaneously, among them the huge *Britannic,* which had been intended as a sister of the ill-fated *Titanic* before war intervened. Whether these ships succumbed to submarine torpedoes or to submarine-laid minefields was never decisively determined, but the results were similar. Casualties were surprisingly light, but death was always gruesome. Escaping from *Britannic,* one elderly British nursing matron saw a propeller from the slowly sinking ship "cut a boat in half and fling its mutilated victims into the air, but for the sake of the young women for whom she was responsible, she never uttered a sound or moved a muscle of her grim old face." A decade after the Armistice, Admiral Lewis Bayly, who was responsible for sending Britain's Q ships to sea, recalled, "Perhaps one of the most dreadful sights in the war was the arrival on shore of numbers of women and children saved from a ship torpedoed by an enemy submarine. Half-clothed, wet and cold, many of the women did not know whether their children were saved or not, and many had lost all they possessed." The "Submarine Menace," as it came to be called, "was something different: our commerce was subject to attack by an 'unseen' enemy, to be sunk by a torpedo before any signal for help could be sent or any escape could be attempted; liners, tramps, fishing craft, men, women, and children, were all at the mercy of an 'unseen enemy.'"[14]

No nation that employed submarines—and minefields—could now be certain of escaping the stigma of terrorism. The first ship lost in World War II—just twelve hours after its inception—was the 13,500-ton British passenger liner *Athenia,* which went down some 250 miles off the northwest coast of Ireland after being torpedoed by the submerged U-30. Five years later almost to the day, three American submarines, *Pampano, Sealion,* and *Growler,* attacked a Japanese convoy in the South China Sea containing two transports and sank both. What the American skippers did not know at the time (though they quickly learned as they began rescuing the handful of pitiful survivors) was that the ships were carrying 2,200 British and Australian prisoners of war from Southeast Asia to the Home Islands. According to journalist and historian Gearoid O'Neill, only 136 survived.[15] The following spring and summer, submarines (and air force B-29s) began mining Japan's Inland Sea in an effort to choke off the transport of supplies and troops from the Asian mainland to Japanese ports. Undoubtedly, innocent fishermen and perhaps a small interisland passenger vessel or two or more went down with loss of life. By that time the world had become so numbed to casualties of any kind that such sinkings, if known, would have been dismissed as the fortunes of war.

Confronted by the universal moral condemnation of a world that could still be thrilled with horror, the German Admiralty stayed its hand throughout the last months of 1915 and all of 1916, submitting grudgingly to American demands that the U-boat campaign be restricted to surface attacks, while Berlin repeatedly tried to convince the always skeptical Wilson of the plight under which imperial Germany labored. It was a difficult task, of course, for the Germans refused to admit publicly how badly the British blockade was affecting their war effort. But that blockade itself could be condemned as a weapon of terror since it not only flagrantly flouted traditional neutral rights in several respects but also included foodstuffs in the list of contraband. If British policy makers, civilians all, were trying to starve German women and children, was it immoral when U-boat commanders, warriors, with hungry wives and infants at home, inadvertently killed British noncombatants or accidentally drowned neutrals traveling on British ships? Dogger Bank had demonstrated the apparent impotence of the High Seas Fleet; Jutland had confirmed it. Yet Germany had to wage a successful war at sea or perish. Combat against an island nation even more vulnerable to blockade than the fatherland could be prosecuted only with a new weapon system whose physical limitations dictated that it be employed with stealth. The Germans thus had some valid points to make, but Wilson and his people were never sufficiently impressed to reverse policy.

The president's willful ignorance of the brutal realities of modern industrial warfare fueled German desperation. All too soon, in a self-fulfilling prophecy, the kaiser's military and naval advisers—though not Wilhelm himself—began calling for the kind of sustained barbarism at sea that the *Lusitania* incident had prefigured. Alfred von Tirpitz led the charge toward "military-political brinkmanship," but by the autumn of 1916 conditions were so desperate that not only his sailors and the army marched beside him but so did a surprisingly broad segment of public and political opinion. Combat on the western front was bleeding Germany white while the navy had done nothing of consequence. At home the blockade and a disastrous harvest strained German resources to the utmost. The enemy was arming his merchant ships faster than Germany could produce submarines. But the navy insisted that unrestricted submarine warfare could rescue the situation at a stroke and lead to dramatic victory. If the U-boats could sustain a six-month campaign, destroying an average of six hundred thousand tons of enemy shipping each thirty days, Britain would be finished, for "the exceptionally poor harvest of grain, including feed grain," had proved to be worldwide, hitting North America as well as Europe and the British Isles exceptionally hard. Only Britain's ability to import foodstuffs from as far away as Argentina, India, and Australia kept Albion's war machine running, and that machine in turn was the fulcrum of the entire Allied war effort, for Italy and France "are already so severely weakened in their economic foundations that they are kept in the fight only through England's energy and resources. If we succeed in breaking" the "backbone" of the British war effort, its merchant fleet, "the war will be immediately decided in our favour." Suddenly, the war at sea seemed to hold the key to victory in the exhausting, bloody war on land.

Three days before Christmas 1916, Admiral Henning von Holtzendorff, a Tirpitz protégé and "the driving force behind the German declaration of un-restricted U-boat warfare," dispatched a lengthy memorandum containing the above views to Royal Field Marshal and Army Chief of Staff Paul von Hinden-burg. In his concluding paragraphs, Holtzendorff confronted the twin specters of a U.S. entry and Germany's fate. The first he dismissed; the second he clearly feared. "It is my firm belief that war with the United States is such a serious matter that it should by all means be avoided. In my view, fear of a diplomatic rupture, however, should not lead us to recoil from making use at the decisive moment of a weapon that promises victory for us." The "decisive moment" had clearly arrived.

> From the moment back in autumn 1916 when I declared the time had come to strike against England the situation has steadily improved in our favour. The [global] crop failure, in conjunction with the effects of the war on England up to now, gives us the opportunity to force a decision before the next harvest. If we do not make use of what may well be the last opportunity, then I see no other option than that of mutual exhaustion, without our succeeding in bringing the war to an end on terms that would secure our future as a world power.

Holtzendorff insisted that "to achieve the desired results, the campaign of un-restricted submarine warfare has to be launched on 1 February [1917] at the very latest." So it was. Hindenburg and the army immediately supported the navy, and at a conference at Pless (Pszczyna) early in January 1917 Theobald von Bethmann Hollweg discovered that his kaiser had been won over to the new policy. The chancellor's will collapsed in the face of royal, military, and (not far in the background) public insistence on yet another ruthless war policy.[16] Following Holtzendorff's recommendation, Germany inaugurated unrestricted submarine warfare on February 1, 1917. President Wilson broke off diplomatic relations within the week and after the deaths of several American citizens on torpedoed vessels asked Congress for a declaration of war on April 2. Four days later the United States was formally at war with Germany.

From its inception undersea warfare generated as much self-pity as self-justification. To their victims U-boats were like a knife in the back coming suddenly out of the dark. To their crews the "pig boats" were hideous coffins. To be abruptly torpedoed was a dreadful ordeal. The murder of *Lusitania* was like the terror bombing of a great glittering hotel. Indeed, several hundred passengers were just finishing their luncheon in the sumptuous dining hall when the torpedo struck. But unlike the victims of a hotel or department store bombing, those who survived the immediate horrors of torpedoing had to endure the further trauma of being suddenly pitched into chilly or icy waters, where most of them perished. The faces on many of the corpses recovered from Saint George's Channel in the days after the *Lusitania* massacre were frozen in expressions of inexpressible woe.

But submariners had their own agonies. Going to sea in the tiny, cramped undersea craft of both world wars was an ordeal that could daunt or warp the strongest person. Dying in such vessels was beyond imagining. Antisubmarine technology and tactics in the First World War were, of necessity, quite crude. "Asdic" and its advanced system, "sonar," lay a decade and more in the future. When under way U-boats could be detected only by "hydrophones" that picked up the sound of their engines, or by sight, if their small periscopes left a sufficient trail through the water. When attacking individual ships far at sea from a submerged position, the boats were thus nearly invulnerable. Only with the institution in 1917 of the convoy system was the menace tamed, for the boats were then forced to move into shallow coastal waters to find suitable prey. There they were liable to comparatively ready detection, not only by hydrophone and periscope sightings but also by glimpses of their submerged hulls in clear water. Destroyers, "subchasers," and aircraft had a far better chance to detect and destroy them. British submarine crews operated almost exclusively in the shallow waters off German or German-held ports in the Channel, the North Sea, and the Baltic.

Whether far at sea or operating close ashore, the submarine skippers and crews of 1915–1918 and 1939–1945 could endure only by youthful bravado, impudence, and daring. A tale from the earliest days of the submarine era illustrates how men survived or tried to survive an essentially inhuman existence. At the outbreak of World War I Lieutenant Max Horton sailed his E-9 right into Heligoland harbor, hunting for enemy warships. He found none tempting enough, and so, instead of departing, he simply took his ship down to the shallow bottom (sixty feet) and waited, sending the crew to their bunks for rest while he, the executive officer, and the navigator settled in for several rounds of three-handed bridge. "We could hear enemy ships scuttling about overhead," one of Horton's ratings remembered,

> when sudden like I hears something clang against us way for'ard. The war hadn't been going long enough for us to know all we did later, as you might say, but it was plain to know what it was. They was sweeping, and their sweeps was hooked across our bows.
>
> I cups me head in me hand, wondering when the explosions would begin, when I hears the Captain say, "Your play, Chapman." Mr. Chapman, I noticed, was a bit interested in this here row up for'ard too.
>
> The wire slipped and scraped. It was so plain you could see it all. Her [the submarine's] skin might've been glass. The chains worked along the bow, scratched over the jumping wires, hitched up against the periscope standard, and after what seemed like a couple of weeks dragged clear. Just as it did, Mr. Chapman says, "Sorry, Horton old chap, but you are down one trick doubled."
>
> The Captain laughs. A nasty laugh, it seems to me. "Don't you believe it, Chapman," he says. "You revoked just when the wire hooked on. You forfeit two tricks." Then he turns to the navigating officer who was keeping score, tells him what to put down, and says, "Bridge, gentlemen, is a game you've simply got to keep your mind on if you hope to play it well."[17]

But when the luck finally ran out and all the guile, competence, and cunning that U-boat skippers (or their counterparts on British or U.S. boats) possessed was exhausted, death was inevitable. Drowning helplessly in a crowded, smelly, sinking submarine that had been rammed or holed by shell fire from a presumably harmless enemy merchantman was terrible enough. But to perish during a depth-charge attack while already trapped several hundred feet beneath the surface was indescribable. Many submarine crews survived hours of depth bombing before the final moment. Every man knew when every attack was coming because he could clearly hear the screws of the approaching enemy warship churning through the water above (Chuff-cHuff-cHuff-cHuff-cHuff), and even the splash of the depth charges as they hit the sea after rolling off the enemy's stern. There were long seconds of unbearable waiting, bracing for what might be the final shock, then the awful, driving thunderclaps as explosion after explosion rocked the small boat from stem to stern, often blowing out electrical systems, snapping off lightbulbs, bursting waterlines, and throwing men violently against machinery or to the deck in the sudden dark.

Dazed sailors determined whether they were indeed still alive, then rushed to make the frantic repairs needed to survive while trying to elude the next attack. All too often the final, shattering blow was struck. If men were lucky, their ship blew up and they went to eternity without a thought. But many had time to realize that their craft was mortally damaged and could not reach the surface. All they could do was to stand or slump in darkness in the midst of a rising flood of freezing seawater, waiting stoically for the end or screaming frantically at the captain or someone to do something. Either they would drown in the rising waters, or their bodies would implode as the entire leaking hull drifted inexorably into the depths to be finally crushed by the terrible ocean pressure.

Only the stoutest characters could serve on such ships day after day and week after week of a long war cruise. Since Germany used its submarines far more actively and aggressively in European waters than did the Allies, the U-boat experience was particularly harrowing. Within hours after leaving port the air was foul with stale food and sweating bodies. If forced to the surface during bad weather, the tiny U-boats of 1914–1918 (and 1939–1945!) pitched and rolled even worse than the smallest destroyers or corvettes. All aboard knew that a successful mission had to include at least one or two depth-charge attacks. In such circumstances the psyche was coarsened and brutalized beyond recognition. German U-boat crews often behaved inhumanly, and their adversaries on the surface tracked them down and drowned them with relish. Those U-boat crewmen who survived a cruise often returned to port completely broken in spirit.

Because the collapse and demoralization of imperial Germany in November 1918 led to an only partial preservation of German submarine records, no authoritative study of the undersea war of 1914–1918 exists.[18] The lack of a comprehensive history of U.S. naval operations in World War I exacerbates the problem. Therefore, the relative efficiency both of the German U-boat war and of Allied countermeasures has, until recently, been difficult to determine with precision. Statistics, although fascinating, have been contradictory and incomplete. According to recent information U-boats in 1914 sank 3 British merchantmen totaling 2,950 tons. The next year, as Berlin finally recognized their potential, German submarines sent 640 civilian vessels totaling 1,189,031 tons to the bottom. In 1916, despite being ostensibly leashed to the traditional provisions of commerce warfare, the kaiser's submarines destroyed 1,301 ships totaling 2,194,420 tons. And in 1917, when unrestricted undersea warfare was most intense, German U-boats sank 3,170 Allied and neutral ships totaling nearly 6 million tons. In April 1917 alone the U-boats sent more than 860,000 tons of shipping to the bottom, and "the chance of [an Allied] vessel safely completing a round voyage from the British Isles to a port beyond Gibraltar was now only one in four." Not only had Holtzendorff's 600,000-ton monthly sinking target been exceeded, but the steadily increasing number of sinkings threatened outright Allied defeat as well. In the last year of the war, when the Allied convoy system became fully operational, losses were reduced by nearly two-thirds. But even then 1,280 ships totaling more than 2.5 million tons perished. According to these figures, approximately 11 million tons of Allied and neutral shipping were destroyed over the course of the war.

In 1919 a knowledgeable British analyst, L. H. Hordern, presented much lower figures on submarine sinkings.[19] He investigated how many Allied merchant vessels sunk by submarines were torpedoed and how many were torpedoed without warning, the real test of terrorist warfare. Hordern broke his study into three phases. During Phase 1, which lasted until January 29, 1915, submarines used no torpedoes against Allied merchant ships; a surfaced U-boat stopped every vessel and allowed its crew and passengers to escape before the ship was destroyed. Only 4 British merchant ships were lost in this period. In Phase 2, which lasted until February 1, 1917, Britain lost 544 ships and 3,066 lives (including 1,198 on *Lusitania*) to German submarines (an average of 22 ships per month). Of the vessels lost, 269, or nearly half, were sunk by torpedoes and 148 of them without warning. A further 129 vessels were damaged with some loss of life. Hordern broke Phase 3, the period of unrestricted submarine warfare from February 1917 to the Armistice, into three subcomponents. During the seven months from roughly February 1 to August 31, 1917, German submarines sank 736 vessels, an average of 105 per month, or five times the rate in Phase 2. Of these, 572, or more than 75 percent, were torpedoed and 505, or 69 percent, were sunk without warning. From September 1, 1917, until the blockading of the Belgian submarine bases in April 1918, submarines sank 548 Allied merchantmen, an average of 68.5 per month. Of these, 448, or 82 percent, were torpedoed, all but 4 without warning. In the last six-plus months of the war from May 1 to November 11, 1918, German U-boats sent 252 Allied vessels to the bottom, an average of 42 per month. Two hundred twenty-eight, or 90 percent, were sunk by torpedo, all with no warning.

And how did the U-boats fare? Admiral Eduard von Capelle, in evidence given before the Reichstag War Failures Committee in 1919, stated that Germany built 390 submarines during or before World War I. These included 19 boats completed for the surrender after November 11, 1918. According to Capelle, 178 boats were definitely lost, 176 others surrendered, 14 were scuttled, 7 were lost en route to surrender, and 5 were ceded. Another 8 were broken up in Germany, and 2 others were interned elsewhere and not surrendered. Nearly eighty years later, in 1997, naval scholar Paul Kemp completed a detailed study of German submarine losses in both world wars. Kemp agreed with the figure of 178 destroyed between 1914 and 1918, though a careful count of his figures indicates that 11 more U-boats were killed than he and other authorities have stated. According to Kemp, 5 German U-boats were lost in 1914, 21 more in 1915, 24 in 1916, 25 in the period January to June 1917, and 43 in the last six months of 1917. Seventy-one were destroyed by Allied ships, aircraft, and mines between January 1 and November 11, 1918, for a grand total of 189.[20] Whatever the statistics, it cannot be denied that after 1916 the U-boat war at once deflected and tied down British naval energies and resources and that the subsequent U.S. naval effort focused almost entirely on the enemy submarine offensive. "In November, 1917, a balance sheet of the forces engaged on either side, which the head of the Anti-Submarine Warfare Department of the Admiralty drew up for Admiral Sir John Jellicoe showed that '. . . on the German side there were about 178 U-boats. Against these the British were using 277 destroyers, 30 corvettes, 49 steam yachts, 849 trawlers, 687 drifters, 24 mine sweepers (paddle boats), 50 small dirigibles, 194 aircraft, 77 Q-ships . . .' and well over 100,000 mines as well."[21]

Did U-boat sinkings ever disrupt Allied shipping sufficiently to imperil the war effort? The answer seems to be no, though they probably would have without the intervention of U.S. sea power. If Hordern's figures are correct (and it was in the British interest to inflate, not deflate, sinking rates to emphasize the barbarism and terror of the German submarine campaign so that it would be outlawed in the future), then the U-boat war was not yet the life-and-death crisis that it seemed at the time. And once the Allies began employing vigorous countermeasures, especially convoying, the German sea offensive was contained within a matter of months.

The kaiser and his military and naval advisers simply outsmarted themselves in pursuing submarine warfare. Before February 1917 Germany was not sinking enough British and French vessels to seriously jeopardize the Allied war effort. To do that it had to resume unrestricted submarine warfare. But, as knowledge-able Germans realized, such an act would bring the United States into the war with its own merchant marine (augmented by a large number of German vessels impounded in American ports), and its unprecedented industrial capabilities including rapid shipbuilding. Thus, Berlin's submarine campaign was frustrated at every point.[22]

Even before Wilson asked Congress for a formal declaration of hostilities, he directed the navy to dispatch an immediate mission to London to explore joint planning with the Admiralty. The obvious candidate was William Sims, now a rear admiral who in late March sailed for England in mufti aboard an American passenger ship and met his old friend Jellicoe just hours after the United States had become, in Wilson's careful calculation, an associate member of the Allied cause.

Jellicoe had shocking news. The Allies were not winning the war; Germany was. Opening a drawer, he handed Sims a report of merchant-marine losses for the previous several months. According to Admiralty figures, German U-boats had sent 536,000 tons of Allied shipping to the bottom in February and 603,000 tons in March. The amount for April, if sinkings continued at the same rate, could reach 900,000 tons (and in fact losses were very close to that estimate).[23] Jellicoe could not know, but could guess, that his enemies across the North Sea were jubilant. General Erich Ludendorff had even urged in February 1917 that hospital ships be sunk without warning, since the perfidious English were doubt-less employing them for military purposes. Ludendorff's suggestion was appar-ently accepted, for within three months enemy submarines had destroyed two British hospital vessels.[24]

Sims was amazed at the figures Jellicoe presented. What was Britain doing to stop this terrible hemorrhage? Everything it could, Jellicoe replied. Shipyards were frantically constructing destroyers, trawlers, and any other vessels that could be used as antisubmarine platforms. Every small craft then on the seas was being requisitioned to hunt U-boats. But the situation was serious, "and we shall need all of the assistance we can get." When Sims asked what solutions there might be to the U-boat "problem," his old friend replied, "Absolutely none that we can see now."[25]

Several months later, when the first half-dozen American destroyers sent to European waters under Lieutenant Commander Joseph Taussig were about to begin their first antisubmarine patrols, the British commander of the western approaches, Admiral Lewis Bayly, called the captains to Admiralty House in Queenstown (now Cobh) for a briefing. He delivered a short speech, which he would give to every one of the nearly one hundred U.S. destroyer skippers who rotated through during the war; indeed, it was a speech that would have been appropriate for anyone venturing into the Battle of the Atlantic a quarter century later, for it set forth in stark terms the British view of the U-boat war:

> When you pass beyond the defenses of the harbor you face death, and live in danger of death until you return behind such defenses. You must presume from the moment you pass out that you are seen by a submarine and that at no time until return can you be sure that you are not being watched. You may proceed safely, and may grow careless in your watching; but let me impress upon you the fact that if you do relax for a moment, if you cease to be vigilant, then you will find yourself destroyed, your vessel sunk, your men drowned.[26]

By its nature war is a prolonged exercise in hysteria; however, it may be overlaid by apparent rationality. In an atmosphere of incessant crisis, mature and dispassionate judgment is often the first quality to be jettisoned. But it must also be regained if victory is to be achieved. The Royal Navy responded to events and to Sims's proddings by initiating convoys with greater rapidity and imagination than contemporaries or many historians credited them. Once the Anglo-Americans settled on the convoy system in the late summer of 1917, the U-boats were doomed.

The Americans were an absolutely crucial element in the victory over the German submarines. The navy that entered the war in April 1917 was a half-trained, understrength service, but it was eager for a fight and determined to become a preeminent if not the predominant maritime power on earth. Its president stood confidently behind it.

Back in December 1915 Wilson had sent to Congress a "comprehensive plan for putting the navy upon a final footing of strength and efficiency" within five years. No less than 16 capital ships and nearly 100 support vessels, including submarines, would be added to the fleet, which would also "immediately" recruit 10,000 sailors and 1,500 marines. The following month Wilson made a brief but intensive train tour from Washington, D.C., to Kansas City and back to generate popular sentiment for "preparedness." Over the past three years of his administration, the president told a Chicago audience, Congress had "poured out more money" for the navy than ever before in the nation's history. "All the subsidiary arms of the service have been built up," most especially aviation.

Whereas in 1912 only 4 officers were assigned to flying duties—without a single usable aircraft at hand—"now there are thirty-seven airships, 121 commissioned officers," a large number of enlisted support personnel, and a "school of practice at Pensacola." Naval administration had been completely reorganized and centralized with a chief of naval operations responsible for overall service efficiency and the formulation of mission responsibilities. "The defense of the nation," Wilson added, demanded a strong fleet. "The Navy," he said several days later, "sees that nobody interferes with us."[27]

The president calculated, erroneously it would seem, that the U.S. fleet in 1915 was no better than fourth in size in the world (it was probably third by this time behind Britain and Germany). Wilson was careful, however, to emphasize the defensive character of the nation's rapidly expanding sea service. "Do you realize the task of the navy?" he asked a St. Louis audience, inviting his listeners to consider "the enormous stretch of coast from the [Panama] canal to Alaska—from the canal to the northern coast of Maine. There is no other navy in the world," he concluded to applause, "that has to cover so great an area . . . as the American navy, and it ought, in my judgement, to be incomparably the greatest navy in the world."[28] Whether he meant size, capability, or both, the president did not say, but foreign observers could not mistake his meaning.

The navy bill finally reached both House and Senate floors in the summer of 1916, and the handful of opponents who argued its folly, its cost, and the ability of the nation's coastal defenses to beat back an enemy invasion were swept aside. By this time the stalemate at Jutland had revealed substantial weaknesses in the British fleet, and preparedness advocates campaigned successfully to compress the proposed five-year building-plan program into three.[29]

The debates revealed how disillusioned and cynical the country had become with the bloodshed overseas and the duplicitous diplomacy it had fostered around the world. As Antony Preston has observed, the purpose of the 1916 legislation, Wilson's protestations to the contrary notwithstanding, "was quite simply to displace the British as the world's leading power, by building a navy . . . which could, if necessary, achieve its aims by force."[30] Given German barbarism at sea as well as ashore, British high-handedness in prosecuting the blockade (and ineptitude in defeating the High Seas Fleet), and long-standing racial if not political tensions with Japan, the United States would have been foolhardy to consider any foreign navy either its friend or its shield. A shattered postwar world would need American goods, credits, and services. A strong merchant marine would be the key to future national prosperity, and it was essential to protect U.S. vessels with warships flying the Stars and Stripes.

The naval bill of August 29, 1916, provided for a continuous program of construction of more than 150 ships, all of which were to be laid down by July 1, 1919. Above all, the new legislation provided for a much more balanced fleet. Gone was the juvenile obsession with huge battleships at the expense of other types of vessels. The old passions had been replaced by an understanding that modern naval warfare, especially the emergence of the submarine, required the services of cruisers and large numbers of "auxiliary" vessels, particularly destroyers. The United States thus committed itself to build 10 new battleships, 6 battle cruisers, 10 scout cruisers, 50 destroyers, 9 oceangoing submarines, and 58 coastal submarines. Provision was also made for the substantial increase in personnel of all ranks and rates needed to man the new ships.[31] But long before the program could be properly started, Germany resumed unrestricted submarine warfare and dispatched the Zimmermann telegram.[32] The U.S. Navy suddenly found itself in a war it had never envisioned.

The naval legislation had presumed sufficient time to enlist and train the thousands of sailors needed to man more than 100 different ships. Suddenly, there was no time. Five years earlier 3,094 officers and 47,515 enlisted men had manned the fleet. Now the number of officers had more than doubled to 8,038 regulars and reserves on active duty. The enlisted ranks had increased 360 percent to 171,133 regular, reserve, and "National Naval Volunteers." Eighteen months later, on November 9, 1918, only two days before the Armistice, there were 32,474 active-duty officers in the fleet and 497,030 enlisted men. In six years the U.S. Navy had increased tenfold.[33]

But it proved up to the challenge. For years the service had ranked just behind the army as the largest procurement agency in the federal government. Late-nineteenth-century administrative reforms and reorganization had given the Navy Department six centrally coordinated bureaus and a modern and efficient supply system. In 1917–1918 John M. Hancock, who headed the Purchasing Division in the Bureau of Supplies and Accounts, carefully bought along commodity lines, stressed competitive bidding whenever possible, and employed "tough" safeguards against abuse in negotiated contracts.[34]

While several thousand naval reserve officers were rushed through a "strenuous" three months' course at the naval academy, a flood of recruits overwhelmed the training depots and ships, and most of the older pre-dreadnoughts were pressed into service as training vessels.[35] Despite its dramatic growth, the U.S. Navy never found enough men to run its ships. Even the splendid new battlewagons like *Arizona, Oklahoma,* and *Nevada* were undermanned, and their crews contained many novices who had to be drilled and drilled by senior seamen, petty officers, and officers before the ships could be considered even minimally efficient.[36] Education for enlisted men was conducted at a frantic pace everywhere and at all levels, and its immediate rewards were chaotic and haphazard, leading to strains in the fleet between the comparative handful of old-timers, who had slowly worked their way up the promotion ladder, and the horde of new, rapidly trained boys, who often had responsibilities and perquisites beyond their years and initial capabilities.

Young Charlie Crooks enlisted just days after Wilson urged his countrymen to make the world safe for democracy.[37] The precocious seventeen year old had spent an indifferent year at the University of Chicago, and this impressed navy recruiters, who rushed him through basic training and then sent him to a slapdash three-week gunnery course, from which he emerged as a first-class gunner's mate. Assigned to the destroyer *Fanning*, Charlie proudly walked up the gangplank with his new "crow" and three chevrons and was met by the officer of the deck, a grizzled, old chief petty officer of perhaps thirty-seven or so who may have been a veteran of 1898. The chief approached the boy with a disarming smile and said: "My, my, that's certainly a handsome watch you have there." Charlie agreed. His father, a prominent Chicago lawyer, had given him the expensive, elegant timepiece as a going-away present. "May I see it?" the chief asked in his kindly voice. Charlie obligingly took the watch off his wrist and handed it to the chief, who promptly walked to the lines and with a delicate gesture dropped the watch overboard. Then he turned around and snarled, "Now get below, sonny!"

Charlie and several hundred thousand other shocked recruits quickly learned the rigors of naval discipline and in record time became good sailors. Around them their country buckled down to wage a modern war as no other nation ever had. In a year the United States Army recruited, trained, and transported to France 2 million soldiers; the navy, with major assistance from the British and French, less so from the Italians, safely escorted every one of them through the submarine-infested sea-lanes. The United States built the terminals and bases in France to efficiently receive and distribute the sudden flood of doughboys and their multitude of supplies. It also built bases and aerodromes in France and Britain for the many hundreds of destroyers, subchasers, and aircraft that provided the critical escorts through the enemy submarine lanes. By the spring of 1918 thousands of Americans were arriving in France daily, and that country of placid farms and charming châteaus became a huge American cantonment. The United States also produced thousands of mines and built the mine-laying vessels to sow them in the upper reaches of the North Sea, where they would interdict the sea-lanes between the enemy submarine bases and the western approaches. And finally a substantial number of American destroyers and subchasers were dispatched to the Mediterranean, where they played an important role in stifling German and Austrian U-boat campaigns. "The wonder of the war," wrote American naval officer Thomas Frothingham in 1921, "has been the fact that the peaceful United States proved to be the one nation that coordinated the functions of its military, naval, and industrial forces, to accomplish its full strategic objective, in the time set by a crisis and on the enormous scale demanded by the World War."[38]

Laissez-faire business principles were immediately suspended, and through a series of emergency boards and committees the Wilson administration raised the federal government to the position of director, occasionally even dictator, of the economy. Navy secretary Josephus Daniels, Chief of Naval Operations William S. Benson, and Commander in Chief of the Atlantic Fleet Henry T. Mayo gradually hammered out a coherent national naval policy in conjunction with Sims and the British Admiralty during the spring and summer of 1917. Meanwhile, the War Industries Board mobilized production, including frantic construction of cargo and transport ships; the War Trade Board licensed imports and exports; the Capital Issues Committee regulated investment; the War Finance Corporation lent funds to munitions industries; and the Food and Fuel Administrations set production, consumption, and pricing standards. "This is a crisis," a government bureaucrat told steel industry leaders, "and commercialism, gentlemen, must be absolutely sidetracked."[39]

Although the board was never able to get ships to sea in the eighteen months before the Armistice, it did produce a flood of merchant vessels in late 1918 and on into 1919 that would have to find employment—or be scrapped—when peace came. Meanwhile, the foundations of a substantial American transport fleet were readily available elsewhere. No fewer than thirty of the largest passenger liners in the kaiser's merchant service—among them the huge new *Vaterland, Grosse Kurfürst,* and *Friedrich der Grosse*—either were already in New York or had turned back to that neutral harbor at the beginning of the war. America's entry "precipitated, in effect, the Jutland of the German merchant marine." The enemy vessels immediately became legitimate prizes of war; their crews were sent to Ellis Island pending formal internment, and the ships themselves were moved to dockyards in Brooklyn and Hoboken, where hundreds of workers immediately swarmed aboard to convert them to troop transports.[40]

When the ships reappeared, the navy's Cruiser and Transport Force promptly prepared them for their first voyages overseas. Most had been given a dazzling camouflage of wildly colored stripes and strips that subsequently frustrated many submarine skippers maneuvering for the kill. "Some U-boat commanders were so bothered by the lurid emerald greens, pinks and purples used in ships' color-schemes that they had the eye-pieces of their periscopes fitted with color-filters."[41]

Only days after Congress declared war, Foreign Minister Arthur Balfour and an Anglo-French naval mission under Vice Admiral Montague Browning arrived in the United States and with tactful diplomacy began to construct a formal naval alliance. Browning met with Daniels, Benson, and Mayo at Norfolk and again at the Navy Department in Washington, D.C., and begged for at least one destroyer in European waters as a symbol of American intentions. After hours of polite badgering Daniels finally turned to Mayo and asked if such a ship could be detached. The admiral replied, "We can send a division and should not send less than that." Lieutenant Commander Joseph Taussig was designated skipper and was soon on his way to Ireland. The six little (eleven hundred–ton) destroyers attempted a constant sea speed of fifteen knots on their way across, "but during about half the passage were forced to slow to 12 on account of heavy beam seas and water coming aboard." Repairs to a condenser aboard *Wainwright* also slowed the small fleet for about ten hours. Nonetheless, Sims cabled Secretary Daniels, Taussig brought them all into Queenstown "in excellent condition" little more than four weeks after Wilson's declaration of war. As previously arranged, the division was met by a British destroyer that brought them into port through a swept channel in a recently seeded German minefield. News of their departure from the United States had appeared in Berlin news- papers shortly before their arrival in European waters. "On arrival in harbour," Sims continued, "our Destroyers commenced oiling immediately and the Com- manding Officers went ashore and paid official calls to Vice-Admiral Sir Lewis Bayly, Commanding British Naval Forces" in the area, and others. In an exchange that would go down in U.S. naval history, Bayly asked young Taussig how soon he could be ready for sea. "We are ready now, Sir," Taussig replied. "This appar- ently was a considerable surprise to the Vice Admiral, who then gave them four days before taking up active work."[42]

Balfour also persuaded Benson to dispatch several more squadrons of destroy- ers to Queenstown as soon as possible, and the Americans also agreed to provide merchant shipping on the crucial North Atlantic run. Complete Anglo-American cooperation was finally achieved at a series of naval conferences in London in the autumn of 1917 and culminated in establishment of the Allied Naval Council to coordinate policy and activities, which began meeting in Paris at the end of the year. At the same time a joint Anglo-American naval-planning section was established in Sims's office.[43] France and Italy, as well as Britain, also supplied troopships to transport the U.S. Army "over there." Britain's enormous merchant service could provide nearly half the carrying capacity, with French and Italian vessels transporting a mere fraction of the American men and equipment. U.S. warships took five out of every six American doughboys through the submarine danger zones to France.[44]

The Germans were thunderstruck by the U.S. effort; the Allies were amazed. "Would [the United States] appear in time to snatch the victor's laurels from our brows?" Hindenburg wondered. "That, and that only, was the decisive question! I believed I could answer it in the negative." The new chief of staff of the German army (who had replaced Erich von Falkenhayn following the hideous standoff at Verdun-sur-Meuse) was wrong, and he lost the war because of this miscalculation. America's entry "was like an avalanche," British Prime Minister David Lloyd George marveled. "The world has never seen anything like it."[45]

At Queenstown Taussig's six ships were soon followed by others, and by Independence Day 1917 there were thirty-five U.S. destroyers there. By November the number had grown to fifty-two, covering the waters between southern Ireland, France, and Gibraltar. Five of the American vessels had steamed all the way from the Philippines. The Americans were throwing every destroyer they possessed into the U-boat campaign. The destroyers, together with twenty-seven yachts that were sent over during the summer and early autumn, were employed almost exclusively upon convoy-escort work in the submarine zone. The U.S. reinforcements made the convoy system possible, for without them the Royal Navy would have had to reduce the number of destroyers to well below the margin required to safely support the Grand Fleet in any future battles with Reinhard Scheer and Franz von Hipper.[46]

At first the Queenstown escorts traveled "light," that is, they took a convoy to sea; got it past the last-known German submarines, perhaps three hundred miles or so beyond the Irish coast; and then returned to port. But by the end of 1917 the Admiralty had timed convoy departures and arrivals so that when the escorts "handed off" one outbound convoy for the United States, they immediately or soon thereafter picked up a convoy coming in from Canada, New York, or Boston. Only a few convoys were escorted exclusively by destroyers; most were covered by a few destroyers and a number of armed trawlers, sloops, subchasers, and even Q ships. The senior destroyer captain suddenly found himself burdened with a new title and responsibility: escort commander. Most of them handled the job with competence and aplomb.

Convoying proved a complex, time-consuming process requiring prodigious effort and considerable skill, attributes not well understood either by impatient publics of the time or by some historians thereafter.[47] Two factors were decisive in ensuring success: introduction of the depth charge, which the British had steadily elaborated since the beginning of 1915, and the ever growing volume of destroyers, P-boats, sloops, and subchasers.[48] Beyond the ships and weapons a whole new infrastructure was needed to respond to a novel means of warfare. The air and naval bases in the British Isles and France required support personnel, accommodation for staff and stores, recreation areas and canteens, hospitals, and docking, refueling, and repair facilities on a large scale. Training and inspection facilities had to be built and manned. With only a few exceptions the bases were staffed by reservists and women, who for the first time in the industrial era made a major contribution to naval warfare. The work of the Women's Royal Naval Service, popularly known as the Wrens, was not confined to clerical or intelligence occupations. Many were employed fitting depth charges and wire nets, "even in boiler cleaning."[49]

It took time for sailors to understand exactly how an antisubmarine convoy system could best be organized and how it could best function.[50] Eventually, the Anglo-American antisubmarine forces of 1917–1918 developed patterns of warfare that were still standard practice in the much broader conflict a quarter century later. The task began ashore, before sailing, for escort commanders had to ensure that their prospective convoys were well organized and ready to move. For this responsibility they could rely on the help of Bayly and his excellent staff at Queenstown, who drew up detailed sailing instructions for each merchant ship and warship captain in the forthcoming operation. Bayly's methods were soon adopted by convoy managers on the other side of the Atlantic in New York and Boston. Instructions included time of departure, the order in which each ship would pass through the antisubmarine nets or boom, directions for proceeding through the mine-swept channel, a sketch showing the position of all vessels in the convoy, the courses the convoy was to steer and the various navigation points it would pass on the ocean while remaining intact, information on what to do if the escorts had to depart before the planned dispersal point was reached, the speed of the convoy, and the type of zigzag pattern to use and its duration. In addition, the escort commander received a special sealed envelope containing orders, information, and instructions regarding the inbound convoy he would meet once the outbound convoy passed beyond his point of responsibility.

He was also given data about all the convoys that either were then at sea or would be at sea while he and his escorts were out in the Atlantic or in the Irish Sea. According to Taussig such information was provided so that one convoy would not blunder into another at night on the increasingly crowded western approaches.

Convoys began leaving U.S. ports on a weekly basis as early as May 1917 as the great buildup in Europe slowly got under way. A year later convoys left Hampton Roads, New York, or Boston daily. American shipyards halted battleship construction and started frantically churning out more than 200 destroyers (only a handful of which were completed in time to see action in 1918), countless merchant vessels, and 440 subchasers—tough, 110-foot, lightly armed, oceangoing power yachts designed not so much to destroy U-boats as to drive them away from convoys.[51]

On the day of departure escorts usually left harbor about two hours before the convoy and then spread out to conduct an antisubmarine sweep for a distance of ten miles beyond the lightship. After satisfying themselves that no U-boats were lurking about the harbor entrance ready to pounce as the convoy laboriously put itself together, the escorts moved back to the lightship to rendezvous with their charges. Then began the tedious process of "rounding up" and "shepherding" the merchant vessels into their various columns. Once that was accomplished, the convoy could proceed into the Atlantic, often on a zigzag course. At sea the escort commanders and their captains experienced numerous difficulties. Radio was still a crude, uncertain instrument as late as 1918, and many vessels carried only one operator, who unfortunately required food, drink, and a bit of sleep to function acceptably. Moreover, few merchant ships were equipped with searchlights that could be used as signaling lamps. When destroyer or trawler captains could not rouse a recalcitrant or dilatory skipper by radio, they had to resort to hailing the bridge with megaphones. But in the vicious winter days and nights on the North Atlantic howling winds often tore the words right out of the escort commander's mouth; as the war reached a climax in mid-1918, with ships, troops, and supplies literally pouring into Europe, many merchantmen had crews of Scandinavians, French, or Italians, and escorts found it nearly impossible to communicate with some deliberately ignorant skippers. Fog and rain often made semaphoring—and thus communication by internationally recognized signals—impossible.

Breakdowns were frequent among the merchantmen; occasionally, cargoes shifted dramatically in heavy seas, which could cause ships to capsize. No greater difference could be found between the antisubmarine war of 1917–1918 and the 1940–1943 Battle of the Atlantic than the response to these crises. The escort commanders of the later war often either came alongside the broken-down merchantman or used blinker lights to wish the poor devil and his crew the best of luck before sailing on with the rest of the convoy. The U-boats had become so deadly, the cargoes for Britain so desperately essential, that an entire convoy or its escort (or both) could not be jeopardized to save one ship. But in 1917–1918 the stricken vessels were almost invariably taken in tow, and none were lost while approaching British shores.

The Admiralty always feared that the German battle cruisers might somehow break out of the North Sea or even the Channel to wreak havoc. Thus, convoys had to be protected from enemy surface raiders not only in the submarine zones around Europe but at midocean as well. The Americans were able to deploy their arsenal of old, comparatively slow but powerfully gunned armored cruisers for the purpose. Chronic European coal shortages required the cruisers to drop their convoys when their bunker fuel was reduced to half. But within a few hours if not minutes, the convoys were picked up by the destroyers, so that the escort was practically continuous.

Once an outbound convoy from Europe reached the ocean safety point beyond the known range of U-boat activity, it usually dispersed and the escorts assumed a scouting line searching for the incoming convoy from the United States. Unless hindered by fog, darkness, or occasionally extremely heavy seas, rendezvous was usually achieved routinely. Thousands of doughboys heading for France on their transports—and a handful of congressmen and senators sailing the big ocean liners on their way to fact-finding tours of the western front—were amazed to see the little destroyers and trawlers suddenly racing up from the horizon, dark smoke pouring from their funnels, at just the time and from just the compass point that members of their ship's crew had said to expect them. "For the grateful passengers in the big ship it was a dramatic moment. They loved the Navy. It was magnificent. The country had never appreciated its noble bluejackets." On one ocean liner in a convoy an appreciative senator "laid aside his life-belt, invaded the smoking-room, and swore he would vote for any naval appropriation desired."[52] The escorts usually had to shepherd their new charges into different columns in order to separate ships into divisions going to various ports in Britain or France. The incoming escorts would contact the local or inshore escorts from Plymouth or Liverpool via radio so they could hand off each column as appropriate.

The destroyer crews, subchaser seamen, and trawler sailors of World War I did not have to endure the many awful sub-Arctic voyages (to say nothing of the Arctic convoys) that their sons and nephews would experience years later. But they did live through some terrible winter storms in the western approaches, the Channel, and off the coast of France. Those on the subchasers suffered the worst, for although these vessels had powerful engines and were beautifully designed to swoop over the heaving swells and absorb the crashing waves of the North Atlantic, they inevitably rolled wildly in all except the mildest seas. One subchaser captain said that when his tiny craft did its "usual dance" at sea, the sun "looked 'like a maltese cat flying across a horizon of scrambled eggs.'" The destroyers were not immune to the effects of stormy North Atlantic winter, and a wit on *Wadsworth* composed a sardonic little ditty about a landlubber caught on the cruel sea:

> Oh Mr. Captain stop the ship,
> I want to get out and walk!
> I feel so flipperty, flopperty, flip,
> I'll never reach New York—
> Oh Mr. Captain stop the ship,
> I'm sick of the raging main,
> Hi! Hi! Call me a cab,
> And take me home again.[53]

Despite Bayly's dramatic warnings about the ubiquity of the U-boat danger, antisubmarine warfare in 1917–1918 was conducted with a latitude and civility that escort captains and commanders in the next war would have found both astounding and criminally negligent. One night in the autumn of 1917, for example, lookouts informed the officer of the deck on Taussig's ship, *Wadsworth,* that they had just seen a phosphorous wake astern, which indicated a half-submerged U-boat heading for the convoy. *Wadsworth,* which was passing the rear of the convoy, immediately headed off in pursuit of the wake and dropped several depth charges on it. Minutes later a sister ship, *Trippe,* reported that she had struck an underwater object that had tilted her fifteen degrees on impact. The two vessels dropped several more charges but could see nothing and carried on with their routine escort duties. A half hour later radiomen aboard *Wadsworth* picked up signals from a heavily damaged submarine nearby asking for assistance. Taussig and his mates concluded that the enemy had been injured either by the depth charge attack or by *Trippe's* inadvertent ramming, and they proceeded on their way. Twenty-five years later Johnnie Walker would have rushed over and killed the beast.[54]

Convoying by itself was not the entire solution to the U-boat menace. To be effective it required augmentation by aircraft, minefields, "barrages" of booms and nets (thrown across the narrow Strait of Dover and from Otranto at the mouth of the Adriatic), other submarines, and above all adequate intelligence. Minefields varied considerably in both size and purpose. Some were designed to be used against surface craft, others against submerged U-boats. In some cases both purposes were combined.[55]

In mid-May 1917, Lieutenant Ronan Grady, an intelligence officer with the Office of Naval Operations in Washington, D.C., cabled Sims in London that "most of the German submarines and especially the large ones after clearing the mine field off the German coast head directly for Fair Island between the Orkneys and Shetlands Islands and do not hesitate to pass through to the Atlantic," subsequently making a landfall at St. Kilda west of the Hebrides before heading south to the vicinity of Fastnet and the Isles of Scilly. "The British have found it wholly impracticable to net this passage." The Americans decided to give it a go in a rather desperate attempt to overcome the persistent shortage of destroyers and other antisubmarine craft. The task, begun in early 1918, was prodigious, and one that the British viewed skeptically (they did not trust the efficiency of American mines) until the first destroyed U-boat was confirmed. After that the Royal Navy was converted, and one British analyst later wrote that "a minefield had a very disturbing effect on enemy submarines, and they would not willingly enter it if they knew where it was."[56]

By 1918 the Americans had joined the British, using submarines themselves, as U-boat hunters and killers. In February the first of eleven U.S. submarines arrived at Berehaven (Castletownbere) on the southwestern coast of Ireland, "around the corner" from Queenstown. In the last nine months of the war they may have sunk one U-boat, although it was not clear whether an American torpedo or one of the U-boat's own destroyed the German craft.

The British and U.S. naval-air arms in Europe swelled to enormous size by November 1918, ably assisted by smaller French forces, and their number-one duty was antisubmarine warfare. Only a handful of German submarines were directly destroyed from the air, because the crude, fragile planes of 1917–1918 possessed little offensive punch. Moreover, British air crews, at least initially, proved ignorant in the ways of submarine hunting. As late as March 1918, the director of the Air Division of the Naval Staff complained that "few [Naval] Air Service Officers have more than the vaguest idea of the capacity of the various classes of enemy submarines to remain submerged and the depth of water in which they can rest on the bottom, or the speeds at which submarines cruise submerged or on the surface." Captain F. R. Scarlett urged that a pamphlet be prepared "giving all the information relating to the various types of enemy submarines" including but not confined to submarine cruising capabilities, types of attack, mine-laying operations, and hunting tactics.[57]

Perhaps the chief contribution made by Allied aircraft was their drastic curtailment of submarine operations near convoys and in coastal areas. "When aircraft could provide aerial cover for a convoy, the convoy was virtually immune." British and American airmen detected enemy submarines in a broad arc from the southern North Sea through the Channel and the Dover Straits around to the Irish Sea. Initially, U-boats operating at the limit of their range in the eastern Atlantic off Ireland were immune to detection and assault from the air due to the limited range of British and U.S. aircraft. But the inauguration of the convoy system forced the U-boats to seek independently steaming prey in the coastal waters around the British Isles. Here flying boats, the smaller seaplanes, and land-based naval aircraft, together with reconnaissance blimps, could spot them readily and send them beneath the surface for hours at a time while shipping was rerouted or nearby antisubmarine vessels were directed against them. The average daily strength of the Royal Air Force (RAF) against the U-boats during the last six months of the war was impressive: 85 large flying boats, 216 seaplanes, 189 land-based aircraft, and 75 airships. America's naval-aviation buildup in the European theater was nothing short of stupendous. On April 6, 1917, the day Congress formally declared war against Germany, the United States Navy and Marine Corps possessed 54 aircraft—45 seaplanes, 6 flying boats, and 3 land-based aircraft. Nineteen months later, on Armistice Day, the navy and marine corps squadrons had 2,107 machines in hand: 695 seaplanes, 1,170 flying boats, and 242 land-based aircraft. The navy established hasty, forced-draft training programs on university campuses, on new air bases, and even in private industry. Most of the aviators and ground-support personnel were naval reservists. Twenty-five hundred officers and twenty-two thousand enlisted men flew or serviced the aircraft, auxiliary kite balloons, and the 3 dirigibles operating from three large bases in France and Britain as well as smaller installations in the Azores. U.S. naval aircraft flew more than three million nautical miles and attacked and damaged a dozen U-boats. Not only did American seaplanes and flying boats provide essential aerial reconnaissance and protection over the convoys, but land-based naval and marine corps aircraft also participated (with the RAF's new Handley Page heavy bombers) in major air raids against German U-boat facilities at Zeebrugge, Ostend, and Brugge, and for a time air units near Calais and Dunkirk directly supported the British army in Flanders.[58]

The key to the success of the convoy system was the incorporation of Room 40 with its priceless wireless intercepts, which allowed convoy managers ashore to pinpoint the location of enemy U-boats on a convoy's route and to alert the escorts either to expect battle or, if there was sufficient time, to reroute the convoy out of harm's way. By early 1918 the British Admiralty had established a convoy room with a large wall map showing the location of every convoy at sea as well as the latest position of enemy U-boats determined by Room 40's wireless intercepts. By thus visualizing a vast, watery battlefield, the Allies were able to overcome the most serious menace to their essential supremacy at sea.[59]

The successes of Room 40 in the battle against the U-boats were more substantial than its earlier efforts to track the movements of the German High Seas Fleet. In the first place, British radio intelligence improved steadily throughout the war years as the intercept specialists gained more experience and their superiors came to rely more confidently on their skills. Second, the antisubmarine war of 1917–1918, unlike the surface sweeps and occasional battles of 1914–1916, was conducted more comprehensively. Analysts in the Royal Navy's convoy room could employ not only radio intelligence but also aerial reconnaissance and surface-ship contacts and sightings to draw a fairly complete picture of enemy activities. A quarter century later, the British, Canadian, and U.S. navies would establish even more elaborate convoy rooms to monitor and manipulate the Battle of the Atlantic against Hitler's sea wolves, employing and combining even more sophisticated technologies and intelligence and reconnaissance capabilities.

The convoy system with support from above and beneath the waves had two fundamental objectives: to make it difficult for enemy submarines to find targets and to add considerably to the danger when they did. Convoys were designed to be magnets, defensive shields, and offensive platforms, luring U-boats in order to destroy them. German submariners responded feebly at best. Karl Dönitz, then a young submarine captain in the Mediterranean, recalled bitterly:

> The introduction of the convoy system in 1917 robbed [the U-boat] of its opportunity to become a decisive factor. The oceans at once became bare and empty; for long periods of time the U-boat, operating individually, would see nothing at all; and then suddenly up would loom a huge concourse of ships, thirty or fifty or more of them, surrounded by a strong escort of warships of all types. The solitary U-boat, which most probably had sighted the convoy purely by chance, would then attack, thrusting again and again and persisting, if the commander had strong nerves, for perhaps several days and nights, until the physical exhaustion of both commander and crew called a halt.

After all this effort the submarine might have sunk one or two vessels, but that was "a poor percentage of the whole. The convoy would steam on."[60]

From the beginning, the western sea approaches to Great Britain were the obvious locus of U-boat interest. Certainly, the Mediterranean was a profitable field of endeavor, and Berlin sent U-boats there as early as 1915. But even decimating enemy shipping between Gibraltar and Greece (and the handful of U-boats made a good attempt) could not whittle down British maritime trade sufficiently to induce hunger, shortages, and surrender.[61] Successful raids against enemy supply routes in the Channel were largely precluded by the presence of the Dover Patrol and the many destroyers of the Grand Fleet (although Flanders-based U-boats usually managed to avoid the Dover Patrol and escaped into the Atlantic by running the Channel at night). Moreover, most of the vessels in the Channel trade were comparatively small. The England-to-Norway shipping lanes could always be assaulted, but, as in the Mediterranean, the volume of traffic there was not large enough to cause a total crisis should the U-boats attack Allied shipping.

The essential hunting grounds were the Atlantic and the Irish Sea. Here a sufficient number of large enemy merchant ships could be sunk to threaten Britain's defeat. But U-boat deployment was restricted to the High Seas Fleet port of Wilhelmshaven (where about two-thirds of the vessels were stationed) and the Flanders ports of Ostend and Zeebrugge. The Flanders submarine force was occasionally distracted by joint missions with German destroyers to raid Britain's Dover Patrol. And after the spring of 1918 the British used repeated raids to make the Belgian ports untenable. To reach the western approaches, U-boat commanders had to take their vessels either around the northern coast of Scotland or through the Channel and along the Cornish coast and past the Isles of Scilly, consuming not only time but also precious fuel, which cut down the days they could spend patrolling off the southern tip of Ireland or in Saint George's Channel.

Such factors had not been decisive before convoys. But when the Royal Navy changed policy, the Germans failed to implement countermeasures, the most effective of which would have been the concentration of many submarines for a more or less simultaneous attack (that is, the "wolf pack") and assaults by night. U-boat captains employed neither practice with any consistency during World War I. When in April 1918 one of the submarine command staff proposed converting a two thousand–ton "cruiser U-boat" into a radio-command vessel that would sail into the western approaches to detect approaching convoys and direct U-boats onto its course, his superiors ordered the big ship to the Azores, where enemy traffic, although undefended, was very light.[62] Instead of wolf packs operating at night, individual submarines continually sought out enemy convoys by day and often lurked about uncertainly until they were spotted and either chased away or destroyed.

German submarine commanders had one other option: the introduction of a handful of large, long-range, heavily gunned (5.9-inch) cruiser U-boats after 1915 allowed the German war effort to expand far out into the Atlantic. Extensive raids by these huge submarines against shipping in U.S. coastal waters was an obvious alternative to increasingly frustrating operations in European waters. But the kaiser and a majority of his government initially favored ignoring the American war declaration, hoping to lull Washington into inactivity. For most of 1917 Germany did not make a counterdeclaration of war, and German admirals did not send their U-boats to American shores. The next year proposals in the German Admiralty for a North American submarine offensive foundered because of too few appropriate U-boats and Chancellor Georg von Hertling's hopes for a compromise peace based on President Wilson's celebrated Fourteen Points. Only a handful of the large submarines finally got to their posts off New England and the middle Atlantic states where they scrupulously operated according to the agreed prewar international rules of cruiser warfare. They did comparatively little damage because of well-escorted coastal convoys.[63]

By December 1917 it became clear to German strategists that the U-boats could neither starve England into submission nor prevent hundreds of thousands of American troops from crossing the Atlantic to the trenches of France. Late the following spring as Germany launched its last desperate offensive on the western front in hopes of breaking the Anglo-French armies before U.S. forces could be fully brought to bear, the U-boat war at last foundered. An Admiralty memorandum of June 4 noted that from the German press "we learn that the enemy Naval Staff has been severely criticised for not building the submarines in sufficient quantities effectively to carry out the war against the Allies' commerce at sea. The German public is clearly disappointed that England has neither yet been beaten, nor is within measurable distance of being beaten, by the shortage of supplies brought from overseas."[64]

The memorandum identified three basic reasons the U-boat campaign was failing: first, the convoy system; second, the Allied antisubmarine counteroffensive, especially the activities of the British Auxiliary Patrol, which generally worked inshore and was largely composed of small commandeered civilian vessels; and third, "the resulting caution, almost amounting to a lack of enterprise, shown by a large proportion of the German Submarine Commanders, who have always in face of them the fact that so many of their friends do not return while the cause of their destruction is unknown." The Admiralty memorandum went on to exhort all elements in the antisubmarine campaign to work especially strenuously during the forthcoming months of good weather and short nights to rout the U-boats once and for all. The Admiralty provided ten illustrations of successful attacks on U-boats first sighted on the surface or found with hydrophones following a merchant ship sinking. The attacks occurred in the North Sea and off Dover, Falmouth, Kingston, Gibraltar, and Cueta or when Allied destroyers or auxiliary vessels were awaiting the arrival of convoys in the Channel or off Ireland. Admiralty writers insisted that good seamanship, vigilance, quick reactions, and fighting efficiency were key to finding and sinking a U-boat.[65]

But in the overall history of antisubmarine warfare, the illustrations would prove to be fatally misleading. As presented by the Admiralty, enemy submarines in nearly every instance were readily found and even more readily destroyed or damaged by almost perfunctory depth-charge—or (if surfaced) gunnery—attack. Allied analysts failed to consider that by this late date in the war, the U-boats were circumscribed by both the convoy system and very limited deployment opportunities from just a few easily watched ports on the European coast directly opposite the British Isles. In the twenties and thirties, the Admiralty would develop and deploy asdic, essentially a greatly advanced hydrophonic underwater detection system, and be content that it alone was sufficient to defeat the U-boat. It was not. In the next world war in which longer-range German U-boats with more daring and innovative captains deployed from nearly the entire western European coast and attacked convoys all over the North Atlantic rather than close inshore to Great Britain, the submarine menace would expand exponentially.

The harmony required to sustain Allied momentum was fragile at best. American admirals with long memories recalled that Britain had been considered a primary potential enemy until the final years of the previous century if not later. Britain's blockade constantly rankled American seamen, both civil and military. The idea of "perfidious Albion" lingered in the upper echelons of the U.S. Navy, especially among the more unimaginative officers like William S. Benson, the first chief of naval operations. When Sims was about to embark on his mission to London several days after the U.S. declaration of war, Benson warned: "Don't let the British pull the wool over your eyes. It is none of our business pulling their chestnuts out of the fire. We would as soon fight the British as the Germans."[66]

Sims's own insistent personality compounded the underlying tension in Anglo-American naval relations. For nearly half a year he persistently bombarded his superiors at home on the need to reorient U.S. naval construction and policies toward antisubmarine warfare. Not surprisingly, his views antagonized both Benson and Daniels, who believed, with some justification, that Sims was building his own bureaucratic empire in London.[67] Was American policy to be wrenched out of context merely to satisfy British demands? Was the U.S. Navy to become simply an auxiliary of the Grand Fleet? Was there not something sinister in British insistence that antisubmarine warfare had suddenly become more important than destroying German battlewagons? Britain, after all, remained allied with Japan, which had quickly responded to Wilson's determination to build a sea service second to none by reconfirming its own plans for a new "eight-eight" navy: eight battleships and eight battle cruisers armed with huge new sixteen-inch guns.[68] Sims became convinced that Benson, Daniels, and even Wilson did not grasp the seriousness of Britain's plight, and the British Admiralty concluded that the United States was unresponsive and slow in waging war. Benson, Daniels, and Wilson, on the other hand, believed that the Royal Navy had lost its courage after Jutland and had become timid and incompetent.

Professional respect and cordiality were more easily and quickly achieved on the working level as Britons and Americans got to know each other. Taussig had served with Jellicoe on the China Station at the time of the Boxer Rebellion, but the first sea lord had greatly outranked the American and Taussig had no reason to believe that Jellicoe would remember him. When the American flotilla reached Queenstown, however, Taussig found a flattering letter from Jellicoe awaiting him. The Briton was "delighted" that Taussig had been selected to lead the vanguard of American ships that were coming "to help us fight for freedom, humanity, and civilization: we shall have our work cut out to subdue piracy." After succinctly giving his opinion of the enemy, Jellicoe proceeded to give his opinion of the new ally: "I must say... [t]here is no navy in the world that can possibly give us more valuable assistance, and there is no personnel in any navy that will fight better than yours. My China experience tells me this."[69]

The British wasted no time getting their allies into the fight. Signalmen and gunners were seconded to each American destroyer, and "schools" were held on the U.S. ships daily. Liaison officers spent hours patiently answering their Yankee visitors' tactical and operational questions. Taussig claimed that he and his men had never heard of depth charges, although during the Civil War the Federal Bureau of Ordnance had developed crude prototypes of these weapons. Soon, however, the fantails of the American ships were festooned with "ash cans," first lashed to lines, then mounted on racks. The sailors also installed Y guns to shoot depth charges off either side of the swiftly moving vessel so the explosive pattern could be spread over a wider area.[70]

Bayly left Taussig responsible for the upkeep and provisioning of his ships and the training and disciplining of his men. "It was simply a case of my going to the Admiral and saying: 'Here are six United States destroyers placed at your disposal, for the purpose of helping to win the war. I will keep them in the best possible condition as to material and personnel; we will go and do whatever in your judgment you deem proper.'" The arrangement worked perfectly: the two men gained great respect and affection for each other, resulting, Taussig later wrote, "in an efficiency of operation throughout the war which was beyond anything I had dreamed possible."[71]

Such warm and fuzzy feelings did not extend to Washington, where Benson continued to view the British "cousins" with no little skepticism and even dislike. In late July 1917 Jellicoe invited Sims up to the Firth of Forth for "consultations" with David Beatty, the Grand Fleet commander. "The result," Sims cabled home, "is that Admiralty request that the four strongest coal-burning battleships with six destroyers be sent to join" a Grand Fleet that was rapidly reshuffling ships and men in a constant effort to stay atop Scheer's slowly expanding High Seas Fleet. Sims and his British allies agreed "that moral effect would be very great also mutual benefit of exchange of ideas and methods." Ten days later, Sims informed Washington that two junior officers in the London embassy had just returned from an inspection trip "to tell . . . about the number of things they found in the Grand Fleet in which we are distinctly inferior," including fire control and concentration.[72]

Benson fired back that the United States believed that "the strategic situation necessitates keeping battleship force concentrated, and cannot therefore consider the suggestion of sending part of it across." Sims returned volley. "I have explained in my cables and letters why it is that the British fleet needs a reinforcement of some of our dreadnoughts. I cannot see that the sending of this division of ships would be any disintegration of our fleet, but merely an advance force interposed between us and the enemy fleet." Evidently weakening, Benson wrote in the margin of Sims's message: "But this is a division of the main force which is always faulty if not fatal. Show us the plan and we will make our decision."[73]

Benson went over to London in early November, and was promptly converted. In an undated memorandum, he set forth a number of cogent reasons for sending a division of modern battleships to the Grand Fleet: direct exposure to wartime conditions, the further strengthening of a British fleet whose undoubted superiority over the enemy had been frequently compromised in past actions by poor weather and visibility, the fillip given to American opinion. "But the major consideration," Benson concluded, "is prestige. . . . There should be no possibility of an impression at home or abroad, among the hostile, allied or neutral, that we are performing an auxiliary or secondary part in the military prosecution of the war." Washington had sent destroyers to the Atlantic front, then cruisers, small patrol vessels crewed "largely by partly trained reserves." Submarines were on their way across even as Benson wrote, and a mining force to close the North Sea would not be far behind. Sending a division of older coal-burning dreadnought battleships would cap this substantial naval effort.[74]

On November 13, Secretary Josephus Daniels informed Benson, still in London, that four coal burners would be sent across, ranging in age from the USS *New York,* commissioned in 1914 (which would see service again in World War II as an elderly but effective convoy escort), to the seven-year-old USS *Delaware.* Hastily docked for last-minute repairs, the ships were under way to Europe in less than a month.[75]

When Rear Admiral Hugh Rodman arrived at Scapa Flow on December 7, 1917, to reinforce the hard-pressed Grand Fleet with Battleship Division 9 of the Atlantic Fleet (flagship *New York* and *Delaware* along with *Wyoming* and *Florida*), the British were as glad to see these vessels as they had earlier been to see Taussig and his destroyers. As coal burners, the American vessels fitted comfortably into the British supply system since only the most recently commissioned British dreadnoughts ran on oil. The United States, itself a major oil producer at the time, had turned to oil fuel for its newest big ships like *Arizona, Pennsylvania, Nevada,* and *Oklahoma,* which were kept in home waters through most of the war.[76] The Grand Fleet band greeted the Americans, and Rodman promptly placed himself under Beatty's command. Beatty proclaimed that the day "marks an epoch in the history of England and America!" Rodman both charmed and amused his new superior by remarking that unlike the rigidly disciplined Royal Navy, the U.S. fleet was pretty informal: "I don't believe much in paper work," Rodman confessed. "Whenever you have anything to bring to my attention, come and see me." Beatty replied, "I'll just do that, Admiral."[77]

By proclaiming a historic alliance Beatty was actually more right than he knew. The U.S. battleship sailors settled in as comfortably with their British hosts as had the destroyer crews at Queenstown, and each side at Scapa Flow was careful to avoid friction and antagonism. Rodman and his men forged a close, cooperative link with the Royal Navy at the operational level that was gradually reflected further up the line in the Anglo-American and Allied staff and planning committees. British admirals yearned to trumpet the fact that the Grand Fleet had now been stiffened with a division of Yankee battlewagons. "It was a gloomy winter [of 1917–1918] in London," wrote one American shortly thereafter. "Not so much discouragement as realization that the collapse of the Russian military power had made a finish of the war seem far remote. France and England would hold fast until the last regiments died in their tracks, but they gazed across the sea and waited for America to put its back into the conflict." Britons would be "thrill[ed] . . . to know your big ships are in the war zone," an admiral told American correspondent Ralph Paine, who was with the battleships. "You have no idea how it would buck them up. Why, when I first heard it, I rushed around among my friends in the service and passed them the word." Certainly, the Grand Fleet was capable of dispatching the Hun on its own, "but it's the idea of the thing. Splendid! It's all hands together, destroyers, battleships and the rest of the show." Alas, it was not to be. Censors insisted until very late in the game that Scheer and his sailors be kept in the dark as to exactly what forces confronted them.[78]

From the start, service with the Grand Fleet was a tough chore for Yankee sailors. "At home it had seemed almost impossible that battleships could be kept ready to dash to sea at from two to four hours notice, through month after month, independent of navy yards and docks." But British seamen had been doing it for three and a half years when their cousins from the New World steamed in. The Americans would learn to do it, too, though "the work was hard, the strain incessant."[79]

When their gunnery and seamanship improved, the American battleship crews at Scapa Flow received more and more responsibility, steaming with the Grand Fleet in response to alarms that the enemy might be at sea, otherwise protecting the crucial Scandinavian convoys. Correspondent Ralph Paine memorably described one dramatic, but not unusual, nighttime sortie from the vast, windswept anchorage followed by a brutal passage through the upper North Sea. Long after the decks had been piped down for the night and most of the twelve hundred–odd men aboard the flagship *New York* were asleep in their hammocks, the word came: anchors aweigh at 0300. Most of the crew continued their slumber as the officers were awakened and the deck parties mustered. Paine found Rodman, a broad- and jovial-faced mariner, in his cabin calmly drinking "smoking hot" coffee, his "burly figure" wrapped in oilskins. Orders had been given; there was nothing more to do. Soon the captain of the flagship came in to report; he, too, exuded calm and confidence. So, too, did the captain of *Texas*, which had just arrived to increase the American battleship component

to five. He reported his big, powerful, modern warship ready for sea in all respects. After a time the crew was piped to reveille, then quarters, for leaving
harbor. Rodman lumbered up to the bridge as "blinker lights flashed from scores
of British ships" and the low hills round the anchorage reverberated to the
sound of a hundred and more anchor chains coming up through the hawser
pipes. "After that the black night and silence, and great ships stealing slowly
toward the headlands and the fairway to the sea." Most were invisible from
New York's bridge and decks through the murk and rain gusts. In this preradar
era, the great war fleet blindly but carefully "passed out" of the anchorage "so
many hundred yards apart, steering close to rock-bound islands whose merest
touch would have ripped a battleship's hull."

Where this vast assemblage was bound and why were known only to the admirals and their captains. Paine was deeply moved by the scene. "This trained
obedience, the flawless coordination of these many thousand men at the prompting of a few words was profoundly impressive. The Fleet had a soul and a purpose. It was human, not so many masses of floating steel, but it had the tenacity
of tested metal." Such tenacity would be needed out in a North Sea lashed by
winter gales and storms where "inflexible vigil" was required "in lonely waters
far to the north." Dawn brought seventy-mile-per-hour winds that "tumbled
the sea this way and that" so that even the 27,000-ton, 573-foot *New York* was
hurled about. Belowdecks it was "damp, gloomy, dismal . . . with the hatches
battened." Bare-legged sailors baled frantically as water poured through
open gun ports. Chairs were lashed down, eating a proper meal was impossible,
and officers and enlisted men alike subsisted on coffee and lukewarm or cold
hash. But the ship and her sisters had suffered worse off the Grand Banks as
they steamed across to Scapa Flow, and the men were philosophic. Life aboard a
battleship in the North Sea was infinitely preferable to life in the trenches of
the western front. "The guy who beefed about staying wet and losing sleep for
twenty-four hours or so was a short-card sport."

As Rodman "stolidly propped himself" on the open bridge, taking "the wind
and spray as it came," the men around him gazed and blinked through the wet,
swirling gloom and wondered uneasily "what would happen should a German
fleet loom out of this rain and spindrift at point-blank range." In this respect
Rodman's sailors, and those of Beatty around him, were no better off than the
Tars of Nelson's day or Blake's time or, indeed, any seamen in an Age of Sail
stretching back nearly to the dawn of recorded time. " 'A short and merry scrap,
take it from me,' said a quartermaster with his glasses at his eyes. 'The lads that
got in the first punch would have it all their own way. Wow! With this rotten

visibility? Fairly bumping into each other? Excuse me! Would there be anybody left to tell about it, I wonder? Salvos of big guns at two or three thousand yards? Well, it may break that way some day. You can't pick your weather in this game.'"

In the constantly heaving seas where even a battleship's tall bow scooped into the brine and took heavy water, life above decks could be deadly. A gang of sailors ordered at first light to rig safety lines forward watched in horror as one of their careless or unfortunate mates was suddenly swept overboard to disappear forever amid the raging waters. There was no possibility of launching a boat; the only recourse was to toss the poor devil a line or life belt as he drifted by on the crest of a wave. But he was never seen, and soon his hushed mates gathered quietly below to mourn him.[80]

"It is not that it blows any harder in the North Sea than in many other parts of the world," Rodman wrote to Benson in mid-January 1918, "but that it seems to be almost continually blowing, shifting rapidly from one point of the compass to another and kicking up a rough cross sea which has again demonstrated the disadvantage of having our 5 inch guns mounted too low" in the hull. New York's gun deck was so heavily flooded "in our last run" that not only were the guns useless but the ports also had to be kept closed to keep the water from flooding the entire deck. During the unusually cold European winter of 1917–1918 the U.S. battlewagons plowing through rough North Sea waves were also pelted with persistent "snow, hail, sleet, and rain, often coupled with fog and mist." Life at sea during these long winter days was barely less tolerable than life around the anchor chain. Entering the narrow, often storm-tossed Pentland Firth that divides the northern coast of Scotland from the Orkneys after one cruise, "with the British battleships leading" in column, the Americans encountered a "strong spring tide running against the wind" that repeatedly smothered or submerged the main decks of their big vessels with tons of water. Rodman reported, "Our ships, with higher free boards, made better weather of it" than the Royal Navy. But then, "unusually heavy snows, with temperatures much below normal, have prevailed at the northern base, in consequence of which there has been much suffering amongst the inhabitants ashore, and a shortage of food." Rodman did not say whether shortages extended to the fleet, but he suggests that they may well have.[81]

And so it went for nearly a year, operating out of either Scapa Flow or Rosyth, the sweeps through the upper North Sea, the long days and nights of convoying up to Norway in winter storms and through pleasant summer waters. Sims informed Benson with evident pride in mid-February that Rodman "is certainly persona grata with everybody and is spoken of in the highest terms not only by the British but by all our people who come in contact with him." Following an inspection trip to Rosyth in the spring, Captain Dudley Knox reported that "the Grand Fleet, including the American battleships, is thoroughly indoctrinated with the single mission of destroying the High Seas Fleet at the earliest possible moment." So deep had the idea seized hold of all minds that the old British fear of enemy submarines was "seldom" expressed. After three and a half years of grinding war patrols and occasional battle, British Tars were also impressed with "the manner in which our ships are kept up, both as regards their cleanliness and mechanical efficiency." *New York* had been thoroughly inspected by "every Admiral in the British Fleet," each one of whom then sent the captains of his squadron over "at odd times to inspect" the Yankee battleship.[82]

In August 1918 the Admiralty at last prevailed upon Benson and the Navy Department to send a squadron of three battleships—two of them the brand-new oil-burning *Oklahoma* and *Nevada*—to Berehaven at the southern tip of Ireland to help guard against a widely feared breakout of Hipper's battle cruisers into the Atlantic that in fact never materialized. Instead, the enemy broke internally, then mutinied, and suddenly it was all over. As the defeated German battle fleet finally steamed forlornly down the line of Allied ships and into internment at Scapa Flow in November 1918, Rodman's battleship squadron was right in the center of Beatty's huge, vigilant formation.[83]

Who were the real victors in the Great War, and what had they won? On land Allied armies pushed back their exhausted enemies to the frontiers of the Reich but no farther. As Norman Friedman has observed, the mass armies of 1914–1918 simply could not defeat one another.[84] Since their advanced war-making technologies were similar, they were stalemated. The government in Berlin surrendered long before most soldiers were willing to do so, and there were no Allied victory parades down the Unter den Linden. It seemed equally difficult to identify the winners at sea. The Imperial German Navy had apparently shamed itself irretrievably. Designed by its creator to be the embodiment of "Germandom" at home as well as abroad, it had mutinied against its own people and government. On June 21, 1919, seven months after steaming into ignominious surrender under British guardianship, the High Seas Fleet compounded the felony by scuttling itself in protest over the severity of the Versailles peace terms. The navy thus forfeited its legitimacy and respect in the eyes of both Germany and the world.

But a close examination shows that the humiliation of the German navy was ambiguous. The surface sailors had mutinied; their brothers in the U-boats had not. The kaiser and his generals and admirals had never assigned the High Seas Fleet a realistic tactical or strategic role in the overall scheme of national security and expansion. Scheer, Hipper, and their men did their best with the tasks and equipment they were given. The submariners were a different breed entirely. Before 1914 no one had imagined, no one could imagine, such a weapon. By 1917 the U-boat had become a major strategic instrument of war, perhaps the preeminent such instrument. Because of the craft's unique combination of range, stealth, and destructiveness, an essentially landlocked, geopolitically disadvantaged state like Germany might project its power to literally global dimensions, holding potential hostage any nation that depended on oceangoing commerce for its survival. Other participants in the Great War possessed submarine fleets; none employed them with remotely the same diligence and ruthlessness as Germany. Overcome at last by the convoy system and the critical infusion of Americans arms at sea as well as in France, the U-boat sailors could claim, if not victory, then a kind of twisted honor in never quitting. German arms thus did not fail in the Great War. Soon enough a twisted genius of evil like Adolf Hitler would understand this and use it to his own advantage. For German submarine sailors the Great War was indeed merely the first round of an eternal conflict with arrogant Britain for control of the world ocean.

If the Imperial German Navy did not truly lose the Great War at sea, the Royal Navy most certainly did not win it. Only its superior numbers in capital ships, the convoy system, and the sporadically brilliant capabilities of Room 40 saved it from disaster. In large measure this was due to a chronic, systemic breakdown between the Admiralty and the fleet that sensitive observers, like Filson Young, instantly grasped when he joined Beatty's battle cruisers in November 1914.

> The naval officer, whether in peace or war, had the sense that the Admiralty cared very little about his interests, did not wish to hear his point of view, and, what concerned him a great deal more, seemed to care very little whether the Navy was or was not properly equipped for the work it had to do.... The Admiralty's point of view was that everything was safe in its hands, and that all the naval officer had to do was to keep quiet and do what he was told.

Staffed by many able characters and brains, "the spirit informing the whole was ... narrow and lifeless ... expressing itself everywhere in the policy that the means were more important than the end." Britannia continued to rule the waves, and in its successful exercise of sea power, including the blockade, the Royal

Navy fulfilled its basic if undramatic function. Once the German army's massive spring offensive of 1918 bogged down, the Allied blockade at last became decisive; the German people had had enough.[85] But British dominance after 1914 was always a near-run thing. England's sailors failed at Dogger Bank and at Jutland because of faulty intelligence, communication, and ship design, and they failed for much too long to counter an unrestricted U-boat campaign that threatened their nation and empire. In 1914 British naval planners believed that the war would be short. They had made no provision for further construction of heavy vessels, and after Jutland they paid the price with an unacceptably narrow margin of superiority over the High Seas Fleet. At the end of the war the Royal Navy possessed only a handful of fast, modern, efficient battleships—the five *Queen Elizabeth*s, which were as poorly armored about the decks and therefore as vulnerable as their predecessors—and it was threatened by both friends and putative enemies, eager to displace or at least complement British sea power. The Admiralty was at bay and knew it.

Without its capital ships firing one shot in anger, the Imperial Japanese Navy was a decided victor in the Great War. Its role was obscured by the greater and lesser European sea powers and after 1917 by the U.S. Navy. But the Japanese were surprisingly active. Their fleet chased Maximilian Graf von Spee and his squadron all over and then out of the western Pacific while seizing nearly all of Germany's strategically critical islands in the process. Soon thereafter, the withdrawal of the Royal Navy from beyond Suez gave the Japanese the opportunity and pretext to roam the entire Far East on behalf of the Allied cause.

In February 1915 then vice admiral Thomas Jerram at Singapore invited a Japanese squadron to base itself at Britain's strategic outpost, which remained largely undeveloped in terms of facilities but nonetheless controlled one of the key choke points on the world ocean. "From that time up till the present," a Japanese naval officer wrote in 1919, "our Squadrons, though many changes in commanders and units have taken place, bear the responsibility of patrolling the vast area of the China Sea, Java Sea, Batan Sea, Sulu Sea, Celebes Sea, and the northern part of the Indian Ocean." When *Leipzig* and *Dresden* appeared off the American West Coast in the autumn of 1914, "this exposed our trade routes, both British and Japanese, to attack." A Japanese cruiser was dispatched to North American waters, followed by a battleship and another cruiser. For a while these ships roamed the sea-lanes off British Columbia, the Pacific Northwest, and California. After the Germans hurried away, the Japanese rendezvoused in western Mexican waters, touching off a hysterical reaction in the United States that was ably abetted by the German propaganda service.

Daily in Berlin, all during the winter of 1914, highly placed German visitors called upon United States Ambassador [James W.] Gerard to whisper the great danger that threatened America from Japan and relay confidential reports that Mexico was full of Japanese colonels and America full of Japanese spies. In Washington the German press attaché, Baron von Schoen, transferred from Tokyo when Japan joined the Allies, publicly proclaimed upon his arrival in September that Japan's intense hatred for the United States, coupled with her strong pro-Mexican feeling, made war "unavoidable."[86]

The Germans played incessantly on American racism and credulity. Several weeks after Schoen's warning, rumors swept the West Coast that a Japanese army had landed in Mexico. After the war German documents revealed that the message had originated on one of von Spee's smaller cruisers, *Geier,* which had briefly visited Honolulu and sent the rumors out over the wireless while the ship's band played afternoon concerts to cover the sound of transmission.[87]

American hysteria was understandable. Japan had been dallying with the Mexicans for years, feeding their anger over the long-ago loss of Texas, New Mexico, and Arizona to the arrogant Yankees. Rumors persisted for years in Washington that Japan had signed a secret treaty with Mexico for a naval base in Magdalena Bay. There were constant reports that Japanese troops were in Mexico, and Japanese officials visiting the country incessantly emphasized the ostensible racial similarities between the two peoples. In 1911 Grand Admiral of the Japanese Fleet Yashiro visited Mexico City and after wine and a sumptuous meal rose unsteadily to toast the "'fraternal feast'" and to promise unspecified common actions against an unspecified common enemy.[88]

In April 1915 word raced across the arc of cities and towns from Dallas to San Francisco that the Japanese battle cruiser *Asama* was "mysteriously maneuvering" in Turtle Bay on the coast of Baja California. The Hearst press, the most rabid proponent of the Yellow Peril, screamed that the United States was about to be invaded, and rumors crisscrossed the nation that Japanese troops had been in Baja for months if not years, that Tokyo was building naval bases at various points along the western Mexican coast, and that thousands of Japanese fishermen speaking two or three languages were establishing villages throughout Baja. The commander in chief of the U.S. Pacific Squadron promptly asked for reinforcements and ordered the cruiser *New Orleans* south to investigate. The Americans found several Japanese cruisers anxiously hovering around *Asama,* which was ostensibly stuck in the mud. Eventually, the big ship freed itself or was freed, and the Japanese squadron sailed off. But Japan's naval presence in the Western Hemisphere had been confirmed. Tokyo was not displeased.[89]

By 1918 Japan could boast that it had (marginally) helped the Allies track down a few German raiders, had routinely patrolled hundreds of thousands of square miles of eastern ocean for the Allied cause, and had sent some small and medium surface combatants to the Mediterranean. Japanese diplomacy would soon win significant concessions on both the Asian mainland and in the islands of the Pacific. At the Paris Peace Conference, nearly all of Germany's valuable possessions in China and Oceania fell into Japan's lap. Tokyo's new island possessions lay directly astride the tenuous commercial, supply, and communication lines between the American West Coast and U.S. possessions in Oceania and off East Asia.

The Japanese triumph occurred at the moment when a seismic shift was shaking domestic politics to its roots. From the beginning of the Meiji era, "two governments had grown up: military and civilian, separate and equal." The great clans that had engineered the Meiji revolution remained in power for decades thereafter through their senior representatives, the genrō, who dominated both governments. But the parliamentary democracy of the 1890s introduced a powerful solvent to the rule of the genrō, and in the ensuing struggle for control of both governments, "the civilians" in the cabinet at last gained "the right to set general military policy on troop strength and organization, while the military maintained the right to run actual operations independently." In the Imperial Japanese Navy this translated to civilian control over construction tonnage and its devotion to various warship classes. The system continued to work well, with comparatively few frictions prior to 1919, but the question of Japan's role and mission responsibilities in the postwar world generated ultimately unbearable tensions. Tokyo's appetite for an ever greater power in and influence over the international scene, fanned to a heat in large part by the navy's participation in World War I, sowed the seeds for a great Pacific war that might, under perfect circumstances, conclude in Japan's favor.[90]

But it was the United States that now possessed the power to shape international affairs if and as it chose. In eighteen months of combat America had proved to be incontestably the greatest military-industrial complex on earth. Beyond the two million doughboys who provided the margin of victory in Europe, beyond the antisubmarine campaign, the enormous buildup of naval airpower, the great North Sea mine "barrage," and the handful of initially questionable but increasingly useful battleships that sailed with the Grand Fleet, was a single important truth that at least one American observer fully grasped: "The United States has shown that it has the quickest turnover of man-power in the world, especially adapted to receive training through contact with an infusion of skilled officers and men."[91] This ability to produce millions of combat-capable people, coupled with an unmatched industrial capability, made the United States potentially the world's preeminent military and naval power any time the government and people concluded that circumstances demanded that it become so.

The Great War revolutionized sea power. Naval combat expanded to include the skies above and the depths below. Pax Britannica was gone forever, and so was the supremacy of the line-of-battle ship, whether wood or steel, that had created and sustained it. But the dimensions of the new world order remained obscure as the guns at last fell silent. In future years the global community tried to heal itself through collective security, but the hatreds and appetites remaining from an essentially inconclusive war led to a gradual breakdown of international order. It was in this atmosphere that naval statesmen and planners struggled to comprehend the world bequeathed by one war so they would be prepared to wage the next.

Preface

1. Phillips Payson O'Brien, introduction to *Technology and Naval Combat in the Twentieth Century and Beyond,* edited by O'Brien, ix; Brian R. Sullivan, "Italian Warship Construction, 1873–1915," in ibid., 3.

2. Peter Truscott, *Kursk Russia's Lost Pride,* 50.

3. For Hattendorf, see especially *Naval History and Maritime Strategy: Collected Essays;* Friedman, *Seapower as Strategy: Navies and National Interests.*

Prologue. The Master: Alfred Thayer Mahan

1. Alfred Thayer Mahan to Charles R. Miles, November 22, 1888, in *Letters and Papers of Alfred Thayer Mahan,* edited by Robert Seager II and Doris Maguire, 1:667–68; John B. Hattendorf, "In a Far More Thorough Manner," *Naval History* 19:2 (April 2005): 38–43; Randy C. Bolano, "U.S. Navy Owes T. B. M. Mason," *Naval History* 19:3 (June 2005): 26–27, 29–30 (quote). Roosevelt's review in the *Atlantic Monthly* (October 1890) is reprinted in William H. Harbaugh, ed., *The Writings of Theodore Roosevelt,* 36–41 (quote on pp. 36–37).

2. The essence of Mahan's argument is in chapter 1 of *The Influence of Sea Power upon History, 1660–1783,* 25–89. Unless otherwise noted, the following summary and quotations are from this source.

3. John Keegan, *The Price of Admiralty: The Evolution of Naval Warfare,* 101–2.

4. Mahan, *Influence of Sea Power,* 1, 2, 506.

5. Winston S. Churchill, *The World Crisis, 1911–1918,* 1:3, 151.

Chapter 1. The Architects: Theodore Roosevelt, Alfred von Tirpitz, and John "Jacky" Fisher

1. William H. McNeill, *The Rise of the West: A History of the Human Community,* 623.

2. Robert Thorne's missive to Henry VIII is quoted in Samuel Eliot Morison, *The Great Explorers: The European Discovery of America,* 99. Raleigh is quoted in the

frontispiece to Peter J. Hugill, *World Trade since 1431: Geography, Technology, and Capitalism.*

3. Wolfgang Wegener, *The Naval Strategy of the World War,* 14–15; Fisher quoted in John Keegan, *The First World War,* 266.

4. Ludwig Dehio, *The Precarious Balance: Four Centuries of the European Power Struggle,* 19–219 (Napoléon quoted on p. 164).

5. Arno J. Mayer, *The Persistence of the Old Regime: Europe to the Great War,* 307; Reginald C. Hart, "A Vindication of War," *Nineteenth Century* (August 1911), quoted in Arthur J. Marder, *From the Dreadnought to Scapa Flow: The Royal Navy in the Fisher Era, 1904–1919,* 1:3.

6. Bernard Brodie, *Sea Power in the Machine Age,* 127, 150.

7. Ibid., 105–7; William Oliver Stevens and Allan Westcott, *A History of Sea Power,* 271.

8. Brodie, *Sea Power,* 151, 235–36.

9. Karl Lautenschläger, "Technology and the Evolution of Naval Warfare," 182–84.

10. Ira Nelson Hollis, "The Uncertain Factors in Naval Conflicts," 728.

11. Ibid.

12. James Morris, *Pax Britannica: The Climax of an Empire,* 421.

13. "American Comments," *Times* (London), weekly edition, July 2, 1897, 421; "On the Continent," ibid.; Robert K. Massie, *Dreadnought: Britain, Germany, and the Coming of the Great War,* xvii–xxxi.

14. Fred T. Jane, "Naval Warfare: Present and Future," 234–35, 240–41.

15. See a photo of *Boston* in Edward Shippen, *Naval Battles of the World: Great and Decisive Contests on the Sea; Causes and Results of Ocean Victories and Defeats; Marine Warfare and Armament in All Ages: The Growth, Power and Management of Our New Navy and Its Pride and Glory of Swift Cruiser, Impregnable Battle-ship, Ponderous Engine and Deadly Projectile,* 720.

16. Edward L. Beach Jr., *From Annapolis to Scapa Flow: The Autobiography of Edward L. Beach Sr.,* 28, 37, 51.

17. Ibid., 17–112 (quotes on pp. 29, 34). See also Shippen, *Naval Battles,* 719–30.

18. Beach, *Annapolis to Scapa Flow,* 43; Walter R. Herrick Jr., *The American Naval Revolution,* 39–192; Norman Friedman, "Transformation a Century Ago," *Naval History* 19:2 (April 2005): 32, 34–35.

19. Frederick Jackson Turner, "The Significance of the Frontier in American History," reprinted in Ray Allen Billington, ed., *Frontier and Section: Selected Writings of Frederick Jackson Turner,* 39; Billington, *America's Frontier Heritage,* 6, 12.

20. Friedman, *Seapower as Strategy,* 48.

21. James A. Field Jr., "American Imperialism: The Worst Chapter in Almost Any Book," 667.

22. Ibid., 657–58.

23. Howard K. Beale, *Theodore Roosevelt and the Rise of America to World Power,* 50, 51; see also p. 64.

24. Theodore Roosevelt, "Expansion and Peace," *Independent,* December 21, 1899, reprinted in Harbaugh, *Writings of Roosevelt,* 32.

25. Martin G. Netsky and Edward L. Beach Jr., "The Trouble with Admiral Sampson," 10.

26. Frank Freidel, *The Splendid Little War,* 25; Beach, *Annapolis to Scapa Flow,* 90–93.

27. Ira Nelson Hollis, "The Navy and the War with Spain," 605, 606, 610.

28. George Modelski and William R. Thompson, *Seapower in Global Politics, 1494–1993,* 74–79.

29. Gordon Brook-Shepherd, *Royal Sunset: The European Dynasties and the Great War,* 85–86.

30. Holger H. Herwig, *Politics of Frustration: The United States in German Naval Planning, 1889–1914,* 18; Fritz Fischer, *Germany's Aims in the First World War,* 3–49.

31. John Leyland, "The Naval Expansion of Germany," in *The Naval Annual, 1909,* edited by T. A. Brassey, 121.

32. Niall Ferguson, *Empire: The Rise and Demise of the British World Order and the Lessons for Global Power,* 165.

33. William L. Langer, *European Alliances and Alignments, 1871–1890,* 494. See also Archibald Hurd and Henry Castle, *German Sea-Power: Its Rise, Progress, and Economic Basis,* 97–101.

34. Churchill, *World Crisis,* 1:88.

35. Alfred von Tirpitz, *My Memoirs,* 1:12, 13, 33. See also Daniel Jonah Goldhagen, *Hitler's Willing Executioners: Ordinary Germans and the Holocaust,* 74.

36. Tirpitz, *My Memoirs,* 1:53.

37. Ibid., 86–87, 108–9, 111.

38. Ibid., 110–11.

39. Carl-Axel Gemzell, *Organization, Conflict, and Innovation: A Study of German Naval Strategic Planning, 1888–1940,* 53–56.

40. Ibid., 11.

41. Hurd and Castle, *German Sea-Power,* 119.

42. Ivo Nikolai Lambi, *The Navy and German Power Politics, 1862–1914,* 146.

43. Wolf von Schierbrand, "Germany as a World Power," 139.

44. Stevens and Westcott, *History of Sea Power,* 287 (italics in original).

45. A good discussion of the role of naval interests—especially coaling stations and foreign bases—in driving and directing German imperial policies is Albert Harding Ganz, *The Role of the Imperial German Navy in Colonial Affairs.*

46. Herwig, *Politics of Frustration,* 21; see also p. 33.

47. Churchill, *World Crisis,* 1:92–93.

48. J. Morris, *Pax Britannica,* 424; Michael Lewis, *The Navy of Britain,* 253–54, 393; Anthony Carew, *The Lower Deck of the Royal Navy, 1900–1939: The Invergordon Mutiny in Perspective,* 49; Filson Young, *With the Battle Cruisers,* 55. See also Correlli Barnett, *The Swordbearers: Supreme Command in the First World War,* 189.

49. J. Morris, *Pax Britannica,* 425.

50. Peter Kemp, "From Tryon to Fisher: The Regeneration of a Navy," in *Naval Warfare in the Twentieth Century, 1900–1945: Essays in Honour of Arthur J. Marder,* edited by Gerald Jordan, 16, 19.

51. Archibald Hurd, "Progress or Reaction in the Navy," 707–8; Marder, *Dreadnought to Scapa Flow,* 1:7. See also Kemp, "From Tryon to Fisher," in *Naval Warfare,* edited by Jordan, 19.

52. Keegan, *Price of Admiralty,* 99.

53. Kemp, "From Tryon to Fisher," in *Naval Warfare,* edited by Jordan, 16, 18.

54. Archibald Hurd, "A Dreadnought Naval Policy," 1027, 1029 (italics in original).

55. William Jameson, *The Fleet That Jack Built: Nine Men Who Made a Modern Navy,* 90. The following discussion of the reforms of the Fisher era is based primarily on Marder, *Dreadnought to Scapa Flow,* 1:7, 8, 12–45; Jameson, *Fleet That Jack Built,* 1–170; Barnett, *Swordbearers,* 189–90; Jon Tetsuro Sumida, *In Defense of Naval Supremacy: Finance, Technology, and British Naval Policy, 1889–1914;* Peter Padfield, *The Battleship Era,* 163–203; Churchill, *World Crisis,* 1:53–58; Carew, *Lower Deck of the Royal Navy,* 3–71; Nicholas A. Lambert, *Fisher's Naval Revolution;* Stephen Roskill, *Churchill and the Admirals,* 22–31; and two superb contemporary analyses by Hurd, "Progress or Reaction" and "A Dreadnought Naval Policy."

56. Marder, *Dreadnought to Scapa Flow,* 1:12, 35 (italics in original); Percy Scott, *Fifty Years in the Royal Navy,* 234. See also Jameson, *Fleet That Jack Built,* 156.

57. Lambert, *Fisher's Naval Revolution,* 76–85, 280–84.

58. Fisher's colleague Admiral Sydney Fremantle quoted with emphasis in Marder, *Dreadnought to Scapa Flow,* 1:28 (see also p. 15); Churchill, *World Crisis,* 1:54–55. See also Roskill, *Churchill and the Admirals,* 21. Rumors of Fisher's spying upon fellow and junior officers is in Young, *With the Battle Cruisers,* 49. Fisher's own comment is quoted in Jon Tetsuro Sumida, "Sir John Fisher and the *Dreadnought:* The Sources of Naval Mythology," 59, 619. Fisher's public impact, along with that of his great rival, Tirpitz, is discussed in Paul M. Kennedy, "Fisher and Tirpitz: Political Admirals in the Age of Imperialism," in *Naval Warfare in the Twentieth Century,* edited by Jordan, 48–49, 57.

59. Hurd, "Progress or Reaction," 715.

60. Ibid., 716–17.

61. Roskill, *Churchill and the Admirals,* 28–29; Arthur J. Marder, *Portrait of an Admiral: The Life and Papers of Sir Herbert Richmond,* 21.

62. See, for example, Michael Bronner, "The Recruiters' War," *Vanity Fair,* September 2005, 303–18.

63. Tristan Jones, *Heart of Oak,* 15, 36; Kemp, "From Tryon to Fisher," in *Naval Warfare,* edited by Jordan, 17–18; Christopher McKee, *Sober Men and True: Sailor Lives in the Royal Navy, 1900–1945,* 5, 8, 17–22, 24. McKee's effort represents a rather typical academic exercise in history "from the bottom up" that is at once formal, stilted, overly mannered, and, in the end, uninformative. McKee admits, for example, that he has ignored such critical formative factors as the often brutal experience of the boy

training ships (5). Even less excusably, he completely ignores the Invergordon mutiny of 1931 that uncovered most but not all of the most unlovely truths about life on the lower decks of British men-of-war. The "shilling-a-day men" quote is from Keegan, *The First World War,* 133; Cecil H. Fox, R.N., *Manual of Seamanship for Boys and Seamen of the Royal Navy, 1904* (London: Eyre and Spottiswoode, 1905), was reprinted in 2003 by Algrove Publishing.

64. McKee, *Sober Men and True,* 44–45.

65. Carew, *Lower Deck of the Royal Navy,* xviii.

66. Len Wincott, *Invergordon Mutineer,* 21, 23–26, 45.

67. Fox, *Manual of Seamanship.*

68. Churchill, *World Crisis,* 1:156, 169; Roskill, *Churchill and the Admirals,* 23, 302n25. A comparison of Royal Navy diets at the close of the eighteenth and the beginning of the twentieth centuries may be made by consulting the "Table of the Daily Proportion of Provisions Allowed to Every Person on Board His Majesty's Ships" (1797) in Anne Chotzinoff Grossman and Lisa Grossman Thomas, *Lobcouse and Spotted Dog: Which It's [sic] a Gastronomic Companion to the Aubrey/Maturin Novels,* 98 with the list of "Provisions . . . Supplied to all H.M. Ships" in Fox, *Manual of Seamanship,* 298. The 1914 daily rations standard is reprinted in McKee, *Sober Men and True,* 239–40.

69. Young, *With the Battle Cruisers,* 122, 128–29 (quote).

70. T. G. N. Haldane to Admiral Herbert William Richmond, March 26, 1930, folder RIC/2/4, Richmond Papers; Young, *With the Battle Cruisers,* 55, 58–59.

Chapter 2. Scorpions in a Bottle

1. A. P. Thornton, *The Imperial Idea and Its Enemies: A Study in British Power,* 135; Herwig, *Politics of Frustration,* 39.

2. Sumida, *In Defence of Naval Supremacy,* 329; Lambert, *Fisher's Naval Revolution,* 21–29.

3. Barbara W. Tuchman, *The Guns of August,* 21.

4. Beale, *Roosevelt and America,* 324–31 (quote on p. 329).

5. Diana Preston, *A First Rate Tragedy: Robert Falcon Scott and the Race to the South Pole,* 3, 105; Rudyard Kipling, "The Long Trail."

6. Tirpitz, *My Memoirs,* 1:121. Tirpitz's eternal commitment to a large, aggressive, and tactically sophisticated fleet is discussed in Patrick J. Kelly, "Strategy, Tactics, and Turf Wars: Tirpitz and the Oberkommando der Marine, 1892–1895," 1049, 1059.

7. Lambi, *Navy and Power Politics,* 76.

8. Ibid., 77, 79. John Keegan's summary of Tirpitz's strategic thought misses much of what the German admiral believed the High Seas Fleet could accomplish as an instrument of "Germanism" and might accomplish in denying a British army access to the Continent in the event of a Franco-German war. See Keegan's limited summary of Tirpitz's "risk theory" in *Price of Admiralty,* 100, 110–11.

9. Lambi, *Navy and Power Politics,* 125.

10. Ibid., 143.

11. Ibid.

12. Ibid.

13. Ibid., 42–43, 49–54; Herwig, *Politics of Frustration,* 33, 41.

14. Daniel Horn, *The German Naval Mutinies of World War I,* 4 (quote), 5; Holger H. Herwig, *The German Naval Officer Corps: A Social and Political History, 1890–1918,* 5–33; James Goldrick, *The King's Ships Were at Sea: The War in the North Sea, August 1914– February 1915,* 43–44; Tirpitz, *My Memoirs,* 1:33.

15. Alfred von Tirpitz discussed the creation and curriculum of the academy at Kiel in *My Memoirs,* 1:29, 31. Franz von Hipper's naval education is recounted in Tobias R. Philbin III, *Admiral von Hipper, the Inconvenient Hero,* 2–6. Erich Raeder discussed his own education in *My Life,* 6–10.

16. Philbin, *Admiral von Hipper,* 4; see also p. 2.

17. The fullest account of German naval officer training before World War I is found in Captain von Kühlwetter, "The Personnel of the German Navy," *The Naval Annual, 1913,* edited by Viscount Hythe, 135–37 (quotes on pp. 136, 137).

18. Ibid., 137.

19. Philbin, *Admiral von Hipper,* 6; Tirpitz, *My Memoirs,* 1:29.

20. Philbin, *Admiral von Hipper,* 6.

21. Hurd and Castle, *German Sea-Power,* 157–69 (quotes on p. 159).

22. Horn, *German Naval Mutinies,* 7.

23. Ibid., 7–8.

24. Ibid., 8–9.

25. Ibid., 11; Hurd and Castle, *German Sea-Power,* 169–71 (quote on p. 170); Reinhard Scheer, *Germany's High Seas Fleet in the World War,* chap. 2, p. 2.

26. Horn, *German Naval Mutinies,* 12.

27. Kelly, "Strategy, Tactics, and Turf Wars," 1054–58; Goldrick, *King's Ships,* 47.

28. Herwig, *German Naval Officer Corps,* 6–8; Tirpitz, *My Memoirs,* 1:131, 143.

29. David Lyon, *Sea Battles in Close-Up: The Age of Nelson* 7–28 (quote on p. 7). See also Roger Morris, *The Royal Dockyards during the Revolutionary and Napoleonic Wars;* Leyland, "Naval Expansion of Germany," in *The Naval Annual, 1909,* edited by Brassey, 120–33 (quotes on German shipbuilding expansion on p. 131); and Churchill, *World Crisis,* 1:88.

30. A. Maurice Low, "Foreign Affairs" (1906), 179; Sydney Brooks, "England and Germany"; Edwin D. Mead, "England and Germany," 399–400.

31. Low, "Foreign Affairs" (1906), 180; Excubitor, "The British Reply to Germany's Dreadnoughts," 466.

32. The following discussion is based on the exhaustive analyses by contemporary British naval authorities. See Excubitor, "The German Naval Bill," 73–82; Hurd and Castle, *German Sea-Power,* 140–41; and Hurd, "A Dreadnought Naval Policy."

33. Excubitor, "The German Naval Bill," 73–75.

34. Ibid., 74–75.

35. Ibid., 74.

36. Schierbrand, "Germany as a World Power," 139.

37. Archibald S. Hurd, "British Sea-Power, 1900–1930, Read at the Spring Meetings of the Seventy-second Session of the Institute of Naval Architects, March 25, 1931," folder RIC/2/1, Richmond Papers.

38. Ruddock F. Mackay, "Historical Reinterpretations of the Anglo-German Naval Rivalry, 1897–1914," in *Naval Warfare,* edited by Jordan, 35–36; Paul M. Kennedy, "The Development of German Naval Operations Plans against England, 1896–1914," 55–65.

39. Holger H. Herwig, introduction to *Naval Strategy,* by Wegener, xviii.

40. Paul G. Halpern, *A Naval History of World War I,* 66.

41. Hurd, "A Dreadnought Naval Policy," 1017, 1018.

42. Massie, *Dreadnought,* 469; D. R. Morris, "Homer Clark Poundstone and the All Big-Gun Ship," *United States Naval Institute Proceedings* /4 (June 1948): 707–21.

43. The article is summarized in Hurd and Castle, *German Sea-Power,* 130–32.

44. Marder, *Dreadnought to Scapa Flow,* 1:43–44; Antony Preston, *Battleships,* 49; John Maxtone-Graham, *The Only Way to Cross,* 15–21.

45. Frederick L. Oliver, review of "Homer Clark Poundstone and the All Big-Gun Ship," by D. R. Morris, *United States Naval Institute Proceedings* 74:11 (November 1949): 1427; Hurd and Castle, *German Sea-Power,* 132.

46. Karl Lautenschläger, "The Dreadnought Revolution Reconsidered," in *Naval History: The Sixth Symposium of the U.S. Naval Academy,* edited by Daniel M. Masterson, 122, 123.

47. Keegan, *Price of Admiralty,* 105.

48. John Roberts, *Battlecruisers,* 10–11.

49. G. Lowes Dickinson, *The International Anarchy, 1904–1914,* 375–76 (quote on p. 375); Churchill, *World Crisis,* 1:23–25.

50. P. Kennedy, "Development of Operations Plans," 65–66.

51. Ibid., 67–68.

52. Year-by-year British and German dreadnought construction and completion figures are in Massie, *Dreadnought,* 909–11; see also pp. 468–97, 609–25, 698–711. Halpern, *Naval History,* 7, lists thirty-one British and twenty German capital ships in commission in August 1914, a number that agrees with John Moore et al., *Jane's Fighting Ships of World War I,* 35–41, 43–45. Halpern adds two capital ships to the British list that were originally built for Turkey. Fisher's preference for a preemptive strike before Germany could get its dreadnought program fairly under way was understood by Tirpitz and others in Berlin as early as 1908. See Massie, *Dreadnought,* 701. Additional materials are from Churchill, *World Crisis,* 1:23–24; Dickinson, *International Anarchy,* 377; Keegan, *Price of Admiralty,* 105–6 (which includes Fisher's "Copenhagen" suggestion); and

Oscar Parkes, *British Battleships, Warrior 1860 to Vanguard 1950: A History of Design, Construction, and Armament,* 518. The British publicist is quoted in Mead, "England and Germany," 397.

53. A. Preston, *Battleships,* 51–65; Keegan, *Price of Admiralty,* 104–6, 109–12; Padfield, *The Battleship Era,* 199–203; Barnett, *Swordbearers,* 190–93.

54. A. Preston, *Battleships,* 60–61. See also Halpern, *Naval History,* 9; Barnett, *Swordbearers,* 193; and John Irving, *The Smoke Screen of Jutland,* 66n2.

55. Barnett, *Swordbearers,* 191; V. E. Tarrant, *Jutland, the German Perspective: A New View of the Great Battle, 31 May 1916,* 17–18.

56. Norman Friedman, "World Naval Developments: The Typhoon Saga Ends," *United States Naval Institute Proceedings* 125:2 (February 1999): 92.

57. Sumida, *In Defense of Naval Supremacy,* 51–61; "strategic cavalry" is from Churchill, *World Crisis,* 1:66; "big cats" and related quotes are from typescript copy of an interview with Fisher in *The Times* (London), September 1919, titled "Changes in Men and Ships," folder RIC/2/1, Richmond Papers. See also David C. Evans and Mark R. Peattie, *Kaigun: Strategy, Tactics, and Technology in the Imperial Japanese Navy, 1887–1941,* 153.

58. For various rated and estimated speeds of British capital ships by contemporary naval experts, see Moore et al., *Jane's Fighting Ships of World War I,* 35–41. Both Andrew Gordon and Karl Lautenschläger emphasize that by 1914 the most advanced battleship and battle-cruiser designs on *both* sides of the North Sea were converging, that is, the British *Lion*-class battle cruisers and *Queen Elizabeth*-class battleships were close to each other in speed and armament, and the same was true of similar German types (Gordon, *The Rules of the Game: Jutland and British Naval Command,* 13; Lautenschläger, "The Dreadnought Revolution Reconsidered," in *Naval History,* edited by Masterson, 134). However, it should be pointed out that at least one edition of *Jane's All the World's Ships* rated the latest battle cruisers *Queen Mary* and *Tiger* at 33 knots, whereas Jellicoe observed shortly after Jutland that the Fifth Battle Squadron composed of the "fast battleships" of the *Queen Elizabeth* class were either incapable of keeping speed with Beatty's battle cruisers or, more important, incapable of running away from the enemy's battle cruisers. "The highest mean speed attained by H.M.S. *Barham* on the recent measured mile trials was 23.97 knots. It is known that H.M.S. *Valiant's* speed is less than that of H.M.S. *Barham,* and it is therefore fairly evident that the Fifth Battle Squadron cannot get away from the German Third Battle Squadron when they are in range" (Jellicoe to the secretary of the Admiralty, July 12, 1916, in *The Jellicoe Papers: Selections from the Private and Official Correspondence of Admiral of the Fleet Earl Jellicoe,* edited by A. Temple Patterson, 2:25).

59. Scott, *Fifty Years,* 235–45 (quotes on pp. 239, 244).

60. Sumida, *In Defense of Naval Supremacy,* 331.

61. "In fact the concept of the all-big-gun ship with high speed was not intrinsically flawed. The helm-free fire control system developed by Pollen—the first really practical analogue computer capable of high-order differentiation—allowed for the first time in

history, maneuvering ships to engage maneuvering targets out to the effective range of their guns in the visibility prevailing. When the fire-control system was allied with the director principle developed by. . . Percy Scott through which elevation, training, and firing could be coordinated automatically from one position in the ship, vessels so equipped could fight at ranges at which their otherwise equally matched opponents could not hope to achieve results, whatever the size of their main battery. . . . The extraordinary results achieved by the Royal Navy in the opening years of the Second World War with visual fire-control systems that were in essence those developed by Pollen and his engineers are an indication of what a technological advantage the Royal Navy could have had over its opponents" in 1914–1918 (James Goldrick, introduction to *With the Battle Cruisers,* by Young, xvi–xvii).

62. Sumida, *In Defense of Naval Supremacy,* 331. A post-Jutland Admiralty Committee reached the devastating conclusion that Britain's battle cruisers "are unequal to the duties assigned to them, as their protection is insufficient to enable them to encounter the capital ships of the enemy without undue risk of destruction" (Gordon, *Rules of the Game,* 13).

63. Barnett, *Swordbearers,* 191.

64. On submarine development, see Antony Preston, *Submarines,* 6–27; and the terse but authoritative summaries by Thomas Parrish in *The Submarine: A History,* 3–41, and Wolfgang Frank in *The Sea Wolves,* 11–14. A short but illuminating discussion of the problems of effective submarine propulsion both on and beneath the surface is in Hugill, *World Trade since 1431,* 138–39. Early enthusiasm for the submarine among the kaiser's sailors is discussed in James Edward Sultow, "The Imperial German Navy, 1910–1914," 522–23; and Gary E. Weir, *Building the Kaiser's Navy: The Imperial Navy Office and German Industry in the von Tirpitz Era, 1889–1919,* 107–8. See also Edwyn Gray, *Submarine Warriors,* 3–8; Gemzell, *Organization, Conflict, and Innovation,* 61; Churchill, *World Crisis,* 1:260; and Halpern, *Naval History,* 101–2.

65. Ferguson, *Empire,* 245.

66. Moore et al., *Jane's Fighting Ships of World War I,* 44, 105; A. Preston, *Battleships,* 66.

67. Keegan, *Price of Admiralty,* 105.

68. Unless otherwise noted, the following discussion is based on information in Barnett, *Swordbearers,* 190–93; Keegan, *Price of Admiralty,* 104–6, 109–12; Padfield, *The Battleship Era,* 199–203; and A. Preston, *Battleships,* 51–65.

69. Henry Reuterdahl's article is discussed in George T. Davis, *A Navy Second to None: The Development of Modern American Naval Policy,* 186–87; and Harold Sprout and Margaret Sprout, *The Rise of American Naval Power, 1776–1918,* 277. See also Admiral Viscount [John] Jellicoe, *The Grand Fleet, 1914–1916: Its Creation, Development and Work,* 173–74; and David Beatty to Ethel Beatty, September 29, 1914, in *The Beatty Papers: Selections from the Private Official Correspondence of Admiral of the Fleet Earl Beatty,* edited by B. McL. Ranf, 1:137.

70. A. Preston, *Battleships,* 61–62.

71. Ibid., 65–67; Halpern, *Naval History,* 9.

72. Gary E. Weir, "Tirpitz and Technology," 41; A. Preston, *Battleships,* 65.

73. German industrial weaknesses in World War II are mentioned in Craig Haffner and Donna E. Lusitana, producers, *Sink the* Bismarck! (Greystone Productions: Arts and Entertainment Network, 1996); Theodor Krancke and H. J. Brennecke, *Pocket Battleship: The Story of the* Admiral Scheer, 8–9; Burkard Baron von Müllenheim-Rechberg, *Battleship* Bismarck: *A Survivor's Story,* 38–39; Richard Overy, *Why the Allies Won,* 51, 57, 118; and Raeder, *My Life,* 205–6.

74. I. F. Clarke, *Voices Prophesying War, 1763–1984,* 30–50, 137–38, provides a concise summary of pre-1914 European war fiction (quotes on pp. 44, 138). The contemporary quotes are from Mead, "England and Germany," 400.

75. Mead, "England and Germany," 400–401.

76. Hurd, "A Dreadnought Naval Policy," 1019; Mahan's observation is in James R. Reckner, "The Great White Fleet in New Zealand," 26. See also Churchill, *World Crisis,* 1:73, 86; Halpern, *Naval History;* Lambert, *Fisher's Naval Revolution,* 249–61; Varne Light, "Our Too Domestic Navy," 225, 227; and Marder, *Dreadnought to Scapa Flow,* 1:41, 106–11.

77. Light, "Our Too Domestic Navy," 224, 227.

78. Mead, "England and Germany," 401; Cecil Battine, "The Surrender of the Mediterranean," 263; Archibald Hurd, "The Peril of Invasion: Italy's 'Bolt from the Blue,'" 1044.

79. Editorial in *The Naval Annual, 1903,* edited by T. A. Brassey, iii.

80. Dickinson, *International Anarchy,* 376–77.

81. The following account is based on Churchill, *World Crisis,* 1:29–34 (quote on p. 29); and Tirpitz, *My Memoirs,* 1:275–76.

82. Tirpitz, *My Memoirs,* 1:275; Churchill, *World Crisis,* 1:32–33.

83. Churchill, *World Crisis,* 1:33.

84. J. Ellis Barker, "The Armament Race and Its Latest Developments," 660; [Theobald] Theodore von Bethmann Hollweg, *Reflections on the World War, Part I,* 57; Fischer, *Germany's Aims,* 31.

85. Barker, "Armament Race," 659–60.

86. Hurd and Castle, *German Sea-Power,* 142–43.

87. Barker, "Armament Race," 655.

88. Holger H. Herwig, *"Luxury" Fleet: The Imperial German Navy, 1888–1918,* 89, 91; Herwig, "The Failure of German Sea Power, 1914–1945: Mahan, Tirpitz, and Raeder Reconsidered," 80; Weir, *Building the Kaiser's Navy,* 99–100, 112.

89. Tirpitz, *My Memoirs,* 1:277; Lambi, *Navy and Power Politics,* 372.

90. Hurd and Castle, *German Sea-Power,* 143, 144.

91. Sydney Brooks, "England and Germany," *Forum,* 97–98.

92. Lord Haldane is quoted in Dickinson, *International Anarchy,* 374; Fischer, *Germany's Aims,* 29.

93. Tirpitz, *My Memoirs,* 1:288–96.

94. Tuchman, *The Guns of August*, 72.

95. Bethmann Hollweg, *Reflections on the War*, 58, 59.

96. Herwig, *"Luxury" Fleet*, 89–90.

97. Marion C. Siney, *The Allied Blockade of Germany, 1914–1916*, 15; Churchill, *World Crisis*, 1:114–15. The physical description of Scapa Flow is from Young, *With the Battle Cruisers*, 70, 72.

98. Gemzell, *Organization, Conflict, and Innovation*, 86–87.

99. Fischer, *Germany's Aims*, 32. See also Lambi, *Navy and Power Politics*, 382–83.

100. Lambi, *Navy and Power Politics*, 382–83.

101. Halpern, *Naval History*, 17.

102. Just what orders the kaiser gave his sailors and when is a matter of debate. According to Paul Kennedy, John Keegan, and others, Wilhelm issued his final war directive to the German navy on December 3, 1912, stipulating—according to the official memorandum drawn up shortly thereafter—that the naval war "is to be carried out from the German [that is, Heligoland] Bight." Its "chief war task should be to damage the blockading forces of the enemy as far as possible through numerous and repeated attacks day and night, and *under favorable circumstances* to give battle with all the forces at your disposal." In other words, the High Seas Fleet, unless exceptionally favored, should not court its own demise by an all-out offensive against Britain. According to Lambi, however, the kaiser dispensed his final fleet orders five days later, on December 8, 1912, in a meeting with the military, naval, and diplomatic leadership. At that time, the kaiser issued his remarks about the inevitability of a European war (based on recent assurances by the British that they would come to the aid of France if it was attacked by Germany). The kaiser then stated that the fleet must concentrate against Britain rather than Russia and that "it was also to attack British troop transports to the Continent." Army chief Moltke "strongly supported the Kaiser. He stated that war was inevitable and wanted it to occur as soon as possible." Although some have dismissed the meeting's importance, others have characterized it "as the war council for 1914." See Kennedy, "Development of Operations Plans," 69 (which contains the quoted portions of the kaiser's war directive approved on December 3; unfortunately, it is unclear if the italicized portion is in the original or has been emphasized by Professor Kennedy); Keegan, *The First World War*, 267; Fischer, *Germany's Aims*, 31–33 (though not commenting directly on the December 1912 war conferences, it does reflect the increasingly rabid nature of the kaiser's thought at this time); and Lambi, *Navy and Power Politics*, 382–83.

103. Lambi, *Navy and Power Politics*, 384.

104. Goldrick, *King's Ships*, 47; Gemzell, *Organization, Conflict, and Innovation*, 139. The German operational plan of August 4, 1914, is quoted in part in Wegener, *Naval Strategy*, 11n.

105. "Admiral Sir George Callaghan's Review of the War Plans after Maneuvers, 1913"; D. Beatty to E. Beatty, July 23, 27, 28, 1913, both in *Beatty Papers*, edited by Ranf, 1:77–79, 82.

106. Lambert, *Fisher's Naval Revolution*, 289 (quote), 249–61, 291–300.

Chapter 3. Rengo Kantai

1. Edwin A. Falk, *Tōgō and the Rise of Japanese Sea Power,* 13–97 (quotes on pp. 13, 22); Shizuo Fukui, *Naval Vessels, 1887–1945: Mitsubishi Zosen Built,* 2; M. D. Kennedy, *Some Aspects of Japan and Her Defence Forces,* 39; Hector C. Bywater, *Sea-Power in the Pacific: A Study of the American-Japanese Naval Problem,* 131–34; Hansgeorg Jentschura, Dieter Jung, and Peter Mikel, *Warships of the Imperial Japanese Navy, 1869–1945,* 11; Edwin O. Reischauer, *Japan: Past and Present,* 114–16.

2. Thomas C. Smith, *The Agrarian Origins of Modern Japan,* 205.

3. J. Charles Schencking, *Making Waves: Politics, Propaganda, and the Emergence of the Imperial Japanese Navy, 1868–1922,* 27–47; G. A. Ballard, *The Influence of the Sea on the Political History of Japan,* 137. Ballard is a particularly interesting source for the period. Writing in 1921 after a forty-five-year career, the retired British vice admiral doubtless knew many of Victoria's naval officers who had gone to the Far East to train the fledgling Japanese navy, and he writes with verve and authority.

4. Schencking, *Making Waves,* 38–43 (quotes on pp. 38, 43).

5. R. J. B. Bosworth, *Explaining Auschwitz and Hiroshima: History Writing and the Second World War, 1945–1990,* 179.

6. Evans and Peattie, *Kaigun,* 10.

7. G. Ballard, *Influence of the Sea,* 137–38.

8. Schencking, *Making Waves,* 82–83; Falk, *Tōgō and Sea Power,* 176–98; Evans and Peattie, *Kaigun,* 38–46; Bywater, *Sea-Power in the Pacific,* 137; [Neville D. Kirk], "The Rise of Japanese Naval Power," in *Seapower: A Naval History,* edited by E. B. Potter, 350–52.

9. Masanori Ito and Roger Pineau, *The End of the Imperial Japanese Navy,* 7–8; G. Ballard, *Influence of the Sea,* 153. See also Bywater, *Sea-Power in the Pacific,* 141.

10. Shippen, *Naval Battles,* 776.

11. The most thorough account of Japanese naval operations during the 1894–1895 war with China is G. Ballard, *Influence of the Sea,* 150–75. See also Evans and Peattie, *Kaigun,* 46, 48; Hans-Joachim Krug et al., *Reluctant Allies: German-Japanese Naval Relations in World War II,* 25; and Jonathan D. Spence, *The Search for Modern China,* 223. The Royal Navy study is discussed in William H. Homan, "Kamikazes, Turtle Backs, and Torpedoes That Made U-turns," *Naval History* (summer 1990): 22–23.

12. Kirk, "Rise of Japanese Naval Power," in *Seapower: A Naval History,* edited by Potter, 353. The German blunder is recounted in Morinosuke Kajima, *The Emergence of Japan as a World Power, 1895–1925,* 15–16. See also Schencking, *Making Waves,* 84.

13. Evans and Peattie, *Kaigun,* 25.

14. Ibid., 49, 57–65 (quotes on pp. 57, 49, 61); Schencking, *Making Waves,* 84–85.

15. Schencking, *Making Waves,* 84–86 (quote on p. 86).

16. Carlos R. Rivera, "Big Stick and Short Sword: The American and Japanese Navies as Hypothetical Enemies before 1922," 32–59.

17. Earl Hancock "Pete" Ellis in a letter from Cavite naval base in 1902, quoted in Dirk A. Ballendorf and Merrill L. Bartlett, *Pete Ellis, an Amphibious Warfare Prophet, 1880–1923,* 33.

18. Stephen Howarth, *To Shining Sea: A History of the United States Navy, 1775–1991,* 276. An excellent history of the Philippine insurrection is Stuart Creighton Miller, *"Benevolent Assimilation": The American Conquest of the Philippines, 1899–1903,* esp. 96–98, 135–36, 167–68, 201–52. See also Kenneth J. Hagan, *This People's Navy: The Making of American Sea Power,* 229.

19. Margaret Leech, *In the Days of McKinley,* 424; Kemp Tolley, *Yangtze Patrol: The U.S. Navy in China,* 12–20, 54–55; *Dictionary of American Fighting Ships,* vol. 1, s.vv. "U.S.S. *Brooklyn*," "U.S.S. *Kentucky*"; Hagan, *This People's Navy,* 231; Max Boot, "A Century of Small Wars Shows They Can Be Won," *New York Times,* July 6, 2003, 10.

20. S. Miller, *"Benevolent Assimilation,"* 135.

21. The purpose of the General Board of the navy is quoted in Edward S. Miller, *War Plan Orange: The U.S. Strategy to Defeat Japan, 1897–1945,* 15. See also Theodore Roosevelt, *The Works of Theodore Roosevelt,* pt. 1, 582–83; and G. Davis, *Navy Second to None,* 157, 164–65, 167.

22. T. Iyenaga, "Japan's Mission in the Far East," 459.

23. Adachi Kinnosuke, "The Birth of the New Nippon," 263.

24. Iyenaga, "Japan's Mission," 460.

25. Ibid., 461.

26. Ito quotes in ibid., 461, 465.

27. Okakura-Kakuzo, *The Awakening of Japan,* 4, 6, 106.

28. The following discussion is based on Mark R. Peattie and David C. Evans, "Satō Tetsutarō and Japanese Strategy," 36–39; and Evans and Peattie, *Kaigun,* 133–51.

29. M. Kennedy, *Aspects of Japan,* 43–47.

30. Julian S. Corbett, *Maritime Operations in the Russo-Japanese War, 1904–1905,* 2:5–6. See also Schencking, *Making Waves,* 103.

31. Unless otherwise noted, the following account of naval operations during the Russo-Japanese War is taken from G. Ballard, *Influence of the Sea,* 225–87; Corbett, *Maritime Operations,* vol. 2; Falk, *Tōgō and Sea Power,* 278–427; Kirk, "Rise of Japanese Naval Power," in *Seapower: A Naval History,* edited by Potter, 354–63; and Stevens and Westcott, *History of Sea Power,* 287–302. Recent sources for the naval aspects of the Port Arthur campaign include Evans and Peattie, *Kaigun,* 94–110; and William H. Homan, "Nightmare at Port Arthur," 21–27.

32. Rivera, "Big Stick and Short Sword," 66–82, 110–28.

33. Kirk, "Rise of Japanese Naval Power," in *Seapower: A Naval History,* edited by Potter, 353, 354.

34. Corbett, *Maritime Operations,* 2:8.

35. Falk, *Tōgō and Sea Power,* 86–97; Albert M. Bledsoe, "The Japanese Naval Academy," *United States Naval Institute Proceedings* 75:2 (March 1949): 331.

36. Bledsoe, "The Japanese Naval Academy," 330; Fred T. Jane, *The Imperial Japanese Navy,* 257–58; Bywater, *Sea-Power in the Pacific,* 179.

37. The origins of professional training in the Imperial Japanese Navy are discussed in M. Kennedy, *Aspects of Japan,* 34–38; and Bywater, *Sea-Power in the Pacific,* 178–79. A brief, informed discussion of Eta Jima and its curriculum is in Bledsoe, "The Japanese Naval Academy," 329–33 (quote on p. 330).

38. Shippen, *Naval Battles,* 727.

39. Tameichi Hara, Fred Saito, and Roger Pineau, *Japanese Destroyer Captain,* 15–16.

40. Jane, *The Imperial Japanese Navy,* 283, 293–94, 299.

41. Bywater, *Sea-Power in the Pacific,* 184–88 (Jane quoted on p. 85).

42. Ibid., 186, 187, 188.

43. Hesibo Tikowara, *Before Port Arthur in a Destroyer: The Personal Diary of a Japanese Naval Officer,* 3; Peattie and Evans, "Satō and Japanese Strategy," 34–39.

44. The following account of the experiences of Japanese enlisted men is from Bywater, *Sea-Power in the Pacific,* 179–80, 189–90; Hara, Saito, and Pineau, *Japanese Destroyer Captain,* 18; and Jane, *The Imperial Japanese Navy,* 303–7.

45. Saburo Sakai, Martin Caidin, and Fred Saito, *Samurai!* 7–8, 9.

46. Bywater, *Sea-Power in the Pacific,* 189–90.

47. Robert J. Casey, *Torpedo Junction: With the Pacific Fleet from Pearl Harbor to Midway,* 102–3.

48. Tikowara, *Before Port Arthur,* 2; Ronald H. Spector, *At War at Sea: Sailors and Naval Warfare in the Twentieth Century,* 8.

49. A good account of the Battle of the Yellow Sea is G. Ballard, *Influence of the Sea,* 235–44.

50. The standard accounts of the Russian Baltic Fleet in the war with Japan are Richard Hough, *The Fleet That Had to Die;* Corbett, *Maritime Operations,* 2:185–344; and Constantine Pleshakov, *The Tsar's Last Armada: The Epic Journey to the Battle of Tsushima.* Briefer accounts are in Padfield, *The Battleship Era,* 172–81; and the sources cited in note 31.

51. [Colonel A. C. Repington], *The War in the Far East, 1904–1905: By the Military Correspondent of "The Times,"* x, 60.

52. Kirk, "Rise of Japanese Naval Power," in *Seapower: A Naval History,* edited by Potter, 358.

53. Pleshakov, *Tsar's Last Armada,* 70, 75.

54. Repington, *War in the Far East,* 409, 411. 569.

55. Pleshakov, *Tsar's Last Armada,* 205.

56. A. Novikoff-Priboy, *Tsushima,* 131–32. Novikoff-Priboy claims to have been part of the Baltic Fleet and taken part in the Battle of Tsushima as an enlisted "paymaster's steward." He alleges that his notes on the cruise and battle were lost for some time and that in any event they could not have been published under the czar. His prejudices are that of communism's everyman for the foibles and tyrannies of the monarchical age, but the narrative does ring true. Nonetheless, it should be treated with caution.

57. Repington, *War in the Far East,* 563; Hough, *The Fleet That Had to Die,* 96 (quote).

58. Kirk, "Rise of Japanese Naval Power," in *Seapower: A Naval History,* edited by Potter, 360; Spector, *At War at Sea,* 8.

59. Kirk, "Rise of Japanese Naval Power," in *Seapower: A Naval History,* edited by Potter, 360.

60. Hough, *The Fleet That Had to Die,* 163.

61. I have used the translation of this quotation in Ito and Pineau, *Imperial Japanese Navy,* 7. Hough's slightly different translation is in *The Fleet That Had to Die,* 163.

62. Spector, *At War at Sea,* 19.

63. Rating the relative rank of the world's fighting fleets in 1905, or 1913, was a difficult task. Britain retained its numerical supremacy in nearly all types of warship down to World War I; France in 1905 was doubtless second. After that, the rapidly developing German and U.S. navies were clearly superseding the defeated Russian fleet.

64. Repington, *War in the Far East,* 577.

65. Shencking, *Making Waves,* 112–35 (quotes on pp. 131–32).

66. A. Maurice Low, "Foreign Affairs," (April–June 1908): 468.

67. Chester Holcombe, "Some Results of the Eastern War," 24–25.

68. Repington, *War in the Far East,* 579.

69. Holcombe, "Some Results," 28, 30.

70. Beale, *Roosevelt and America,* 43.

71. Norman A. Graebner, *An Uncertain Tradition: American Secretaries of State in the Twentieth Century,* 48.

72. Harold C. Ridgely, "Are the Japanese Unfriendly?" 483–85.

Chapter 4. The Boast of the Red, White, and Blue

1. Beach, *Annapolis to Scapa Flow,* 113–22; Reckner, "The 'New' Sailor," 44–49.

2. William S. Sims, "Naval Morale after War," *United States Naval Institute Proceedings* (September 1922): 1467; Arthur A. Ageton, *The Naval Officer's Guide,* 144–45 (italics in original); Hattendorf, *Naval History and Maritime Strategy,* 29, 31.

3. An expert survey of the African American experience with the United States Navy is Bernard J. Nalty, *Long Passage to Korea: Black Sailors and the Integration of the U.S. Navy* (quotes on pp. 13, 14–15). Brief summaries are in Reckner, "The 'New' Sailor," 45–47; Spector, *At War at Sea,* 265–71; and Jonathan G. Utley, *An American Battleship in Peace and War: The U.S.S.* Tennessee, 7, 62–63.

4. For many years the standard work on Annapolis was Kendall Banning, *Annapolis Today.* The best brief account of the spirit and mission of the U.S. Naval Academy— and the source of the following quotations (523, 524)—is Richard S. Craighill, "The Navy University," *United States Naval Institute Proceedings* 75:5 (May 1949): 523–35; it is also perhaps the most idealistic. A cogent discussion of the late-nineteenth-century hazing scandal is in D. R. Morris, "Homer Clark Poundstone" (see chap. 2, n. 42). Peter

Karsten's often harshly skeptical *The Naval Aristocracy: The Golden Age of Annapolis and the Emergence of Modern American Navalism* is an occasionally welcome antidote to the idealism of most histories of the Brigade of Midshipmen. Interestingly enough, the Nimitz Library at the Naval Academy has no less than a half-dozen copies of the work.

5. Paul A. C. Koistinen, *Mobilizing for Modern War: The Political Economy of American Warfare, 1865–1919*, 43.

6. The establishment and development of the Naval War College at Newport is traced in Herrick, *The American Naval Revolution*, 10–171; and John B. Hattendorf, B. Mitchell Simpson III, and John R. Wadleigh, *Sailors and Scholars: The Centennial History of the U.S. Naval War College*, 1–35.

7. Karsten, *Naval Aristocracy*, 11.

8. A good overall account of this issue is B. C. Bryan, "An Analysis and Discussion of Various Systems of Promotion in the Navy, with Outlines of a Proposed New System of Transfer from the Active List," *United States Naval Institute Proceedings* 47:8 (August 1921): 1251–70 (quote on p. 1251). Information on the appalling length of time that many ensigns and lieutenants spent in grade at the end of the nineteenth century was provided by Captain Frederick L. Oliver, Annapolis class of 1898, in his comments on D. R. Morris's article, "Homer Clark Poundstone" (see chap. 2, n. 45); ongoing criticism of the navy's promotion policies is in F. A. L. Vossler, "Promotion in the Navy," *United States Naval Institute Proceedings* 47:1 (January 1921): 7–20 (quote on p. 7).

9. Karsten, *Naval Aristocracy*, 15–16; Robert L. O'Connell, *Sacred Vessels: The Cult of the Battleship and the Rise of the U.S. Navy*, 134–35.

10. William Sowden Sims, *The Victory at Sea*, 7–8; Sprout and Sprout, *American Naval Power*, 273–75; Brayton Harris, *The Age of the Battleship, 1890–1922*, 122–30; D. R. Morris, "Homer Clark Poundstone," 707–21.

11. Frederick S. Harrod, *Manning the New Navy: The Development of a Modern Naval Enlisted Force, 1899–1940*, 20–21; Shippen, *Naval Battles*, 747–49.

12. Quoted in Harrod, *Manning the New Navy*, 21.

13. John D. Alden, *The American Steel Navy: A Photographic History of the U.S. Navy from the Introduction of the Steel Hull in 1883 to the Cruise of the Great White Fleet, 1907–1909*, 266; Harris, *Age of the Battleship*, 132; Marder, *Dreadnought to Scapa Flow*, 1:8.

14. See, for example, Hector C. Bywater, *The Great Pacific War: A Historic Prophecy Now Being Fulfilled*, 77.

15. Quoted in Sprout and Sprout, *American Naval Power*, 251.

16. E. Miller, *War Plan Orange*, 23.

17. Ibid., 13, 23.

18. The following discussion and quotations are from ibid., 24–25.

19. Robert A. Hart, *The Great White Fleet: Its Voyage around the World, 1907–1909*, 32.

20. Homer Lea, *The Valor of Ignorance*, 306–8.

21. Hart, *Great White Fleet,* 31.

22. Ibid., 23; Beale, *Roosevelt and America,* 285 (quote). Unless otherwise noted, the following account of the U.S. Navy's 1907–1909 world cruise is based on Hart's splendid account in *Great White Fleet* and James R. Reckner's equally fine *Teddy Roosevelt's Great White Fleet.*

23. Theodore Roosevelt, *An Autobiography,* 563–64.

24. Hart, *Great White Fleet,* 29.

25. Ibid., 34.

26. Ibid., 37.

27. Reckner, *Roosevelt's Great White Fleet,* 46; Sydney Brooks, "The Voyage of the American Fleet," 201–11.

28. The Roosevelt Corollary, set forth in the president's State of the Union message to Congress in December of that year, stipulated that in order to guarantee the inviolability of the Western Hemisphere from European intervention, the United States would step in and exercise "international police power" in cases of "flagrant" wrongdoing or impotence on the part of any Western Hemispheric government. See Dexter Perkins's still authoritative and dispassionate discussion in *A History of the Monroe Doctrine,* 239–40.

29. Brooks, "Voyage of the American Fleet," 207.

30. Ibid., 208, 210–11.

31. Reckner, "New Zealand," 26–27.

32. A. Maurice Low, "Foreign Affairs: Japan and the Saxon," 309–10.

33. Reckner, "New Zealand," 29.

34. Low, "Foreign Affairs: Japan and the Saxon," 311.

35. Hart, *Great White Fleet,* 221.

36. Ibid., 229. See also E. B. Potter, *Bull Halsey,* 95.

37. Sperry is quoted in Reckner, *Roosevelt's Great White Fleet,* 159; Potter, *Bull Halsey,* 94–95; Thomas B. Buell, *The Quiet Warrior: A Biography of Admiral Raymond A. Spruance,* 19–21. Young Chet Nimitz, just a few years ahead on the seniority list, visited Japan aboard the Asiatic Fleet flagship *Ohio* in 1905, shortly after Tsushima, and spoke with Tōgō himself. Nimitz was surprised when the revered Japanese admiral addressed him in flawless English. "The scene made a deep impression on the midshipman, as did the Japanese and their country." Twenty-two years later, Nimitz attended Tōgō's funeral. Alan Schom, *The Eagle and the Rising Sun: The Japanese-American War, 1941–1943; Pearl Harbor through Guadalcanal,* 166.

38. Henry F. Pringle, *Theodore Roosevelt: A Biography,* 347. Roosevelt's message to the fleet is in Roosevelt, *An Autobiography,* 573–74 (quote on p. 574).

39. [Shailer Matthews], "The Prophet with the Big Stick," *World To-Day* 16:3 (March 1909): 229; Francis W. Shepardson, "The Roosevelt Regime," 268.

40. Evans and Peattie, *Kaigun,* 137–38.

41. Peattie and Evans, "Satō and Japanese Strategy," 37.

42. Ibid., 38.

43. G. Davis, *Navy Second to None,* 188–89; Hattendorf, Simpson, and Wadleigh, *Sailors and Scholars,* 61–65. TR's interest and input can be traced in Elting E. Morison et al., eds., *Letters of Theodore Roosevelt,* 6:1446, 1453, 1456–57, 1469–72.

44. Hattendorf, Simpson, and Wadleigh, *Sailors and Scholars,* 73.

45. Rivera, "Big Stick and Short Sword," 113, 154–55.

46. G. Davis, *Navy Second to None,* 182. See also Fletcher Pratt and Harley E. Howe, *The Compact History of the United States Navy,* 195.

47. Archibald Hurd, "The New Navy Estimates," 310.

48. Ibid.

49. See Seward W. Livermore, "The American Navy as a Factor in World Politics."

50. Hart, *Great White Fleet,* 11.

51. Ibid., 11–12; O'Connell, *Sacred Vessels,* 137.

52. See Modelski and Thompson, *Seapower in Global Politics,* 76; and Hilary Herbert, "A Plea for the Navy," 1–13.

53. Hart, *Great White Fleet,* 13.

54. Ibid., 15–16.

55. Ibid., 16.

56. See Ralph Ingersoll, *The Battle Is the Pay-Off.*

Chapter 5. Rush to Conflict

1. Roskill, *Churchill and the Admirals,* 27.

2. Brian Schofield, "'Jacky' Fisher, HMS *Indomitable,* and the Dogger Bank Action: A Personal Memoir," in *Naval Warfare,* edited by Jordan, 60–65.

3. Tirpitz, *My Memoirs,* 1:309.

4. Young, *With the Battle Cruisers,* 21 (quote), 32.

Chapter 6. Standoff, 1914–1915

1. "Ante-Invasion Papers—Synopsis, 1914–1918," folder RIC/2/2, Richmond Papers.

2. Lambert, *Fisher's Naval Revolution,* 289.

3. Bernard Edwards, *Dönitz and the Wolf-Packs,* 11–12.

4. Young, *With the Battle Cruisers,* 92. A good discussion of Britain's dilatory depth charge–development program is in Dwight R. Messimer, *Find and Destroy: Antisubmarine Warfare in World War I,* 76–80.

5. Tuchman, *The Guns of August,* 366; A. Preston, *Battleships,* 81; Young, *With the Battle Cruisers,* 93.

6. Beatty to Churchill, October 17, 1914, in *Beatty Papers,* edited by Ranf, 1:141; D. J. Munro, *Scapa Flow: A Naval Retrospect,* 197.

7. Patrick Beesly, *Room 40: British Naval Intelligence, 1914–18* 48; Jellicoe, *Grand Fleet,* 22–23.

8. Scheer, *Germany's High Seas Fleet,* chap. 2, p. 5.

9. Gemzell, *Organization, Conflict, and Innovation,* 138–39; Philbin, *Admiral von Hipper,* 82; "German Notes on Transportation of the BEF," n.d., RIC/2/1, Richmond Papers.

10. Britain supplied four fresh brigades for the Battle of the Marne, and, in addition, Anglo-French control of the western Mediterranean allowed the French to bring over and place in line the Forty-fifth Division from Algeria (Keegan, *The First World War,* 111–12, 119–21).

11. Roskill, *Churchill and the Admirals,* 35.

12. Ibid.

13. Irving, *Smoke Screen of Jutland,* 7.

14. Fisher's plan is summarized and commented upon in Richard Hough, *Death of the Battleship: The Tragic Close of the Era of Sea Power,* 77.

15. Even less daring, but promising, plans to lure the High Seas Fleet or to destroy its North Sea bases of operations or both were rejected by the British Admiralty in the early stages of the war. At the end of 1914, two young naval commanders who would rise to the very top of the service in coming years proposed a commando-naval raid on the Heligoland dockyards. William Fisher and Dudley Pound argued that such an assault would lure the High Seas Fleet out from Wilhelmshaven and Cuxhaven for a decisive battle in the North Sea. See untitled plan dated December 30, 1914, folder FHR/2, William Wordsworth Fisher Papers.

16. The exploits of these vessels are covered in Churchill, *World Crisis,* 1:237–59; Halpern, *Naval History,* 75–82, 88–100; A. A. Hoehling, *The Great War at Sea,* 9–40, 60–102; Richard Hough, *The Long Pursuit;* Edwin P. Hoyt, *The German Who Never Lost: The Story of the* Königsberg; Hoyt, *Kreuzerkrieg;* Hoyt, *The Last Cruise of the* Emden; Hoyt, *Raider Wolf: The Voyage of Captain Nerger;* S. L. Poole, *Cruiser: A History of British Cruisers from 1889 to 1960,* 33–41; and Dan van der Vat, *Gentlemen of War: The Amazing Story of Captain Karl von Müller and the S.M.S.* Emden.

17. Roskill, *Churchill and the Admirals,* 40.

18. Beesly, *Room 40,* 78–79, 145, 175 (quote on p. 275).

19. Jerram to Mrs. Jerram, typescript copy of undated letter, folder JRM 16/4, Thomas Jerram Papers.

20. A detailed account of the Battle of the Falklands is Julian S. Corbett and Henry Newbold, *Official History of the War: Naval Operations,* 1:416–54. See also Beesly, *Room 40,* 75–76; Halpern, *Naval History,* 91–93; Poole, *Cruiser,* 35–39; and Roskill, *Churchill and the Admirals,* 39–40.

21. The best brief accounts of the *Goeben* incident are Halpern, *Naval History,* 51–59; Marder, *Dreadnought to Scapa Flow,* 2:20–30; and Tuchman, *The Guns of August,* 161–87. An excellent full-length study is Dan van der Vat, *The Ship That Changed the World: The Escape of the* Goeben *to the Dardenelles in 1914.* Churchill's interesting and not totally self-serving account is in *World Crisis,* 1:200–209.

22. A. Preston, *Battleships,* 77.

23. Schofield, "'Jacky' Fisher," in *Naval Warfare,* edited by Jordan, 65–66.

24. Marder, *Dreadnought to Scapa Flow*, 2:21.

25. Churchill, *World Crisis*, 1:206; Tuchman, *The Guns of August*, 186.

26. Halpern, *Naval History*, 30–32; Philbin, *Admiral von Hipper*, 85–86; Goldrick, *King's Ships*, 82–117 (quote on p. 115).

27. Horn, *German Naval Mutinies*, 21.

28. Young, *With the Battle Cruisers*, 156–66 (quotes on pp. 164, 166).

29. German Admiralty staff paper quoted in Tarrant, *Jutland*, 27.

30. Ibid. (italics in original).

31. Ibid., 29; Beesly, *Room 40*, 3–7; Edwin T. Layton, Roger Pineau, and John Costello, *And I Was There: Pearl Harbor and Midway—Breaking the Secrets*, 27.

32. Daniel Goure, "The Leading Edge of Transformation," *Seapower* 45:7 (July 2002): 35–36.

33. Churchill, *World Crisis*, 1:415.

34. The fullest and most accurate accounts of the Scarborough action are in Goldrick, *King's Ships*, 189–226; Halpern, *Naval History*, 42–44; Tarrant, *Jutland*, 28–32; and Young, *With the Battle Cruisers*, 98–115. Young witnessed the action from flagship *Lion*'s signal bridge. Less satisfactory in terms of either completeness or accuracy are Beesly, *Room 40*, 51–55; Churchill, *World Crisis*, 1:414–30; Jellicoe, *Grand Fleet*, 174–79; and Philbin, *Admiral von Hipper*, 97–99.

35. The incident is recounted in Young, *With the Battle Cruisers*, 108.

36. Tirpitz's remarks are quoted in Beesly, *Room 40*, 55; and Philbin, *Admiral von Hipper*, 99; Jellicoe, *Grand Fleet*, 179.

37. Philbin, *Admiral von Hipper*, 108.

38. Tarrant, *Jutland*, 33 (quote), 35, 39; Philbin, *Admiral von Hipper*, 109, 111.

39. Young, *With the Battle Cruisers*, 123, 178. The battle of Dogger Bank is covered in ibid., 176–223; Goldrick, *King's Ships*; Halpern, *Naval History*, 44–47; Keegan, *Price of Admiralty*, 115–18; and Tarrant, *Jutland*, 33–39. As is often the case in battle, there are time discrepancies, depending on the historian's grasp of local time or his emphasis on one or the other fleet.

40. Tarrant, *Jutland*, 35; Schofield, "'Jacky' Fisher," 66–67.

41. Schofield, "'Jacky' Fisher," 67.

42. Commander Goldrick believes Beatty himself made the erroneous sighting. See his editorial comment in Young, *With the Battle Cruisers*, 198n12.

43. Ibid., 38; Keegan, *Price of Admiralty*, 117. Keegan maintains that Beatty ordered up a light cruiser to take him off *Lion*; Tarrant states it was the destroyer *Attack*.

44. Irving, *Smoke Screen of Jutland*, 65.

45. Or so Commander Goldrick believes. See his editorial comment in Young, *With the Battle Cruisers*, 152n4. Beatty's despairing remark is quoted in Halpern, *Naval History*, 46.

46. Tarrant, *Jutland*, 39. By the end of the war German U-boats had dispatched no fewer than nine British dreadnoughts and pre-dreadnoughts, fourteen cruisers, and fifteen destroyers (A. Preston, *Submarines*, 48; Halpern, *Naval History*, 34; Munro, *Scapa Flow*,

197–98; Gray, *Submarine Warriors*, 315). Germany's initial decision to initiate unrestricted submarine warfare came after von Pohl assured Chancellor Bethmann Hollweg and then the kaiser that Germany possessed enough U-boats to destroy British commerce (Messimer, *Find and Destroy*, 17).

47. Halpern, *Naval History*, 48–50, 291–92, 299, 328.

48. Arthur S. Link, *Woodrow Wilson and the Progressive Era, 1910–1917*, 153–54, 206.

49. Siney, *Allied Blockade of Germany*, 245. See also the brief discussion in Messimer, *Find and Destroy*, 12–13.

50. See "Hints for Visiting Officers," n.d., vol. 1 of "Diary of the Grand Fleet: Signal Log of His Majesty's Ship *Marlborough*," folder MAD/1, Charles Madden Papers.

51. Siney, *Allied Blockade of Germany*, 245–46; Halpern, *Naval History*, 49; Link, *Wilson and the Progressive Era*, 157–58. Link states that the British order declaring the entire North Sea a war zone was dated November 3.

52. A. Preston, *Submarines*, 53.

53. Siney, *Allied Blockade of Germany*, 66–244 (quote on p. 246).

54. Halpern, *Naval History*, 50.

55. The reports of De Chair and Tupper, together with an editorial discussion of the various blockade patrol areas north and west of the British Isles between 1914 and 1918, are in John D. Grainger, ed., *The Maritime Blockade of Germany in the Great War: The Northern Patrol, 1914–1918*, 86–99, 489–96.

56. Link, *Wilson and the Progressive Era*, 159.

57. Lynn Montross, *War through the Ages*, 740; Grainger, *Maritime Blockade of Germany*, 14–15.

58. Siney, *Allied Blockade of Germany*, 256; Paul M. Kennedy, *The Rise and Fall of the Great Powers: Economic Change and Military Conflict from 1500 to 2000*, 269–70.

59. Albert Speer, *Inside the Third Reich: Memoirs by Albert Speer*, 7; Siney, *Allied Blockade of Germany*, 256; Horn, *German Naval Mutinies*, 39–57 (quote on pp. 39–40); Beesly, *Room 40*, 48. The most recent analyst of the British blockade concludes that its effectiveness "was thus neither so great as the British navalists claimed nor so minimal as the latest revisionists suggest." Its effect was, above all, cumulative, and it could only be made approximately complete if and when the USA participated in it fully, which, of course, the United States did upon entering the war in early April 1917 (Grainger, *Maritime Blockade of Germany*, 22).

60. Churchill, *World Crisis*, 1:484, 489, 484; Keegan, *The First World War*, 190.

61. Keegan, *The First World War*, 221, 225–26; Churchill, *World Crisis*, 1:486.

62. Goldrick, *King's Ships*, 18–20; Beesly, *Room 40*, 8; Roskill, *Churchill and the Admirals*, 41–65.

63. An appreciation of the Gallipoli campaign can be gleaned from the following sources: Iain Ballantyne, *Warships of the Royal Navy: HMS* London, 48–49; Eric Bush, *Gallipoli;* Corbett and Newbolt, *Official History*, 2:119–382, 3:24–39, 68–107; Halpern, *Naval History*, 109–24; Marder, *Dreadnought to Scapa Flow*, 2:129–328; Alan Moorhead, *Gallipoli;* and John North, *Gallipoli: The Fading Vision*.

64. Halpern, *Naval History*, 110; Harry Albert Austin, "The United States Unprepared for War," 530.

65. Tyrwhitt to Keyes, n.d. ("Early March 1915"), in *The Keyes Papers: Selections from the Private and Official Correspondence of Admiral of the Fleet Baron Keyes of Zeebrugge*, edited by Paul G. Halpern, 1:98; Halpern, *Naval History*, 110 (quote on p. 111).

66. Halpern, *Naval History*, 111.

67. Keyes to [?], March 2, 1915, in *Keyes Papers*, edited by Halpern, 1:98.

68. Ballantyne, *Warships of the Royal Navy*, 48–49.

69. Marder, *Dreadnought to Scapa Flow*, 2:313; William Guy Carr, *By Guess—and by God: The Story of the British Submarines in the War*, 7–80; Gray, *Submarine Warriors*, 7, 46–58; Churchill, *World Crisis*, 2:724.

70. Keyes to Vice Admiral H. F. Oliver, November 29, 1915, in *Keyes Papers*, edited by Halpern, 1:258–62; Halpern, *Naval History*, 123; Keegan, *The First World War*, 248–49.

71. What might have happened had the Allies won at Gallipoli and moved on Constantinople and the Danube has bewitched several historians. Such speculation is beyond the boundaries of this study, but see Keegan, *The First World War*, 267–70; and Friedman, *Seapower as Strategy*, 151–52, 319n.

72. Roskill, *Churchill and the Admirals*, 52–53.

73. Ibid., 53.

Chapter 7. Jutland

1. Irving, *Smoke Screen of Jutland*, 12.

2. The literature on Jutland has grown vast. The briefest accounts are Theodore Ropp, *War in the Modern World*, 235n; and A. J. P. Taylor, *English History, 1914–1945*, 63. The most exhaustive are Corbett and Newbolt, *Official History*, 3:313–424; Holloway H. Frost, *The Battle of Jutland*; and Robert K. Massie, *Castles of Steel: Britain, Germany, and the Winning of the Great War at Sea*, 566–684. The finest are Massie; Marder, *Dreadnought to Scapa Flow*, 3:37–259, which tries to put the best possible face on British efforts throughout the long afternoon and evening, and largely succeeds; Barnett, *Swordbearers*, 113–99; Gordon, *Rules of the Game*, which is contentious and challenging; and Keegan, *Price of Admiralty*, 122–55. The most intriguing contemporary analysis was provided by Japanese officer Ichiro Sato ("The Battle of Jutland: A Brief Tactical Analysis") in Alexander Richardson and Archibald Hurd, *Brassey's Naval and Shipping Annual, 1921–2*, 77–84. See also Herbert Russell, "Battle Tactics: Some Reflections Suggested by 'Jutland Refought,'" *Naval and Military Record* (August 15, 1935), copy in folder RIC/2/5, Richmond Papers. Halpern, *Naval History*, 314–28, is an excellent and dispassionate overview, as is Neville D. Kirk, "Jutland," in *Seapower: A Naval History*, edited by Potter, 432–54. Spector, *At War at Sea*, 79–91, provides an incomparable sailor's-eye view of the battle as both pageant and violent tragedy. The best ac-

count of the battle as seen and interpreted by the German participants is Tarrant, *Jutland*. See also Philbin, *Admiral von Hipper*, 127–37; and Scheer, *Germany's High Seas Fleet*, chap. 10. Irving's *Smoke Screen of Jutland* is an excellent, if biased, account from the British side; more balanced is Donald Macintyre, *Jutland*. I have also drawn on three contemporary accounts: Churchill's narrative and assessment, shamelessly oriented to Beatty, in *World Crisis*, 2:1012–69; Beatty's own dispatches to Jellicoe regarding the battle in *Beatty Papers*, edited by Ranf, 1:323–38; and Jellicoe's own dry and self-serving account in *Grand Fleet*, 304–414. Finally, the limited and frustrating air element in the battle is profiled in Arthur Hezlet, *Aircraft and Sea Power*, 46–56.

3. Keegan, *Price of Admiralty*, 51, 117.

4. Stephen W. Roskill, ed., *Documents Relating to the Naval Air Service*, 186–88 (Captain Bowhill's account); Carl O. Schuster, "Strike Warfare, 1914," 37, 41; Hezlet, *Aircraft and Sea Power*, 29–30; Allen Andrews, *The Air Marshals: The Air War in Western Europe*, 11.

5. Hezlet, *Aircraft and Sea Power*, 34–36.

6. Ibid., 40.

7. Irving, *Smoke Screen of Jutland*, 36, 37.

8. Spector, *At War at Sea*, 79, provides a vivid word picture from contemporary sources. See also Keegan, *The First World War*, 270.

9. Keegan, *Price of Admiralty*, 125.

10. Ibid., 137.

11. Extracts from Jellicoe's proposed revised version of a new appendix to "The Grand Fleet," in *Jellicoe Papers*, edited by Patterson, 2:421.

12. "The Commodore, 2nd Light Cruiser Squadron [Goodenough] reported at 5:40 that the enemy had altered course to N.N.W., and he gave me the *Southampton's* position as Lat. 56°12'N. Long. 5°40'E. No bearing or distance of the enemy was given, but if it was assumed that the centre bore east 10–11 miles from the *Southampton* as reported in the 5 p.m. signal, it put the German van in a position 15 miles to the north-westward of the position which had been worked up from the previous reports. Some little time later, a report came in from the *Black Prince*, also timed at 5:40 p.m., giving a position for the enemy's battle-cruisers, and this placed them another 13 miles to the north-westward of the position in which the *Southampton* placed the German battleships. There was evidently something very wrong, and the assumption was that the ships reported by the *Black Prince* must be our own battle-cruisers. On this basis the German battle-cruisers might be placed some 6–7 miles ahead of the ships reported by the *Southampton* on a N.N.W. course" (ibid., 423).

13. Jellicoe, *Grand Fleet*, 353–57 (quote on p. 353). Jellicoe's signal to *Marlborough* and its reply are quoted in Barnett, *Swordbearers*, 158. Jellicoe's mention of "German battleships" in his proposed revised history of Jutland suggests that at the very least he suspected the entire German fleet might be out and ahead of him.

14. Halpern, *Naval History*, 321; Tarrant, *Jutland*, 133, 135.

15. Halpern, *Naval History,* 320.

16. Extracts from Jellicoe's proposed revision, in *Jellicoe Papers,* edited by Patterson, 2:431.

17. Ibid.

18. Tarrant, *Jutland,* 138; see also p. 137.

19. Keegan maintains that Scheer understood the situation very well and that as his big guns were continuing to hit hard whatever British forces were in front of him he continued on his way, until after "only" ten minutes of heavy shelling from Jellicoe's battleships his "nerve cracked" (*Price of Admiralty,* 129).

20. Jerram's after-action report, June 5, 1916, folder JRM 18/1, Jerram Papers. Damage to the German battle cruisers is discussed in Roberts, *Battlecruisers,* 120.

21. Folder "Grand Fleet, 1916–17," JRM 18/1, Jerram Papers.

22. Ibid.; Keegan, *Price of Admiralty,* 129.

23. Marder, *Dreadnought to Scapa Flow,* 3:128–29; Keegan, *Price of Admiralty,* 129.

24. Philbin, *Admiral von Hipper,* 130. The Grand Fleet's excessive fear of torpedoes was once again in evidence at Jutland. Jerram wrote, "There is some evidence that submarines were close" throughout the primary action between the two battle fleets. He added that the cruiser *Duke of Edinburgh* transmitted three sighting messages, "and my Flag Lieutenant-Commander is certain that he saw the two periscopes of one vessel." Moreover, "the right gunlayer and trainer of 'Y' turret in [flagship] *King George V* state that they saw a torpedo break surface 400 yards short of *King George V*" (Jerram after-action report, June 5, 1916, folder JRM 18/1, Jerram Papers). Such impressions have led British historian Richard Hough to argue that Jutland was decided "more by the threat of the torpedo than the big bang of the big gun" (*The Longest Battle: The War at Sea, 1939–45,* 81).

25. Extracts from Jellicoe's proposed revision, in *Jellicoe Papers,* edited by Patterson, 2:432.

26. Irving, *Smoke Screen of Jutland,* 76.

27. Ibid., 239 (italics in original).

28. Ibid.

29. Ibid., 238; Jerram's after-action report, June 5, 1916, folder JRM 16/4, Jerram Papers.

30. Extracts from Jellicoe's proposed revision, in *Jellicoe Papers,* edited by Patterson, 2:436.

31. Guglielmo Ferrero, "The Dangers of War in Europe," *Atlantic Monthly* 111 (January 1913): 3–4.

32. Irving, *Smoke Screen of Jutland,* 8; Marder, *Dreadnought to Scapa Flow,* 3:233; James Watson Gerard to Robert Lansing, in *The Papers of Woodrow Wilson,* edited by Arthur S. Link, 37:272.

33. Archibald Hurd, "A Visit to the Grand Fleet," 1019–35 (quotes on pp. 1021, 1023, 1025).

34. Hoehling, *Great War at Sea,* 150–51.

35. Hezlet, *Aircraft and Sea Power,* 58–63.

36. Tyrwhitt to Jellicoe, August 21, 1916, in *Jellicoe Papers,* edited by Patterson, 2:46.

37. Halpern, *Naval History,* 330–31, 417–21; Tarrant, *Jutland,* 251–52; Beesly, *Room 40,* 166–67.

38. Barnett, *Swordbearers,* 185.

39. Macintyre, *Jutland,* 195; Keegan, *Price of Admiralty,* 153.

40. Marder, *Dreadnought to Scapa Flow,* 3:259.

41. See the various exchanges between Jellicoe and the Admiralty, July to September 1916, in *Jellicoe Papers,* edited by Patterson, 2:28–70. Beatty's angry letter to Jellicoe, dated July 27, together with Jellicoe's response to the Admiralty are on pp. 31–35.

42. Jellicoe to the secretary of the Admiralty, September 14, 1916; to the First [Sea] Lord, April 27, 1917, in ibid., 71–27, 160–62.

43. Horn, *German Naval Mutinies,* 33, 52.

44. See ibid., 68–198.

45. Viscount Cunningham of Hyndhope, *A Sailor's Odyssey,* 88.

46. Jerry W. Jones, "U.S. Battleship Operations in World War I, 1917–1918," 45–47 (Beatty is quoted on p. 47). See also Beatty's memorandum "The Situation in the North Sea," December 29, 1917, quoted in David F. Trask, *Captains and Cabinets: Anglo-American Naval Relations, 1917–1918,* 190.

47. J. Jones, "U.S. Battleship Operations," 47.

48. Gordon, *Rules of the Game,* 2. For the *Harper Report* summary, including Beatty's signal and Jerram's dilatory and unhappy response, see press clipping titled "Truth," folder JRM 18/2, Jerram Papers. For Jerram's sacking, see correspondence from and to Jerram in folder JRM 20.

49. Gordon, *Rules of the Game,* 542–43.

50. Ibid., 548–55; Masterman's lengthy article is in folder JRM 18/2, Jerram Papers.

51. Gordon, *Rules of the Game,* 472, 486–87, 566; Herbert Russell, "Battle Tactics," 519.

52. Marder, *Dreadnought to Scapa Flow,* 3:vii.

53. Ibid., 2d ed., 228–29.

54. "Address Delivered by Admiral Ernle Chatfield at a General Meeting of Officers Aboard *Nelson,* 28 October 1929, Following Atlantic Fleet Exercise, Autumn, 1929," folder CHT/2/1, p. 1, Ernle Chatfield Papers.

55. Paul M. Kennedy, *The Rise and Fall of British Naval Mastery,* 247.

Chapter 8. Terror at Sea, 1915–1918: The Submarine and Its Consequences

1. Peter Schnall, producer, "The Last Voyage of the *Lusitania*"; Dan van der Vat, *The Atlantic Campaign World War II's Great Struggle at Sea,* 22.

2. Churchill, *World Crisis,* 1:265.

3. See, for example, Colin Simpson, *The* Lusitania.

4. Robert D. Ballard, *Exploring the* Lusitania, 194–95.

5. Diana Preston, Lusitania: *An Epic Tragedy,* 395–401.

6. L. H. Hordern, "The Submarine War on Merchant Shipping," in *The Naval Annual, 1919,* edited by Earl Brassey and John Leyland, 129; D. Preston, *Epic Tragedy,* 420.

7. D. Preston, *Epic Tragedy,* 307; Archibald Hurd, "Outlawry at Sea: An Indictment of the German Navy," 29, 30, 32; Thomas P. Yaroschul, *Floating Palaces.*

8. A. Preston, *Submarines,* 57.

9. Roosevelt is quoted in Hagan, *This People's Navy,* 249; Lansing is quoted in Link, *Wilson and the Progressive Era,* 165n; House and Wilson are quoted in G. Davis, *Navy Second to None,* 212–13. For the president's initiation of a national preparedness program to place the army and navy in a high state of efficiency, strength, and readiness, see Woodrow Wilson to Josephus Daniels, to Lindley Miller Garrison, July 21, 1915, in *Papers of Wilson,* edited by Link, 34:4–5. The unsigned editorial is from "The German Note," 246. See also A. Preston, *Submarines,* 57; and Halpern, *Naval History,* 299.

10. Messimer, *Find and Destroy,* 29–39, contains an excellent discussion of Britain's effective antisubmarine tactics in the early months of the war that frightened and demoralized U-boat captains. An interesting personal account from the Q-ship perspective is Gordon Campbell, *My Mystery Ships.*

11. Angus Ross, "Losing the Initiative in Mercantile Warfare: Great Britain's Surprising Failure to Anticipate Maritime Challenges to Her Global Trading Network in the First World War," 10.

12. Hurd, "Outlawry at Sea," 29.

13. The *Arabic* incident is discussed in many sources. I have relied on Massie, *Castles of Steel,* 542–43. See also Halpern, *Naval History,* 301–2, which claims that Captain Schneider believed *Arabic* was turning toward him to ram.

14. Vera Brittain, *Testament of Youth,* 312–13; Admiral Sir Lewis Bayly, foreword to *My Mystery Ships,* by Campbell, viii–ix, 3. Brittain was a British nursing sister at the time and had traveled to Malta on *Britannic.*

15. Gearoid O'Neill, "One Final Ordeal," *Naval History* (October 2004): 27.

16. See Dirk Steffen, "The Holtzendorff Memorandum of 22 December 1916 and Germany's Declaration of Unrestricted U-boat Warfare." The document is summarized in Halpern, *Naval History,* 337–38.

17. Carr, *By Guess—and by God,* 2–4.

18. Dudley W. Knox, *A History of the United States Navy,* 415.

19. Hordern, "Submarine War on Shipping," in *The Naval Annual, 1919,* edited by Brassey and Leyland, 132–33.

20. Von Capelle's figures are cited in appendix 3A, "The German Submarine Strength," in *The German Submarine War, 1914–1918,* by R. H. Gibson and Maurice Prendergast, 351. Paul Kemp, *U-boats Destroyed: German Submarine Losses in the World Wars,* 7–59. Other sources for statistics on British merchant and German U-boat losses in World War I include Gray, *Submarine Warriors,* 8; Halpern, *Naval History,* 341;

Keegan, *The First World War*, 353–54; A. Preston, *Submarines*, 62–63; and van der Vat, *Atlantic Campaign*, 41.

21. Frank, *The Sea Wolves*, 16.

22. John Leyland, "The Enemy Navies," in *The Naval Annual, 1919*, edited by Brassey and Leyland, 87.

23. Sims, *The Victory at Sea*, 8–9.

24. Trask, *Captains and Cabinets*, 34; Thomas E. Bonsall, Titanic: *The Story of the Great White Star Line Trio—the* Olympic, *the* Titanic, *and the* Britannic, 54; Brittain, *Testament of Youth*, 312–14. The information on the hospital ships sunk by submarines is from J. K. Taussig, "Destroyer Experiences during the Great War," *United States Naval Institute Proceedings* 48:12 (December 1922): 2015–40; 49:1 (January 1923): 39–69; 2 (February 1923): 221–48; and 3 (March 1923): 383–408; see p. 39.

25. Quoted in Sims, *The Victory at Sea*, 9.

26. Taussig, "Destroyer Experiences," 47.

27. "The Ideals of the Navy," presidential address at the Biltmore Hotel, New York, May 17, 1915; "Annual Message to Congress, December 7, 1915"; and "An Address in Chicago on Preparedness" are in Link, *Papers of Wilson*, 33:209–12, 35:299–300, 36: 63–70. Ray Stannard Baker and William E. Dodd, eds., *The Public Papers of Woodrow Wilson: The New Democracy*, 1:329–32, identifies the venue of the New York speech as the Biltmore Hotel. Wilson's brief allusion in St. Louis to the navy's role is in 2:255.

28. "An Address in St. Louis on Preparedness," in *Papers of Wilson*, edited by Link, 36:114–21 (quote on pp. 119–20).

29. Ibid., 218–24; Hagan, *This People's Navy*, 253.

30. A. Preston, *Battleships*, 118.

31. G. Davis, *Navy Second to None*, 227; Harris, *Age of the Battleship*, 153.

32. Intercepted and decoded by Room 40 and promptly sent to U.S. officials, the "Zimmermann telegram" dated January 16, 1917, from Foreign Secretary Arthur Zimmermann in Berlin to German Minister in Washington Count Johann von Bernstorff was in fact two messages. The first informed Bernstorff of Berlin's determination to resume unrestricted submarine warfare on February 1, 1917. The minister was to hold this information in strictest confidence until the German torpedoes began to fly. "Preparing for the belligerency they believed would be America's answer," the German Foreign Ministry included another message that Bernstorff was to pass on secretly to Minister von Eckhardt in Mexico "by a safe route. This cable informed Mexican authorities that should their government come into the war on the side of Germany, Berlin would see to it that the lost territories of Texas, New Mexico, and Arizona would be returned to Mexico as part of a victorious peace package" (Barbara Tuchman, *The Zimmermann Telegram*, 11–12).

33. C. C. Gill, *Naval Power in the War (1914–1918)*, 163–64.

34. Koistinen, *Mobilizing for Modern War*, 182.

35. Taussig, "Destroyer Experiences," 246.

36. J. K. Taussig, "A Study of Our Navy Personnel Situation," *United States Naval Institute Proceedings* 47:8 (August 1921): 1155; J. Jones, "U.S. Battleship Operations," 217–18.

37. I heard this story from Mr. Crooks many years ago.

38. Thomas G. Frothingham, "The Strategy of the World War, and the Lessons of the Effort of the United States," 680.

39. William E. Leuchtenburg, "The New Deal and the Analogue of War," in *Change and Continuity in Twentieth Century America,* edited by John Braeman, Robert H. Bremner, and Everett Walters, 85.

40. Maxtone-Graham, *Only Way to Cross,* 120, 134.

41. A. Preston, *Submarines,* 63.

42. William Sims to secretary of the navy, May 11, 1917, reprinted in Michael Simpson, ed., *Anglo-American Naval Relations, 1917–1919,* 220–21.

43. Taussig, "Destroyer Experiences," 2020.

44. Gill, *Naval Power in the War,* 158–59.

45. Frothingham, "Strategy of the World War," 679n15, 680n18.

46. G. S. Knox, "Allied Navies at War: The United States Navy," in *The Naval Annual, 1919,* edited by Brassey and Leyland, 69.

47. Unless otherwise noted, the following discussion is based on Hordern, "Submarine War on Shipping," in *The Naval Annual, 1919,* edited by Brassey and Leyland, 128–46; and N. A. Leslie, "Convoy and Transport during the War," in ibid., 147–60.

48. Messimer, *Find and Destroy,* 77–80, 147.

49. Hordern, "Submarine War on Shipping," in *The Naval Annual, 1919,* edited by Brassey and Leyland, 140.

50. Taussig, "Destroyer Experiences," 225–41.

51. G. Davis, *Navy Second to None,* 237n; John Rousmaniere, "The Romance of the Subchasers"; Moore et al., *Jane's Fighting Ships of World War I,* 144–48.

52. Ralph D. Paine, *The Fighting Fleets: Five Months of Active Service with the American Destroyers and Their Allies in the War Zone,* 1–2.

53. The subchaser captain's observation is in Rousmaniere, "Romance of the Subchasers," 43; the *Wadsworth* doggerel is quoted in Taussig, "Destroyer Experiences," 406.

54. Taussig, "Destroyer Experiences," 240–41.

55. Ibid., 142.

56. Ibid.; Halpern, *Naval History,* 439. For an account of the Anglo-American mining of the North Sea, see Messimer, *Find and Destroy,* 181–88; and Howarth, *To Shining Sea,* 314–15, 320. Grady's cable to Sims is reprinted in M. Simpson, *Anglo-American Naval Relations,* 223.

57. "Memorandum by Captain F. R. Scarlett, Director, Air Division, Naval Staff," March 7, 1918, reprinted in Roskill, *Naval Air Service,* 635–37.

58. Halpern, *Naval History,* 425–26 (quote on p. 426); Messimer, *Find and Destroy,* 130–39; Hezlet, *Aircraft and Sea Power,* 85–101; Roy A. Grossnick et al., *United States Naval Aviation, 1910–1995,* 23–37, 447; Howarth, *To Shining Sea,* 318–20.

59. Van der Vat, *Atlantic Campaign,* 40–41.

60. Karl Dönitz, *Memoirs: Ten Years and Twenty Days,* 4.

61. Kapitänleutnant Lothar von Arnauld de la Perière in U-35 is credited with sinking 3 warships, 5 transports, and 187 merchant vessels in the Mediterranean and immediate adjacent areas in the Atlantic between January 1916 and the end of 1917. A brief account of his career and methods is in Gray, *Submarine Warriors,* 93–99.

62. Halpern, *Naval History,* 368–69.

63. Herwig, *Politics of Frustration,* 126–33, 138–43.

64. Copy in folder FHR/8, Fisher Papers.

65. Kemp's careful descriptions of each U-boat loss during World War I fully support the Admiralty contentions (*U-boats Destroyed,* esp. 23–59).

66. Benson's remarks have been widely published. See, for example, Trask, *Captains and Cabinets,* 55; and Halpern, *Naval History,* 358. On Benson's less-than-sterling intellect, see Trask, "William Shepherd Benson," in *The Chiefs of Naval Operations,* edited by Robert William Love Jr., 3, 5.

67. The best study of Anglo-American naval tensions and cooperation in World War I is Trask, *Captains and Cabinets.*

68. A. Preston, *Battleships,* 118.

69. Taussig, "Destroyer Experiences," 2033.

70. Ibid., 45; "The Bureau of Ordnance," *United States Naval Institute Proceedings* 75:2 (February 1949): 219 (photo caption); Theodore Roscoe, *Tin Cans: The True Story of the Fighting Destroyers of World War II,* 39–40.

71. Taussig, "Destroyer Experiences," 41. See also Sims to secretary of the navy, May 11, 1917, reprinted in M. Simpson, *Anglo-American Naval Relations,* 221.

72. Sims to OpNav, July 21, 1917; to Pringle, July 31, 1917, reprinted in M. Simpson, *Anglo-American Naval Relations,* 330–31.

73. Benson to Sims, August 20, 1917, ibid., 331–32.

74. Memorandum by Benson, November 1917, ibid., 333–34.

75. Daniels to Benson, November 13, 1917, reprinted in ibid., 335.

76. Friedman, *Sea Power as Strategy,* 69.

77. J. Jones, *U.S. Battleship Operations in World War I,* 54.

78. Paine, *Fighting Fleets,* 289–90.

79. Ibid., 292.

80. Ibid., 293–301; J. Jones, *U.S. Battleship Operations,* 42–43.

81. Rodman to Benson, January 19, 1918, reprinted in M. Simpson, *Anglo-American Naval Relations,* 342–43.

82. Sims to Benson, February 15, 1918, ibid., 343; "Report of Captain D. W. Knox . . . on Visit to Rosyth and Mine Bases," ibid., 346–47.

83. J. Jones, *U.S. Battleship Operations,* 71–73, 100–107.

84. Friedman, *Sea Power as Strategy,* 104.

85. Young, *With the Battle Cruisers,* 56; Friedman, *Sea Power as Strategy,* 104.

86. G. Nakashima, "Japan," in *The Naval Annual, 1919,* edited by Brassey and Leyland, 65, 66; Tuchman, *The Zimmermann Telegram,* 57.

87. Tuchman, *The Zimmermann Telegram,* 58.

88. Ibid., 36.

89. Ibid., 60–63, 76.

90. Stephen E. Pelz, *The Race to Pearl Harbor: The Failure of the Second London Naval Conference and the Onset of World War II,* 13.

91. Frothingham, "Strategy of the World War," 682.

SELECTED BIBLIOGRAPHY

THE FOLLOWING BIBLIOGRAPHY is highly selective, listing only those works that immediately and directly influenced my thinking on the course of early-twentieth-century sea power in the context of international politics and economic, social, and technological development. Citations of the numerous articles from the *U.S. Naval Institute Proceedings* have been excluded for space reasons. Sufficient citations may be found in the appropriate endnotes.

Manuscript Collections

National Maritime Museum, Greenwich, England
Ernle Chatfield Papers
William Wordsworth Fisher Papers
Eric J. A. Fuller Papers
Thomas Jerram Papers
Charles Madden Papers
Herbert William Richmond Papers

Other Sources

Alden, John D. *The American Steel Navy: A Photographic History of the U.S. Navy from the Introduction of the Steel Hull in 1883 to the Cruise of the Great White Fleet, 1907–1909.* Rev. ed. Annapolis: Naval Institute Press, 1989.
———. *Flush Deck and Four Pipes.* 1965. Reprint, Annapolis: Naval Institute Press, 1990.
Alford, Jonathan, ed. *Sea Power and Influence: Old Issues and New Challenges.* Osmun, Sweden: Gower and Allenheld, 1980.
Andrews, Allen. *The Air Marshals: The Air War in Western Europe.* New York: William Morrow, 1970.

Aronson, Theo. *Crowns in Conflict: The Triumph and the Tragedy of European Monarchy, 1910–1918*. Manchester, N.H.: Salem House, 1986.

Austin, Harry Albert. "The United States Unprepared for War." *Forum* 51 (April 1914): 526–33.

Baer, George W. *One Hundred Years of Sea Power: The U.S. Navy, 1890–1990*. Stanford: Stanford University Press, 1994.

———. "U.S. Naval Strategy, 1890–1945." *Naval War College Review* 44:1 (winter 1991): 6–31.

Baker, Ray Stannard, and William E. Dodd, eds. *The Public Papers of Woodrow Wilson: The New Democracy*. 2 vols. New York: Harper and Brothers, 1926.

Ballantyne, Iain. *Warships of the Royal Navy: HMS* London. Barnsely, South Yorkshire: Leo Cooper, 2003.

Ballard, G. A. *The Influence of the Sea on the Political History of Japan*. London: John Murray, 1921.

Ballard, Robert D. *Exploring the* Lusitania. New York: Warner Books, 1995.

Ballendorf, Dirk A., and Merrill L. Bartlett. *Pete Ellis, an Amphibious Warfare Prophet, 1880–1923*. Annapolis: Naval Institute Press, 1997.

Banning, Kendall. *Annapolis Today*. New York: Funk and Wagnalls, 1938.

Barker, J. Ellis. "The Armament Race and Its Latest Developments." *Fortnightly Review*, n.s., 546 (April 1, 1913): 654–68.

Barnett, Correlli. *The Swordbearers: Supreme Command in the First World War*. New York: Signet Books, 1965.

Bartlett, Merrill L. *Assault from the Sea: Essays on the History of Amphibious Warfare*. Annapolis: Naval Institute Press, 1983.

———. "Ben Hebard Fuller and the Genesis of a Modern United States Marine Corps, 1891–1934." *Journal of Military History* 69:1 (January 2005): 73–91.

Battine, Cecil. "How to Postpone an Anglo-German War." *Fortnightly Review*, n.s., 546 (June 1, 1912): 1049–58.

———. "The Surrender of the Mediterranean." *Fortnightly Review*, n.s., 546 (August 1, 1912): 260–71.

Beach, Edward L., Jr. *From Annapolis to Scapa Flow: The Autobiography of Edward L. Beach Sr.* Annapolis: Naval Institute Press, 2003.

———. *Submarine*. New York: Signet Books, 1953.

———. *The United States Navy: 200 Years*. New York: Henry Holt, 1986.

Beale, Howard K. *Theodore Roosevelt and the Rise of America to World Power*. 1956. Reprint, New York: Collier Books, 1962.

Beesly, Patrick. *Room 40: British Naval Intelligence, 1914–18*. San Diego: Harcourt Brace Jovanovich, 1982.

Belloc, Hilaire. *The Elements of the Great War: The First Phase*. New York: Hearst's International Library, 1915.

Bethmann Hollweg, [Theobald] Theodore von. *Reflections on the World War, Part I*. Translated by George Young. London: Thornton Butterworth, 1920.

Billington, Ray Allen. *America's Frontier Heritage*. New York: Holt, Rinehart, and Winston, 1966.

———, ed. *Frontier and Section: Selected Writings of Frederick Jackson Turner*. Englewood Cliffs, N.J.: Prentice-Hall, 1961.

Blennerhassett, Roland. "The Vital Question." *Fortnightly Review*, n.s., 487 (July 1, 1907): 1–11.

Bonsall, Thomas E. Titanic: *The Story of the Great White Star Line Trio—the* Olympic, *the* Titanic, *and the* Britannic. New York: Gallery Books, 1987.

Bosworth, R. J. B. *Explaining Auschwitz and Hiroshima: History Writing and the Second World War, 1945–1990*. London: Routledge, 1993.

Braeman, John, Robert H. Bremner, and Everett Walters, eds. *Change and Continuity in Twentieth Century America*. New York: Harper Colophon Books, 1966.

Braisted, William Reynolds. *The United States Navy in the Pacific, 1897–1909*. Austin: University of Texas Press, 1958.

———. *The United States Navy in the Pacific, 1909–1922*. Austin: University of Texas Press, 1971.

Brassey, Earl, and John Leyland, eds. *The Naval Annual, 1919*. London: William Clowes, 1919.

Brassey, T. A., ed. *The Naval Annual, 1903*. Portsmouth, England: J. Griffin, 1903.

———. *The Naval Annual, 1909*. London: J. Griffin, 1909.

British Marine Officer. "Wanted: An American Merchant Marine." *Atlantic Monthly* 104 (July 1909): 13–21.

Brittain, Vera. *Testament of Youth*. 1933. Reprint, New York: Wideview Books, 1980.

Brodie, Bernard. *Sea Power in the Machine Age*. Princeton: Princeton University Press, 1941.

Brook-Shepherd, Gordon. *Royal Sunset: The European Dynasties and the Great War*. Garden City, N.Y.: Doubleday, 1987.

Brooks, Sydney. "England and Germany." *Atlantic Monthly* 55 (January 1912): 617–27.

———. "England and Germany." *Forum* 62 (January 1912): 90–99.

———. "The Voyage of the American Fleet." *Fortnightly Review*, n.s., 494 (February 1, 1908): 201–15.

Buell, Thomas B. *The Quiet Warrior: A Biography of Admiral Raymond A. Spru-ance.* Boston: Little, Brown, 1974.

Bush, Eric. *Gallipoli.* Boston: Allen and Unwin, 1975.

Bywater, Hector C. *The Great Pacific War: A Historic Prophecy Now Being Fulfilled.* 1925. Reprint, Boston: Houghton Mifflin, 1942.

———. *Sea-Power in the Pacific: A Study of the American-Japanese Naval Prob-lem.* Boston: Houghton Mifflin, 1921.

Campbell, Gordon. *My Mystery Ships.* London: Hodder and Stoughton, 1928.

Carew, Anthony. *The Lower Deck of the Royal Navy, 1900–1939: The Invergordon Mutiny in Perspective.* Manchester, England: Manchester University Press, 1981.

Carr, William Guy. *By Guess—and by God: The Story of the British Submarines in the War.* Garden City, N.Y.: Doubleday, Doran, 1930.

Casey, Robert J. *Torpedo Junction: With the Pacific Fleet from Pearl Harbor to Midway.* Indianapolis: Bobbs-Merrill, 1942.

Chant, Christopher. *Warfare of the 20th Century: Armed Conflicts Outside the Two World Wars.* Secaucus, N.J.: Chartwell Books, 1988.

Churchill, Winston S. *The World Crisis, 1911–1918.* 2 vols. New York: Barnes and Noble, 1993. First published in 4 vols. New York: Scribner's, 1923, 1927, 1929, 1931.

Clarke, I. F. *Voices Prophesying War, 1763–1984.* London: Oxford University Press, 1966.

Coletta, Paolo E. *Admiral Bradley A. Fiske and the American Navy.* Lawrence: Regents Press of Kansas, 1979.

Corbett, Julian S. *Maritime Operations in the Russo-Japanese War, 1904–1905.* 2 vols. Annapolis: Naval Institute Press, 1994 (a study prepared in October 1915 as a confidential publication of the Intelligence Division of the Ad-miralty War Staff and reproduced from the copy held by the Library of the Royal Navy College, Greenwich).

Corbett, Julian S., and Henry Newbold. *Official History of the War: Naval Oper-ations.* 5 vols. plus maps. London: Longmans, Green, 1921–1930.

Cunningham, Viscount, of Hyndhope. *A Sailor's Odyssey.* New York: E. P. Dut-ton, 1951.

Dangerfield, George. *The Strange Death of Liberal England, 1910–1914.* 1935. Reprint, New York: Capricorn Books, 1961.

Davis, George T. *A Navy Second to None: The Development of Modern American Naval Policy.* New York: Harcourt, Brace, 1940.

Davis, Richard Harding, James F. J. Archibald, Ellis Ashmead Bartlett, Henry

James Whigham, Frederick Palmer, Robert L. Dunn, James H. Hare, and Victor K. Bulla. *The Russo-Japanese War: A Photographic and Descriptive Review of the Great Conflict in the Far East.* New York: P. F. Collier, 1905.

Dehio, Ludwig. *The Precarious Balance: Four Centuries of the European Power Struggle.* Translated by Charles Fullman. 1948. Reprint, New York: Vintage Books, 1962.

Dickinson, G. Lowes. *The International Anarchy, 1904–1914.* New York: Century, 1926.

Dictionary of American Fighting Ships. 8 vols. Washington, D.C.: Navy Department, Naval History Division, 1959–1981.

Dingman, Roger. *Power in the Pacific: The Origin of Naval Arms Limitation, 1914–1922.* Chicago: University of Chicago Press, 1976.

Dönitz, Karl. *Memoirs: Ten Years and Twenty Days.* Translated by R. H. Stevens. Cleveland: World Publishing, 1959.

Dreher, James. "The Year in Germany." *Atlantic Monthly* 98 (November 1906): 663–74.

Edwards, Bernard. *Dönitz and the Wolf Packs.* London: Brockhampton Press, 1996.

Evans, David C., and Mark R. Peattie. *Kaigun: Strategy, Tactics, and Technology in the Imperial Japanese Navy, 1887–1941.* Annapolis: Naval Institute Press, 1997.

Excubitor. "The British Reply to Germany's Dreadnoughts." *Fortnightly Review,* n.s., 495 (March 2, 1908): 456–69.

———. "The German Naval Bill." *Fortnightly Review,* n.s., 469 (January 1, 1906): 72–82.

Fairbank, John King. *The United States and China.* 3d ed. Cambridge: Harvard University Press, 1971.

Fairbank, John K., Edwin O. Reischauer, and Albert M. Craig. *East Asia: The Modern Transformation.* Boston: Houghton Mifflin, 1965.

Falk, Edwin A. *From Perry to Pearl Harbor: The Struggle for Supremacy in the Pacific.* New York: Doubleday, Doran, 1943.

———. *Tōgō and the Rise of Japanese Sea Power.* London: Longmans, Green, 1936.

Ferguson, Niall. *Empire: The Rise and Demise of the British World Order and the Lessons for Global Power.* New York: Basic Books, 2002.

Field, James A., Jr. "American Imperialism: The Worst Chapter in Almost Any Book." *American Historical Review* 83:3 (June 1978): 644–68.

Fischer, Fritz. *Germany's Aims in the First World War.* New York: Norton, 1967. First published 1961 in Germany as *Griff nach der Welbmacht.*

Fox, Cecil H., R.N. *Manual of Seamanship for Boys and Seamen of the Royal Navy, 1904.* 1905. Reprint, Almonte, Ontario: Algrove Publishing, 2003.

Frank, Wolfgang. *The Sea Wolves.* Translated by R. O. B. Long. New York: Ballantine Books, 1958.

Freidel, Frank. *The Splendid Little War.* New York: Dell, 1958.

Friedman, Norman. *Seapower as Strategy: Navies and National Interests.* Annapolis: Naval Institute Press, 2001.

———. *U.S. Cruisers: An Illustrated Design History.* Annapolis: Naval Institute Press, 1984.

Frost, Holloway H. *The Battle of Jutland.* Annapolis: U.S. Naval Institute, 1936.

Frothingham, Thomas G. "The Strategy of the World War, and the Lessons of the Effort of the United States." *U.S. Naval Institute Proceedings* 47:219 (May 1921): 669–83.

Fukui, Shizuo. *Naval Vessels, 1887–1945: Mitsubishi Zosen Built.* Nagasaki: Mitsubishi Shipbuilding and Engineering, n.d.

Fuller, J. F. C. *The Decisive Battles of the Western World and Their Influence upon History.* Vol. 2, *1792–1944.* Edited by John Terraine. London: Grenada Publishing, 1970.

Ganz, Albert Harding. "The Role of the Imperial German Navy in Colonial Affairs." Ph.D. diss., Ohio State University, 1972.

Gemzell, Carl-Axel. *Organization, Conflict, and Innovation: A Study of German Naval Strategic Planning, 1888–1940.* Stockholm: Esselte Studium, 1973.

"The German Note." *Forum* 54 (August 1915): 245–46.

Gibson, R. H., and Maurice Prendergast. *The German Submarine War, 1914–1918.* New York: Richard R. Smith, 1931.

Gill, C. C. *Naval Power in the War (1914–1918).* New York: George H. Doran, 1918.

Goldhagen, Daniel Jonah. *Hitler's Willing Executioners: Ordinary Germans and the Holocaust.* New York: Alfred A. Knopf, 1996.

Goldrick, James. *The King's Ships Were at Sea: The War in the North Sea, August 1914–February 1915.* Annapolis: Naval Institute Press, 1984.

Gordon, Andrew. *The Rules of the Game: Jutland and British Naval Command.* London: John Murray, 1996.

Graebner, Norman A. *An Uncertain Tradition: American Secretaries of State in the Twentieth Century.* New York: McGraw-Hill, 1961.

Grainger, John D., ed. *The Maritime Blockade of Germany in the Great War: The Northern Patrol, 1914–1918.* Aldershot, England: Ashgate, 2003.

Gray, Edwyn. *Submarine Warriors.* New York: Bantam Books, 1990.

Grossman, Anne Chotzinoff, and Lisa Grossman Thomas. *Lobcouse and Spotted Dog: Which It's [sic] a Gastronomic Companion to the Aubrey/Maturin Novels.* New York: Norton, 1997.

Grossnick, Roy A., William J. Armstrong, W. Todd Baker, John M. Elliott, Gwendolyn J. Rich, and Judith A. Walters. *United States Naval Aviation, 1910–1995.* Washington, D.C.: Department of the Navy, Naval Historical Center, 1997.

Hagan, Kenneth J. *This People's Navy: The Making of American Sea Power.* New York: Free Press, 1991.

Halpern, Paul G. *A Naval History of World War I.* Annapolis: Naval Institute Press, 1994.

———, ed. *The Keyes Papers: Selections from the Private and Official Correspondence of Admiral of the Fleet Baron Keyes of Zeebrugge.* 3 vols. Boston: George Allen and Unwin, 1972–1981.

Hara, Tameichi, Fred Saito, and Roger Pineau. *Japanese Destroyer Captain.* New York: Ballantine Books, 1961.

Harbaugh, William Henry. *The Life and Times of Theodore Roosevelt.* Rev. ed. New York: Collier Books, 1963.

———, ed. *The Writings of Theodore Roosevelt.* Indianapolis: Bobbs-Merrill, 1967.

Harris, Brayton. *The Age of the Battleship, 1890–1922.* New York: Franklin Watts, 1965.

Harrod, Frederick S. *Manning the New Navy: The Development of a Modern Naval Enlisted Force, 1899–1940.* Westport, Conn.: Greenwood Press, 1978.

Hart, Robert A. *The Great White Fleet: Its Voyage around the World, 1907–1909.* Boston: Little, Brown, 1965.

Hartcup, Guy. *The Achievement of the Airship: A History of the Development of Rigid, Semi-rigid, and Non-rigid Airships.* London: David and Charles, 1974.

Hattendorf, John B. *Doing Naval History: Essays toward Improvement.* Newport, R.I.: Naval War College Press, 1995.

———. *Naval History and Maritime Strategy: Collected Essays.* Malabar, Fla.: Krieger Publishing, 2000.

Hattendorf, John B., R. J. B. Knight, A. W. H. Pearsall, N. A. M. Rodger, and Geoffrey Till. *British Naval Documents, 1204–1960.* London: Scolar Press, 1993.

Hattendorf, John B., B. Mitchell Simpson III, and John R. Wadleigh. *Sailors and Scholars: The Centennial History of the U.S. Naval War College.* Newport, R.I.: Naval War College Press, n.d.

Herbert, Hilary. "A Plea for the Navy." *Forum* 24 (September 1897): 1–13.

Herrick, Walter R., Jr. *The American Naval Revolution.* Baton Rouge: Louisiana State University Press, 1966.

Herwig, Holger H. "The Failure of German Sea Power, 1914–1945: Mahan, Tirpitz, and Raeder Reconsidered." *International History Review* 10:1 (February 1988): 68–105.

———. *The German Naval Officer Corps: A Social and Political History, 1890–1918.* Oxford: Clarendon Press, 1973.

———. *"Luxury" Fleet: The Imperial German Navy, 1888–1918.* 1980. Reprint, Aldershot, England: Ashfield Press, 1987.

———. *Politics of Frustration: The United States in German Naval Planning, 1889–1914.* Boston: Little, Brown, 1976.

Hezlet, Arthur. *Aircraft and Sea Power.* New York: Stein and Day, 1970.

Hoehling, A. A. *The Great War at Sea.* New York: Thomas Y. Crowell, 1965.

Hofstadter, Richard. *The Age of Reform.* New York: Alfred A. Knopf, 1955.

Holcombe, Chester. "Some Results of the Eastern War." *Atlantic Monthly* 96 (July 1905): 24–30.

Hollis, Ira Nelson. "The Navy and the War with Spain." *Atlantic Monthly* 82 (November 1898): 605–10.

———. "The Uncertain Factors in Naval Conflicts." *Atlantic Monthly* 81 (June 1898): 728.

Homan, William H. "Nightmare at Port Arthur." *Naval History* 4 (summer 1990): 21–27.

Hone, Thomas C., and Mark D. Mandeles. "Interwar Innovation in Three Navies: U.S. Navy, Royal Navy, Imperial Japanese Navy." *Naval War College Review* 40:2 (spring 1987): 63–83.

Hone, Trent. "Building a Doctrine: U.S. Naval Tactics and Battle Plans in the Interwar Period." *International Journal of Naval History* 1:2 (October 2002). Reprinted at http://www.ijnhonline.org/volume 1-number 2-Oct02/articles.

———. "Evolution of Fleet Tactical Doctrine in the U.S. Navy, 1922–41." *Journal of Military History* 67:4 (October 2003): 1107–48.

Horn, Daniel. *The German Naval Mutinies of World War I.* New Brunswick, N.J.: Rutgers University Press, 1960.

Hough, Richard. *Death of the Battleship: The Tragic Close of the Era of Sea Power.* New York: McFadden, 1965.

———. *The Fleet That Had to Die.* London: Hamish Hamilton, 1958.

Hough, Richard. *The Longest Battle: The War at Sea, 1939–45.* 1986. Reprint, London: Cassell, 2001.

————. *The Long Pursuit.* New York: Harper and Row, 1969.

Howarth, Stephen. *To Shining Sea: A History of the United States Navy, 1775–1991.* New York: Random House, 1991.

Hoyt, Edwin P. *The German Who Never Lost: The Story of the* Königsberg. New York: Funk and Wagnalls, 1968.

————. *Kreuzerkrieg.* Cleveland: World Publishing, 1968.

————. *The Last Cruise of the* Emden. New York: Macmillan, 1966.

————. *Raider Wolf: The Voyage of Captain Nerger.* New York: Paul Eriksson, 1974.

Hugill, Peter J. *World Trade since 1431: Geography, Technology, and Capitalism.* Baltimore: Johns Hopkins University Press, 1993.

Hurd, Archibald. "A Dreadnought Naval Policy." *Fortnightly Review,* n.s., 480 (December 1, 1906): 1017–32.

————. "Economy on the Fleet: Lord Fisher's Demand." *Fortnightly Review,* n.s., 634 (October 1, 1919): 514–28.

————. "The New Navy Estimates." *Fortnightly Review,* n.s., 529 (January 2, 1911): 300–313.

————. "Outlawry at Sea: An Indictment of the German Navy." *Fortnightly Review,* n.s., 588 (July 1915): 29–43.

————. "Peace and a Naval Holiday." *Fortnightly Review,* n.s., 630 (June 2, 1919): 879–93.

————. "The Peril of Invasion: Italy's 'Bolt from the Blue.'" *Fortnightly Review,* n.s., 541 (December 15, 1911): 1044–55.

————. "Progress or Reaction in the Navy." *Fortnightly Review,* n.s., 472 (April 16, 1906): 707–19.

————. "The Triumph of Germany's Policy." *Fortnightly Review,* n.s., 549 (September 1, 1912): 412–27.

————. "A Visit to the Grand Fleet." *Fortnightly Review,* n.s., 588 (December 1915): 1019–35.

————. "The War-Makers and the Navy." *Fortnightly Review,* n.s., 567 (March 2, 1914): 418–34.

Hurd, Archibald S., and Henry Castle. *German Sea-Power: Its Rise, Progress, and Economic Basis.* London: John Murray, 1914.

Hyatt, A. M. J., ed. *Dreadnought to Polaris: Maritime Strategy since Mahan.* Papers from the Conference on Strategic Studies at the University of Western Ontario, March 1972. Annapolis: Naval Institute Press, 1973.

Hythe, Viscount, ed. *The Naval Annual, 1913.* Portsmouth, England: J. Griffin, 1913.

Ikle, Fred W. "Japanese-German Peace Negotiations during World War I." *American Historical Review* 71:1 (October 1965): 62–76.

Ingersoll, Ralph. *The Battle Is the Pay-Off.* New York: Harcourt, Brace, 1943.

Irving, John. *The Smoke Screen of Jutland.* New York: David McKay, 1967.

Ito, Masanori, and Roger Pineau. *The End of the Imperial Japanese Navy.* Translated by Andrew Y. Kuroda and Roger Pineau. New York: MacFadden Books, 1965.

Iyenaga, T. "Japan's Mission in the Far East." *Forum* 33 (June 1902): 458–66.

Jameson, William. *The Fleet That Jack Built: Nine Men Who Made a Modern Navy.* London: Rupert Hart-Davis, 1962.

Jane, Fred T. *The Imperial Japanese Navy.* London: W. Thacker, 1904.

———. "Naval Warfare: Present and Future." *Forum* 24 (October 1897): 234–45.

Jefferson, Charles Edward. "The Delusion of Militarism." *Atlantic Monthly* 103 (March 1909): 379–88.

Jellicoe, Admiral Viscount [John]. *The Grand Fleet, 1914–1916: Its Creation, Development and Work.* New York: George H. Doran, 1919.

Jentschura, Hansgeorg, Dieter Jung, and Peter Mikel. *Warships of the Imperial Japanese Navy, 1869–1945.* London: Arms and Armour Press, 1977.

Jones, Jerry W. *U.S. Battleship Operations in World War I.* Annapolis: Naval Institute Press, 1998.

———. "U.S. Battleship Operations in World War I, 1917–1918." Ph.D. diss., University of North Texas, 1995.

Jones, Tristan. *Heart of Oak.* Toronto: Bantam Books, 1984.

Jordan, Gerald, ed. *Naval Warfare in the Twentieth Century, 1900–1945: Essays in Honor of Arthur J. Marder.* London: Croom Helm, 1977.

Kajima, Morinosuke. *The Emergence of Japan as a World Power.* Rutland, Vt.: Charles E. Tuttle, 1968.

Kakuzo-Okakura. *The Awakening of Japan.* New York: Century, 1905.

Karsten, Peter. *The Naval Aristocracy: The Golden Age of Annapolis and the Emergence of Modern American Navalism.* New York: Free Press, 1992.

Keegan, John. *The First World War.* New York: Random House, 1998.

———. *The Price of Admiralty: The Evolution of Naval Warfare.* New York: Viking, 1988.

Kelly, Patrick J. "Strategy, Tactics, and Turf Wars: Tirpitz and the Oberkommando der Marine, 1892–1895." *Journal of Military History* 66:4 (October 2002): 1033–59.

Kemp, Paul. *U-boats Destroyed: German Submarine Losses in the World Wars.* London: Arms and Armour Press, 1997.

Kennedy, M. D. *Some Aspects of Japan and Her Defence Forces.* London: Kegan Paul, Trench, Trubner, 1928.

Kennedy, Paul M. "The Development of German Naval Operations Plans against England, 1896–1914." *English Historical Review* 350 (January 1974): 48–76.

———. *The Rise and Fall of British Naval Mastery.* 1976. Reprint, London: Ashfield Press, 1987.

———. *The Rise and Fall of the Great Powers: Economic Change and Military Conflict from 1500 to 2000.* New York: Random House, 1987.

Kinnosuke, Adachi. "The Birth of the New Nippon." *Forum* 38 (October–December 1906): 255–76.

Knightley, Phillip. *The First Casualty: From the Crimea to Vietnam, the War Correspondent as Hero, Propagandist, and Myth Maker.* New York: Harcourt Brace Jovanovich, 1975.

Knox, Dudley W. *A History of the United States Navy.* New York: G. P. Putnam's Sons, 1936.

Koistinen, Paul A. C. *Mobilizing for Modern War: The Political Economy of American Warfare, 1865–1919.* Lawrence: University Press of Kansas, 1997.

Krancke, Theodor, and H. J. Brennecke. *Pocket Battleship: The Story of the Admiral Scheer.* New York: Berkley Publishing, 1958.

Krug, Hans-Joachim, Yoichi Hirama, Berthold J. Sander-Nagashima, and Axel Niestlé. *Reluctant Allies: German-Japanese Naval Relations in World War II.* Annapolis: Naval Institute Press, 2001.

Lambert, Nicholas A. *Sir John Fisher's Naval Revolution.* Columbia: University of South Carolina Press, 1998.

Lambi, Ivo Nikolai. *The Navy and German Power Politics, 1862–1914.* Boston: Allen and Unwin, 1984.

Langer, William L. *European Alliances and Alignments, 1871–1890.* 2d ed. New York: Vintage Books, 1950.

Lautenschläger, Karl. "Technology and the Evolution of Naval Warfare." *International Security* 8:2 (fall 1983): 173–221.

Layton, Edwin T., Roger Pineau, and John Costello. *And I Was There: Pearl Harbor and Midway—Breaking the Secrets.* New York: William Morrow, 1985.

Lea, Homer. *The Valor of Ignorance.* New York: Harper and Brothers, 1909.

Leech, Margaret. *In the Days of McKinley.* New York: Harper and Row, 1959.

Lewis, Michael. *The Navy of Britain.* London: George Allen and Unwin, 1948.

Light, Varne. "Our Too Domestic Navy." *Fortnightly Review,* n.s., 560 (August 1, 1913): 224–29.

Link, Arthur S. *Woodrow Wilson and the Progressive Era, 1910–1917.* New York: Harper and Row, 1954.

———, ed. *The Papers of Woodrow Wilson.* 69 vols. Princeton: Princeton University Press, 1966–1994.

Livermore, Seward W. "The American Navy as a Factor in World Politics." *American Historical Review* 63 (July 1958): 863–79.

Lord, Walter. *A Night to Remember.* Toronto: Bantam Books, 1971.

"The Loss of the *Titanic.*" *Nation* 11:3 (April 20, 1912): 76–77.

Love, Robert William, Jr. *History of the U.S. Navy, 1775–1991.* Harrisburg, Pa.: Stackpole Books, 1992.

———, ed. *The Chiefs of Naval Operations.* Annapolis: Naval Institute Press, 1980.

Low, A. Maurice. "Foreign Affairs." *Forum* 38 (October–December 1906): 165–85.

———. "Foreign Affairs." *Forum* 39 (April–June 1908): 458–78.

———. "Foreign Affairs." *Forum* 39 (October–December 1907): 166–85.

———. "Foreign Affairs: Japan and the Saxon." *Forum* 40 (October–December 1908): 309–12.

Lyon, David. *Sea Battles in Close-Up: The Age of Nelson.* Annapolis: Naval Institute Press, 1996.

MacInnis, Joseph. Titanic *in a New Light.* Charlottesville, Va.: Thomasson-Grant, 1992.

MacIntyre, Donald. *Jutland.* London: Pan Books, 1957.

Maddocks, Melvin. *The Great Liners.* Alexandria, Va.: Time-Life Books, 1978.

Mahan, Alfred Thayer. *The Influence of Sea Power upon History, 1660–1783.* 3d ed. Boston: Little, Brown, 1940.

Marder, Arthur J. *From the Dreadnought to Scapa Flow: The Royal Navy in the Fisher Era, 1904–1919.* Vol. 1, *The Road to War, 1904–1914.* Vol. 2, *The War Years: To the Eve of Jutland, 1914–1916.* Vol. 3, *Jutland and After, May 1916–December 1916;* Vol. 5, *Victory and Aftermath.* London: Oxford University Press, 1961–1970.

———. *From the Dreadnought to Scapa Flow: The Royal Navy in the Fisher Era, 1904–1919.* Vol. 3, *Jutland and After, May 1916–December 1916.* 2d ed. London: Oxford University Press, 1978.

———. *Portrait of an Admiral: The Life and Papers of Sir Herbert Richmond.* London: Jonathan Cape, 1952.

Marvin, Winthrop L. "American Ships and the Way to Get Them." *Atlantic Monthly* 104 (October 1909): 433–41.

Massie, Robert K. *Castles of Steel: Britain, Germany, and the Winning of the Great War at Sea.* New York: Ballantine Books, 2004.

———. *Dreadnought: Britain, Germany, and the Coming of the Great War.* New York: Random House, 1991.

Masterson, Daniel M., ed. *Naval History: The Sixth Symposium of the U.S. Naval Academy.* Wilmington, Del.: Scholarly Resources, 1987.

Maxey, Edwin. "The Isolation of Germany." *Forum* 52 (November 1909): 424–31.

Maxtone-Graham, John. *The Only Way to Cross.* New York: Macmillan, 1972.

Mayer, Arno J. *The Persistence of the Old Regime: Europe to the Great War.* New York: Pantheon Books, 1981.

McKee, Christopher. *Sober Men and True: Sailor Lives in the Royal Navy, 1900–1945.* Cambridge: Harvard University Press, 2002.

McLellan, Alexander G. "A British View of American Naval Expenditures." *Atlantic Monthly* 108 (January 1911): 34–44.

McNeill, William H. *The Rise of the West: A History of the Human Community.* New York: Mentor Books, 1965.

Mead, Edwin D. "England and Germany." *Atlantic Monthly* 101 (March 1908): 397–407.

Melhorn, Charles M. *Two-Block Fox: The Rise of the Aircraft Carrier, 1911–1929.* Annapolis: Naval Institute Press, 1974.

Messimer, Dwight R. *Find and Destroy: Anti-submarine Warfare in World War I.* Annapolis: Naval Institute Press, 2001.

Miller, Ben. *Ocean Liners.* New York: Mallard Press, 1990.

Miller, Edward S. *War Plan Orange: The U.S. Strategy to Defeat Japan, 1897–1945.* Annapolis: Naval Institute Press, 1991.

Miller, Stuart Creighton. *"Benevolent Assimilation": The American Conquest of the Philippines, 1899–1903.* New Haven: Yale University Press, 1982.

Millet, Allen R. *Semper Fidelis: The History of the United States Marine Corps.* New York: Macmillan, 1980.

Modelski, George, and William R. Thompson. *Seapower in Global Politics, 1494–1993.* Seattle: University of Washington Press, 1988.

Montross, Lynn. *War through the Ages.* New York: Harper and Row, 1960.

Moore, John. *Jane's Fighting Ships of World War I.* London: Random House Group, 2001 (based on wartime editions of *Jane's All the World's Ships* that were originally published in 1919).

Moorhead, Alan. *Gallipoli.* London: Hamish Hamilton, 1956.

Morgan, Kenneth O. *The Oxford History of Britain.* New York: Oxford University Press, 1988.

Morison, Elting E., John M. Blum, Alfred D. Chandler, and John J. Buckley, eds. *Letters of Theodore Roosevelt.* 8 vols. Cambridge: Harvard University Press, 1951–1954.

Morison, Samuel Eliot. *The Great Explorers: The European Discovery of America.* 2 vols. New York: Oxford University Press, 1978.

Morris, James. *Farewell the Trumpets: An Imperial Retreat.* San Diego: Harcourt Brace Jovanovich, 1978.

———. *Heaven's Command: An Imperial Progress.* San Diego: Harcourt Brace Jovanovich, 1973.

———. *Pax Britannica: The Climax of an Empire.* San Diego: Harcourt Brace Jovanovich, 1968.

Morris, Roger. *The Royal Dockyards during the Revolutionary and Napoleonic Wars.* Leicester, England: Leicester University Press, 1983.

Mowry, George E. *The Era of Theodore Roosevelt and the Birth of Modern America, 1900–1912.* New York: Harper Torchbooks, 1962.

Müllenheim-Rechberg, Burkard Baron von. *Battleship* Bismarck: *A Survivor's Story.* Translated by Jack Sweetman. Rev. ed. Annapolis: Naval Institute Press, 1990.

Munro, D. J. *Scapa Flow: A Naval Retrospect.* London: Sampson, Low, Marston, 1932.

Nalty, Bernard C. *Long Passage to Korea: Black Sailors and the Integration of the U.S. Navy.* Washington, D.C.: Naval Historical Center, 2003.

Netsky, Martin G., and Edward L. Beach Jr. "The Trouble with Admiral Sampson." *Naval History* 9:6 (December 1995): 8–16.

North, John. *Gallipoli: The Fading Vision.* London: Faber and Faber, 1936.

Novikoff-Priboy, A. *Tsushima.* Translated by Edna Paul and Cedar Paul. New York: Alfred A. Knopf, 1937.

O'Brien, Phillips Payson, ed. *Technology and Naval Combat in the Twentieth Century and Beyond.* London: Frank Cass, 2001.

O'Connell, Robert L. *Sacred Vessels: The Cult of the Battleship and the Rise of the U.S. Navy.* Boulder: Westview Press, 1991.

Okakura-Kakuzo. *The Awakening of Japan.* New York: Century, 1905.

Overy, Richard. *Why the Allies Won.* New York: W. W. Norton, 1996.

Owen, Charles. *The Great Days of Travel.* Exeter, England: Webb and Bowen, 1979.

Padfield, Peter. *The Battleship Era.* London: Rupert Hart-Davis, 1972.

Paine, Ralph D. *The Fighting Fleets: Five Months of Active Service with the American Destroyers and Their Allies in the War Zone.* Boston: Houghton Mifflin, 1918.

Parkes, Oscar. *British Battleships,* Warrior *1860 to* Vanguard *1950: A History of Design, Construction, and Armament.* Annapolis: Naval Institute Press, 1990.

Parkes, Oscar, and Maurice Prendergast, eds. *Jane's Fighting Ships, 1919.* London: Sampson, Low, Marston, 1919.

Parrish, Thomas. *The Submarine: A History.* New York: Viking, 2004.

Patterson, A. Temple. *The Jellicoe Papers: Selections from the Private and Official Correspondence of Admiral of the Fleet Earl Jellicoe.* 2 vols. London: Spottiswoode, Ballantyne, 1966, 1968.

Peattie, Mark R. *Sunburst: The Rise of Japanese Naval Air Power, 1909–1941.* Annapolis: Naval Institute Press, 2001.

Peattie, Mark R., and David C. Evans. "Satō Tetsutarō and Japanese Strategy." *Naval History* 4:4 (fall 1990): 34–39.

Pelz, Stephen E. *Race to Pearl Harbor: The Failure of the Second London Naval Conference and the Onset of World War II.* Cambridge: Harvard University Press, 1974.

Perkins, Dexter. *A History of the Monroe Doctrine.* Boston: Little, Brown, 1963.

Philbin, Tobias R., III. *Admiral von Hipper, the Inconvenient Hero.* Amsterdam: B. R. Grüner, 1982.

Pleshakov, Constantine. *The Tsar's Last Armada: The Epic Journey to the Battle of Tsushima.* New York: Basic Books, 2002.

Poole, S. L. *Cruiser: A History of British Cruisers from 1889 to 1960.* London: Robert Hale, 1970.

Potter, E. B. *Bull Halsey.* Annapolis: Naval Institute Press, 1985.

———, ed. *Seapower: A Naval History.* Englewood Cliffs, N.J.: Prentice-Hall, 1960.

Pratt, Fletcher, and Harley E. Howe. *The Compact History of the United States Navy.* Rev. ed. New York: Hawthorne Books, 1962.

Preston, Antony. *Aircraft Carriers.* New York: Gallery Books, 1979.

———. *Battleships.* New York: Gallery Books, 1981.

————. *Submarines.* New York: Gallery Books, 1982.

Preston, Diana. Lusitania: *An Epic Tragedy.* New York: Walker, 2002.

————. *A First Rate Tragedy: Robert Falcon Scott and the Race to the South Pole.* Boston: Houghton Mifflin, 1998.

Pringle, Henry F. *Theodore Roosevelt: A Biography.* New York: Harvest Books, 1956.

Raeder, Erich. *My Life.* Translated by Henry W. Drexel. Annapolis: U.S. Naval Institute, 1960.

Ranf, B. McL., ed. *The Beatty Papers: Selections from the Private and Official Correspondence of Admiral of the Fleet Earl Beatty.* 2 vols. London: Scolar Press, 1989, 1993.

Reckner, James R. "The Great White Fleet in New Zealand." *Naval History* 5:3 (fall 1991): 26–29.

————. "The 'New' Sailor." *Naval History* 19:2 (April 2005): 44–49.

————. *Teddy Roosevelt's Great White Fleet.* Annapolis: Naval Institute Press, 1988.

Reischauer, Edwin O. *Japan: Past and Present.* New York: Alfred A. Knopf, 1967.

[Repington, Colonel A. C.]. *The War in the Far East, 1904–1905: By the Military Correspondent of "The Times."* New York: E. P. Dutton, 1905.

Richardson, Alexander, and Archibald Hurd. *Brassey's Naval and Shipping Annual, 1921–2.* London: William Clowes and Sons, n.d.

Ridgely, Harold C. "Are the Japanese Unfriendly?" *Forum* 50 (October 1913): 483–85.

Rivera, Carlos R. "Big Stick and Short Sword: The American and Japanese Navies as Hypothetical Enemies before 1922." Unpublished manuscript provided by author.

Roberts, John. *Battlecruisers.* London: Chatham Publishing, 1997.

Roosevelt, Theodore. *An Autobiography.* 1913. New York: Da Capo Press, 1985.

————. *State Papers as Governor and President, 1899–1909.* New York: Scribner's, 1925.

————. *The Works of Theodore Roosevelt, Executive Edition.* 14 vols. Part 1, *Presidential Addresses and State Papers.* New York: P. F. Collier, n.d.

Ropp, Theodore. *War in the Modern World.* Rev. ed. New York: Collier Books, 1962.

Roscoe, Theodore. *Tin Cans: The True Story of the Fighting Destroyers of World War II.* New York: Bantam Books, 1960.

Roskill, Stephen. *Churchill and the Admirals.* London: Collins, 1977.

————, ed. *Documents Relating to the Naval Air Service.* Vol. 1, *1908–1918.* London: Scolar Press, 1969.

Ross, Angus. "Losing the Initiative in Mercantile Warfare: Great Britain's Surprising Failure to Anticipate Maritime Challenges to Her Global Trading Network in the First World War." *International Journal of Naval History* 1:1 (April 2002): Reprinted at http://www.ijnhonline.org/volume 1--number 1/Apr02/article.

Rousmaniere, John. "The Romance of the Subchasers." *Naval History* 6:2 (summer 1992): 42–45.

Sakai, Saburo, Martin Caidin, and Fred Saito. *Samurai!* Toronto: Bantam Books, 1978.

Scheer, Reinhard. *Germany's High Seas Fleet in the World War.* Available online at http://www.richthofen.com/Scheer/.

Schencking, J. Charles. *Making Waves: Politics, Propaganda, and the Emergence of the Imperial Japanese Navy, 1868–1922.* Stanford: Stanford University Press, 2005.

Schierbrand, Wolf von. "Germany as a World Power." *Forum* 34 (July–September 1902): 138–42.

Schnall, Peter, producer. "The Last Voyage of the *Lusitania.*" *National Geographic Explorer.* Turner Broadcasting System, 1994.

Schom, Alan. *The Eagle and the Rising Sun: The Japanese-American War, 1941–1943; Pearl Harbor through Guadalcanal.* New York: W. W. Norton, 2004.

Schuster, Carl O. "Strike Warfare, 1914." *Naval History* 12:1 (January–February 1998): 37–41.

Scott, Percy. *Fifty Years in the Royal Navy.* New York: George H. Doran, 1919.

Seager, Robert, II, and Doris Maguire. *Letters and Papers of Alfred Thayer Mahan.* 3 vols. Annapolis: Naval Institute Press, 1975.

Shepardson, Francis W. "The Roosevelt Regime." *World To-Day* 16:3 (March 1909): 265–68.

Shippen, Edward. *Naval Battles of the World: Great and Decisive Contests on the Sea; Causes and Results of Ocean Victories and Defeats; Marine Warfare and Armament in All Ages: The Growth, Power and Management of Our New Navy and Its Pride and Glory of Swift Cruiser, Impregnable Battle-ship, Ponderous Engine and Deadly Projectile.* Philadelphia: P. W. Ziegler, 1894.

Simpson, Colin. *The Lusitania.* Boston: Little, Brown, 1972.

Simpson, Michael, ed. *Anglo-American Naval Relations, 1917–1919.* London: Scolar Press, 1991.

Sims, William Sowden. *The Victory at Sea.* 1920. Reprint, Annapolis: Naval Institute Press, 1984.

Siney, Marion C. *The Allied Blockade of Germany, 1914–1916.* Ann Arbor: University of Michigan Press, 1957.

Smith, Thomas C. *The Agrarian Origins of Modern Japan.* 1959. Reprint, New York: Atheneum, 1966.

Spector, Ronald H. *At War at Sea: Sailors and Naval Warfare in the Twentieth Century.* New York: Viking, 2001.

Speer, Albert. *Inside the Third Reich: Memoirs by Albert Speer.* New York: Macmillan, 1970.

Spence, Jonathan D. *The Search for Modern China.* New York: W. W. Norton, 1990.

Sprout, Harold, and Margaret Sprout. *The Rise of American Naval Power, 1776–1918.* 3d ed. Princeton: Princeton University Press, 1944.

———. *Toward a New Order of Sea Power: American Naval Policy and the World Scene, 1918–1922.* Princeton: Princeton University Press, 1940.

Steffen, Dirk. "The Holtzendorff Memorandum of 22 December 1916 and Germany's Declaration of Unrestricted U-boat Warfare." *Journal of Military History* 68:1 (January 2004): 215–24.

Stevens, William Oliver, and Allan Westcott. *A History of Sea Power.* New York: Doubleday, Doran, 1942.

Stevenson, William. *A Man Called Intrepid: The Secret War.* New York: Ballantine Books, 1976.

Sullivan, Mark. *Our Times: The United States, 1900–1925.* 6 vols. New York: Charles Scribner's Sons, 1926–1935.

Sultow, James Edward. "The Imperial German Navy, 1910–1914." Ph.D. thesis, Indiana University, 1953.

Sumida, Jon Tetsuro. "Fisher's Naval Revolution." *Naval History* 10:4 (July–August 1996): 20–26.

———. *In Defense of Naval Supremacy: Finance, Technology, and British Naval Policy, 1889–1914.* Boston: Unwin Hyman, 1989.

———. "Sir John Fisher and the *Dreadnought:* The Sources of Naval Mythology." *Journal of Military History* 59 (October 1995): 619–37.

Sweetman, Jack. *The Great Admirals: Command at Sea, 1587–1945.* Annapolis: Naval Institute Press, 1997.

Tarrant, V. E. *Jutland, the German Perspective: A New View of the Great Battle, 31 May 1916.* Annapolis: Naval Institute Press, 1995.

Taylor, A. J. P. *English History, 1914–1945.* New York: Oxford University Press, 1965.

Thiesen, William H. "Professionalization and American Naval Modernization in the 1880s." *Naval War College Review* 49:2 (spring 1996): 33–49.

Thornton, A. P. *The Imperial Idea and Its Enemies: A Study in British Power.* 1959. Reprint, Garden City, N.Y.: Doubleday Anchor Books, 1968.

Tikowara, Hesibo. *Before Port Arthur in a Destroyer: The Personal Diary of a Japanese Naval Officer.* Translated by R. Grant. New York: Dutton, 1907.

Till, Geoffrey. *Seapower: A Guide for the Twenty-first Century.* London: Frank Cass, 2004.

Tirpitz, Alfred von. *My Memoirs.* 2 vols. New York: Dodd, Mead, 1919.

Tolley, Kemp. *Yangtze Patrol: The U.S. Navy in China.* Annapolis: Naval Institute Press, 1971.

Tracy, Nicholas. *The Collective Naval Defense of the Empire, 1900–1940.* London: Ashgate Press, 1997.

Trask, David F. *Captains and Cabinets: Anglo-American Naval Relations, 1917–1918.* Columbia: University of Missouri Press, 1972.

Trimble, William F. *Admiral William A. Moffett: Architect of Naval Aviation.* Washington, D.C.: Smithsonian Institution Press, 1994.

Truscott, Peter. *Kursk Russia's Lost Pride.* London: Simon and Schuster U.K. Pocket Books, 2003.

Tuchman, Barbara W. *The Guns of August.* 1962. Reprint, New York: Bantam Books, 1976.

———. *The Zimmermann Telegram.* New York: Dell Books, 1965.

Uhlig, Frank, Jr. *How Navies Fight: The U.S. Navy and Its Allies.* Annapolis: Naval Institute Press, 1994.

"The United States as a World Power." Pts. 1 and 2. *Forum* 29 (July 1900): 608–22; (August 1900): 673–87.

U.S. Department of State. *Papers Relating to the Foreign Relations of the United States, 1911.* Washington, D.C.: U.S. Government Printing Office, 1918.

———. *Papers Relating to the Foreign Relations of the United States, 1912.* Washington, D.C.: U.S. Government Printing Office, 1919.

Utley, Jonathan G. *An American Battleship in Peace and War: The U.S.S. Tennessee.* Lawrence: University Press of Kansas, 1991.

van der Vat, Dan. *The Atlantic Campaign World War II's Great Struggle at Sea.* New York: Harper and Row, 1988.

———. *Gentlemen of War: The Amazing Story of Captain Karl von Müller and the S.M.S. Emden.* New York: William Morrow, 1984.

———. *The Ship That Changed the World: The Escape of the Goeben to the Dardanelles in 1914.* London: Hodder and Stoughton, 1985.

Wade, Wyn Craig. *The Titanic: End of a Dream.* New York: Penguin Books, 1986.

Wegener, Wolfgang. *The Naval Strategy of the World War.* Translated by Holger H. Herwig. Annapolis: Naval Institute Press, 1989.

Weir, Gary E. *Building the Kaiser's Navy: The Imperial Navy Office and German Industry in the von Tirpitz Era, 1889–1919.* Annapolis: Naval Institute Press, 1992.

———. "Tirpitz and Technology." *Naval History* 4 (winter 1990): 41–44.

Whitehouse, Arch. *Fighting Ships.* New York: Curtis Books, 1967.

Williams, Talcott. "The New Navy." *Atlantic Monthly* 90 (September 1902): 383–93.

Wincott, Len. *Invergordon Mutineer.* London: Weidenfeld and Nicolson, 1974.

Yaroschul, Thomas P. *Floating Palaces.* Expanding Television Properties for the Arts and Entertainment Network, 1996.

Young, Filson. *With the Battle Cruisers.* 1921. Reprint, Edinburgh: Birlinn, 2002.

INDEX

Note: Numbers in italics refer to illustrations

LISLE A. ROSE is the author of eight previous books, including *The Ship That Held the Line: U.S.S.* Hornet *and the First Half of the Pacific War* and *The Cold War Comes to Main Street: America in 1950.* He served in the U.S. Navy from 1954 to 1957 and in the U.S. Department of State's Bureau of Oceans and International Environmental and Scientific Affairs from 1978 to 1989. He lives in Edmonds, Washington.